D1483571

Society at War

SOCIETY AT WAR
The militarisation of South Africa

edited by
JACKLYN COCK & LAURIE NATHAN

St. Martin's Press: New York

TO DAVID WEBSTER

© 1989 David Philip, Publisher

For information, write:
Scholarly and Reference Division,
St. Martin's Press, Inc., 175 Fifth Avenue,
New York, N. Y. 10010

First published in the United States of America in 1989

Printed in South Africa

ISBN 0-312-03551-9

Library of Congress Cataloging-in-Publication Data

Society at war : the militarization of South Africa / edited by
Jacklyn Cock and Laurie Nathan.
    p.   cm.
Includes bibliographical references.
ISBN 0-312-03551-9
1. South Africa-- Politics and government-- 1970 2. Civil-military
relations-- South Africa. 3. South Africa-- Military policy.
4. South Africa-- Social conditions. I. Cock, Jacklyn. II. Nathan,
Laurie.
DT779.952.S63 1989   89-35155
306.2'7'0968--dc20   CIP

Printed by Clyson Printers (Pty) Ltd, Maitland, South Africa

Contents

Contributors

SEAN ARCHER lectures in economics at the University of Cape Town

ANDREW BORAINE works for Planact in Johannesburg, dealing with urban development and housing issues

FRAN BUNTMAN is a research assistant in the Centre for Policy Studies at the University of the Witwatersrand

WILLIAM COBBETT is co-ordinator of Planact in Johannesburg, and has co-edited *Popular struggles in South Africa*

JACKLYN COCK is senior lecturer in the Sociology Department at the University of the Witwatersrand, and author of the study *Maids and madams*

CAROLE COOPER is the associate director (research) of the South African Institute of Race Relations

ROBERT DAVIES is on the staff of the Centre of African Studies, Eduardo Mondlane University, Maputo

GAVIN EVANS, who was a leading member of the End Conscription Campaign, works as a journalist

JEREMY GREST lectures in the Department of Comparative African Government at the University of Natal

NICHOLAS HAYSOM practises as a lawyer in Johannesburg and is associated with the Centre for Applied Legal Studies at the University of the Witwatersrand

KAREN JOCHELSON is at present engaged in research at St Antony's College, University of Oxford

HANNCHEN KOORNHOF is engaged in research in the Department of Comparative Literature at the University of the Witwatersrand

MARIAN LACEY lectures in the Department of Political Studies at Rhodes University, and is the author of *Working for boroko*

LAURIE NATHAN was the national organiser of the End Conscription Campaign in 1985-6, and is at present engaged in research for a doctorate at Bradford University

KATE PHILIP works for the National Union of Mineworkers, organising rural cooperatives

MARK PHILLIPS is a research assistant in the Centre for Policy Studies at the University of the Witwatersrand

DEBORAH POSEL is a research officer in the African Studies Institute at the University of the Witwatersrand

DIANE SANDLER works as a clinical psychologist in Cape Town

KATHY SATCHWELL practises as a lawyer in Johannesburg

JAMES SELFE is a senior research assistant in the Research Department of the Democratic Party

GRAEME SIMPSON is currently studying for a doctorate in history at Middlesex Polytechnikon in London

MARK SWILLING is on the staff of the Centre for Policy Studies at the University of the Witwatersrand

TONY WEAVER is a freelance journalist based in Cape Town; from 1983 to 1985 he was the Namibian bureau chief for the SAAN group of newspapers

HARALD WINKLER is engaged in research in the Department of Religious Studies at the University of Cape Town

Abbreviations

ANC	African National Congress
Armscor	Armaments Development and Production Corporation
AZAPO	Azanian People's Organisation
BOSS	Bureau for State Security
CAP	Civil Action Programmes
CF	citizen force
CIIR	Catholic Institute for International Relations
CONSAS	Constellation of Southern African States
COSG	Conscientious Objectors' Support Group
CSIR	Council for Scientific and Industrial Research
DST	Directorate of Special Tasks
ECC	End Conscription Campaign
EIU	Economist Intelligence Unit
EPG	Eminent Persons Group
FAPLA	military wing of MPLA
FNLA	National Front for the Liberation of Angola
Frelimo	Front for the Liberation of Mozambique
GDP	gross domestic product
HSRC	Human Sciences Research Council
IISS	International Institute for Strategic Studies
ISI	import-substitution industrialisation
JMC	Joint Management Centre
LIC	low-intensity conflict
LLA	Lesotho Liberation Army
MARNET	military area radio network
MCSA	Methodist Church of South Africa
MK	Umkhonto we Sizwe
MNR	Mozambique National Resistance Movement
MPLA	Popular Movement for the Liberation of Angola
Neusa	National Education Union of South Africa
NGK	Nederduitse Gereformeerde Kerk
NIS	National Intelligence Service
NKP	National Key Point
NMS	National Management System
NSMS	National Security Management System
NUM	National Union of Mineworkers
NUSAS	National Union of South African Students
PAC	Pan-Africanist Congress

PF	permanent force
PFP	Progressive Federal Party
PLAN	People's Liberation Army of Namibia
Renamo	Mozambique National Resistance Movement (see MNR)
RSA	Republic of South Africa
SACC	South African Council of Churches
SADCC	Southern African Development Coordination Conference
SADF	South African Defence Force
SAIRR	South African Institute of Race Relations
SAP	South African Police
SIPRI	Stockholm International Peace Research Institute
SSC	State Security Council
SWA	South West Africa
SWAPO	South West African People's Organisation
SWATF	South West Africa Territory Force
TED	Transvaal Education Department
TNIP	Transkei National Independence Party
UDF	Union Defence Force
UDF	United Democratic Front
UN	United Nations
UNICEF	United Nations Children's Fund
UNITA	National Union for the Total Independence of Angola
WHAM	'winning hearts and minds'

Foreword

FRANK CHIKANE

Prior to September 1984 when the South African Defence Force moved en masse into the black townships of the Vaal Triangle, black people who have been on the receiving end of the apartheid state's repressive measures described South Africa as a police state. From time to time, especially after the Soweto uprising in 1976, the army had been seen in action with the police, particularly at roadblocks. But this did not make the perception of a war situation a widespread one. It was only after September 1984 that it became clear the apartheid government was waging a full-scale war against the voteless majority in the country.

The distinction between the army and the police faded away. The government began to talk about the security forces, meaning the joint forces of the police and army, which were set against all those who opposed the apartheid system. Because of the intervention of the security forces, peaceful protests and demonstrations were turned into violent conflicts. The army used lethal armoury against defenceless township residents, and thousands were killed, maimed or wounded. Young blacks responded to this state violence through any means available to them. At the same time the armed wing of the African National Congress, Umkhonto we Sizwe, intensified its armed struggle against the apartheid regime.

These events led me to conclude without any doubt that South African society was at war. In court cases involving captured ANC guerillas, I gave evidence in mitigation of sentence and submitted that from the point of view of the black majority the apartheid regime is waging a war against them. Both the SAP and the SADF are seen as 'enemy forces' waging a war with the sole aim of maintaining white minority rule against the humanity and birthrights of black people. The militarisation of South Africa is therefore seen as a process of militarisation against the oppressed majority. The threat to the white minority state is not in the main an external one. The threat is an internal one. Thus militarisation is directed against the people of South Africa.

The SADF in the black townships is widely regarded as an army of occupation to enforce the law of the apartheid state. This perception is reinforced by the participation of the military in the State Security

Council (SSC) and the elaborate national security network of the Joint Management Centres (JMCs). For the victims of apartheid it is not a civilian government that is ruling them but a military government. We are ruled here by the apartheid army against our will!

The publication of this book is indeed very timeous to help all South Africans, black and white, face the reality of the militarisation of our society and the implications thereof, particularly for the voteless black majority. I would like to call on all peace-loving South Africans to take effective measures at various levels to stall this process of militarisation, and bring those in power to their senses so that they abandon this inhuman apartheid system, and establish a new non-racial democratic South Africa where there will be no need for militarisation.

I am looking forward to that day when weapons of war will be turned into ploughshares. When all will live in peace. For this reason I commend this book to you.

Frank Chikane
General Secretary
South African Council of Churches

Preface

In the late 1970s the South African state and military began speaking of a 'total onslaught' against the country and its inhabitants. According to Defence Minister General Magnus Malan in 1977, this onslaught 'involves so many different fronts, unknown to the South African experience, that it has gained the telling but horrifying name of total war. This different but all-encompassing war has brought with it new methods and new techniques which in turn have to be met by total countermeasures.'

The 'total war' referred to by General Malan was the struggle being waged against apartheid and colonialism by the people of South Africa and southern Africa. Their resistance had intensified dramatically in the mid-1970s with the Soweto uprising and the independence of Angola and Mozambique.

The 'total countermeasures' employed by the state involved the steady militarisation of South African society, and the growing deployment of the SADF in a coercive role inside and outside the country. The tendency towards escalating militarisation and reliance on state violence has been so extensive in the 1980s that we believe that it deserves 'the telling but horrifying name of total war'.

This war is being waged, in brutal and subtle forms, in defence of white minority rule and an iniquitous social system. It is truly 'all-encompassing': it operates at political, economic and ideological levels, affects every area of society, and impinges on the lives of all South Africans. 'Virtually every member of the white and black populations is immersed in the militarisation of society, either as wielders of coercive and restrictive power or as objects or respondents to that power' (Grundy, 1983: 10).

This book seeks to examine the dimensions and manifestations of 'total war'. It aims to describe and analyse the role of the SADF and the militarisation of South African society. Given the infancy of peace research in South Africa, and the difficulties and risks it involves, the book can make no claim to be complete or definitive. It raises as many questions as it answers, and, we hope, will stimulate further investigation in the area.

The various contributions to the book were commissioned in early

1988 and completed by the middle of that year. There have been significant developments in southern Africa since. In late 1988 Pretoria agreed to withdraw its troops from Angola, and to implement United Nations Resolution 435 in Namibia.

We hope that this book not only adds to an understanding of the destructive forces at play in our country, but encourages the reader to work actively against them. All the contributors to the book are involved, as professionals or activists, in the struggle against apartheid and militarisation. Their chapters were written, and the book is presented, in this spirit.

Lastly, we would like to thank our publisher, David Philip, for his enthusiastic response to this project when first approached, and to thank especially Russell Martin for his boundless patience and energy in assisting with the editing process.

Jacky Cock & Laurie Nathan

Introduction

JACKLYN COCK

South Africa as a society at war

'We in South Africa have a war going on. Those who have not realised it are foolish.' This was the perception of the Rev. Frank Chikane, general secretary of the South African Council of Churches, when he spoke at the funeral of 17 African youths killed during a conflict – known as 'the six-day war' – in Alexandra township in 1986. The question of whether the conflict in South Africa can be regarded as a war is, however, strongly contested by the state.[1]

After the state responded to non-violent protest in the 1950s with the Sharpeville shootings and a state of emergency in 1960, the ANC decided to embark on 'armed struggle' as one strand in its strategy for liberation. At its Kabwe Conference in 1985, the ANC adopted the notion of a 'people's war' and committed itself to recruiting and training a greater number of members for military action. Many members of the ANC's military wing, Umkhonto we Sizwe (MK), regard themselves as soldiers fighting in a people's war.

However, in a treason trial in 1988, Brigadier Hermanus Stadler of the South African Police maintained that the ANC cannot be regarded as being at war with the South African government. Instead, he argued, the government is facing a 'revolutionary onslaught'. This argument was advanced in order to deny ANC members prisoner-of-war status which, in terms of the Geneva Protocols of 1977, is granted to people engaged in wars against colonial powers.

In contrast, during the same month, in a different court case, the state did describe itself as being at war. It argued that the activities of the SADF fell outside the court's jurisdiction because the Defence Force is on a 'war footing'. In this case the End Conscription Campaign (ECC) had applied to the Supreme Court for an order restraining the SADF from illegally harassing it.

While Hannah Arendt's definition of war as 'the massification of violence' implies that there is a simple relation between the two phenomena, it is clear that the violent conflict in South Africa does not easily fit into conventional definitions. For example, 'Warfare is socially organised physical coercion against a similarly socially organised opponent' (Kaldor, 1982: 263). 'War is an open armed conflict in which regular, uniformed forces are engaged, on at least one side; the fighters and the fighting are organised centrally to some extent; and there is some continuity between armed clashes' (Kidron and Smith, 1983: 6). MK and the SADF are not 'similarly socially organised opponents'. Nor is there 'continuity between armed clashes'. Much of the violent confrontation that occurs is episodic.[2] For these reasons the conflict in South Africa is understood in this work as a low-level civil war, or a situation of 'low-intensity conflict'. War is viewed along a continuum of violent conflict, ranging from low-intensity conflict through conventional war to nuclear or high-intensity war.

The term 'low-intensity conflict' (LIC) is also used in the literature to describe a military strategy of the state. This is a strategy to defeat liberation movements without engaging in full-scale conventional war. The term has been used to describe current state counter-insurgency strategy in South Africa, which involves the mobilisation of resources at political, economic and ideological levels. The SADF has been a central source of direction in this process.

The impetus for this mobilisation has been provided by the increasing popular resistance to minority rule and the apartheid system. From about 1975 SADF personnel referred to a 'total onslaught' against South Africa. The state's response of 'total strategy' has in turn supplied the basis for legitimising an increasing military involvement in all spheres of national, regional and local government decision-making. In this sense total strategy was the launchpad for the militarisation of South African society.

Militarisation as a contested concept

An informed understanding of militarisation requires that a distinction be drawn between three related social phenomena:

(1) *The military as a social institution* – a set of social relationships organised around war and taking the shape of an armed force.

(2) *Militarism as an ideology,* the key component of which is an acceptance of organised state violence as a legitimate solution to conflict. Other components involve a glorification of war whereby actors and encounters are portrayed in heroic terms, and an acceptance of what have been termed 'military values' – hierarchy, discipline, obedience and the centralisation of authority (Merryfinch, 1981: 9).

(3) *Militarisation as a social process* that involves a mobilisation of resources for war at political, economic and ideological levels.

These phenomena are closely related. Militarisation involves both the spread of militarism as an ideology, and an expansion of the power and influence of the military as a social institution.

One of the difficulties in the existing literature is that these phenomena are sometimes defined very broadly and loosely. For example, militarism has been described as a set of attitudes and social practices which regards war and the preparation of war as a normal and desirable social activity. This is a broader definition than is common among scholars. It qualifies people other than John Wayne as militarists. But in an age when war threatens our survival it is as well to understand any behavior, however mild in appearance, which makes war seem either natural or desirable. (Mann, 1987: 35)

Another difficulty is that the term 'militarism' is used in the literature to mean different things to different people:

first, to mean an aggressive foreign policy, based on a readiness to resort to war; second, the preponderance of the military in the state, the extreme case being that of military rule; third, subservience of the whole society to the needs of the army which may involve a recasting of social life in accordance with the pattern of military organisation; and fourth, an ideology which promotes military ideas. (Andreski, 1968: 429)

It is also used to mean high military spending and large arms industries. However, there is no necessary relationship between these various phenomena. 'Some countries have relatively high military spending but not much arms industry. Others have military dictatorships which show little propensity to war. Many of the states which have most often resorted to war, like Britain, have never been run by the military.' (Smith and Smith, 1983: 11). For Smith and Smith the term 'militarism' is descriptive rather than analytic. It refers to the various phenomena cited above 'in which the common keynote is the maintenance of permanent armed forces' *(ibid.)*. This reduces the concept to a description of a society that maintains a military institution. As the maintenance of armed forces is nearly universal, this clearly does not take us very far.

In much of the literature, analysis hinges on a dualistic model of the 'civil' and the 'military' as two separate and independent spheres. Militarisation is then used to describe a process of intrusion or encroachment. Enloe, for example, follows this approach, but refines it by pointing out that militarisation is a process with both material and ideological dimensions. 'In the material sense it encompasses the gradual encroachment of the military institution into the civilian arena. . . . The ideological dimension implies the extent to which such encroachments are acceptable to the population and become seen as 'common-sense' solutions to civil problems, such as in the case of army intervention to restore services in public sector strikes.' (Enloe, 1983: 9)

Other writers have attempted to 'measure' the degree of this encroachment. Luckham, for example, has constructed a 'grid' which tries to relate several variables, such as the respective strengths of military and civilian institutions, the interaction between the two spheres, and the degree to which military 'boundaries' are open to penetration from outside (Luckham, 1971).

Some analysts have tried to conceptualise this penetration in notions of 'the military–industrial–technological–bureaucratic complex' (Eide and Thee), or the 'military–industrial complex'. Williams refer to this as 'an organised grouping of arms production, military research and state-security interests which has, in effect, moved beyond the control of civil society, and is the true contemporary form of the state itself' (Williams, 1985: 224). But concepts which attempt to delimit the problem have been subject to criticism. For example: 'We speak of "the military–industrial complex" or of "the military sector" or "interest" of the arms lobby. This suggests that the evil is confined in a known and limited place: it may threaten to push forward, but it can be restrained; contamination does not extend through the whole societal body.' (Thompson, 1982: 21) This notion of contamination is the crucial insight in Thompson's analysis. He concludes that 'the USA and the USSR do not have military–industrial complexes, they *are* such complexes' *(ibid.)*. Similarly Bahro has lamented that 'our whole social organism is riddled by the disease of militarism' (Bahro, 1982: 89).

It is tempting to analyse South African society in terms of these concepts of 'contamination' and 'saturation'. However, one of the difficulties with this approach is that the notions become too broad and inclusive to have any analytical usefulness. 'Militarisation' becomes a kind of 'hold-all' into which everything negative and repressive about South African society is thrown.

The approach followed here is to ground analysis in a particular social process – militarisation – that involves the mobilisation of resources for war. This process has developed as a result of intensifying resistance to minority rule. It has been spearheaded by the SADF, and has in turn expanded and extended the power and influence of the military.

South Africa as a militarised society

It is not always an easy task to demonstrate the militarised nature of a particular society. In the process of militarisation the role of the military as a discrete institution may become increasingly obscure. 'The more a society becomes militarised the more difficult it becomes to separate military and non-military structures or to distinguish clearly their purpose and procedures. The military becomes a less discrete and more pervasive element in society.' (Wiseman, 1988: 231) It is not possible 'to agree on a few key variables and to develop a list of criteria against which any given country could be checked' (Berghahn, 1984: 70). Nor is it desirable to restrict analysis to directly observable and measurable cause-and-effect relations. This would impose an analytical straitjacket which would permit only safe and trivial questions. Instead a number of indicators are used here as flags to point the reader to the militarised nature of South African society.

Militarisation at the economic level

(1) An important indicator of the militarisation of South African society is the expanding armaments industry and growing links between the SADF and the private sector. The local armaments manufacturer, Armscor, is now one of the largest corporations in South Africa, and has established the country as the fifth largest arms producer in the world. More than 1 500 private-sector contractors and sub-contractors are engaged in producing components and military materials for Armscor (Simpson, this volume).

Institutional links between the SADF and the private sector are clear in the Defence Manpower Liaison Committees set up in 1982 to discuss the allocation of manpower; the Defence Research and Development Council which links specialists in the private sector with military research needs; and the National Key Points Committee which oversees protection for non-military installations that are considered vital for state security (Philip, this volume).

Such economic and institutional cooperation is not the only important link between the SADF and private industry. There is also the widespread practice of companies making salary and benefit payments to employees serving in the SADF. The support given to the SADF by business is also indicated by the range of companies and products advertised in the official SADF publication, *Paratus.* Numerous advertisements offer concessions to soldiers, such as a 50 per cent reduction at Holiday Inns throughout the country and R300 off the purchase of a Mazda motor car.

The links between the military and capital are likely to become even closer as the SADF privatises more of its equipment and services. According to General Magnus Malan, 'the private sector already provides the SADF with about 75% of all manufactured equipment and services' (*Star,* 16.5.1986). However, South Africa does not yet have a war economy with price controls, rationing and the requisitioning of labour, products and property.[3] Nor does it spend proportionately as much on defence as some other countries.

(2) Defence expenditure is nevertheless high and is often cited as evidence of the growing militarisation of South African society (Archer, this volume). 'Since the beginning of the eighties, roughly 20 per cent of total government expenditure has been fed into the Defence Force' (Frankel, 1984: 73). In June 1987 the Defence budget was increased by 30 per cent over that of 1986, to R6 683 million. Most analysts agree that the real total is much larger. One estimate is that total security-force expenditure is closer to R15 billion or about 28 per cent of the national budget (*Weekly Mail,* 15.7.1988). The Econometrix director, Dr Azar Jammine, estimated in July 1988 that the Angolan war was costing the South African taxpayer R4 billion a year (*Sunday Star,* 3.7.1988). Recently it was revealed in parliament that, according to figures supplied by

General Magnus Malan, nearly R1 million a day is spent on ammunition alone (*Star,* 27.5.1988).

(3) A sophisticated weapons system absorbs some of this military spending. Obviously other societies have larger and more sophisticated weapons systems, but 'the key issue is what the military machine is used for, rather than how large it is' (Blatchford, 1988: 42). It will be demonstrated below that in South Africa it is mainly used for repression.

Of particular concern with regard to South Africa's weapons system is the belief amongst international observers that the country's nuclear industry contains a military component in the form of nuclear weapons (Koeberg Alert Research Group, 1987). There are four reasons for this belief. Firstly, South Africa undoubtedly has the capacity to produce the weapons. It has enough enriched uranium, its weapons experts have the necessary technical skills, and the SADF has the delivery systems capable of launching nuclear missiles. According to *New Scientist,* South Africa's uranium enrichment plant at Velindaba could potentially produce 40–100 atomic bombs a year (cited in *Sunday Tribune,* 12.10.1986).

Secondly, there is evidence that South Africa has actually tested nuclear weapons. The US State Department claims that South Africa detonated a 2,5–3 kiloton bomb off its coast in September 1979 *(ibid.).* Thirdly, the South African government has intimated that it does have nuclear weapons, although it officially denies this. Fourthly, South Africa's consistent refusal to sign the Nuclear Non-Proliferation Treaty has fuelled speculation that it has atomic weapons. The treaty is designed to inhibit the diversion of nuclear material from civilian to military purposes, and would open South Africa's uranium enrichment plants to international inspection.

Militarisation at the political level

There are two different ways of conceptualising the power of the military at this level. The first emphasises its coercive role in protecting white minority rule. The second relates to its increasing influence in state decision-making.

(4) The SADF has played an extensive coercive role in South Africa's regional policy of destabilisation. It has maintained a military occupation of Namibia (Weaver, this volume), and has repeatedly attacked Angola since 1975 (Grest, this volume). The Defence Force has also been responsible for repeated acts of aggression against Mozambique (Davies, this volume), Lesotho, Swaziland, Botswana, Zambia and Zimbabwe.

Pretoria's policy of destabilisation has wrought havoc in neighbouring countries, destroying social life, disrupting economies and infrastructure, and directly or indirectly causing the death and social dislocation of tens of thousands of people (Hanlon, 1986). As a result, the international community regards South Africa as a 'threat to the maintenance of international peace and security', and has imposed an arms embargo on it (Cobbett, this volume).

(5) The SADF has increasingly been used internally to maintain minority rule and the apartheid system. Throughout the 1980s it has been used as a major agency to suppress resistance in arenas as diverse as education, health and labour. It has been deployed to evict rent defaulters, occupy black schools, guard polling booths, invade health clinics to identify the injured, maintain beach apartheid, monitor demonstrations, and suppress resistance to bantustan independence. It has also been involved in forced removals, strike-breaking and the 're-education' of political detainees.

The army's coercive internal role was exercised most extensively during the 1984–6 period of intensified black resistance (Nathan, this volume). In 1985 alone, more than 35 500 troops were used in townships throughout the country. Most of them were conscripts, some of whom were psychologically disturbed by their experience (Sandler, this volume). The troops also generated a high level of violence against and fear amongst township residents.[4] The New York Lawyers' Committee for Human Rights reported a campaign of terror against black children. 'In the past year a terrifying pattern of abuse has emerged in townships with a heavy military presence: soldiers pick up children on the streets, load them into Casspirs and hold them for several nightmarish hours. Inside the Casspirs the children are threatened, intimidated, and assaulted before being turned out to make their own way home.' (*Weekly Mail*, 18.4.1986)

While the SADF was an ubiquitous presence in many black townships, a suggestion that it should be brought into white suburbs to protect shoppers raised considerable controversy. A National Party candidate in the 1988 municipal elections organised a petition signed by some 400 people calling for national servicemen to patrol the Rosebank–Parktown North area of Johannesburg on foot. This provoked opposition MP Peter Soal to ask the Minister of Law and Order whether 'the situation has deteriorated to such an extent that Rosebank is like Beirut and troops should be deployed in the suburbs' (*Rosebank–Killarney Gazette*, 1.6.1988). Many residents of the white suburbs rejected the idea on the grounds that policemen were sufficient.

Ironically the image of 'Beirut' was a real one to many township residents. During the 1984–6 uprising the SADF often acted together with the South African Police. Their activities were indistinguishable to township residents as they fused in a pattern of violence and fear (CIIR, 1988a). The closeness of their relation led many commentators (as well as the state) to link the two in the notion of 'the security forces'. However, to lump the army and the police together in this way can cause one to loose sight of the inappropriateness of the use of the army in internal repression. 'In the twentieth century . . . the military have been primarily a means of inter-state conflict and only secondarily a means of internal repression. In most advanced capitalist countries this function has increasingly become a specialised police concern.' (Shaw, 1988: 110)

By early 1987 the SADF and the SAP had largely crushed the rebellion in the black townships. Their role faded as surrogate black forces in the shape of vigilantes, *'kitskonstabels'* and municipal police came to form the main agents of violence and fear (CIIR, 1988a; Haysom, this volume). This use of surrogate forces is in line with the strategy of low-intensity conflict in which the military assume a covert coordinating role. This leads us to the second way of conceptualising the process of militarisation at the political level, by examining the increasing power of the military within the state.

(6) It is generally agreed by analysts that in South Africa the military is positioned at the centre of state decision-making. For example, Frankel maintains: 'Militarisation is always measured by the appearance of soldiers as public decision-makers, and the growing influence of the South African military is finally, and perhaps most importantly, reflected in the penetration of top government institutions by Defence Force personnel, on either a formal or informal basis' (Frankel, 1984: 103). Vale takes this further to argue that the military constitutes an extra-parliamentary government which actually rules South Africa (quoted in *Star,* 12.2.1988).

The militarisation of the state may be open and explicit, or it may take more indirect 'subterranean' forms. In the latter case, 'the armed forces do not occupy the front line in the political sense. They do not govern directly, but exercise rather tight control over the formal holders of power.' (Lowy and Sader, 1985: 9)

In South Africa such control operates through the National Security Management System which determines total strategies and coordinates resources, and is dominated by the SADF and the SAP (Selfe, this volume). The most significant site of power within the NSMS is the State Security Council (SSC). This has replaced the Cabinet as the most influential state decision-making body. The NSMS gives the military direct influence in decision-making down to local government level. At a regional and local level this influence operates through a complex network of some 500 Joint Management Centres (JMCs), sub-JMCs and mini-JMCs, which coordinate security force activities on the ground and devise local strategies to deal with and possibly pre-empt security problems. The JMCs are chaired by the military and police, and their business is regarded as classified. All participants in the NSMS must take an oath of secrecy which makes them subject to penalties under the Protection of Information Act. Therefore the full gamut of NSMS activities at all levels is by definition covert.

There is a close relationship between the SADF and the SAP in this institutional structure. However, it is important not to lose sight of the specific role of the military by adopting a blurred and inflated notion of the 'security establishment'.[5] The military is positioned at the centre of this covert power structure. Its role in coordinating resources and tying strategies together needs to be understood in relation to modern counter-insurgency theory.

State security strategists in South Africa are clearly drawing on this theory, which emerged from campaigns in Algeria, Cuba, Malaysia and Vietnam, to produce more sophisticated strategies rooted in a long-term view. Swilling and Phillips (this volume) suggest that there has been a shift in state security thinking from 'total strategy', informed by the French strategist André Beaufre, to 'counter-revolutionary warfare' or 'winning hearts and minds' (WHAM), informed by the writings of the American J. J. McCuen. Both 'total strategy' and 'WHAM' are military strategies which involve comprehensive social engineering. Both strategies emphasise the psychological dimensions of counter-insurgency. Both emphasise as well the need for 'economic action', but WHAM takes this further. Swilling and Phillips argue that the 'fundamental difference between "total strategy" as conceived in the early 1980s and the WHAM programme that has been implemented since 1986, is that the latter is no longer concerned primarily with restructuring the access points to political society' (Swilling and Phillips, 1988: 22). Instead the focus is on recasting the foundations of civil society so as to maintain control of the populace. This is achieved through economic development – material upliftment or upgrading of designated townships in a way that is intended to 'win the hearts and minds' of their inhabitants.

It is important to appreciate the extent to which upgrading constitutes a military strategy. In 1987 General Magnus Malan announced that he had taken 'personal responsibility' for the upgrading projects in the townships of Alexandra, Mamelodi (Boraine, this volume), Bonteheuwel and New Brighton. These and other townships are conceptualised as 'strategic bases' from which the SADF and the SAP believe they can regain control over the oppressed majority. General Malan described this strategy as follows: 'I want to see to what extent I can better the living conditions of the people, to what extent I can get the people to accept the government so that they don't break with the authorities and drift into the hands of the terrorists' (*Cape Times*, 30.3.1987). Malan's statement is totally in accord with the current emphasis on 'economic aid', which is a key element of counter-insurgency strategy. Therefore it is not surprising that SADF personnel have been actively involved in upgrading projects in a variety of capacities. For example, soldiers have been used to sell houses in townships in an attempt to 'contain the total onslaught and beat the rent boycott' (SADF spokesman, *Sowetan,* 29.9.1987).

(7) As the SADF's role inside and outside South Africa has escalated over the past 25 years, so its structures have expanded and its size grown markedly (Phillips, this volume). The extent to which the SADF incorporates all white South African males is a further indicator of the militarised nature of South African society. White men are required to complete two years' initial, continuous service in the SADF, followed by camps of a total of 720 days spread over 12 years (Satchwell, this volume).[6] Although black men are not subject to conscription, they are increasingly being drawn into military structures, particularly those in the 'independent' bantustans. The bantustan forces have become yet another link, albeit a vulnerable one, in South Africa's vast security network (Cooper, this volume).

Similarly, white women are not liable for compulsory military service but contribute to the process of militarisation in significant ways, both directly and indirectly at material and ideological levels (Cock, this volume). This incorporation of growing numbers of South Africans into the military is not only physical, but also ideological in that they are exposed to the SADF's understanding of South African society, and especially of 'the threat of communism' and 'the dangers of the revolutionary onslaught'. These dangers are emphasised in the mobilisation of resources for war which is occurring more widely at the level of ideas.

Militarisation at the ideological level

(8) The ideology of militarism, which legitimates state violence as a solution to conflict, is promoted by a number of agencies, particularly the state-owned radio and television networks. These agencies glorify the SADF, criminalise political opponents, and 'demonise' the ANC, which 'is almost invariably reported on in terms of violence and terrorism' (Tomaselli, 1988: 22). The violence of the security forces is presented as necessary and legitimate while township resistance is portrayed as inherently violent, anarchic and 'primitive' (Posel, this volume).

(9) This ideology is linked to a consumerist militarism, which is evident in the popularity of war toys, games and films, and in the frequency of military parades and other displays of armed strength. This consumerist militarism glorifies soldiers and military encounters in an insidious way (Jochelson and Buntman, this volume).

We have become accustomed to the integral militarism of the modern nation-state, at its most formal and official levels. It is not surprising that this has spread to stain the whole society. But we may also be facing something worse than this: a vigorous, spectacular and consumerist militarism, extending from the toy-missile flashes of the children's shops and games arcades, to the military tournaments and air displays of general public entertainment and finally to the televised images of safely distant wars. (Williams, 1985: 239)

In South Africa this process is very much in evidence. War games are advertised as 'the family game of the future'. An advertised demonstration by two of the country's top war-games teams promised 'an ideal opportunity to experience a war-type situation and to have fun at the same time'; experiences included a 'leopard crawl through the bush', and 'hunt a terrorist' (*Northern Review*, 3.7.1987). The process is also clear in the rapid growth of the private security industry, and in a kind of siege mentality in the white community whereby people retreat into a private defensive core.[7]

The effect of all this is to encourage South Africans to accept and share the state's definition of, and solutions to, political conflict. These ideas are also promoted through the militarisation of white schooling.

(10) The militarisation of white schooling has been achieved through veldschools, cadets and Youth Preparedness programmes (Evans, this volume). It has 'involved the conscious creation of a social atmosphere that makes military service seem attractive, military responses to policy issues sensible, and great military strength and expenditure seem acceptable – one which, in general, prepares the population for conditions of siege and war' (Grundy, 1983: 109).

The practice of compulsory SADF registration at the age of 16 for white boys has been described as using schools as 'recruiting bases' for the SADF. One parent complained: 'This method of recruitment is yet another example of the increasing militarisation of our society. Do other parents feel concern about their sixteen- and seventeen-year-old sons signing away two years of their lives without even a family discussion?' (Letter to *The Star*, 7.4.1987)

The school cadet system is coordinated by the SADF and the various provincial education departments. It involves pupils devoting a portion of their week to marching and other military activities. It was described by Captain Willem Steenkamp as an attempt 'to cultivate the military spirit' and 'a positive attitude to the SADF' (quoted by Evans, 1983: 284). Cadets are part of the Youth Preparedness programme, a compulsory subject in white schools, which emphasises military preparedness, discipline and patriotism. Veldschools are an outdoor extension of this programme. The schools are run on military lines, and activities include survival training, tracking and camouflage, marching and practical field-training, as well as group discussions, lectures and films. The pedagogic content includes discussions of the 'communist onslaught' and the need for a military response.

The military nature of the white educational environment has become more marked over time. During 1987 it became known that the Transvaal Education Department had instructed certain teachers to carry guns, and that fences, barbed-wire and high walls had been erected around many white schools.

(11) A final indicator of militarisation at the ideological level is the extent to which the status of soldiers is 'privileged' in white society. Soldiers are held in high esteem, and the media promotes a glamorised image of the SADF generally. One privilege enjoyed by soldiers is their potential exemption from prosecution in the courts. On at least two occasions President Botha has issued certificates of indemnity effectively banning legal proceedings against members of the SADF. In the most recent case the trial of six SADF members arising from the death of a black Namibian was discontinued. These cases illustrate the power conferred on the SADF by the Defence Act (Satchwell, this volume).

Conclusion

The power of the military in South Africa is considerable, and has expanded with the process of militarisation. This introduction has tried to provide readers with a kind of sketch map to assist them in understanding this process. A number of indicators have been used as flags to point to the mobilisation of resources of war at economic, political and ideological levels. While no single indicator alone enables us to grasp this process, their cumulative effect and inter-relation are significant.

The militarisation of South African society cannot be periodised as dating from 1984 when the SADF was used extensively in black townships, but extends back to the initial stages of white colonisation (Seegers, 1986), and particularly to the first two decades after Union (Lacey, this volume). Increasing resistance to minority rule and the apartheid system from inside and outside the country over the past two decades has provided the impetus for the dramatic intensification of this process.

The militarisation of South Africa has not been a smooth and uniform process, however. It has thrown up contradictions, generated new relations of antagonism and provoked important sources of resistance. The church has been the site of much of this challenge (Winkler and Nathan, this volume). Another source of resistance was the End Conscription Campaign (ECC), which constituted one of the most important political developments in white society in recent years (Nathan, this volume). Its banning in August 1988 reflects the extent to which the state felt threatened by its activities. Nevertheless, there is a groundswell of opposition to conscription specifically, and to militarisation generally, that the banning will not eliminate. 'We are a nation in chains with virtually every avenue of peaceful protest cut off. But resistance has not evaporated. Nor will it until the central issue has been addressed – that of transfer of power to the majority.' (Human rights activist, Max Coleman, speaking at the Congress of the Social

Democratic Party of West Germany, September 1988)

It is hoped that this book will make a contribution towards understanding the obstacles to achieving that goal.

PART ONE
The nature and role of the
South African Defence Force

1 The nuts and bolts of military power: the structure of the SADF

MARK PHILLIPS

The security establishment

The instruments of defence and coercion available to the South African state are among the most varied and diffuse in the world. Together they make up the 'security establishment', as the formal apparatuses of repression have come to be known (Grundy, 1986: 41). It is necessary to gain some idea of the extent of this security network before examining in detail the SADF, which is only one (albeit the most important) component. The security establishment includes the Department of Defence, the various intelligence services (Military Intelligence and Counter-Intelligence, National Intelligence Service and Security Police), and the Directorate of Security Legislation. There is also the National Key Points Committee, the civil defence system (National Civil Defence Committee, Directorate of Civil Defence, and civil defence sectors, wards and cells) and the school cadet system. Although the following are autonomous in theory, they can be considered part of South Africa's security establishment: the South West Africa's Territory Force (SWATF), home guard and SWA Police, and the defence forces, security police detachments, police forces and semi-traditional 'chief's police' of the homelands.

The most visible component of the security establishment in most communities is the SA Police. The police force's security arms are the riot squad, 'reaction units', *'kitskonstabels'*, a special guard unit, a special task force, the police reserve and the voluntary reserve police, and the police counter-insurgency units. The armaments industry and its allied research and industrial institutions integrate the security establishment's material needs with the private sector. The security establishment's research and production network involves the Armaments Corporation (Armscor) and some 1 500 private contractors, the Council for Scientific and Industrial Research (CSIR), the Human Sciences Research Council (HSRC), the Defence Manpower Liaison Committees (Demalcoms), and the Defence Research and Development Council. It also includes a number of key parastatals, such as Sasol, Iscor, and SA Transport Services. Other components of the formally acknowledged security establishment are the municipal police, mine police, military police, traffic police, private security companies, game rangers, neighbourhood and business watches, and military–academic think-tanks such as the Joint Defence College, the Military Academy and the Institute for Strategic Studies at Pretoria University. Coordination of the security establishment's functions occurs through the National Security Management System.

Apart from the bodies which are formally part of the establishment, there is a range of semi-autonomous institutions and groupings which operate in a grey area of limited accountability to counter the multitude of threats which security-planners see ranged against white minority rule. These groups include vigilantes, death squads,[1] threat squads,[2] and proxy forces such as UNITA in Angola, Super ZAPU in Zimbabwe, the Lesotho Liberation Army and the Mozambique National Resistance Movement (Renamo). There are also various private initiatives in the field of mobilisation and propaganda, such as the Terrorism Research Centre, Veterans for Victory, Victims Against Terrorism, and Conscript Advisory Boards. Together, these groups play an important role in the defence of apartheid.

The centre of gravity of this network of coercion is no longer the SA Police, as it was for the first thirty years of apartheid. The police state which was constructed under prime ministers Malan, Strijdom, Verwoerd and Vorster has been militarised in the 1980s. The SADF has come to control huge resources of manpower and the lion's share of the security budget. In the face of mounting challenges to white rule, the SADF's overall theory of counter-revolutionary warfare has increasingly led it to play a determinant role in the formulation and implementation of state strategies. This has meant a shift from the heavily repressive 'counter-insurgency' tactics of the old Bureau for State Security (BOSS) and security police to counter-revolutionary war policies which go under the name of 'winning hearts and minds'. Counter-revolutionary war involves strategies of reform and cooption as well as of repression.

The composition of the SADF

The SADF is the largest direct employer of manpower in the country. Except for the Swiss and Israeli armies, it is the most reliant on reserve forces in the world (*SA Barometer*, 1, 1987). The SADF is really two 'distinctive bodies' (Grundy, 1986: 21): a 'full-time' force and a 'part-time' reserve force. The full-time force consists of professional soldiers (the permanent force), conscripted national servicemen, 'service volunteers' (white women, and coloured and Indian men), as well as an auxiliary service and civilian employees. The part-time component comprises the citizen force (CF) and commando force (see Table 1). The full-time force makes up the essential fighting complement of the Defence Force, while the part-time force lies in reserve for back-up duties, 'area defence' and periods of acute emergency. Although the part-time force comprises 68 per cent of total SADF manpower, it normally renders only 13 per cent of SADF service or man-days (Defence White Paper, 1986). The two forces together represent what Frankel (1984: 25) has called a 'dialectic' between an imported British liberal professional army tradition and an indigenous 'sometime-soldier–sometime-citizen' commando tradition.

Table 1.   **Full-time and part-time forces of the SADF**

Full-time component	31,9%	Part-time component	68,1%
Permanent force	9,1%	Citizen force	47,2%
National servicemen	15,6%	Commando force	20,9%
Service volunteers	1,0%		
Auxiliary service	1,1%		
Civilians	5,1%		

A commission of investigation into the future planning of the SADF, headed by Defence Force chief General Jannie Geldenhuys, reported in 1986 that this structure should be retained in principle (Defence White Paper, 1986: 5). Among the considerations it put forward to support this recommendation were: the manpower-intensive nature of the conflict in which the SADF is involved; the necessity of the guaranteed force levels which conscription provides; the need to share skilled manpower with the civilian economy; the need for reserve forces in counter-insurgency (COIN) operations; provision for reserve forces when COIN or conventional hostilities exceed the capabilities of the full-time force; and the need to involve as many persons as possible over the widest geographic area. There is also an unstated reason for maintaining the system of compulsory national service. According to Seegers (1987: 163), it 'constitutes a very important mechanism of racial solidarity. . . . By its very nature, National Service moderates intra-white cleavages, creates bonds that override social and other distinctions, and circumvents the problem of self-selection among volunteers.'

The relationship between the part-time and full-time forces can best be understood in terms of the typical Defence Force career of a white male. All white men must register for military service at 16, while still at school. They are then liable for service in the full-time force. Those who do not make a career in the permanent force are required either before or after tertiary education to render two years of national service in one of the five arms of the Defence Force. After this they are placed in the part-time citizen force for twelve years, during which time they must serve up to 720 days in annual 30-, 60- or 90-day 'camps'. Then they are placed in the active citizen force reserve for five years and may be required to serve 12 days a year in a local commando until the age of 55. Finally, they are placed on the national reserve until they are 65.

Although blacks have increasingly been drawn into the ranks of the security establishment and its proxy forces since the 1970s, the base of the SADF itself remains conscripted white manpower. According to the 1986 Defence White Paper, 76 per cent of full-time personnel are whites. The part-time force is also made up of whites, with the exception of a small minority of coloureds, Indians and Africans in the commandos (some 12 per cent of total commando strength, according to the Defence White Paper), and a small number of black citizen force volunteers. Together, these figures indicate that fully 90 per cent of SADF personnel are whites (although less than 15 per cent of the population is white). This reliance on the white population, in conjunction with the variety of threats perceived by Defence Force planners, explains the complex structure of SADF staffing and the life-long demands made on white conscripts.

Estimates of the total force the SADF can mobilise vary considerably. Most often cited is a figure around 400 000–500 000 (*Armed Forces*, May 1985; Heitman, 1983: 53; Leonard, 1983: 99; Davies *et al.*, 1984: 186; Grundy, 1986:21). This is also the figure cited by State President P. W. Botha in defence of the system of conscription (*Beeld*, 5.3.1988). The *Rand Daily Mail* (23.3.1982, 24.3.1982) estimated that up to one million men can ultimately be drawn into the military machine. However, the real significance of these figures lies less in the total number who could be fielded in a full-scale conflict (mobilising all 500 000 would rapidly bring the economy to its knees) than in the overall level of preparation in the white community for war. This includes preparation for conventional, counter-insurgency, border and area warfare.

The army

Until the mid-1970s, the SADF was divided into the traditional service arms of army, navy and airforce. It has responded to the increasing level of conflict in South Africa and southern Africa with the establishment of a further arm, the medical services, and a fifth arm under a separate command structure – the special forces (Spesmag). The highest responsible body in the SADF to oversee the operation of these five arms is the Defence Command Council, chaired by the chief of the SADF. A Defence Planning Committee is responsible for financial management and arms production. Internal SADF management is handled by a Defence Staff Council. Overall SADF operations fall under the guidance of the State Security Council.

By far the largest and most significant of the five service arms is the army. Its standing force at any one time totals about 75 000 (*SA Barometer*, 1, 1987). The 261-unit-strong infantry is the backbone of the SADF. Some 15 armoured units, 16 field artillery units and 11 anti-aircraft units complement the infantry force. With about 80 per cent of total SADF manpower (*SA Barometer*, 1, 1987) and almost 40 per cent of the annual defence budget (Defence White Paper, 1986), the size and expenditure of the army reflect the extent of SADF operations inside and outside the country, and the increased importance of the land-based threat posed by guerilla struggle and popular uprisings. As the 1986 Defence White Paper put it, 'the space between the RSA and its enemies has narrowed alarmingly'. Southern Africa has accordingly been divided into four 'operational areas'. The Western operational area has its headquarters in Windhoek and includes Zambia and Angola. The Northern operational area is based in Pietersburg and covers Zimbabwe and Botswana. The Eastern operational area is head-quartered in Nelspruit and includes Mozambique and Swaziland. Finally the internal operational area covers South Africa itself.

There are three components to the army – a conventional force, a counter-insurgency (COIN) force (also known as the territorial force), and elements falling directly under the chief of the army such as the Army College and the Army Battle School. The COIN force is, not unexpectedly, by far the larger of the two operational forces.

The conventional force – 1 SA Corps – consists of only two divisions, the 7th Infantry and 8th Armoured Divisions, and a parachute brigade (44 Parachute Brigade). Each division has three brigades – one armoured and two mechanised – with some 5 000 troops per brigade. A typical brigade consists of two battalions of mechanised infantry and two tank regiments (or three battalions of mechanised infantry and no tanks), an artillery unit of G-5s or G-6s or both, a targeting unit, a regiment of armoured cars, and an anti-aircraft unit. These are all backed by support units such as an engineer regiment, radio communications, maintenance units, field workshops and a large number of reservists (Frankel, 1984; Heitman, 1988; Larteguy, 1988). The parachute brigade has three battalions and a regiment equipped with mortars.

Only the formation commanders of conventional force brigades, certain principal staff commanders and an administrative skeleton are permanent force members. The conventional force is otherwise dependent on the citizen force for most of its officers as well as for most of its men (Larteguy, 1988; Heitman, 1988: 6). 1 SA Corps was established in 1974 in the face of the impending collapse of the Portuguese colonial empire. It is trained at the Army Battle School at Lohatla in the northern Cape.

The territorial force comprises the largest part of the army infantry. It is organised into ten regional commands and the Walvis Bay military area. Far North and Eastern Transvaal Command have conventional as well as COIN roles. As the backbone of 'area defence' in what General Magnus Malan called the 'second front' of the war, the territorial force takes responsibility for the internal operational area (*Rand Daily Mail*, 5.2.1982; Larteguy, 1988). Unlike SWAPO, the internal 'enemy' is seen

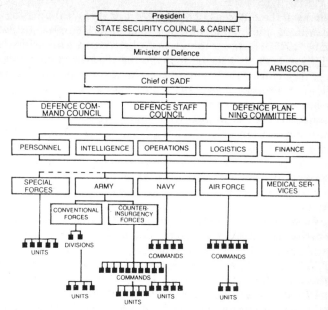

Figure 1: The structure of the SADF

as fighting not a border but an 'area' war against the SADF. The term 'area defence' was used for the first time by former SADF chief, General Constand Viljoen, in 1982. Referring to the ANC, Viljoen said:

> They apparently do not have a border war in mind. They are going to fight an area war. . . . If we had to deal with this using the full-time force the demands on the system would be too great. But we are going to deal with it by using Area Defence. . . . people living in an area must be organized to defend themselves. (*Financial Mail*, 15.1.1982)

Part-time soldiers in the commandos and the citizen force are the first-line of defence in this war, with the full-time force acting as a 'reaction force'. The aim has been to make the defence network more suited to the type of operations expected, with functional structures and discipline in which small combat groups receive greater attention (Davies *et al.*, 1984: 185).

Both the commando and CF units consist largely of light infantry battalions. Three types of commandos exist – rural, urban and industrial. Commandos are generally established as and when a need for them is perceived. So-called 'Dad's Army' commando units (involving men up to 55 years old) have been established throughout the northern, eastern and western Transvaal and Natal border regions. Commandos were also established in the Eastern Cape, Border and northern OFS within six months of the outbreak of the September 1984 Vaal uprising. The first coloured commando unit was established in Queenstown in December 1985 in response to riots in the local African township (Evans and Phillips, 1988: 137). Each commando can be backed up if necessary by three mechanised regiments of armoured vehicles and by a special anti-riot battalion (Larteguy, 1988). Supporting the commando forces in the border regions is the military area radio network, MARNET. This functions both as an intelligence warning system and as an SOS system to protect farmers, who are linked through MARNET to the nearest military base. With 83 base stations and more than 2 500 non-military users, MARNET has recently been expanded to cover the Eastern Province and OFS (Defence White Paper, 1986: 22).

Special forces

The most highly trained troops in the SADF are the reconnaissance commandos ('Recces'). The Recces fall under their own command system – special forces – and are answerable only to the head of the SADF. There are five Recce regiments based at Durban, Pretoria, Phalaborwa and Langebaan. They are specialists in what the SADF journal *Paratus* (May 1985) called 'unconventional warfare'. They are allegedly responsible for many of the attacks on the frontline states and for the training and deployment of proxy forces such as UNITA and Renamo. Recce commandos have also sabotaged oil installations and refineries in Angola.[3]

Other specialist units include the Defence Headquarter's Pathfinder Company of 44 Brigade, the Police Special Task Force, the SWA Police Special Task Force, the SWA Specialists (which use motorcycles, tracker dogs and pack hounds) and the SWA COIN unit, formerly known as Koevoet. To this list should be included 32 Battalion which is made up of mercenary troops, primarily from the defeated Angolan FNLA movement. Troops of 32 Battalion wear unmarked uniforms, use non-SADF equipment (such as AK-47s) and are alleged to be paid cash bounties for killings (BBC, 7.2.1981). According to a deserter, British mercenary Trevor Edwards, the battalion frequently acted together with or on behalf of UNITA and was responsible for 'scorched earth' tactics in southern Angola (*Guardian*, 29.1.1981).

The navy

The SA Navy is the smallest and most poorly funded of the SADF's operational arms. Its total standing force is about 10 000 (*SA Barometer*, 1, 1987). The navy is organised into two area commands directly responsible to naval headquarters in Pretoria. Naval Command West at Silvermine in the Western Cape has Simonstown as its major base. Naval Command East headquartered in Durban has its major base at Salisbury Island. The termination of the Simonstown Agreement with

Britain in 1975 ended joint use of the naval base at Simonstown. This setback and the imposition of the mandatory United Nations arms embargo in 1977 seriously affected the navy. It was subsequently forced to drop its task of protecting the Cape sea route to concentrate on regional interests such as coastal patrol, harbour protection and supporting destabilisation campaigns in Mozambique and Angola (BBC, 30.5.1985; *Sowetan*, 3.6.1985). With the possible exception of submarines, its blue-water capability is presently virtually zero. The navy's main operational units are the strike-craft flotilla, the submarine flotilla, and the mine counter-measures flotilla. The frigate squadron is not operational as both frigates are in reserve awaiting modernisation (Heitman, 1988: 12). The navy also has a counter-insurgency role, for which a thousand-strong Marine Brigade was established in 1979. Marine units are specialised infantry units responsible for harbour, base and national key-point protection. Marines are also deployed in the northern Namibian operational zone and have seen service on township patrols since 1984 (Defence White Paper, 1986).

The airforce

The SA Air Force is organised into two regional commands – Western and Southern – and four functional commands – Airspace Control, Tactical Support, Training, and Logistics. Western Air Command has its headquarters in Windhoek. It controls airforce operations in the Namibian–Angolan war zone. Southern Air Command (formerly Maritime Command) shares the Silvermine complex near Cape Town as its headquarters with the navy. It controls all the airbases along the coast. Since the retirement of the obsolete Shackletons, the SAAF has lacked a long-range maritime patrol capability (Heitman, 1988: 10). Airspace Control Command is sub-divided into a Highveld Sector and a Lowveld Sector, covering the western and eastern Transvaal respectively. It is responsible for both early warning and air defence. Tactical Support Command has the task of establishing and operating within 72 hours temporary air bases wherever the airforce may need them (Heitman, 1988: 9–10). The SAAF numbers about 13 000 personnel (*SA Barometer*, 1, 1987).

Although it is relatively modern and extremely well funded, the airforce is becoming the weak link in the SADF's armour as a result of the increasingly sophisticated air-defence and air-strike capabilities of the frontline states, Angola in particular. The arms embargo has affected it more than any other branch of the SADF. *Paris Match* military corres-pondent Jean Larteguy, who was able to conduct and publicise an unprecedented series of interviews with SAAF personnel, reported that the airforce is no longer confident of its abilities to deal with its adversaries. He quotes an airforce colonel as follows:

Our aircraft are too old. Our Mirage 111s and Cheetahs and our Mirage F1s, armed with Kukri air-to-air heat-seeking missiles can hold their own against the MiG 21s, thanks to the superiority of our pilots, but they are outclassed by the MiG 23s. . . .

Their radar covers not only Angola but extends 100 kilometres over our lines into South West Africa. It has become extremely dangerous to fly over this zone. If we wanted to give cover to our forces operating in Angola we would soon be detected and taken out by the SAMs and the MiG 23s. It is a classic case of Soviet deployment and without the right equipment we are powerless against it. What we need are modern fighter aircraft. (Larteguy, 1988)

Armscor

The Armaments Corporation of South Africa (Armscor) falls under the authority of the Minister of Defence. Its board of directors reflects the close cooperation between the defence establishment and the private sector, which provides seven of Armscor's ten directors (SAIRR, 1980: 378). Armscor, South Africa's largest exporter of manufactured goods, employs over 20 000 people directly and over 100 000 indirectly through its more than 1 500 private sub-contractors (Grundy, 1986: 46; Steenkamp, 1983: 53). Although Armscor claims it now satisfies 90 per cent of SADF requirements, its successes have largely been in the field of production and technology adaptation rather than design. It still relies for the most part on imported technology. The arms embargo, together with fiscal constraints, has put some costly but crucial technologies, components and weapons systems beyond the reach of the SADF. As a result, serious shortcomings remain, particularly in the navy and airforce.

The SADF and civilian society

The civil defence structure, although a predominantly civilian system that aims at coordinating and maintaining essential services in times of emergency, is also integrated into the military command system. According to the Director of Civil Defence (an army brigadier), the system 'is needed to maintain the national morale in war' as it strengthens the 'ability of the nation to resist any form of external or internal attack' (*Rand Daily Mail*, 31.1.1979). The Civil Defence Directorate falls under the Ministry of Defence. Civil defence functions are coordinated by one of the State Security Council's inter-departmental committees. Provincial supervision is by army territorial commands, while each local authority's civil defence director liaises with the local army commander. Civil defence units incorporate most local authority employees, as well as volunteers from the community who sign contracts binding them to a certain number of hours of voluntary service. Pretoria has the most comprehensive and well-prepared civil defence system in the country. It includes a semi-underground control centre and is divided into seven regions, each with main cells, cells, sectors and blocks (*Citizen*, 14.2.1985). The various civil defence organisations are also integrated into the area defence network, which is tested through regular exercises involving commandos, reaction troops, police units and the primarily civilian-staffed civil defence units.

Also falling under SADF area command is the high-school cadet programme. This involves over 200 000 white school pupils in paramilitary activities such as intelligence and counter-intelligence procedures, fieldcraft, drill, first-aid, tracking, camouflage and marksmanship. Some pupils also learn curfew, ambush and bomb-alert procedures, martial arts and commando techniques, use of artillery and anti-aircraft weapons, and receive lectures on the nature of the 'total onslaught' (Evans and Phillips, 1988; Evans, 1983). The system is headed by a central cadet directorate at army headquarters in Pretoria. The SADF also runs racially segregated 'leadership training camps' for high-school youth of all four 'race groups'. The SADF has set up university military units on the campuses of the white Afrikaans-speaking universities, but strong resistance from the English-speaking universities has prevented the extension of the system.

The Military Academy at Saldanha Bay, which awards degrees under the auspices of the Faculty of Military Science at Stellenbosch University, and the Joint Defence College in Pretoria have been responsible for developing the overall counter-revolutionary war theories which inform state policy in the 1980s. Many of their ideas feed into the planning sub-division of the SADF's operational division at Defence Headquarters in Pretoria. This sub-division defines the SADF's role in national strategy, undertakes and supports strategic research, and formulates coordinated strategies for the various departments of state (Grundy, 1986: 42).

The army's 'total strategy' and counter-revolutionary theories have reached their main institutional expression in the National Security Management System, now often known simply as the National Management System. Military personnel occupy key positions at every level of the system, from the State Security Council to the more than 500 Joint Management Centres. Although soldiers do not necessarily head every JMC, in accordance with the maxim that 'the expert need not be on top as long as he is on tap', many JMCs evidence clear military predominance. For example, the OFS JMC is chaired by Brigadier Reg Otto of the army, the Security Committee chairperson is army colonel Robbie Coetzee and the JMC's secretary is Colonel Hansie Steyl (*Beeld*, 9.7.1988).

Allied forces

Under formally separate command from the SADF but functionally integrated into its operations and planning are the defence forces of the four 'independent' homelands. The 1986 Defence White Paper makes it clear that as far as Africans are concerned, 'the emphasis is on the development of ethnic regional units in the various national states. After independence such units are absorbed by the defence force of the independent states.' Each of the Transkei, Ciskei, Bophuthatswana and Venda homelands have thus acquired defence forces. According to the 1982 Defence White Paper,

military agreements are entered into with these States when they attain their independence. This leads to the creation of a joint management body to co-ordinate co-operation. . . . The SADF recognizes the supportive capabilities of the Independent States and encourages their participation in an overall Southern African military treaty against a common enemy.

The 1980s have seen the steady 'Namibianisation' of the conflict in the northern Namibian war zone. Since the creation of the South West Africa Territory Force (SWATF), the introduction of compulsory conscription for all Namibians, and the establishment of the 9 000-strong home guard in the northern war zone, the burden of fighting the war has increasingly fallen on Namibians themselves. This has led some commentators to suggest that black Namibians are being used as cannon fodder in South Africa's war (Grundy, 1983: 203). SWATF was created in 1980 out of what was formerly the SWA regional command of the SADF. This followed the passing of UN Security Council Resolution 435 which declared that all but 1 500 SADF troops should be removed from Namibia during a transitional period towards independence. The force 'is intended and being developed to form South West Africa's own defence force after independence' (Defence White Paper, 1986).

Although SWATF and SADF troops are deployed together in the war zone, SWATF has rapidly assumed an identity of its own with six ethnic battalions. These are 201 Battalion (Bushmen), 101 Battalion (Ovambo) and 202 Battalion (Kavango) as well as 203, 701, and 102 Battalions. They consist of partly conscripted, partly volunteer light infantry troops trained for COIN warfare. There is also one large conventional brigade, 911 Battalion, based at Windhoek. Although formally multiracial, SWATF is broken down into segregated companies. It also incorporates 26 largely white reserve 'area force units' – similar to South African commandos – and a reserve squadron flying light aircraft (Leonard, 1983: 105). With a total force in excess of 20 000 (*SA Barometer*, 1, 1987), SWATF now provides 51 per cent of all soldiers deployed in the operational area (1986 Defence White Paper). Also integral to SWATF military operations, although formally part of the SWA Police, is the COIN unit (Koevoet) which 'has never had anything other than a military function' (Manning and Green, 1986: 126).

The most difficult relationships to trace between the South African military and its allies are those between the SADF and organised proxy forces of destabilisation – the Mozambique Resistance Movement (Renamo), UNITA, the Lesotho Liberation Army (LLA), and the so-called Super ZAPU of Zimbabwe. There is a wealth of evidence confirming active arming, training, supplying, and deployment by the SADF of such forces (see Martin and Johnson, 1986; Grundy, 1986: 95). However, the relationship between the integration of these groups into SADF operational structures on one hand, and their independence on the other, is not always clear and has varied over time.

No study of the structure of the SADF would be complete without some mention of the relationship between military and police forces in South Africa. The 1988 White Paper on the Organisation and Functions of the South African Police includes as the first of the police force's responsibilities 'the preservation of internal security'. The 1977 Defence White Paper formulated the relationship between the police and military in this way: 'The responsibility for combating internal and especially urban unrest rests primarily on the SAP. Nevertheless, the SA Army must at all times be ready, on a country-wide basis, to quickly mobilize trained forces to render assistance to the SA Police.'

In both its border counter-insurgency and internal security roles the SADF works hand in hand with the SA Police. Internally this has involved SADF units cordoning off townships during SAP swoops, staffing joint roadblocks, participating in squatter demolition and strike-breaking activities, halting meetings, occupying university campuses, and patrolling townships. At the same time, the number of police taking courses in counter-insurgency warfare and riot control has increased from 3 383 in 1977 to 12 917 in 1987 (Annual Report: 1977 and 1987). 'Combat-ready' riot units are now deployed in each of the 19 police divisions country-wide (Ministry of Law and Order, 1988: 18). There is also evidence that the police have worked together with the SADF in providing support for Renamo (Frankel, 1984: 102; *Weekly Mail*, 19.8.1988).

Conclusion

The SADF, its various formal and informal formations, and the security establishment as a whole constitute a formidable coercive network which impinges in one way or another upon the lives of most South Africans. Large and powerful structures and sophisticated technology alone do not, however, necessarily mean that the system which this establishment defends is invincible. Elsewhere in this volume it is suggested that the counter-revolutionary strategy pursued by the SADF and its security allies will not necessarily realise their objectives.[4] A secure future for South Africa lies not in the structures of its defence force or in the further extension of an already bewildering security network, but in the achievement of a non-racial democracy.

2 'Platskiet-politiek': the role of the Union Defence Force (UDF) 1910–1924

MARIAN LACEY

We have to-day in South Africa civil government suppressed by what is nothing less than military autocracy. . . . Instead of the ordinary tribunal of the country, the judicial functions have been usurped by military courts. There is military administration everywhere; civil administration plays only a subordinate part. The freedom of the press . . . has been restricted to eulogies of the Government and the authorities. . . . The people have been robbed of their fundamental and constitutional rights. Freedom of speech – the only place for that is the gaol. There is freedom of public meetings only for Government supporters. Sir, in the place of right and justice . . . there has been nothing but arbitrary despotism. That is the state of affairs under which this country has been suffering . . . it is a state of affairs under which this country is still suffering at the present time. (General J. B. M. Hertzog, House of Assembly Debates, 1914)

Reading General Hertzog's statement almost 75 years later reveals that very little new is to be learnt about the way in which men of power have used, and continue to use, the military to protect and defend their social order. Circumstances, of course, have changed. So have the actors and the social order in South Africa. But has the role and nature of the military? If so, in what way?[1]

This chapter attempts to analyse and explain the historical role and nature of the military, focusing on the period 1910-24. Histories have been written on this period, especially on the Union Defence Force, South Africa and the First World War, and the 1914 Boer Rebellion, but they are either highly ritualised or cast in a stereotyped mould of Boer–British relations. In this context, writing on the military has always been a highly political affair, unashamedly used by imperial and nationalist historians to further their respective political objectives. This chapter seeks to redress some of these shortcomings by casting the role of the military in a new perspective. It deals with the role of the state and the military against worker and popular struggles, in the context of class conflict and class formation in the first two decades after Union.

We first examine how the armed forces were used to confront and brutally defeat militant struggles waged in the main by white workers in the 1913–14 and 1922 strikes. We then assess the role of the military in crushing the popular uprising in 1914. These struggles challenged the social order imposed by the Union government which was determined to defend and further the interests of foreign and domestic mining capital. Having quelled these early attempts by whites to challenge the social order, state repression gave way to reform and restructuring. From 1922 onwards, struggles by white workers have been characterised by compromise, cooption and class collaboration. The use of military force after this was directed against black resisters who challenged the imposed social order.

The military and class war: the strikes of 1913–14 and 1922
   The strikes of 1913–14 and 1922 have been selected for analysis. This is not simply because troops were called in and martial law was declared, but also because state action in suppressing the strikes elucidates most clearly the military's role in a period in which class struggle was transformed into class war. As Ralph Miliband reminds us, class struggle is a two-way process; but it is in the first instance a struggle waged by the dominant class, with the state acting on its behalf, against the workers and subordinate classes (Miliband, 1973: 413). In this struggle, the effective power is that of the state backed by the military as the armoured fist of the ruling class. At such times, when the ruling class believes that their social order is being threatened, Miliband argues,

> there is a vast difference to be made – sufficiently vast as to require a difference of name – between on the one hand 'ordinary' class struggle, of the kind which goes on day in and day out in capitalist societies . . . and which is *known* to constitute no threat to the capitalist framework within which it occurs; and on the other hand, class struggle which either does, or which is thought likely to, affect the social order in really fundamental ways. . . . This latter form of struggle requires to be described not simply as class struggle, but as class war.

With the shutdown of all the gold mines across the Reef in July 1913, the course was set for the declaration of class war and the biggest struggle between labour and mining capital to date. The opening shots were fired by the newly appointed mine manager at the Kleinfontein mine, Edward Bulman. Bulman's appointment was not a haphazard choice, for as F. D. P. Chaplin of Consolidated Gold Fields wrote in a letter to J. X. Merriman:

> The Kleinfontein Company had allowed the mine to become a hotbed of 'Labour'. The miners were allowed to earn an exorbitant amount of money, and the result was that they subscribed more in 1912 to the Miners' Association than was subscribed by the men of any other individual mine. The management at last arrived at the fact that they were losing a good deal of profit and appointed a new manager [Bulman] to 'cleanse the stable'. (Katz, 1976: 382)

Bulman's announcement that underground mechanics would have to work a full-day on Saturdays was the immediate cause of the dispute, for under the Industrial Disputes Prevention Act he was required to give a month's notice of any intended changes. The men who refused to work the extra half-day were dismissed and replaced by non-union men. A strike committee, which included representatives of the newly formed Federation of Trade Unions, demanded the reinstatement of the dismissed workers and the abolition of Saturday afternoon work. The chairman of the Kleinfontein mine, with the full support of the Chamber of Mines, refused to negotiate with the strike committee, claiming that a step of such 'magnitude' would 'create a precedent' which would affect the whole mining industry (U.G. 56–13: 9). A strike was then declared on Kleinfontein mines and the issue of trade-union recognition became a central issue on the strikers' agenda. This, the use of scab labour and the company's refusal to dismiss 59 strike-breakers and reinstate the dismissed men, brought matters to a complete deadlock within a month. The strike had turned into a battle between two parties, the Federation and the Chamber of Mines, 'each of which would be satisfied only with the unconditional surrender of its opponent' (Katz, 1976: 397). By 28 June, delegates of unions affiliated to the Federation agreed that all the affiliated unions would ballot for a general strike. Events moved very rapidly after the meeting; by 4 July a total of 63 mines were already out, and by the following day every mine and power station on the Witwatersrand, comprising 19 000 workers, had joined the strike.

The government was neither equipped nor prepared for a strike of this magnitude. A mass meeting scheduled for 2 p.m. at Market Square in Johannesburg was banned by the chief magistrate acting under orders of the Minister of Defence, J. C. Smuts. The ban was only communicated at 1.30 p.m. when the huge crowd had already assembled. Refusing to disperse, the meeting was broken up by a charge of police and the imperial troops. The latter had been called up belatedly by Smuts, as the Union Defence Force (UDF) still only existed in embryonic form and was therefore unable to handle the crisis. Later that afternoon violence broke out and continued through the night until the following day. By then the general strike was complete. Businesses and shops were closed. The previous night the *Star* offices were burnt, and Park Station was attacked by incendiaries. When disturbances occurred outside the Rand Club, bastion of the Randlords, the order to shoot was given. Firing indiscriminately into the crowd, troops killed 25 people, some of whom were innocent bystanders. Only then did the Prime Minister, Louis Botha, accompanied by Smuts, rush to the Rand. After a meeting held at the Carlton Hotel, a two-hour truce was declared. The Federation leaders agreed to 'stop the disorder' if all the Kleinfontein strikers were reinstated and the government guaranteed to redress the miners' grievances. Smuts and Botha at a second meeting with representatives of the Chamber of Mines outlined the strikers' demands and warned that without sufficient troops the government could not guarantee to defend mine property. The

Chamber of Mines was also forced to capitulate.

The strikers were victorious: the mine-owners promised reinstatement. A judicial commission found the miners' grievances were justified.[2] Thereafter both the Chamber of Mines and the government were obliged to recognise the miners' union, and rules for the future negotiation of industrial disputes were laid down. Commissions were also appointed to investigate the eight-hour day, the cost of living, and railwaymen's wages. Emboldened by their success, the Federation prepared for their next battle. The next time round, six months later, they found Smuts militarily prepared. Backed by the armed forces, the state inflicted a humiliating defeat on the workers.

Towards the end of 1913, the white coal miners of Natal struck. The new year opened with rumours of an impending railway strike. With the threatened retrenchment of 2 000 railwaymen, plans for a general railway strike were set in motion. The South African Federation of Trades was approached to secure sympathy action from the gold miners. With the gold mines threatened again with closure, Smuts responded immediately. Following the debacle of the previous July, Smuts went to extraordinary lengths to reassert his authority. In order to achieve this, he planned in advance a full-scale military operation to pre-empt the strike call. How this was achieved is detailed by Piet van der Byl, at the time a captain in the permanent force, and later Minister of Native Affairs. 'Smuts,' Van der Byl records, 'put into operation his carefully prepared plans for our 18-months-old Defence Force' (1971: 86). In terms of existing legislation, to declare a state of emergency the Cabinet would have to submit a request to the Governor-General advising him to gazette a proclamation; only then could troops be mobilised and martial law imposed. Moreover, the decision of the Governor-General would be made after careful discussion with legal advisers, imperial advisers, and personal agonising. In essence, it would take time 'and here time was of the essence'.

Humiliated by his defeat at the hands of the workers six months earlier, and in order to 'expedite matters' (as Van der Byl would have it), Smuts ensured that the Cabinet prepared both its request and the Governor-General's proclamation well in advance. The proclamation was printed in the correct gazette form, and telegrams to be sent to every unit of the UDF were written. On the day the labour leaders met in Johannesburg, martial law proclamations were already being posted up. Within minutes of the decision to call a general strike being taken, Smuts had signed the Cabinet request, which ten minutes later had the Governor-General's assent. As Van der Byl proudly noted:

Within minutes of the Labour leaders' decision, their whole organisation was paralysed. One man, unable to get through by telephone to Pretoria and trying to make it by road, was stopped by a Police road-block. By morning press censorship was enforced; private telegrams were held up; telephones cut off;

travel on the roads stopped and strike leaders out of touch with their colleagues in other areas. Wild rumours were rampant. This time Smuts had not been caught unprepared. (1971: 87–8)

Unable to be 'blooded' in 1913, the UDF in 1914 was successfully launched as the armoured fist of the ruling class.

With the declaration of martial law 60 000 men from both the commando system and the newly formed UDF[3] were on standby. General De la Rey and his machine-gunners were ordered to surround the Trades Hall and force the surrender of the trade-union leaders.

The imposition of martial law in South Africa on 10 January 1914 signified that the state had, in effect, declared class war against the workers. The country was transformed into an armed camp in defence against its 'internal enemies'. Mass arrests were followed by the illegal deportation, in great secrecy and equal haste, of nine trade-union leaders.

The Indemnity and Undesirables Special Deportation Bill was put before the House shortly after these actions took place. Martial law was still in force, although on the prime minister's own admission the country was calm as it had been throughout this period. Why then the military intervention and the declaration of martial law?

In parliament, speaker after speaker painted a picture of a country 'under siege', and of the imminence of the violence and unrest threatened by 'red terrorists'. Worse even than this was the 'black peril' which, once unleashed by 'red' insurgency, would engulf and erase 'white civilisation'. The government used this parliamentary alarmism to rally conservative forces to its side in its battle with the workers. It also rallied support for the required indemnification following the arbitrary use of force, mass detentions and illegal deportation of union leaders carried out under martial law. Because the actions of the state had been taken against white workers, they required juridical indemnification and public acceptance.

Justifying the imposition of martial law, Prime Minister Louis Botha referred in parliament to the events of July 1913, six months earlier. He insisted that behind these events stood members of the Labour Party and their 'terrorist' cohorts. Their intention, he asserted, was to disrupt the social order:

it was not an ordinary strike, but a revolutionary movement. . . . It was not less than war against society at large. The public were in a state of panic. The position he had beheld . . . was the most terrible he had ever seen in his life. He had seen things in war – he had seen serious panics and serious assaults at arms – but here he saw a thing that was more serious, namely a determined assault on the life of the people. (HAD, 1914, col. 330)

With this alarmist rhetoric Botha denied the basis of the strikers' grievances and went on to describe the events of 4–5 July as a declaration of war against the women and children. It had been a murderous attack on the freedom of the people. . . . The whole movement had not been with an idea to bring the so-called grievances to an end – these had been beside the question – but the whole attempt had been to overthrow society in South Africa. (*Ibid.*)

The state-appointed commission of inquiry showed that the miners had been unjustly treated, and that looting and the burning of the *Star* offices had only followed the intervention of imperial troops. Disregarding this evidence, and foreshadowing South Africa's current rulers, Botha insisted that a few 'agitators' were responsible and that 'there could be no freedom of the people if a minority wanted to rule. It was nothing but tyranny which had wanted to rule South Africa.' Who was this 'minority' whom Botha berated as 'undemocratic and uncaring of the desires of all peace-loving citizens'? The accusations were hurled at the Labour Party members sitting on the cross benches. They were accused of being 'the generals of the hooligans'. But, argued Botha, real power was in the hands of the strike leaders, whom he accused of all being syndicalists or anarchists intent on the violent overthrow of the state through the general strike.[5] These men he painted in dark terms to convince the House of their evil intentions.

The government's use of the armed forces was supported in speech after speech in parliament. J. W. Jagger, a leading representative of commercial capital, joined the general throng and warned of the 'reckless methods' of the strike leaders. Their aim, he claimed, was the financial ruin of the country; their action 'had practically amounted to Syndicalism', which was their goal. This included the repatriation of the black workforce which could result only in 'the utter disorganisation of the life and business of Johannesburg . . . and the credit of the country' (HAD, 1914, col. 318). The 'red peril' theme was followed and reinforced by the assertion that the '*swart gevaar*' – the black peril – could have been provoked into action either in solidarity with the strikers or on its own account. This possibility was seen to be an even greater threat to the ruling class. For this reason alone, military intervention was justified. Unsurprisingly, the prime minister was least restrained in describing this possibility. Drawing on all the archetypal nightmares of whites, he warned the country that 'the reds'

had the natives driven to a state of panic by the revolution and the acts and threats of the Labour Party. Natives did not understand going on strike, but what they did understand was that, when the king sang his war song it was war, and when 'The Red Flag' was sung and the meaning of it explained to them, they felt it was war . . . if peace had not been concluded that evening all along the Reef that night there might have been the most terrible incendiarism imaginable. (HAD, 1914, col. 332)

In 1914, when African miners struck at Jagersfontein and state troopers shot two strikers, the worst fears of the white ruling class were seemingly confirmed: namely, that white workers by their action were spreading revolutionary ideas across the colour line (Hirson, 1987). Black strikes had been illegalised; a decade later Africans were banned from becoming members of official trade unions. Clearly, by denying Africans both the vote and worker rights, the state possessed the key means of keeping African labour ultra-exploitable as well as docile. The events described above show that the use of state troops continued to be an essential factor in maintaining white supremacy and were freely used in its service.

The first decade and a half after Union was clearly of crucial importance. It saw established an industrial social order which was to endure for the following 70 years. The military played a key role in the establishment of this order by emasculating the white labour movement. As Major Nicholson predicted: '. . . of one thing we may be absolutely certain, that not in this generation or the next will the serpent of revolutionary syndicalism raise its head in South Africa' (HAD, 1914, col. 346).

Workers within the first two decades of Union had certainly been divided and disorganised. But as valid as Nicholson's comment was a warning from Labour Party member C. H. Hagger, passing judgment on Botha's 'sneer at democracy': 'It had always been the story that the heretics of one age were the heroes of the next and the gods of the third. The policy of repression and curtailment of rights and justice would like a boomerang return upon the man who threw it and always in increasing momentum, until the man who threw it would fall a victim to his own deed.' (HAD, 1914, col. 365)

The words seemed prophetic when Smuts's government fell after the next major confrontation with organised labour during the Rand Revolt of 1922, during which Smuts used even more violent counter-measures than he had in 1914. Not content with merely unleashing the army against the striking white workers, Smuts brought the newly formed airforce into play, bombing the liberated zones of the strikers in various Johannesburg suburbs as far as Benoni and beyond. The death toll reached 270, with over 1 000 injured; all were white. This massive military operation, however, signalled the end of a particular phase of class conflict in South Africa. It was the last occasion on which white workers had their protests crushed by direct military action, and closed the first brutal cycle of repression of South African workers.

General Hertzog, leader of the National Party opposition, rightly accused the government of constantly engaging in *platskiet-politiek* – the politics of 'shooting down':

everywhere General Smuts had indulged in a policy of shooting down. The passive resistance movement was the first occasion. Then came the shooting in

1913, and then the illegal deportations. . . . Then the rebellion – shooting down and murder. Then the war, which had distracted the Prime Minister's attention. Then the native trouble at Port Elizabeth – shooting again; and then the trouble on the Rand – shooting again. (Hancock, 1962: 87)

He could have added that *platskiet-politiek* was also used in suppressing the strike by 42 000 African mineworkers in 1920, and in the Bulhoek and Bondelswarts massacres.

But it was more than an 'indulgence' of force. Our analysis shows that the state's main concern at that time was to establish a social order in which the mining industry would flourish. The strikes of 1913 and 1922 were clearly a direct threat to mining profitability and the state therefore intervened. Similarly, the 1914 Rebellion led by Afrikaner farmer commandos was perceived as a threat to the interests of mining and foreign capital, and military force was used to crush it. The perceived threat to mining interests and the different role played by the military in this event are analysed in the following section.

The military and class formation: the 1914 Rebellion

The outbreak of the First World War in August 1914 provided the signal in South Africa for an Afrikaner rebellion against the dominant role of British imperialism in South Africa's political economy. The main declared aim of the uprising was the reinstatement of Afrikaner independence and the need to vindicate the thousands of men, women and children who had suffered during the Anglo–Boer War. Most writers agree that these motives, together with the demand that South Africa remain neutral in what was seen as a war between competing imperialist forces, constituted the prime reasons for the outbreak of the rebellion.[4]

These certainly were important motives. However, re-examination of the rebellion, and the military's role in crushing it, reveals another interpretation – that the military was used by the Botha government to undermine the growing resistance by Boer farmers to the changing nature of capitalist relations of production. In this context it has been argued in general terms that the military does not only play a repressive role in defence of dominant class interests (as it did in the strikes) but it can also play a modernising role in class formation. The role of the military in class formation has been demonstrated elsewhere in cases where the middle class challenges traditional landed oligarchies, and the military is used to dislodge the latter (Huntington, 1968). A brief examination of the farmers' grievances, which are relevant in understanding the 1914 Rebellion, reveals the military playing a similar role.

In the first place, the farmer-commandos who rose did so to secure and defend, through armed protest, a traditional social order which they believed was being undermined by the pro-imperialist policies of the Botha–Smuts regime. Hertzog's National Party argued that government policies, in favouring the interests of mining and foreign capital, were forcing some farmers into bankruptcy and squeezing others off the land. This was in fact occurring as the result of a deliberate policy designed to transform and modernise capitalist relations of production in the countryside. The maize producers who persisted in using traditional forms of farming were badly hit in the process.

Even before war broke out in 1914, farmers and maize producers in particular were up in arms. After a three-year drought which had ravaged the countryside, drought relief was only offered to capitalised farmers who could prove they had farmed profitably before the onset of the drought. The small farmers thus faced bankruptcy. In addition to this, Smuts, as Minister of Finance, was threatening to levy a tax on undeveloped land. Farmers who maintained reservoirs of seasonal labour on unoccupied farms, as many maize farmers did, found this measure particularly abhorrent. But there were other threats to the farmers' labour supply. The Natives Land Act of 1913 made it illegal to hire, lease or sell land to Africans residing outside of the reserves scheduled under the Act. Many undercapitalised and small farmers who still farmed under the half-share or share-cropping system, whereby landless African tenants hired or leased land and in return surrendered a share of their crop to the absentee white landowner, suddenly found their livelihood threatened. Furthermore this anti-squatting clause was to apply with immediate effect in the Free State because capitalist farmers in that province were most strident in their demand for state intervention to increase the labour supply (Lacey, 1981). But the implementation of the anti-squatting laws had the completely opposite effect to what was intended: African tenants affected by these harsh new laws fled the Free State farms in their tens of thousands and took refuge in the reserves. This exacerbated the acute labour shortage, as did the farmers' competition with the mine-owners for labour.

On top of this, with the price of maize soaring during the drought, the Chamber of Mines demanded that, since maize was the staple food for mineworkers, either the price of locally produced maize should be lowered, or the government should continue to import much cheaper maize from the United States. As Walker correctly argued, 'those British who had half feared that Smuts or Botha would use their power for purely rural Afrikaner ends were convinced of their error' (Walker, 1959: 559).

In this context, it is not surprising that the dissident commandos, operating under Generals De Wet in the northern and eastern Free State, Kemp in western Transvaal, and Beyers in northern and southern Transvaal, found a high degree of anger and a ready response to their call to rebel. Writing to Smuts in September 1914, Deneys Reitz described conditions in the northern Free State, where burghers were resisting even before the call to rebel was made: 'The Hertzog leaders are, of course, making capital out of the German South West expedition and the Boers in this district are in commotion . . . they stand in groups on every street corner inveighing against the Government and even the Commandant [De Wet] declares he will support the burghers in resisting commandeering orders.' (Hancock, 1966: 196)

Contrary to conventional wisdom, the rebel faction comprised not simply staunch pro-republican NP supporters. Among the farmer-commando recruits were many South African Party constituents from the maize-growing areas, and among the rank-and-file recruits were many poor white indigents who, through the capitalisation of agriculture and the farmers' preference for cheap African labour, had been thrown off the land. Many had gravitated to the dry diggings at the diamond fields, but with the outbreak of the war and the collapse of the diamond industry found themselves jobless again. They too were more than ready to rise to the call.

The prime minister was also Minister of Agriculture and so was well aware of the grievances of maize farmers. Indeed when the Hertzog faction broke away from the South African Party in 1912, it had drawn most of its support from the maize-growing areas. Despite this loss of support, the government heeded the demand by mining capital that maize farming be transformed and made more cost-efficient. In the process many non-progressive farmers were sacrificed.

When the rebellion broke out, martial law was declared and recruits were commandeered to crush the rebellion. During the debate on the Indemnity and Special Tribunals Bill the following year, a majority in parliament ratified the arbitrary use of force by Botha's loyal commandos against their former comrades-in-arms.

This analysis also explains why, in the aftermath of the rebellion, the discriminatory process continued. The poor who had rebelled were further impoverished by high fines and imprisonment, and as a result were proletarianised. The affluent rebels by contrast were treated with greater leniency and discretion both during the war and afterwards. Martial law, as Hertzog's quotation at the beginning of this chapter shows, resulted in the suspension of civil liberties. Nonetheless, as Merriman pointed out, even military rule was a political affair. The inequalities inherent in the process of class conflict and class formation ensured discrimination in favour of some rebels as against others. Merriman wrote to Smuts:

What I wanted to express was the feeling of myself and a good many others, Dutch as well as English, that this palavering with avowed rebels had gone altogether too far. Just look at the facts. On the 26th October de Wet at the head of a band of ragamuffins, . . . destroys the railway, inflicting severe loss and damage on public property. On the 28th, having in the interval stolen (commandeered!) arms and property he appears at Reitz, makes a ridiculous and seditious harangue, damages public property, seizes private goods and proclaims that he is in rebellion. . . . *Is* there no law? Are the crimes of robbery, sedition and public violence merely venial eccentricities when committed by a certain section of the community? (Hancock, 1962: 387)

Merriman insisted that poor and rich alike should all be treated as common criminals and charged with public violence.

A final point which needs to be made in our revaluation of the 1914 Rebellion is that there has been an erroneous assumption in the literature that civil–military relations after Union were patterned on the British model where the military is subordinate to the civil authority. The 1912 Defence Act certainly made provision for modernising the army along these lines. But the activities of dissident elements in the UDF in 1914 demonstrates that the British model was still an alien tradition to Afrikaners of the former Republics. As Hertzog himself stressed in the 1914 Indemnity Bill debate, the Boer commandos had historically always played a key role in moderating power between ruling factions, and an interventionist role in class formation and racial oppression. From his point of view and that of his supporters, the 1914 uprising represented from the outset a traditional form of 'armed protest'. In resigning their commissions and responding to the rebellious farmers in their regional command areas, Generals Beyers, De Wet, Kemp and others were therefore acting as had their forefathers. As Walker noted, the rebellion could be seen as the 'old armed demonstration, the appeal from votes in the Volksraad to the clicking of triggers at the door of the Volksraad chamber which Henry Cloete had heard in Maritzburg in 1843 and more than one republic President since' (Walker, 1959: 563).

This chapter has pointed towards the role of the military in class conflict and class formation, situated within the class war of the first two decades of Union. The use of military intervention to secure political goals was regarded by a significant sector of South African society as an acceptable form of activity; militarisation, suspension of the rule of law, and parliamentary sanction for the arbitrary use of force were not generally regarded as the hallmarks of an aberrant society. As Hertzog correctly pointed out in 1914, these aberrant forms represent the South African way of life:

[If] there was a cause, it was this: the loss by the people of all confidence in Constitutional self-government. This lies at the very root of the rebellion or whatever you may like to call it. The people in this country have no inherited love for the Constitution as the Englishman has. Constitutional government is not . . . an integral part of the life of the nation. Constitutional principles are not, as with the English, taken up from his very infancy, and growing with his life. . . . These people still have to learn what constitutional government means. . . . What must their idea of Constitutional self-government be when interpreted in the light of the actions of the Minister? . . . But an arbitrary lawlessness such as appears to be guiding the actions of the Minister at present and during the last eighteen months can only lead to one thing, and that is chaos. (HAD, 1914, col. 283)

3 The power to defend: an analysis of various aspects of the Defence Act

KATHY SATCHWELL

In 1957 the Defence Act consolidated the law relating to the defence of South Africa. The Act determined the legal position of the South African Defence Force and its members, confirmed the existence of the permanent and citizen forces, and provided for a new military code of discipline and the establishment of a system of commandos. It also constituted the statutory authority for the existence of the SADF. The Act is supplemented by general regulations which have been published in the *Government Gazette*, as well as certain Defence Force Orders which are issued by the chiefs of the Defence Force and the army, navy and airforce.

In terms of the Act, the SADF or any portion or any member thereof may be employed on service 'in the defence of the Republic; in the prevention or suppression of terrorism; in the prevention or suppression of internal disorder in the Republic; and in the preservation of life, health or property or the maintenance of essential services.' While employed on such service, the SADF and its members may be used to carry out the police functions mentioned in Section 5 of the Police Act of 1958 (Section 3(2) of Defence Act).

These already broad functions are even more widely defined in the Act. For example, 'operations in the defence of the Republic' are: 'military operations in time of war or in connection with the discharge of the obligations of the Republic arising from agreement or for the prevention or suppression of any armed conflict outside the Republic which, in the opinion of the State President, is or may be a threat to the security of the Republic' (Section 1 of Defence Act).

Over the past ten years, the SADF has exercised these functions extensively both inside and outside South Africa. It has played a coercive role in black townships, and in Namibia, Angola, Zimbabwe, Lesotho, Swaziland, Mozambique and Zambia. In this context, certain aspects of the Defence Act have been particularly important. Conscription has become a vital issue to the state as more and more young men are required to serve in the SADF. This in turn has fuelled opposition to both conscription and the activities of the SADF. Growing international and domestic opposition has resulted in the SADF's becoming less subject to public scrutiny, and information about military activities becoming more restricted. The activities of the SADF, particularly in Namibia, have also required its members to be indemnified against prosecution for unlawful actions.

This chapter examines the provisions and application of three aspects of the Defence Act: firstly, the liability of a citizen to render service in the SADF, the circumstances under which one might be exempted from service, and the penalties imposed upon those who refuse to serve; secondly, the powers created in the Defence Act to prohibit and limit information about Defence Force activities; and thirdly, instances of blatant interference in the legal process so as to render the SADF beyond the reaches of courts of law.

Liability for service in the South African Defence Force

Section 3(1)(b) of the Defence Act provides: 'Every citizen between his 17th and 65th year, both included, shall be liable to render service in the South African Defence Force. . . .'

A 'citizen' is defined as a South African citizen within the meaning of the South African Citizenship Act No. 44 of 1949. In terms of that Act every person who is born in the Republic after 1949 shall, subject to certain provisions, be a South African citizen. A recent amendment to the Citizenship Act provides that any alien who is entitled to permanent residence and who has been ordinarily resident in the Republic for a period of at least five years shall be a South African citizen by naturalisation as from when he attains the age of 15 years and 6 months, unless his responsible parent or guardian makes a declaration stating that he does not wish to become such a citizen (Section 11A).

Section 63 of the Defence Act requires every male citizen to apply to the SADF registering officer for registration at the beginning of the year in which he becomes 16 years old. Any person who becomes a citizen before he attains the age of 55 years shall also apply for registration within 30 days after the date upon which he becomes a citizen. On registration each person shall furnish his address and thereafter is required to notify the registering officer of every change of his address.

The registering officer shall, with due regard to the requirements of the SADF and subject to any decisions of Exemption Boards or Boards for Religious Objection, allot persons to the citizen force or the commandos as provided for in Section 67.

The liability to render service in the citizen force continues over a period of 14 years reckoned from the date upon which training commenced in the citizen force for the first time (Section 21.1). Such service consists of an initial period of 24 continuous months of national service, and thereafter during the next 12 years of periods of service which shall not exceed 90 days at a time (Section 22(3)(a) and (b)). The period of service may be extended by the Minister of Defence whenever he considers it to be necessary in the interests of the SADF or the public interest.

Exemptions and religious objectors

The Minister of Manpower, in consultation with the Minister of Defence, appoints Exemption Boards in terms of Section 68 of the Defence Act. Any person who is liable to serve may apply to an Exemption Board for deferment of or exemption from service. The Board is empowered, with due regard to any general instructions issued by the Minister of Manpower in consultation with the Minister of Defence, to grant such an application. It does so where 'in its opinion it is justified':

(a) in order to prevent the interruption of the course of education studies of the person concerned; or

(b) by reason of the nature and extent of such person's domestic obligations or any circumstances connected with any trade, profession or business in which he is engaged; or

(c) on the grounds of physical defect, ill-health or mental incapacity on the part of such person; or

(d) on the grounds that such person is being compulsorily detained in an institution; or

(e) on any other ground it may deem sufficient (Section 70 bis (1)).

An application will only be granted by the Board where it is satisfied that undue hardship would otherwise be caused, or that it is in the public interest that the application be granted. The Board has the power to direct that the person concerned be allotted to a commando instead of granting him deferment of or exemption from service. The Board is also empowered to withdraw or amend its decision where it is satisfied that the facts upon which such decision was founded have changed (Section 70 ter).

During 1983 and 1984 a series of amendments to the Defence Act were promulgated to provide for religious objectors who refused to serve in the SADF and who either were not eligible for or had been refused an exemption from service.

The Minister of Manpower appoints Boards for Religious Objection in terms of Section 72A of the Act. The chairman of the Board shall be a judge or a retired judge of the Supreme Court of South Africa, three members of the Board shall be theologians who belong to different religious denominations, and two members shall be members of the South African Defence Force (one of whom shall be a chaplain). If an applicant for classification as a religious objector belongs to a religious denomination which is not represented on the Board, then the Board may coopt a theologian who belongs to that religious denomination. Where no such theologian indicates his willingness to serve on the Board, then the application may be considered by the Board without such a theologian having been coopted.

Any person who has been allotted to the citizen force or commandos may apply to the Board to be classified as a religious objector. Such an application must set out, inter alia, the category of religious objector in which the applicant wishes to be classified, and the facts and grounds upon which the application is based. It must also state the books of Revelation and the articles of faith upon which the religious convictions of the applicant are based. The onus of proving that he is a religious objector rests upon the applicant. The Board may grant or refuse an application.

Where it grants an application for classification as religious objector it may classify the applicant:

(i) as a religious objector with whose religious convictions it is in conflict to render service in a combatant capacity in any armed force;

(ii) as a religious objector with whose religious convictions it is in conflict to render service in a combatant capacity in any armed force, to perform any maintenance tasks of a combatant nature therein and to be clothed in a military uniform; or

(iii) as a religious objector with whose religious convictions it is in conflict to render any military service or to undergo any military training or to perform any task in or in connection with any armed force (Section 72D(1)(a)).

A person classified as a religious objector in terms of Section 72D(1)(a)(i) shall render service in a non-combatant capacity in the SADF. A person classified in terms of Section 72D(1)(a)(ii) shall render service which shall be one-and-a-half times as long as the periods to which he would otherwise have been liable, wearing clothing other than a military uniform, and the service shall be rendered by performing prescribed tasks of a non-combatant nature. A person who is classified as a religious objector in terms of Section 72D(1)(a)(iii) shall render service to be known as 'community service', which shall be completed in a single continuous period equal to one-and-a-half times as long as the aggregate of all periods of service which would otherwise have been applicable. The community service shall be rendered as ordered by the Minister of Manpower in a department as defined in the Public Service Act or in an institute or body contemplated in the Republic of South Africa Constitution Act.

Religious objector status: a case study

Allan Goddard was appointed to a permanent teaching position in the Transvaal Education Department at Queens High School in Kensington, Johannesburg. Shortly thereafter, he applied to the Board for Religious Objection to be classified as a 'religious objector'. On 24 March 1986 the Secretary of the Department of Manpower advised him that his application had been granted by the Board for Religious Objection and that he had been classified as a 'religious objector' in category 72D(1)(a)(iii). In June 1986 Mr Goddard attended a job interview in the Department of Manpower in Johannesburg. At the interview he pointed out that he was employed as a teacher at Queens High School and that it seemed sensible that he should perform his community service there. He was told by the Department of Manpower that if the Transvaal Education Department allowed him to perform his community service in a teaching post, then it would be more than happy to count that as 'community service'.

Later, however, the Department of Manpower informed Goddard's lawyer that in the case of teachers working for the Education Department, obstacles had been encountered, and the Department of Manpower therefore had to place 'religious objectors' in non-teaching positions.

Eventually, the Department of Manpower informed Goddard that he was to commence his community service, and he was sent as a clerk to the accounts department of the Boksburg Regional Office of the Transvaal Education Department. He was given a job filling in forms but it was made quite clear to him that his presence was not really required. There was not even a desk for him, and he had insufficient work to occupy his time.

An application was brought to the Supreme Court of South Africa (Witwatersrand Local Division) against the Director-General of the Department of Manpower and the Director of Education of the Transvaal Education Department. Goddard asked, inter alia, for an order that set aside the decision of the Department of Manpower requiring him to render community service as a clerk in an accounts department, as well as the decision of the Transvaal Education Department that he was not permitted to continue teaching (case no. 6955/87, Witwatersrand Local Division).

The Transvaal Education Department filed an affidavit which outlined its decision, taken with other provincial Directors of Education, that practising teachers who were classified as 'religious objectors' and who were allocated to 'community service' would be placed in administrative positions, if available, in the Education Department.

Unfortunately, the affidavit did not disclose the basis for this decision. However, the intent is very clear. Persons who are qualified as teachers and who are already employed as teachers are to be removed from the classroom once they become 'religious objectors'. It is not unreasonable to speculate that the motivation for the decision is that the education authorities do not wish 'religious objectors' to have contact with school pupils.

It does not seem unreasonable to suggest that these authorities have taken a decision based upon a political approach which is out of sympathy with the provisions of Section 72 of the Defence Act itself. The decision conflicts with the fact that the views of 'religious objectors' have been given legal approval by the Defence Act and the Board for

Religious Objection. The two departments in the Goddard case were prepared to allow a man, with proven skills and commitment, to utilise neither of these as a clerk in an office where he was not required.

Refusing to render military service: a case study

Any person who is liable to render service in the SADF and who refuses to render such service or who fails to report for service shall be guilty of an offence in terms of Section 126A of the Act. A refusal to render service carries the penalty of imprisonment for a period one-and-a-half times as long as the total period of service which the offender would otherwise have been compelled to render, or for a period of 18 months, whichever is the larger. A failure to report for service carries a penalty of imprisonment or detention for a period not exceeding 18 months, or a fine. Any person who has served the full period of imprisonment imposed upon him shall be exempt from his liability to render service. However, if a person who has been convicted gives notice to the Adjutant-General before the expiry of his term of imprisonment that he is now willing to render service or to undergo training, then he shall be exempted from serving the remaining portion of his sentence of imprisonment, provided that he does render the service or undergo the training.

David Bruce was sentenced on 25 July 1988 to serve a term of imprisonment of six years. He had been found guilty by the Magistrate's Court in Johannesburg of a contravention of Section 126A(1)(a) of the Defence Act in that he had refused to obey his call-up to serve an initial two years' national service. He was arrested, charged and subsequently stood trial (case no. 062/00388/889, Johannesburg Regional Court).

Bruce gave evidence to explain why he was not prepared to serve in the SADF:

From quite an early age I was aware of being opposed to racism. From when I was in primary school I became aware of the kind of thing that happened in Germany during the period of the holocaust and became aware that my own family or my mother's family had suffered as a result of those things and as a result of racism; so from quite an early age, I became aware of being opposed to racism and I also became aware of the fact that I was living in a society that was itself fundamentally racist. And so I was aware of being opposed to the present political system in some way.

He elaborated: 'the majority of people in this country are excluded from the status of full citizenship in this country on the grounds of race, but there are all kinds of ways that racism is manifested through the political and economic system of this country.'

Bruce was asked why he refused to serve in the SADF, and he answered: 'my understanding is [based on] the role that the SADF plays in this country. It is not the role of a neutral peace-keeping force or its

46   *Nature and role of SADF*

role is not one of defending the country against its external threat. The basic function which the SADF plays in this country is one of upholding and defending a racist political system.'

Bruce felt that there was no role for him in the SADF that would not involve his upholding the system to which he was opposed. He conceded that at times the SADF did useful things like assisting people who were affected by floods, but he felt unable to involve himself in the structures of the SADF because of the broad role that it played in South Africa and neighbouring countries.

Bruce did not argue that he was a pacifist. He would be prepared to serve in any army 'that is involved in fighting for the people of the country as a whole, that was not involved in fighting what I understand to be essentially a civil war'.

In sentencing Bruce, the court stated that it was 'not the purpose or duty of this court to consider the political structure in South Africa in any way'. However, the court pointed out:

no State exists where the final authority is not vested in an organised Defence Force. The competence to apply an armed force in order to combat any armed resistance and thereby securing and maintaining State security, law and order results typically from the historical foundation of any State. In South Africa too, the State has the duty to protect all individuals by securing law and order. In that regard the State is competent to compel and prescribe to its subjects in order to compile an effective defence force. It is also the duty of the subject in return to respect the aforementioned claim by the State. That is the basis to the obligation to render service in the Defence Force.

In view of the fact that Bruce was liable to an initial period of two years' national service, to be followed by a further total period of two years of intermittent camps, the court imposed a sentence of six years' imprisonment. It stated that Section 126A of the Defence Act provides for a mandatory sentence of imprisonment of one-and-a-half times the period of military service outstanding.[1]

SADF secrecy[2]

The State President has been given far-reaching powers to establish and provide for censorship over all communications passing into or from the Republic (Section 110 of Defence Act). In addition, no person shall publish any information relating to the composition, movements or disposition of the Defence Force (Section 181(1)(a)).

Section 118 of the Defence Act contains a number of prohibitions against what is termed the 'improper disclosure of information'. There is a presumption that 'any information relating to the defence of the Republic is secret or confidential' (Section 118(5)(a)). No person shall publish any statement relating to any member of the SADF or any activity of the SADF or any force of a foreign country which is calculated to prejudice or embarrass the government in its foreign relations or to alarm or depress members of the public (Section 118(1)(b)).

The only reported case involving Section 118(1)(b) is that of *Minister van Verdediging* v *John Meiner (Edms) Bpk* 1976(4) SA 113 (SWA). This case involved an article published in 1976 in the South West African newspaper *Algemeine Zeitung*, which stated that members of the South African Police Reserve had been called up over the weekend, and commented that 'terrorists' had apparently been successful in the north of the country and were now operating further to the south. The Minister of Defence applied for an urgent interdict against the publisher and, inter alia, relied on the provisions of Section 118(1)(b).

The presiding judge found that, although the information contained in the article was known to everyone in the vicinity, there was a reasonable probability that the article would alarm the public or cause it to be dejected. Members of the public would certainly gain the impression that terrorists had now entered the area, that the ordinary police were no longer able to cope with the situation, and that it was therefore necessary to call up reserve units. The court found, however, that the activities mentioned in the newspaper article referred to the activities of the reserve units of the police force, and not to the activities of the army. The provisions of the Defence Act were therefore not applicable.

Case studies

In 1981 a journalist, Du Plessis, was convicted by the Appellate Division of certain contraventions of Section 118 (1983(3) SA 382 (AD)). The trial and the appeal were held *in camera* and court orders were made with regard to what could and could not be published about the case. In formulating the appeal judgment, the judge stated that he specifically avoided reference to any factual details which might be prejudicial or embarrassing to the state.

The evidence was that the accused had written a book about Rhodesia after the declaration of UDI, with special reference to the bush war. While the publisher was in the process of editing the manuscript, it was seized by the security police. The indictment stated that the manuscript contained information on military matters relating to the SADF, but the accused was acquitted on the basis that there was no evidence to show that he had formed a final and definitive intention to publish the secret information. However, the accused was convicted of a contravention of the then Official Secrets Act, No. 16 of 1956, by reason of his communication of the secret information in the manuscript to his publishers. Du Plessis argued, inter alia, that inasmuch as the secret information was already well known at the time of communication, no prejudice to the safety or the interests of the Republic was in fact caused. It was broadly his case that the factual allegations constituting this secret information were matters which had often been canvassed in overseas newspapers and journals; that certain of these publications were available to readers in South Africa; consequently they were matters which were well known; and, therefore, no prejudice to the safety of the Republic resulted from the communication and the manuscript. This argument was rejected by the judges of appeal, who stated that the book contained secret and confidential information concerning South African military matters. In their opinion 'the unauthorised disclosure of these matters would, *prima facie,* be prejudicial to the interests of the Republic'.

Finally, the accused was charged with receipt and retention of secret documents in contravention of the Official Secrets Act, and was convicted. From the judgment it appears that much of the information in question concerned the activities of the South African government beyond the borders of the Republic; moreover, reference was made specifically to 'the UNITA document' which related to the arms needs of UNITA. The appeal judge stated that 'secret State documents cannot be allowed to be bandied about in this way'.

Section 118(4) of the Defence Act renders it an offence for a person to disclose any secret or confidential information relating to the defence of the Republic which came to his knowledge by reason of his membership of the SADF or by reason of his employment in the public service of the Republic or in his employment in any post under the government.

Roland Mark Hunter is presently (1988) serving a term of imprisonment in Pretoria Central Prison. On 27 September 1984 he was convicted in the Supreme Court of South Africa (Transvaal Provincial Division) of a contravention of Section 118(4) of the Defence Act, and received the maximum sentence of five years' imprisonment. The trial was held *in camera.*

In 1984 the full text of the indictment against Hunter appeared on the front page of the *Sunday Tribune.* That indictment charged Hunter with one count of high treason, to which there were alternatives of contraventions of the Prevention of Information Act No. 84 of 1982, the Internal Security Act No. 74 of 1982 and the Publications Act. The substance of the charges as set out in the indictment was that Hunter was attached to the Directorate of Special Tasks with SADF Intelligence. He communicated with the ANC and passed on intelligence information to that body. This he did at various meetings in Johannesburg and in Gaborone, having copied and removed a variety of intelligence documents and items concerning military structures, personnel and operations, which the indictment alleged to be classified matters.

The defence requested further particulars to the indictment since the accused required to know details of the allegations against him especially with regard to the alleged conspiracy, the identity and nature of the Directorate of Special Tasks, the authorisation in law for the work of the Directorate, the duties of Hunter and details of the information allegedly communicated by Hunter to the ANC. The prosecution provided certain of the information which, by order of court, was to be kept confidential. The Attorney-General withheld certain documents on the basis that he considered their disclosure to be contrary to the public interest. Hunter's legal advisers were informed that the Attorney-General was in possession of a certificate signed by the Minister of Defence, issued in terms of the Internal Security Act, in terms of which he was of the opinion that the documents in question affected the security of the state and that their disclosure would prejudicially affect the security of the state. Eventually, the documents were made available to the defence under strict conditions of secrecy and control which did not allow for their retention or copying. The documents had to be studied under the supervision of the Security Branch of the South African Police.

During the trial and subsequently, foreign newspapers and magazines published considerable detail of the duties allegedly carried out by Hunter whilst he was serving in the Directorate of Special Tasks, as well as the various operations and code names under which certain activities were carried out by the Directorate in Mozambique, Angola, Lesotho and Zimbabwe.

Non-liability for unlawful SADF activities

Section 103 ter of the Defence Act creates an indemnity 'in connection with the combating of terrorism'. The import of the section is that:

No proceedings, whether civil or criminal, shall be instituted or continued in any court of law against the State, the State President, the Minister, a member of the South African Defence Force or any other person in the service of the State by reason of any act advised, commanded, ordered, directed or done in good faith by the State President, the Minister or a member of the South African Defence Force for the purposes of or in connection with the prevention or suppression of terrorism in any operational area.

If legal proceedings have at any time been instituted in a court of law against the state, the State President, the Minister of Defence, a member of the SADF or any other person in the service of the state, and the State President holds the opinion 'that it is in the national interest that proceedings shall not be continued', he shall authorise the Minister of Justice to issue a certificate directing that the proceedings shall not be continued. Such authorisation shall only be given to the Minister of Justice after the State President has considered a report by the Minister of Defence setting forth the circumstances under which the act in question took place, as well as the factors indicating that the act was done in good faith and for the purposes of preventing or suppressing terrorism in an operational area. No court shall have the power to review or set aside or otherwise question the validity of the certificate.

Section 103 ter has been invoked by the State President on several occasions. One of these involved the case of Immanuel Shifidi who was stabbed to death at a SWAPO meeting in Katutura township, Windhoek, on 30 November 1986. An inquest was held where evidence was given that more than 50 members of the SADF's 101 Battalion at Ondangwa had been ferried to Windhoek with the express intention of disrupting the meeting. Violent action by the soldiers resulted in chaos and Shifidi's death. In September 1987 the Attorney-General of South West Africa announced that six SADF members were to be prosecuted on a charge of murder. Two were black soldiers and four were white soldiers. The trial was set down for hearing in the Windhoek Supreme Court on 22 March 1988.

On that date it was announced that the State President had issued a certificate in terms of the Defence Act directing that the proceedings should not be continued. The grounds advanced were that this was in the 'national interest' and that the actions complained of were performed 'in good faith'.

The daughter of the deceased applied to the Supreme Court for an order that the certificate be declared invalid, inter alia, on the grounds that the State President had acted with 'gross unreasonableness', in that he had either not applied his mind to the matter or had acted in bad faith when terminating the prosecution. The legal representative of the State President and other respondents argued that the national interest superseded the interests of individual wrongdoers, and it was for that reason that the State President had halted the trial. In March 1989 the Supreme Court invalidated the certificate, though the State President filed for leave to appeal against the ruling.

In terms of regulations promulgated under the current state of emergency in South Africa, the liability of SADF members is also limited in respect of certain acts committed inside the country.

The Defence Act of 1957 does more than determine the legal position of the SADF and establish the statutory authority for its existence. It also provides the legal basis for SADF actions which the international community and the majority of South Africans regard as illegal. The Act sanctions internal and external military aggression, and protects the armed forces from public scrutiny and criminal prosecution. A review of the Act and its application indicates the extent to which South African society is militarised, and state control is exercised through coercive means.

4 Manpower and militarisation: women and the SADF

JACKLYN COCK

... the SADF is mainly dependent on the white male as a source of manpower. (1986 White Paper on Defence and Armaments Supply: 17)

The SADF generally defines manpower in both race- and gender-specific terms. In this sense 'manpower' is an ideological construction. However, this construction obscures the important ways in which women contribute to the militarisation of South African society. In this chapter it is argued that a direct connection between the two is apparent in the increasing use of white women within the SADF in a variety of roles, from nursing through to radar, intelligence work and cartography. There is also an indirect incorporation that is extensive, as women provide a considerable degree of support – both ideological and material – for the SADF.

The distinction between these direct and indirect linkages cannot be drawn in clear terms. One of the defining features of South Africa as a society engaged in war is that the battlefield comprehends the entire society. This blurs the connection between militarisation and gender. If the military is viewed as a bastion of male identity, then

it must categorise women as peripheral, as serving safely at the 'rear', on the 'home front'. Women as women must be denied access to 'the front', to 'combat'. . . . The military has to constantly define 'the front' and 'combat' as wherever 'women' are not. (Enloe, 1983: 15)

In a low-intensity civil war such as that being waged in South Africa, the landscape of combat is redrawn as the experience of war becomes dispersed among the general population. In this process an important breach in the ideological constructions of gender is threatened. As Ruddick has written: 'Dividing the protector from the protected, defender from defended, is the linchpin of masculinist as well as military ideology' (Ruddick, 1983: 472, cited by Schweik, 1987: 552).

For this reason considerable efforts are made to avoid this breach and elaborate a traditional but expanded notion of femininity for women within the SADF. This chapter examines this process, and the direct and indirect incorporation of white women in the militarisation of South African society. It also considers white women's participation in anti-apartheid activities, and the possibility of compulsory military service being extended to include them.

Indirect incorporation: material and ideological

There are three ways in which white women contribute materially to the militarisation of South African society: they are active in support organisations such as the Southern Cross Fund and Operation Ride Safe; they are active in civil defence and commando units; and they are engaged in armaments production for Armscor.

The Southern Cross Fund is an important agency through which white women provide material support for the SADF. Their work has been described by Mr Pik Botha, Minister of Foreign Affairs, as 'memorable, inspiring and dignified' (*Paratus,* July 1986). The Southern Cross Fund works for both the SADF and the SAP, and its motto is, *'They are our security.'* It has 250 branches throughout the country and raises money for the security forces on a full-time basis. Since its inception in 1968 it has raised over R14 million (*Citizen,* 31.5.1986). The money is used for humanitarian purposes, particularly to provide aid and comfort to soldiers in the 'operational area'. For example, it has donated recreational facilities such as snooker tables, swimming pools and television sets, and sends regular parcels to conscripts.

Basics can't be all that bad, not with the useful packages handed out by the Southern Cross Fund . . . the parcels consist of an elegant brief folder in which one can find writing paper, envelopes, a pen knife, a tin opener, nail clippers, pens, cleaning utensils and many other useful artifacts that the troopie would find a need for during his Army service. (*Paratus,* May 1987)

Members of the Southern Cross also visit hospitalised soldiers at No. 1 Military Hospital near Pretoria regularly. According to Frankel, 'the actual effect of Southern Cross activity is to market militarisation in a way which encourages public identification' (Frankel, 1984: 98).

Organising lifts for national servicemen has also provided an important expression of support, reflecting a similar ideology. According to an SABC advertisement, 'They keep us safe in our homes. Let's give them a safe ride to theirs.' The *Bel-en-Ry* (Phone and Ride) organisation was started in 1977 and involved women nationwide in 52 towns from Beaufort West to Zeerust (*Paratus,* May 1987).

White women are increasingly active in civil defence organisations in urban areas. The civil defence programme was consolidated by the Civil Defence Act of 1977. The aim of the programme is to 'provide, by means of planning and provision of emergency measures, with a view to an emergency situation, the RSA and its inhabitants with the greatest measure of protection and assistance and to curtail civilian disruption in the most effective manner' (White Paper on Defence, 1977: 36).

Civil defence involves people in various activities such as traffic control, fire-fighting, first-aid, drill, fieldcraft, crowd control, identification of explosives, weapon training, roadblock routines, anti-riot procedures, and lectures on internal security. One such course in Bloemfontein, aimed specifically at women, included warnings from an SADF lecturer on 'the revolutionary onslaught' and the comment, 'Men get involved in the defence of the country through national service but womenfolk do not get even half of this exposure' (*Paratus*, April 1987).

The civil defence programme provides such 'exposure' and attempts to mobilise the general civilian population for the military defence of the apartheid state. It fits neatly into the overall programme of total strategy.

White women are also increasingly active in commando units in rural areas. In 1982 provision was made for men who had completed their national service to be put on the controlled reserve for five years and then be liable for allocation to their local commandos. Men who have had no training at all are allocated to the national reserve. Both reserves can be called upon to do commando duties in certain 'primary areas' which correspond roughly with the country's border areas. These include the whole of northern Natal and a number of northern and western Transvaal districts.

The commando units are involved in counter-insurgency in these areas, and white women play an increasingly useful part in this function. 'My men cannot be everywhere at once but by training farmers *and their wives* in the use of weapons and communication systems we have an answer to terrorism in the area' (Colonel Swanepoel in *Paratus*, February 1987; emphasis added).

In this process of incorporation, traditional notions of femininity are restructured and expanded. For example, in the Soutpansberg military area, commando members gathered recently for an evaluation. According to *Paratus*, 'In the past two years the Soutpansberg Military Area Unit has concentrated on taking counter-insurgency skills to the farming folk in the area, turning Oumas and housewives into trained auxiliaries of the Defence Force' *(ibid.)*. This strategy is anchored in the Voortrekker tradition. On one occasion, 'Ouma Marina Hogenboezen strode into the evaluation with a rifle under her left arm and picknick [*sic*] basket in her right hand, and said, "Shooting comes as naturally as baking in the kitchen." ' *(Ibid.)*

It is important to stress that traditional notions of femininity are not abandoned in this restructuring. For example, on this occasion the day's programme included a fashion show: 'Bidding to take the best-dressed category the women's teams paraded in a variety of colourful outfits. Red bush-hat cum stetson, safari suit pulled in with red leather belt and red pumps was about the best' *(ibid.)*.

At the indirect material level, the final and most important linkage between women and militarisation in South Africa is to be found in the involvement of women in armaments production for Armscor.[1] Armscor has twelve nationalised subsidiaries whose activities are controlled by the corporation. It distributes work to over a thousand private industry contractors and sub-contractors. Many defence industry workers are women. For example, Pretoria Metal Pressings is an Armscor affiliate which produces a large variety of ammunition and employs a high percentage of women (Ratcliffe, 1983: 81). So does Naschem, an Armscor affiliate which fills and assembles large-calibre ammunition and bombs, and produces explosives and propellants. Lyttleton Engineering Works makes guns and components for guns, cannons and mortars. 'Its workforce consists mainly of women who are increasingly replacing men in production' (Ratcliffe, 1983: 83).

It is extremely difficult to gain information about the composition of the workforce in the armaments industry. However, Ratcliffe has identified a clear pattern in which women appear to be the predominant sector. He suggests this is because 'women are one of the weakest sections of the workforce. Women are perceived to be less militant than men and are thought to have greater dexterity for intricate assembly-line production.' (Ratcliffe, 1983: 85)

The increasing and extensive involvement of women in such 'militarised work' is a global phenomenon. However, much of this work is distanced from the final product so that the military connection between women's daily work and soldiers' killing is obscured.

In addition to being incorporated into the militarisation of South African society in these indirect material ways, women also provide a crucial source of ideological support for soldiers. The importance of this ideological support has been expressed by SADF leaders on numerous occasions. Its function in maintaining soldiers' morale was noted by General C. L. Viljoen, then chief of the SADF.

My congratulations to all those who worked so hard to make this exercise [Exercise Thunder Chariot] the success it was. I would especially like to thank those who stayed at home to keep the fires burning while the men were at the P. W. Botha Training Area. Without the support of their loved ones at home the men on the ground would not have been as successful as they were. The support from their loved ones is an important factor for the morale of the men who took part. (*Paratus*, October 1984)

Colonel L. J. Holtzhausen, Officer Commanding the 7th Division's Mobilisation Unit, gives even greater significance to women as a source of ideological support. He believes women to be 'the mightiest weapon against the current threat'. But gender roles must remain intact: 'Remember the woman must remain a woman and keep on allowing her man to feel like a man because the men are fighting throughout our country not for material things but for their women, children and loved ones' (*Paratus*, February 1984).

Each woman is enjoined to develop these manipulative qualities in order that the SADF may reach her man. A good deal of effort is invested in this process of indirect recruitment. For instance, a girls' school was asked to supply partners for conscripts serving in a parachute battalion in Bloemfontein. Afterwards the girls and their mothers were invited to visit the unit. The wife of the commanding officer explained the rationale: 'We want to reach the woman and try through her to work on the man. A mother has influence over her son and a girlfriend over her boyfriend.' (*Paratus*, September 1983)

The importance of 'working on the man' lies in the fact that it 'is never easy for the armed forces to acquire the manpower they claim they need' (Enloe, 1983: 75). In South Africa manpower is acquired directly by the conscription of white males into the SADF, and indirectly through an ideological conscription into militarism. It is in this latter respect that white women are crucial. They reproduce an ideology of gender roles which links masculinity to militarism. In this process they provide a vital source of emotional support and an incentive to men to 'act like men' both in battle and during their national service.

The significance of this connection between masculinity and militarism should not be underestimated. According to William James one of the main functions of war is 'preserving manliness of type'. He points to a pervasive anxiety about the construction of masculinity, the fear that martial experience alone can make a man, and the belief that war is necessary to the social construction of masculinity.[2]

This connection between masculinity and militarism is reinforced by women. They socialise men into a particular definition of masculinity that is violent in nature and consequence. Mothers do so from an early age by providing their sons with war toys and censuring emotional expression. The army then carries this process to an extreme.

A soldier must learn to dehumanise other people and make them into targets, and at the same time to cut himself off from his own feelings of caring and connectedness to the human community. His survival and competence as a soldier depend on this process. Military training is socialisation into masculinity carried to extremes. (Roberts, 1984: 197)

This process has been detailed by Eisenhart (1975) who describes how a brutalised masculine identity is built into the US Marine Corps' basic training. While no comparable research data are available in South Africa, accounts from conscripts suggest the same linkage. This linkage between militarism and masculinity is frequently the subject of emotional appeals. For example, the Minister of Defence, General Magnus Malan, once described the male members of the ECC as 'mommy's little boys' (*Eastern Province Herald*, 16.4.1987). Military training is often justified in terms of its appropriateness in teaching masculine independence and discipline: 'do bear in mind that soldiering is, after all, a task for a man and the army has to train and discipline our sons to this end.' As a result young men achieve 'the ability to stand on their own feet and become independent individuals able to cope with their own lives' (Letter to *Star*, 24.4.1987). This letter urged 'anxious army mums [to] give your sons all the moral support you can and help them to adopt a positive attitude to their training'.

However, it is as wives that women are an important source of ideological legitimation and emotional support. Wives of serving members of the SADF automatically belong to the Defence Force Ladies Association. This Association strives to promote 'sympathetic understanding and active support for the husband's duty as defender of the Republic of South Africa' (White Paper on Defence, 1982, cited by Ratcliffe, 1983: 70).

The responsibility of soldiers' wives, as motivated by the Ladies Association and the Defence Force, includes the following:

(1) *A knowledge of communism.* 'Knowledge of communism remains of the utmost importance . . . because . . . communism leads to disloyalty' (Mrs Viljoen, national president of the Defence Force Ladies Association, quoted in *Paratus*, April 1983).

(2) *Meticulous grooming.* 'Soldiers do enjoy a status in the community and their lady friends should be an asset to them, even if they are only doing shopping together. Certain standards are expected of him when wearing his uniform and the same applies to the woman accompanying him.' This requirement of meticulous grooming implies an elaborate cultivation of 'femininity', so as to mirror the soldier–husband's status in the community. This clearly illustrates Virginia Woolf's insight in *A room of one's own* where she argues that women serve as 'magnifying mirrors' which show men at twice their natural size. Such mirrors, she claims, 'are essential to all violent and heroic action' (Woolf, 1928: 35–6).

(3) *Self-knowledge.*

Happiness always has a woman in the picture. In the first place happiness is a woman who knows Who has made her. She is the crown of creation and no afterthought or accessory. Happiness also is a woman who knows why she was made. . . . Happiness is also a woman who knows to whom she belongs. This radiates from her own family, to the community and then the nation. The easiest way to break a nation is to break bonds. That is why a mother is so important. Happiness is also a woman who is not naive about an enemy's attack on the Republic of South Africa. (Mrs Viljoen, wife of the then chief of the SADF, quoted in *Paratus*, July 1983)

(4) *Optimism.* 'We must prevent thinking that we could lose. What we are dealing with is total onslaught – it is a total war on all aspects of our lives.' (Speaker at a two-day conference hosted by admirals' and generals' wives, quoted in *Paratus*, April 1983)

(5) *Shared values.* 'The loyal wife is bound to her husband by a shared

love of your fatherland, people and Provider' *(ibid.).*

(6) *Domestic competence.* 'The wife must know where her husband's salary is paid out, and where accounts must be paid. She must be able to drive a car. She must be able to fix fuses and taps. She must assume responsibility for locking doors and windows and for turning off water and electricity after use. . . .' (SADF booklet, *While he is away,* cited in Human Awareness Programme, 1986)

(7) *Regular correspondence.* 'It's up to you to make sure that your letters and actions while he's away show him beyond any doubt that you love him just as much as always, and you're going to wait for him, no matter how long. One very important way to show your love for your man is through the post. A family that does not write weakens the whole platoon.' *(Ibid.)*

(8) *Independence.* 'The wife of a man in uniform has to show responsibility to her calling as wife, believer and citizen. The first phase of the psychological war takes place in the home as the smallest unit of the population. If the enemy succeeds in winning the wife away from her task then half his battle is won. Therefore the wife has to form her own opinion and has to develop in a dexterous manner, to cope with all the demands that are presented.' (Mrs Naudé, wife of the Chaplain-General, quoted in *Paratus,* January 1987)

(9) *Support.* 'Being a wife implies being supportive of her husband in all areas. It implies a job and is hard work. The current life style with its tendency towards democratising and questioning of authority, pessimism and lack of concern are little pricks which work on us daily and lead to disloyalty.' (Speaker at a two-day conference hosted by admirals' and generals' wives, cited in *Paratus,* April 1983)

All these aspects of the responsibility of soldiers' wives emphasise an ideology of domesticity that lays stress on the importance of the home. Furthermore, they suggest the notion of an 'incorporated wife' who is entirely submerged in her soldier–husband's role, and lacking any autonomous identity. The extent to which the wife is incorporated in this way is well illustrated by the Johannesburg City Council's decision to restrict paid maternity leave to women employees whose husbands were presently doing or had done military service. Those to be excluded were 'specifically the wives of religious objectors' as well as all blacks, coloureds, Indians and single women.[3]

The incorporated wife is only one source, albeit crucial, of the ideological legitimation and emotional support which connects women to the social process of militarisation. Other crucial sources are women in their roles as mothers, though here the ultimate point is the theme of sacrifice,[4] and as providers of entertainment and diversion.

Much of the content of this entertainment reinforces an ideology of domesticity in which women and 'loved ones' provide a rationale for the soldier's privations. The message is conveyed through radio and television programmes, and tours of the 'operational areas' by female entertainers. Their contribution to maintaining soldiers' morale has not gone unrecognised. July 1987 marked the twenty-fifth anniversary of the popular radio programme for soldiers 'Forces Favourites'. For the past twenty years this has been prepared and presented by Patricia Kerr. Her commitment earned her the Order of the Star of South Africa 'for exceptional service of military importance' (*Paratus*, April 1987). Her programme sends over 300 messages a week of love and support to and from soldiers, makes pen-pal arrangements, and so forth. Many of these messages reinforce the ideology of gender roles referred to above. Gail Adams, who was producer of the Sunday evening radio programme 'Salute', reported that she 'fell in love about forty times' on her four-hour visits to seventeen base camps. After this experience she planned to 'feature girls regularly, in the form of a "radio centrefold" which could be a chat-up with a reigning beauty queen' (*Paratus*, February 1983).

This 'centrefold'-type use of women is a further component in the linkage between masculinity and militarism. A sexist abuse of female sexuality is evident in at least two different ways: indirect visual abuse of women as sex objects in 'pin-up' illustrations and direct physical abuse of women in the case of rape. As regards the former it is interesting that *Paratus* used to have a monthly 'pin-up' page. A photograph of a woman, either fully clothed or in a bathing costume, filled the final page of every issue until mid-1977 (Fine and Getz, 1986: 30). This clearly reinforced a splintered and contradictory image of women – an image fractured between the extremes of moralism and sexuality, 'damned whores and God's police'.[5]

Unfortunately it is as 'damned whores' that women frequently suffer at the hands of soldiers. Historically rape is often associated with war (Brownmiller, 1976). In some war situations rape has been extremely widespread. For example, during the Bangladesh conflict in 1970–1 an estimated 200 000 women were raped by Pakistani soldiers (Brownmiller, 1976: 79). Rape does occur in the war presently being waged in South Africa.

I live with my husband at 71 Mazosiwe Street, Lingelihle, Cradock. On Saturday 3 August I saw two vehicles patrolling the streets around my house. I think they are called Hippos. In the late evening I walked to a relative's home. I was alone. A Hippo drove up behind me and stopped. Two white soldiers jumped out. One said, 'Here walks a bitch, alone at night, probably looking for a man. We'll help her.' The words were in Afrikaans. One soldier lifted me by my shoulders and one by my ankles. I struggled and said, 'Where are you taking me?' The same soldier said, 'You'll see.' There were other soldiers in the Hippo, but I don't know how many. The Hippos drove to the national road and went towards Port Elizabeth. The soldiers did not speak or interfere with me, but the same two held me. A few kilometres away the Hippo stopped. The one soldier jumped out and the other pushed me out. The two soldiers lifted me over the fence and climbed over. The Hippo drove in the same direction. I can identify the spot. The two soldiers were very young. The one held my arms while the other lifted my dress and removed my slip and panties. I said, 'What are you doing, children?' The one replied, 'Ons gaan jou naai. As jy nie wil, gaan ons jou doodmaak.' (We are going to fuck you. If you don't comply, we'll kill you.)

They then pushed me down with my hips on a big stone. The one soldier held my arms over my head on the ground. The other soldier (who had done all the talking) raped me. He was rough and I was bleeding when he finished. The other said, 'Maak gou. Ek is haastig. Ek wil ook naai.' (Hurry up, I'm in a hurry. I also want to fuck.) The two men switched positions. The one held my hands over my head. The other raped me. He was also rough. . . .

On Monday 5th August I went by taxi to the police station. It was early. In the charge office was one white man in civilian clothes. He heard my story in Xhosa and told me to go to SANLAM – the normal term for security police headquarters. [Local branches of the security police often have offices in privately owned buildings.]

I saw one coloured and one black security policeman together and told them the story in Xhosa. They recorded the facts and asked questions. I was not asked to sign anything. They asked if I knew the soldiers or the Hippo number. They said they would contact me but have not done so. The coloured policeman was flippant. (Sworn statement made by Lena Rasmen, a 70-year-old woman, to Mrs Blackburn, 10.8.1985, Cradock)

It might be thought that the linkage between masculinity and militarism would be eroded by the increasing incorporation of women directly into the armed forces – a process that is occurring both globally and in South Africa. However, in the next section it will be argued that this incorporation preserves the ideology of gender roles, and that the definition of femininity is expanded rather than fundamentally reworked.

The direct incorporation of women into the SADF

Throughout the world women are increasingly used to fill various positions within the armed forces. This may be related to a number of factors such as manpower constraints stemming from falling birth rates, a general militarisation of many different societies, and ironically the rise of 'equal rights feminism'.

Armed forces everywhere are distinctively patriarchal institutions. The patriarchal nature of many societies facilitates connections between the armed forces and other institutions. For example, Enloe writes of the military–industrial complex as a patriarchal set of relations thoroughly imbued with masculine-defined militarist values. The network 'depends on male bonding, male privilege, and militarily derived notions of masculinity'. Several dimensions of the intimate relationships that are cultivated between military officials, arms industry executives and scientists are only comprehensible 'if they are examined as one more manifestation of militarism's reliance on and perpetuation of a gender ideology that constructs "maleness" in a peculiar fashion' (Enloe, 1983: 193).

'Maleness' in this ideology of gender is a relational concept; it implies a dichotomous relation with an opposing set of qualities which comprises 'femaleness'. Militarism is structured upon this dichotomy. As Mason describes it, 'militarism is an organising principle of social life which necessarily magnified the distinctions between the sexes and was predicated upon overt or total male supremacy' (1976: 87). It is this dichotomy which explains women's exclusion from combat roles. However, this exclusion may be eroded under the pressure of 'manpower' constraints and shortages. When this occurs usually attempts are made to keep the ideology of gender roles intact. For example, approximately 65 per cent of Israeli women serve in the army through their two years of compulsory military training (*Jerusalem Post*, 8.11.1986). According to an Israeli army spokesperson, 'CHEN, the Hebrew acronym for Women's Corps, as a word means "charm" and indeed CHEN adds to the Israeli Defence Force the grace and charm which make it also a medium for humanitarian and social activities' (*Spokesman*, 1980: 91). In South Africa there are frequent injunctions to women in the SADF not to allow their role to contaminate their femininity. Physical appearance must be carefully cultivated: 'With good grooming any women can look as good in her uniform as out of it' (*Paratus*, May 1979).

According to the most recent estimates available there are now about a thousand women in the SADF permanent force. Women therefore constitute a significant proportion of its 18 000 members. This proportion has increased steadily in recent years. However, women are excluded from combat roles. This is justified on a number of different grounds:

(1) *Women are unable to cope.* 'It's the task of women to give life and to preserve it. Women can provide invaluable assistance in the support services. I know there are women who could cope but, generally, the female has no place on the battle front.' (Colonel Hilda Botha, Senior Staff Officer Women, quoted in the *Rand Daily Mail*, 18.3.1980)

(2) *Women's socialisation is inappropriate.* 'Women encounter nothing like the extreme physical discomfort and danger of combat in their everyday life so they're not taught to cope with this sort of thing. The men on the other hand experience something like it with blood sports.' (Psychologist Alma Hannon, *Rand Daily Mail*, 18.3.1980)

(3) *Women are incapacitated through physiological function such as menstruation.* 'Some women suffer from premenstrual tension and, at this time, they may be less mentally agile and well co-ordinated than at other times. A percentage are also more accident-prone during this time. If this sort of thing were not checked at the outset it could put

certain women at a definite disadvantage on the front lines.' (Senior consultant in gynaecology at the Johannesburg Hospital, *Rand Daily Mail*, 18.3.1980)

(4) *Male chivalry.* 'It would be very difficult to use women in an operational task. The physical implications like toilet and sleeping facilities would create endless difficulties. Men would find it difficult to prevent themselves saying things like "after you" or "I'll take that, it's too heavy for you".' (Commander Jurie Bosch, Commanding Officer of the South African Irish Regiment, *Rand Daily Mail*, 18.3.1980)

This exclusion from combat roles is essential for maintaining the ideological structure of patriarchy. It is essential because the notion of experiencing military 'combat' is central to the social construction of masculinity. 'To be a soldier of the state means to be subservient, obedient and almost totally dependent. But that mundane reality is hidden behind a potent myth: to be a soldier means possibly to experience "combat" and only in combat lies the ultimate test of a man's masculinity.' (Enloe, 1983: 13)

Although women in the SADF are not used in combat, they are no longer relegated to the traditional female roles of medical and welfare work. They are involved in telecommunications and signals, logistics and finance, military policing and instructional activity. Women volunteers are trained at the SA Army Women's College which opened in George in 1971. Volunteers must be under 22, have matric or its equivalent, be bilingual, never have been married and be physically fit. Initial basic training lasts one year. The women are allowed to specialise in different fields according to their interests, such as telecommunications, cartography, administration and stores administration (*Paratus*, February 1983). The emphasis is on girls who can present the image of women in uniform positively (*Paratus*, September 1984). The crucial point is that there is no contradiction between femininity and serving in the SADF. Thus the ideology of gender roles is preserved.

Inducements to women to serve in the SADF are posed in terms of appeals to a mixture of patriotism and self-improvement. The women will acquire self-discipline, independence and self-reliance, and fulfil their patriotic duty. 'The defence of this country cannot be regarded as an exclusive male prerogative. We women have to come forward and stand by our men against the multi-faceted onslaught against this country.' (Captain Fiona Coughlan, *Paratus*, December 1979) Women in the SADF will also enjoy job satisfaction and career opportunities. 'I regard my work as dynamic, intelligent and fulfilling. The decision I made to join the SADF is one which I'll never regret. I have total job satisfaction.' *(Ibid.)*

However, the image of women serving in the permanent force tends to be inflated to 'superwoman' proportions. The SADF superwoman usually combines her highly responsible job with domestic responsibilities to husbands (often SADF personnel) and children. These women tend to be physically active, and enjoy 'robust' hobbies such as sports and orienteering. They have boundless energy and enthusiasm for their jobs and are often portrayed as extremely attractive. All enjoy cooking. In short the definition of femininity operating in this image has been expanded – the domestic role has not been abandoned but enlarged to include martial as well as domestic skills.

Attractive Sergeant-Major Lauretta Corcher of Signals Unit, Orange Free State Command, has made quite a name for herself in the provincial biathlon arena, but few realise the superfit 29-year-old is a veritable 'superwoman'. In an apron she is a master of bobotie. In the garden she has the flair that lifts every marigold head and at work she runs an efficient operation, overseeing two dozen people. All this the slim sergeant-major shrugs off as merely 'a busy schedule'. What is important is the enjoyment, she says. 'There's never a dull moment in the Defence Force.' (*Paratus,* May 1987)

The inducements such as self-improvement, patriotism and career opportunities point us towards an explanation of why women volunteer for the SADF. Such an explanation is necessary in view of what we know of war as devastating and often meaningless. More often than not, soldiers have to be coerced into war.

. . . why do the men who are called upon to do the actual fighting do so? In large part it is because of coercion. In wartime men are drafted. They are punished if they refuse to serve. Their basic military training is highly compelling, and intended to teach unquestioning obedience, compliance, submission, i.e. coercion is used to make coercion unnecessary. (Stiehm, 1983: 371)

This coercion includes socialisation into an ideology of militarism which compels both men and women.

It is significant that the increasing incorporation of women as a minority of the armed forces has not seriously breached the ideology of gender roles or the sexual division of labour. The most common functions women fulfil in militaries are clerical, administrative and servicing. These are jobs highly similar to those held by women in the wider labour market. They do not contaminate the ideology of femininity which reinforces the sexual division of labour. It is therefore difficult to see how this increasing use of women as a military resource can be hailed as advancing equality between the sexes: '. . . women's participation in the military has failed to challenge traditional and very basic sexist ideologies. It reinforces a sexual division of labour sharper and more rigid in the armed forces than in civilian life.' (Stiehm, 1983: 371)

The almost universal exclusion of women from direct conscription resonates with the much wider subordination and exclusion of women from power and prestige in society. This exclusion is necessary to maintain the existing ideological order. That is why the SADF devotes so much attention to deflecting any potential contradiction that may arise between 'femininity' and participation in the army. Yet while the majority of white women do contribute to the process of militarisation, a small minority of them are a source of resistance to it.

White women's resistance to militarisation

The incorporation of women both directly and indirectly, materially and ideologically, into the militarisation of South African society is not a smooth, uniform process. It is complex and straddles contradictions which are embedded deep in the peculiar social conditions of South Africa. While white women contribute to the process of militarisation, they are also more active than white men in the extra-parliamentary struggle against apartheid. Their involvement will be illustrated by pointing to their participation in two organisations, the End Conscription Campaign and the African National Congress.

Among the small number of whites convicted in South African courts of furthering the aims of the banned ANC, women form a significant proportion. There have been a number of famous cases – Barbara Hogan, Helene Pastoors, Jansie Lourens, Trish Hanekom and Marion Sparg.[6] The last-mentioned, a former journalist, was sentenced in 1986 to 25 years' imprisonment on charges of high treason and arson. She is the first white South African woman known publicly to have served as a member of the ANC's military wing, Umkhonto we Sizwe. Pleading guilty on all the charges against her, Sparg admitted planting limpet mines which exploded in Johannesburg's police headquarters and an East London police station in 1986. She said she knew it was possible policemen or civilians would die in the blasts: 'But my motive was not to injure or kill people. It was one of a soldier in Umkhonto we Sizwe, a military army. I followed orders just like any other soldier.' (*Weekly Mail*, 7.11.1986)

The politics of gender – the power relations structured around opposing concepts of masculinity and femininity – were used to deny and trivialise the validity of such choice and commitment. Shortly after her arrest in March 1986 several South African newspapers depicted Sparg as a failed woman – a lonely, overweight, unattractive female who had turned to revolutionary politics not out of commitment but out of a desire to belong and win acceptance. As a woman, she could not have acted independently but had to be manipulated by a man of special persuasive powers. Sparg was described as acting under the influence of Arnold Geyer, whom Major Craig Williamson of the security police described as 'a sort of Charles Manson figure' (*The Observer*, 31.3.1987). A similar theme was used to denigrate the activities of Barbara Hogan, now serving a ten-year sentence. She was described as 'an academic and trade unionist who was the first person convicted of high treason without committing violent acts. She had run an ANC cell for ten years after being recruited by her black boyfriend, Pindile Mfeti.' *(Ibid.)* Similarly Jansie Lourens, now serving a four-year sentence for treason, was said to be influenced by her boyfriend (now husband) Karl Niehaus.

Ironically their status as white women had also provided a degree of camouflage. It has been suggested that white women attract less attention than men, and under the guise of their femininity are able to travel more freely around the country fulfilling vital roles in the underground war (Major Craig Williamson in *The Observer*, 31.3.1987).

Another challenge to the militarisation of South African society in which white women are extremely active is provided by the peace movement and in particular by the (now banned) End Conscription Campaign. Many of its members and supporters were white women. Women were an important source of commitment and energy at a leadership level as well.

Women supporters of the ECC were in many cases moved by their maternal role, by their sense of responsibility to their children. 'The South African way of life allows a great many myths to exist in our society. One of the greatest of these is the one that goes "the army will make a man of your son" . . . we allow the might of the army to swallow the boys we, as mothers, have spent eighteen years turning into civilised human beings, caring and considerate of others, and in two years turn them into efficient, largely unthinking, killing machines.' (Letter to *Star*, 15.4.1986)

Clearly this issue generates conflict for mothers. A local study has described 'the dilemma experienced as a result of the mothers' opposition towards conscription and their simultaneous feelings that, as mothers, they should be committed to supporting their sons' (Feinstein *et al.*, 1986: 77). Yet it is significant that in this study 'the issue of conscription was hardly discussed by the families. Discussion between mother and son on the issue of conscription was almost non-existent. All mothers felt that their sons should be informed, but distanced themselves from the process.'

Women's resistance to militarisation has historically often been rooted in their maternal roles. Sometimes the content of their resistance has echoed and reinforced such roles, as for example in the wording of the appeal from the International Women's Suffrage Alliance in 1914 to avoid war: 'In this terrible hour, when the fate of Europe depends on decisions which women have no power to shape, we, realising our responsibilities as mothers of the race, cannot stand passively by. Powerless though we are politically, we call upon the governments and powers of our several countries to avert the threatened unparalleled disaster.' (Cited by Orr, 1983: 11)

While the politics of gender is often used to deny the validity of women's independent, autonomous political action, paradoxically it also gives them space for such action. There is no white male equivalent of the white women's civil rights organisation, the Black Sash, nominated for the Nobel Peace Prize in 1985. Their silent protest stands are reminiscent of the 'Mad Mothers' of the Plaza de Mayo in Buenos Aires since 1976.

The conscription of white women

Although the politics of gender has protected women from conscription in the past, it is uncertain whether this will continue. Increasing resistance to the apartheid state could create serious 'manpower' problems for the SADF.

For both the Full-time Force and Part-time Force, the SADF is mainly dependent on the white male as a source of manpower. The escalating threat makes greater demands on the RSA's manpower resources, and white males can no longer bear the security burden alone without harming the economy. The SA Defence Force will therefore be increasingly reliant on other manpower resources. (White Paper on Defence and Armaments Supply, 1986: 17)

One important response to this problem has been the restructuring of the ideology of Defence Force 'manpower' as 'white'. The SADF claims that more coloured and Indian people apply for voluntary service than it can handle (SAIRR, 1985: 417; *Star*, 28.4.1986). The 1986 Defence White Paper clearly envisages extending conscription to coloured and Indian youths in the long term. It suggests taking them through the same stages of military service as whites, i.e. a voluntary system followed by a compulsory ballot system, and then universal conscription. At present the inclusion of Africans within the SADF is primarily tied to the bantustans.

The obvious question that arises is whether the ideological construction of 'manpower' will be restructured to include white women. There has been some talk of this since 1981. In that year Prime Minister Botha said: 'Compulsory national service for women might be instituted in the distant future' (cited in Human Awareness Programme, 1986). However, the question of conscription for white girls is not an issue of frequent debate in South Africa, although it has occasionally taken a somewhat bizarre form. For example, the leader of the right-wing Kappiekommando organisation, Mrs Marie van Zyl, issued a statement challenging Prime Minister Botha to guarantee that if young girls were forced to join a multiracial army, it would not be 'for the purpose of prostitution'. Her concern did not only relate to the possibility of inter-racial sex. She was also reported as saying that 'only lower-class women' joined the Defence Force during the Second World War and were 'used for prostitution' (*Rand Daily Mail*, 24.3.1982).

Generally, conscription for women is still rare. Despite assertions of gender equality there are only a few states (Israel, Mali and Guinea) in which women are conscripted into the armed forces. Women are in the minority in such forces (Enloe, 1983: 127–31).

Future policy on the conscription of white women will hinge on the tension between the need to mobilise women as soldiers (under the pressure of manpower shortages and increasing resistance to apartheid) and the need to avoid any contamination or dilution of the ideological construct of 'femininity'. This construct is crucial as a source of legitimation for the connection between masculinity and militarism. The identification of manhood with soldiering is of such ideological importance that it cannot be breached. The present chapter has attempted to demonstrate this and to show that even without direct coercion into the SADF in the form of conscription, white women contribute directly and indirectly, materially and ideologically, to the militarisation of South African society.

5 Troops in the townships, 1984–1987

LAURIE NATHAN

*Today! Today's army is lions! They hate a person. If one of the police or army come
towards you, you are so scared. You know that the first thing they may do is beat you up,
and then shoot you. We don't accept what's going on today. We don't accept the army.
It's not going to solve the problem, the actions they are doing.* (Crossroads squatter,
Out of Step, May 1987)

Black resistance to white domination in South Africa reached an
unprecedented level in the mid-1980s. Entire communities were
involved in struggles around their economic conditions and lack of
political rights. National political organisations like the United
Democratic Front (UDF), together with trade unions and the military
wing of the African National Congress (ANC), mounted the most
serious challenge to the apartheid state since 1948. The South African
Police were unable to handle the situation alone, and at the end of 1984
the SADF was sent into the townships to assist them.[1]

As the crisis deepened, the government imposed a series of states of
emergency. It virtually outlawed extra-parliamentary opposition and
detained without trial tens of thousands of people. It banned community
organisations and newspapers, and repeatedly introduced new press
restrictions. It also equipped the police and army with extraordinary
powers to suppress the uprising.

This chapter describes the deployment of troops in the black
townships between 1984 and 1987. Four phases are identified. From late
1984 to mid-1985 the army played a back-up role in relation to the SAP.
After the imposition of the 1985 state of emergency, soldiers acquired
new powers and their activities became virtually indistinguishable
from those of the police. The 1986 state of emergency led to an
intensified effort by the combined security forces to crush the
insurrection. By early 1987 they had largely succeeded in their efforts
and began to play a less prominent and direct role; conservative black
forces assumed the front-line of attack and the state stepped up its non-
military efforts to consolidate control over black communities.

The chapter also examines opposition to the deployment of troops
from the black community. What emerges is that the high level of state
violence had contradictory effects. It succeeded in containing the
uprising, but at the same time it dramatically intensified black resent-

ment and militancy. It also heightened international protest and action, and provoked a new wave of anti-apartheid and anti-conscription activity among white opposition groups.

The first invasions

On 3 September 1984 workers and students in Vaal townships observed a stayaway in protest against rent increases. Thousands of residents marched through the streets, attacking apartheid institutions like schools and municipal offices. Police sealed off the townships and moved in with teargas and guns. Over the next few months, battles between police and residents were so fierce that the Minister of Law and Order declared: 'as far as we're concerned it is war, plain and simple' (*Leadership SA,* October 1984).

As the resistance spread across the country, the Minister warned that there would be 'closer co-operation between police and the Defence Force in controlling unrest' (*Argus,* 6.10.1984). Two days later troop carriers entered Soweto and Eastern Cape townships (*Cape Times,* 8.10.1984). Black residential areas in Grahamstown were placed under virtual military occupation and were lit up at night by spotlights placed on nearby hills (*Daily Dispatch,* 8.10.1984).

On 23 October, Operation Palmiet (Bullrush) was launched. At 2 a.m., 7 000 policemen and soldiers in armoured vehicles rolled into Sebokeng township, which lay at the heart of Vaal resistance. The police conducted a house-to-house search, while soldiers armed with R1 rifles lined the streets at 10-metre intervals to ensure that residents stayed indoors. According to one resident:

They knocked on the door as if they wanted to kick it in. When I opened the door they didn't greet me or ask if they could search – they just asked for a house permit, switched on the light and demanded to know who [the sleeping occupants] were. Before they left they stuck a sticker on the cupboard, saying 'Trust me – I am your friend.' (*SASPU National,* December 1984)

Although the raid was conducted 'to root out revolutionaries', as the Minister of Law and Order put it, it led only to the arrest of 354 people on pass law, influx control, pornography and drug offences (*Cape Times,* 24.10.1984). From Sebokeng the police and soldiers moved quickly into the nearby townships of Boipatong and Sharpeville to repeat the operation.

In response to the increased repression, an alliance of trade unions and UDF organisations called a two-day stayaway in November. One of their demands was the immediate withdrawal of troops and police from the townships. The stayaway was at that time the largest ever known in South Africa's history. Thousands of soldiers were deployed in affected areas to patrol the streets and man roadblocks.

Embarrassed by the widespread negative reaction that followed these operations, the government banned all information about Defence Force involvement in joint police–army activities. The blanket of secrecy imposed placed black residential areas 'in the same category as war zones or battlegrounds' (*Cape Times,* editorial, 8.11.1984).

The 1985 state of emergency

The police and army in combination were initially unable to contain the rebellion. By mid-1985 it had spread to rural areas and was increasing in intensity. Government ministers claimed that the ANC and UDF were intent on making the country ungovernable (*Star,* 19.6.1985).

On 21 July, President Botha declared a partial state of emergency on the Witwatersrand, in the Eastern Cape and later in the Western Cape. SAP and SADF officers were given far-reaching powers of arrest and detention. They were also empowered 'to apply or order the application of such force as [they] under the circumstances may deem necessary in order to ward off or prevent . . . suspected danger' (*Government Gazette,* 21.7.1985).

In mid-December special government regulations extended additional powers to soldiers. They were given authority to man roadblocks, search buildings and cars without police assistance, prevent prohibited meetings, disperse 'unlawful gatherings', and arrest or detain any person. A *Star* editorial observed that the powers created a situation of 'martial law in all but name' (*Star,* 3.1.1986), though the Minister of Defence represented them as 'nothing new' (*Star,* 20.12.1985).

The government initially attempted to counter criticisms of the SADF's role by insisting that it was only being used in a 'support capacity' in relation to the SAP. The distinction lost its validity, however, once soldiers acquired police powers. Whatever the difference between police and army tactics and strategies, township residents increasingly saw them as one and the same, and the government itself began referring to the two collectively as the 'security forces'.

According to a national serviceman on township duty in the Eastern Cape in 1985:

Almost throughout these four months the army has been mixed in with the police, with a couple of police in each Buffel [military vehicle] and usually a few more SADF members in the police vehicles. So, for the black population, there has never been an opportunity to differentiate between the two forces, and the SADF almost immediately inherited the lack of credibility and bad reputation of the police. (*Sunday Tribune,* 8.9.1985)

The national serviceman added that while discipline and communications were 'greatly superior' in the SADF, the separation of troops into small combined units allowed them 'to get into the spirit of being a law unto themselves, and mirror the bad behaviour of the police'.

The blurring of police and army roles also highlighted the extent to which the SAP has begun in recent years to operate as a paramilitary force.[2] The rising level of guerilla activity and popular resistance after 1976 brought about the militarisation of SAP training, weaponry, technology and internal organisation (Van der Spuy, 1988). This process intensified after the start of the 1984–6 uprising. The police perceived the escalating conflict as a situation of 'war' and viewed the human targets of their action as 'the enemy' (Shärf, 1988). In two acknowledged incidents, senior police officers invoked classic counter-insurgency terminology when they gave orders to 'eliminate' protesters and 'ring leaders'.[3] In February 1985 'riot control' training, which had previously been restricted to specialist units, was extended to all policemen (Brewer *et al.*, 1988: 177).

During the emergency, the security forces harassed and detained community leaders, disrupted political meetings and black funerals, and attempted to break stayaways, consumer boycotts and strikes. They enforced night curfews in townships and manned roadblocks to prevent non-residents from entering them. On a daily basis they patrolled black urban areas, regularly sealing them off to conduct house-to-house searches. They also maintained a provocative presence inside and outside school premises to prevent student mobilisation and organisation.

According to the Minister of Defence, 35 372 troops were deployed in 96 townships in 1985. The Minister added that a full list of the occasions on which they were used would 'take months to compile and run to hundreds of pages' (House of Assembly, parliamentary questions no. 878, 1986). Many conscripts were put on 24-hour standby, and call-ups for 30-day township camps were doubled to 60 days (*Cape Times*, 4.7.1985).

During this period the SADF repeatedly claimed that its presence in the townships was intended to protect black civilians from 'radicals' and 'criminals'.

If one is prepared to look objectively at the situation, one must see many many people who simply ask for protection of their lives and property. Must we turn a deaf ear to these people? No government worth its salt can allow blatant intimidation to establish itself and to destroy, eventually, the fabric of civil society. (Major-General Van Loggerenberg, Chief Director Operations, *Citizen*, 21.9.1985)

However, township residents saw the SADF as an aggressive force. According to Archbishop Desmond Tutu, 'as a black person I know we don't regard the police and army as our friends. No, let me put it more strongly. We regard them as our enemies.' (Speech at ECC rally, Cape Town, May 1986)

Township residents fight back

The deployment of troops provoked intense opposition from black religious and political groups, trade unions and the community media. The United Women's Organisation, a UDF affiliate, summed up their feelings when it declared:

> The United Women's Organisation calls on troops to leave our townships. We who know the joy of motherhood also know the pain of children being beaten, detained and killed by troops. We know the pain of troops taking young women, of raping and of fear of walking in our streets because of the troops. We call on young conscripts to refuse to go into our areas. We do not want you there. (Speech at ECC rally, Cape Town, October 1985)

Independent surveys confirmed that this view was shared by the majority of township residents. In 1985 a human rights organisation, Women for Peace, conducted opinion polls amongst blacks on the Witwatersrand. Their perceptions of the police and army were overwhelmingly negative. Roughly 90 per cent felt threatened rather than protected by them (Women for Peace, 1985). In addition, more than 90 per cent of residents surveyed in Lamontville township near Durban felt that the security forces did not make their area safer, and 45 per cent thought they increased the level of violence. Some 70 per cent believed the security forces were there to repress community organisations, search for weapons or collect police evidence, while only 8 per cent felt they were there to 'maintain law and order'.[4]

In mid-1985 the conservative mass-circulation Natal newspaper, *Ilanga*, published a front-page editorial in English for the first time.

> We do so for two reasons: Firstly, so that we may add our voice to the call on the government to appoint a judicial inquiry into police and army action in black townships. Secondly, we wish to support the call in a language we can trust the authorities to understand.
>
> The presence of members of the Defence Force and heavily armed police in troubled black townships is never going to work in the way the government thinks or hopes. It is counter-productive and ineffective, as the grim toll of daily killings in these townships shows. . . . You are simply creating a tragic and quite unnecessary civil war situation that may soon develop into a second Lebanon. (Cited in *Argus*, 17.7.1985)

Township residents opposed the army in two ways. They undertook highly effective school and consumer boycotts, and they engaged the security forces in physical battle.

Throughout 1985 and 1986 school boycotts spread like wildfire across the country, involving almost a quarter of a million pupils. Their demands included the release of student leaders from detention, the recognition of democratically elected student representative councils, and the withdrawal of troops from their schools and communities (Muller, 1987).

Nationwide consumer boycotts similarly focused on the SADF's presence in black areas. In one notable incident in Port Elizabeth, the boycott led to negotiations between township organisations and local white business and local government. The negotiations resulted in the temporary withdrawal of the army and the release of political detainees. A director of the Port Elizabeth Chamber of Commerce reported that these moves had curbed violence in the region 'quite dramatically' (*Star*, 25.11.1985).

As the security forces acted to break the boycotts, residents prepared themselves for combat. Militant youths, known as the 'Young Lions', declared that while they did not have guns 'we don't have to fight the Boers [security forces] barehanded. In a people's war, there are other weapons – you make them out of whatever you have.' (*Weekly Mail*, 30.4.1987)

In many townships youths dug trenches across roads to trap military vehicles, and strung lengths of barbed wire across the street at the height of a man standing in an armoured car. They lured army patrols into backstreet ambushes, and fired rivets and sparkplugs from home-made catapults. They hurled petrol bombs at military and private vehicles, and attacked government buildings and the homes of community councillors.

The important thing is not what we can turn into weapons – almost anything can be made lethal – but our will to fight. You can see that will when someone goes against a Casspir with all its armour and the Boers with all their guns inside, and he has only a petrol bomb in his hand. When this will is developed and strengthened, then we will be ready for guns, and when we are ready for guns, we will have them. (*Ibid.*)

In early 1986 there was a spate of violent attacks on political activists. Unidentified assassination squads appeared to have been formed to eliminate them and destroy their homes. Township residents responded by forming 'people's militias' and 'defence committees'. The Soweto Civic Association stated:

The fact that the police, the SADF, [community] councillors and their henchmen have been seen at scenes of petrol bombings and other savage acts of brutality is cause for concern. . . . We can no longer stand by idly while our wives, children and property are being attacked. We have no option but to defend ourselves. (*Weekly Mail*, 2.5.1986)

The behaviour of the security forces heightened black anger and militancy immeasurably. As in the suppression of the 1976 uprising, many young people fled South Africa to join the ANC and would return as trained guerillas. Now, in addition, a generation of children had emerged as 'battle-hardened soldiers *inside* the country' (*City Press*, 20.4.1986; my emphasis).

The 1986 state of emergency

By mid-1986 the government was desperate to end the still intensifying resistance. Township residents had effectively brought about the collapse of local black urban authorities. They were moving beyond 'making the townships ungovernable' to 'building organs of people's power'. Embryonic structures of 'alternative power' were developing through civic organisations, street committees and people's courts. On 12 June the government imposed a national state of emergency, renewed in 1987 and 1988, to eliminate these structures and regain control.

The security forces went about their task with even greater determination than in 1985. Although their role had consistently been an aggressive one, during the 1986 emergency they appeared to rely increasingly on offensive rather than defensive military tactics and weaponry. Whereas previously they had patrolled the streets in relatively cumbersome vehicles loaded with 'riot' equipment, they now used open jeeps with mounted machine guns and highly mobile armed commandos on horseback.

A doctor working at Baragwanath Hospital in Soweto noticed this shift in tactics in the pattern of 'unrest-related' injuries. There was a marked decrease in *sjambok* (whip) and birdshot injuries and an increase in gunshot wounds. The wounds were no longer 'mainly peripheral – i.e. arms, hands, head – but more related to core organs like the heart. It's clear the security forces are shooting to kill.' (Interview with doctor, September 1986)

The nature of the gunshot wounds also indicated that the security forces had replaced low-velocity with high-velocity bullets.

A low-velocity bullet generally causes a hole not much larger than the bullet itself. A high-velocity bullet in comparison is spinning about its axis, so when the bullet hits its target it generates an incredible shock wave. . . . There was a case of a young man who was allegedly caught in crossfire and shot, and the bullet hit his toe and took off the entire lower leg. If it hits you in the abdomen or the chest it's like a tornado – it just whips everything up inside you and you're finished. It's obviously a weapon designed to kill. It's a weapon used in a traditional war situation. (*Ibid.*)

According to the Soweto doctor, in previous years the majority of injured patients at Baragwanath Hospital were 35–45-year-old victims of gang violence. During the 1986 emergency the majority were children aged 14–18. This was because the security forces had made a priority of ending the nationwide school boycotts.

Police and army actions fuelled the boycotts, however. Pupils at Kgothalang Secondary School in Bekkersdal, for example, stayed away from school in protest against what a teacher called 'the invasion of our classrooms'. Armed troops had entered the school and demanded to see class registers. They 'harassed the students' and 'roughed up' teachers who objected (*Weekly Mail*, 22.8.1986).

The Soweto Parents' Crisis Committee and the National Education Crisis Committee repeatedly stressed to senior education officials that peace was not possible under the SADF occupation. Dr Nthato Motlana, Soweto Civic Association president, stated:

We did our best to send the children back to school at the beginning of the year, and are still doing so even now. But the authorities do not seem to be interested. What can be done now to remedy the deteriorating situation? The answer is still the same as when we met [Deputy Minister of Education] de Beer and others: withdraw the troops from our schools and from our townships. (*Star*, 24.8.1986)

The security forces were also active at black universities, which were described by journalists as 'battlegrounds more than academic enclaves' (*Weekly Mail*, 3.10.1986). In mid-1986 the SADF set up camp inside Turfloop (the University of the North) in Lebowa. Students had to produce special identity cards to enter and leave the university. On a daily basis foot patrols marched past lecture theatres, and convoys of military vehicles drove through the campus (Stockenström, 1988).

Media coverage of the security forces in 1985 had galvanised international opposition to apartheid. In 1986 the government introduced a series of far-reaching press restrictions to prevent further exposure. The restrictions prohibited the publication of news and comment about any 'security action', and banned journalists from being present in 'unrest areas'. The Minister of Law and Order was empowered to seize or ban any publication that contravened the restrictions (Armstrong, 1986).

The press curbs considerably reduced the level of information available about SADF activities in 1987. There were, however, reports of soldiers involved in strike-breaking (*Citizen*, 6.2.1987), 'crime prevention operations' (*Weekly Mail*, 26.6.1987), assaults on workers and youths wearing political tee-shirts (*New Nation*, 16.7.1987), the detention and torture of young people (*Business Day*, 24.4.1987), and forced removals of people from where they had resided (*City Press*, 19.4.1987).

Human rights abuses

Allegations of gratuitous and excessive violence were repeatedly made against the security forces. A special Catholic Bishops' Conference report in 1984 accused the police of 'indiscriminate and unprovoked aggression' (Southern African Catholic Bishops' Conference, 1984). In 1985 a Port Elizabeth newspaper stated that accounts of Defence Force misconduct had reached 'alarming proportions' (*Weekend Post*, 2.8.1985). A random survey conducted by the *Eastern Province Herald* revealed that one in three township residents claimed to have been assaulted by policemen or soldiers (13.11.1985).

Human rights organisations compiled reports of security forces throwing teargas into school rooms, beating and detaining children and teachers, and opening fire on them with birdshot, buckshot and rubber bullets.[5] Teachers at township schools described a situation of military siege:

> The riot police and soldiers come and go from our schools constantly. They terrorise the children and have threatened some of them with detention, torture and even sodomy. Some of the kids are scared to death, others are angry. The atmosphere is so tense and the teachers are caught in the middle. It is impossible to carry on classes under these conditions. (Cooke, 1986: 66)

The Detainees' Parents Support Committee reported a pattern of SADF abuses against young people. Soldiers would pick children off the streets and hold them for several hours in military vehicles, or take them to remote areas of veld. The children described being beaten with fists and rifle butts, and subjected to electric shock treatment. They also testified to being doused in petrol and held near open flames (Detainees' Parents Support Committee, 1986).

There are several factors to consider in understanding why the security forces committed such atrocities. Key amongst them was the racist ideology propagated in white schools and in the armed forces that denigrated the value of black life.

> It is not so much the acts of violence that shock as the level of racism that allows them to flourish: so many people [soldiers] who are normally fair and reasonable simply 'hate kaffirs'. . . . There is a tremendous sense of power in beating someone up: even if you are the most put-upon, dumb son-of-a-bitch, you are still better than a 'kaffir' and can beat him up to prove it. (National serviceman, *Sunday Tribune*, 8.9.1985)

> After beating a person, shooting a person, to pull a person as a bag of coal and to throw a person into a Casspir or a [police] van as if they are throwing a bag of potatoes! I don't know how, because even if you throw a bag of maize you cannot just throw it. You will think about how much you paid for it. (Crossroads squatter, *Out of Step*, May 1987)

Another contributing factor to the widespread abuses was the government's determination to protect the security forces from prosecution and public scrutiny. In addition to introducing stringent press restrictions, the emergency regulations granted policemen and soldiers indemnity from civil and criminal prosecution for any act done 'in good faith' (Proclamation R201, *Government Gazette* no. 9993, 26 October 1985). One newspaper concluded that 'the term "law enforcement officer" no longer applies to the security forces or its government' (*Natal Witness*, 4.11.1985).

The police routinely dismissed calls for independent commissions of inquiry into accusations of unlawful conduct, insisting that all complaints be lodged with them. The SADF similarly set up more than twenty offices to hear the increasing number of public complaints about troop action; after the first two months only 16 complaints had been received (*Sowetan*, 26.11.1985).

Township residents believed it 'fruitless to lay complaints to the men you are accusing' (Katlehong resident, *Star*, 25.9.1986). Their concerns did not seem unfounded. In February 1986 the Minister of Law and Order disclosed in parliament that 500 complaints had been lodged against the security forces. Only one policeman had been convicted. Disciplinary steps had been taken against seven policemen and eight soldiers (*Cape Times*, 17.2.1986).

Members of the SAP and SADF who were prosecuted and convicted in civil courts often received extraordinarily light sentences. For example, an army sergeant who beat up three black reporters and a photographer in Soweto was given a suspended sentence of R100 or 90 days' imprisonment (*Argus*, 11.12.1985). A soldier who raped a township woman was sentenced to R80 or 40 days (*Cape Times*, 24.2.1987).

New forms of control

By early 1987 the security forces had broken the back of the rebellion. The state withdrew most of the troops from black areas, directed its repression at individual activists and organisations rather than at whole communities, and replaced its policy of 'maximum policing' with a more sophisticated counter-revolutionary strategy. The strategy, developed by the military and the broader security establishment, entailed two new forms of control.

The first involved the security forces moving into the background as conservative black groups took up the front-line of attack. These groups included vigilantes, municipal police and special constables *(kits-konstabels)*.

Vigilantes first emerged in 1985 in areas where progressive organisations were strongest. The government portrayed their attacks on community activists as 'black-on-black violence', which necessitated the 'neutral' military presence in the townships. The vigilantes in fact often operated with official approval or collusion. They employed similar though often more brutal methods to those wielded by the security forces, but without reinforcing the impression of a minority regime waging war on the majority of its people.

In late 1986 the phenomenon of 'black-on-black violence' developed into one of 'black-on-black policing' (Shärf, 1988). Vigilante activities were effectively taken over by newly formed black police forces – municipal police responsible to black local authorities, and SAP *kits-konstabels* ('instant constables'), so-called because their training only lasts several weeks. By 1987 some 16 000 blacks had been recruited into the two forces, increasing the number of policemen in the country by a third (CIIR, 1988). Because the black police have a greater knowledge of township dynamics than their white counterparts, and because their repressive actions do not reflect on the government in quite the same way, they have been able to 'neutralise' resistance more effectively (Shärf. 1988).

Township residents fear the municipal police and *kitskonstabels* even more than the security forces. Many of them have been charged with murder, rape and robbery, and have been frequently restrained by court orders from assaulting residents (CIIR, 1988a). The Western Province Council of Churches described them as 'a monster that is clearly getting out of hand . . . law enforcement officers that do not obey the law themselves' (Western Province Council of Churches, 1988).

The second key aspect of control in the new counter-revolutionary strategy centres around economic and social upliftment schemes in selected black areas. These entail allocating resources to 'welfare problems' that could potentially become 'security problems'. The aim is to undercut resistance by addressing the 'grievances exploited by revolutionaries'.

This WHAM ('winning hearts and minds') programme is coordinated by the National Security Management System, a secret network of local and regional structures known as Joint Management Centres (JMCs). The JMCs are dominated by the security forces and are also responsible for coordinating the latter's coercive activities. According to the Minister of Defence it was the JMCs that 'stabilised' many parts of the country during the state of emergency (*Argus,* 12.3.1986).

Conclusion

At the time of writing the state has regained control of the country. It is confident that the security establishment's mixture of 'hard war' and 'soft war' tactics will prevent a recurrence of the 1984–6 uprising, and provide the space to reconstitute the black urban authority structures that were destroyed.

This confidence is misplaced. The WHAM programme and the government's reform strategy are fatally flawed by being premised on the continued denial of full political rights for blacks, and by the repression that preceded and still accompanies them. Township residents will not forget the physical and psychological damage inflicted on them by the very institutions that now seek to win them over.

Nor is the international community likely to ease its pressure on the government. The campaign to isolate apartheid, which had slowly built momentum over two decades, became unstoppable in 1985 as people overseas watched daily television coverage of the security forces in action.

In the white community too, the state paid a heavy price for its excessive use of force. By compelling young white men to take up arms against their fellow citizens, it made itself vulnerable to a significant degree of opposition from within the ruling class.

The overall effect of the deployment of troops was accurately forecast in 1985 by political scientist Dr Simon Barnham.

When highly trained and powerfully armed soldiers – who are equipped for a combat role and thus may take on the appearance of an army of occupation – are called in to support the civil power, it is going to escalate the level of violence. Military weaponry and training are designed for killing on a battle-field, not for subduing crowds. Using a sledgehammer to crack a nut is unlikely to have the desired result. (*Sunday Star*, 14.7.1985)

6 The psychological experiences of white conscripts in the black townships

DIANE SANDLER

All they can do is make you as hard as they can with the training, toughen you completely; and make you absolutely resilient so that you can withstand anything and then send you out to get the job done. (Interview with conscript)

I'm normally quite adaptable to situations. I can normally handle most things that happen in my [life]. But this time I don't know. (Interview with conscript)

Since October 1984, thousands of young white male conscripts have been deployed by the South African Defence Force in black townships throughout South Africa. Little is known of their experiences. Less is known about the psychological processes involved. This chapter is an exploratory investigation in this area. It first reviews the literature on the psychological effects of war on soldiers and then presents the findings of a study on the experience of South African conscripts.[1]

Post-traumatic stress disorder

Psychological material on the effects of war on soldiers is not extensive.[2] Although through the centuries both popular literature and various commentators on war have referred to psychological casualties, it was only during the American Civil War that the Union Army's Surgeon-General clinically identified a state of 'nostalgia', in which men with no physical evidence of disease showed various symptoms, including fatigue, insomnia and psychotic features. The same condition was again observed in the Franco–Prussian, Spanish–American and Anglo–Boer wars, and named 'combat fatigue' (Simpson, 1986).

During the First World War psychological damage sustained by soldiers was officially recognised. Those who reported psychological problems as a result of fighting in the war were labelled as having 'shell-shock' – even if they had never in fact been exposed to exploding shells. For the first time, psychiatrists came to form part of the military medical corps, and psychological treatment close to the battle-front became possible in some cases.

However, the psychological lessons of the First World War were widely ignored and virtually no follow-up research was done. During the Second World War, psychological casualties, for example in the US

Army, were widespread, affecting one in ten soldiers (Simpson, 1986). Various labels were given to this disorder, including 'combat neurosis', 'traumatic war neurosis', and 'gross stress reaction'.

In 1951 the disorder entered the nomenclature of the Diagnostic and Statistical Manual of Psychiatric Disorders (DSM I, 1951), the official publication of the American Psychiatric Association, in a category called 'gross stress reaction'. It was deleted by the mental health profession in DSM II (1968). This indicated a decline of psychiatric interest in the syndrome.

Interest was revived by the US military intervention in Vietnam. Almost three million American soldiers were active in Vietnam, and 1,2 million were involved in direct combat. Today it is estimated that between 500 000 and 700 000 veterans of the war experience significant emotional turmoil as a direct result of their experience. However, it was only in the late 1970s that the mental health community in the USA acknowledged the extent and reality of the effects of combat. This was the result of a realisation that psychological problems can emerge months or years after the initiating trauma, and may in fact worsen over time.

Post-traumatic stress disorder, as we now know it, became an official category in DSM III (1982). Military combat forms part of this classification.

The essential feature of this disorder is the development of characteristic symptoms following a psychologically distressing event that is outside the range of usual human experience (i.e. outside the range of common experiences such as simple bereavement, chronic illness, marital conflict). The stressor producing the syndrome would be markedly distressing to almost anyone. . . The most common traumata involve either a serious threat to one's life or physical integrity; a serious threat or harm to one's children, spouse, or other close relatives and friends; sudden destruction of one's home or community; or seeing another person who has recently been, or is being, seriously injured or killed as the result of an accident or physical violence. . . . The trauma may be experienced alone (e.g. rape) or in the company of groups of people (e.g. military combat). Stressors producing this disorder include natural disasters (e.g. floods), accidental disasters (e.g. airplane crashes) or deliberately caused disasters (e.g. bombing, torture, death camps). . . . The disorder is apparently more severe and longer lasting when the stressor is of human design. The traumatic event can be reexperienced in a variety of ways: (1) recurrent and intrusive distressing recollections of the event; (2) recurrent distressing dreams; (3) sudden acting or feeling as if the traumatic event were recurring (includes a sense of reliving the experience, illusion, hallucination, and dissociative [flash-back] episodes); (4) intense psychological distress at exposure to events that symbolise or resemble an aspect of the traumatic event, including anniversaries of the trauma. There is persistent avoidance of stimuli associated with the trauma or numbing of general responsiveness (not present before the trauma), as indicated by at least three of the following: (1) efforts to avoid thoughts or feelings associated with the trauma; (2) efforts to avoid difficulties or situations that arouse recollections of the trauma; (3) inability to recall an important aspect of the trauma (psychological amnesia); (4) markedly diminished interest in significant activities; (5) feeling of detachment or estrangement from others; (6) restricted range of affect, e.g. unable to have loving feelings; (7) sense of a foreshortened future. . . . [and at least two of the following:] (1) difficulty in falling or staying asleep; (2) irritability or outbursts of anger; (3) difficulty concentrating; (4) hypervigilance; (5) exaggerated startle response; (6) physiologic reactivity upon exposure to events that symbolise or resemble an aspect of the traumatic event. (DSM III, revised, 1988)

The psychological complex of 'war trauma' seems to centre specifically around the following features: severe survivor guilt and self-punishment; feelings of being a scapegoat; episodes of severe rage and violent impulses towards what may be indiscriminate targets; psychic numbing; alienation from one's own feelings; doubt about whether one can ever love or trust someone else again; loss of trust in self; and pessimism about the very nature and purpose of life itself.

Current understanding of the effect of combat on the soldier has its roots in the literature emerging from the Vietnam war. This extensive and ongoing body of work deals with a range of social and psychological problems common to Vietnam veterans. These include such indicators as an increase in alcohol and drug abuse; greater incidence of divorce; higher rates of suicide; higher unemployment; and greater use of violence (Laufer and Gallops, 1985; Yager, 1975, 1984). Also included in the literature are discussions about veterans without post-traumatic stress disorder (Hendin and Haas, 1984), issues relating to depression (Helzer *et al.*, 1979), and involvement by soldiers in atrocities (Haley, 1974).

The 'psychology of slaughter'

Two seminal contributions to the Vietnam literature have been made by Robert Jay Lifton (1973) and W. B. Gault (1971). Gault introduced the idea of the 'psychology of slaughter'. By combining the dictionary definition of that activity ('the extensive, violent, bloody or wanton destruction of life; carnage') with a psychological emphasis upon the victim's defencelessness ('whether . . . a disarmed prisoner or an unarmed civilian'), he distinguishes 'slaughter from the mutual homicide of the actual combatants in military battle'. He sets himself the interpretative task of explaining how 'relatively normal men overcame and eventually neutralised their natural repugnance toward slaughter'. His argument is based on a recognition of six psychological themes or principles he believes contribute to slaughter.

(1) *'The enemy is everywhere' or 'the universalisation of the enemy'* (1971: 83). The soldier realistically experiences intense hatred and apprehends immediate physical threat from all quarters. He knows he cannot

distinguish peasant farmer (read in the South African context 'township resident') from 'terrorist', innocent youth from Viet Cong spy (read 'ANC or SWAPO member'). In a land of swamps, malaria, and great hostility, he can only rely on his immediate unit. Everyone else, young or old, man or woman, is identified as his enemy.

(2) *'The enemy is not human' or 'the cartoonisation of the victim'* (1971: 83). The image of the degraded enemy is essential to the psychology of a homicidal combat team. The local Vietnamese people were referred to by American soldiers as 'gooks' and 'dinks'; they were said to be 'like children', and were inscrutable, strange and different.

(3) *The 'dilution' or 'vertical dilution of responsibility'* (1971: 84). The soldier has the sense that responsibility for the death of a specific victim is not his but is shared by his platoon, and that the order to kill was given by the battalion command; thus his dismay is not as great as if he had been alone, and had consciously and deliberately killed a particular person.

(4) *'The pressure to act'* (1971: 84). A soldier is expected to be aggressive. Military principles emphasise the need to act swiftly, strike first, search and destroy, etc. Furthermore, inaction is virtually unbearable – the soldier is in fact anxious to engage.

(5) *'The natural dominance of the psychopath'* (1971: 84). In an atmosphere where accepted conventions and prohibitions are widely suspended, the man of blunted sensibilities and ready violence, unburdened by empathy, guilt or compassion, finds himself at last in a world suited to his character – he can do anything.

(6) Such is the terrifying force of *sheer firepower* that 'terrified and furious teenagers by the tens of thousands have only to twitch their index fingers, and what was a quiet village is suddenly a slaughterhouse' (1971: 84).

Gault concludes that 'in Vietnam a number of fairly ordinary young men have been psychologically ready to engage in slaughter and that moreover this readiness is by no means incomprehensible' (1971: 86). The combination of external historical factors and prevailing military policies provided the matrix for an internal sequence that constituted the psychological dimension, enabling anyone to enter the 'psychology of slaughter'.

The 'hero as warrior'
A further psychological dimension that plays an integral part in the psyche of a soldier is Campbell's (1956) notion of the 'hero as warrior'. In the mythology of war and warrior heroes, the soldier has always laid claim to our emotions. He has been celebrated by virtually all known cultures for his individual courage and for the collective glory he makes possible. In mythology the hero as warrior acts in the service of man's spiritual achievement; he becomes the giver of immortality; he

kills not to destroy life but to enlarge, perpetuate and enhance life. Throughout history, warrior myths have been readily absorbed by specific societies, and recreated in their own hierarchical, power-centred images. The killing of the enemy is enacted in order to consolidate and reaffirm the existing social order. When this is the function, the soldier becomes no longer a warrior hero, but in Lifton's (1973) words the 'socialised warrior'.

The worth of the socialised warrior comes to be measured by concrete acts of killing. It is through killing that he achieves honour, fellowship, and something close to a state of grace. However, to reach the desired psychological state to be able to kill, the socialised warrior requires some kind of initiation process, a symbolic form of death and rebirth that may and usually does coincide with his attainment of adulthood. In that rite (now called basic training), his civil identity with its built-in restraints is eradicated, or at least undermined, and set aside in favour of the warrior identity, with its central focus upon killing. Only through such a process can the warrior become psychically numbed towards killing and dying. The 'socialised warrior' thus becomes a distorted and manipulated version of the 'hero as warrior'. Skill in killing and surviving is cultivated, and even though this skill may combine courage, loyalty and technical proficiency, it no longer serves the purpose of the original heroic quest.

The mythology of war – as cleansing, necessary, inevitable and heroic – and of soldiers as 'warrior heroes' is deeply ingrained in South African society, specifically in the psyches of young white men. Indeed, the militarisation of South African society forms the bedrock from which the psyches of white conscripts have grown. It has two major requirements of individuals. Firstly, that they be submissive to and supportive of the defined authorities, and secondly, that they be aggressive towards the defined enemy. This implies a readiness for active hostility or violent aggression towards the enemy.

The soldier and authority

The process that shapes individuals to meet these requirements has been analysed by Adorno (1969). This is not a linear process, but certain specific stages can be delineated. The first stage involves individuals being encouraged to identify with authority. Authority is represented by symbols, leaders, and institutions of social, political and military power, as well as by the ruling group and its values. This is summed up in Adorno's notion of 'conventionalism', which is based upon the individual's adherence to the standards of the collective powers, with which he, for the time being, is identified. The outcomes of identification are: internalising opinions propagated by the authority so that individuals accept the authority's goals and definition of the conflict; submitting to control by the authority; deriving a sense of power from the authority, especially with regard to military power; and taking pleasure or pride in the 'achievements' of authority.

However, many people have ambivalent and even rebellious feelings about authority. Some tolerate it and others fit Adorno's notion of 'authoritarian submission', which is a way of handling ambivalent feelings towards authority figures. Underlying hostile and rebellious impulses are held in check by fear, and behaviour involving respect, obedience and gratitude is exaggerated. The negative feelings are often all directed towards the enemy. Once the individual has convinced himself that there are people who ought to be punished, he is provided with a channel through which his deepest aggressive impulses may be expressed, even while he thinks of himself as thoroughly moral. Adorno argues that this 'authoritarian aggression' may take the most violent forms if the individual's external authorities lend their approval.

Identification is based both on rewards as well as on fear of being punished and rejected, and enhances a feeling of submissiveness. This is a primary characteristic of 'basic training', which Lifton describes as a 'systematic stripping process' in which the civilian self is 'deliberately denuded' so that the soldier can 'reject his pre-existing identity [and] envelop himself instead in the institutional identity of the military organisation' (1973: 28).

Adorno suggests that the second element in the process involves inducing a feeling of being mortally threatened by the enemy, who is depicted as ruthless, violent and evil. A person who experiences such threat also feels the need for a solution to the threat. Force is projected as the only solution. The threat, however, does not disappear even in the face of demonstrations of superior military power and the ability to annihilate the enemy. It becomes permanent, both objectively in the form of ongoing resistance and ideologically in the form of ongoing propaganda.

The individual's submission to authority is mirrored by an authoritarian attitude towards subordinates and an attempt to impose rules on them. The real autonomy which is lost is replaced by a false autonomy which Adorno has called 'self-glorification'. This is false because it is externalised: the person derives a sense of self-worth from identifying with the powerful authority and also from denigrating and exercising power over others who are weaker. Other people do not count as people – they only count as things to be used or as enemies to be subdued or annihilated.

The South African context

This process of dehumanisation is integral to acts of violence and killing. *Pace* Lifton (1973), this can be referred to in the South African context as the 'Kaffir-syndrome'. 'Kaffir' serves the psychological function of image-replacement – the enemy is no longer a human being, but sub-human and dirt. Some such dehumanising term is always involved in the perpetration of widespread violence and killings – in the South African context for the soldier to cease to feel the humanity of black township residents. It is much easier to eliminate 'Kaffirs' than men, women or children. Adorno found that people who are prejudiced against one group are also prejudiced against other groups. This generalisation of the 'enemy' results in an extension of the identified 'enemy' in South Africa – from Russian imperialism and the ANC, to encompass virtually all black people.

In the psychological environment of the white conscript in South Africa, two themes are especially relevant. Firstly, certain beliefs are held about the current civil war. The unrest and resistance are thought to be the work of a small number of agitators and terrorists. Moreover, the military is seen as neutral and as merely providing support for the police in maintaining 'law and order'.

The second important theme relates to the objective features of the civil war in the townships, including the state of emergency which provides indemnity for all security force action; overwhelming power, especially based on arms; and a white, male army entering a black civilian area. These illusions and features form the psychological environment in which the conscript exists.

A study of conscripts' experiences in black townships
This section sets out to develop a phenomenology of the experiences of white conscripted soldiers operating in South Africa's black townships. Eight individuals were asked to describe the positive and negative aspects of their experiences in the townships, and to focus on a day that stood out in their memory. Not all the interviewees were opposed to the role of the troops in the townships on political or moral grounds. The following themes emerged from their accounts. The themes are generalised and do not necessarily reflect the experience of all conscripts deployed in the townships.

The soldier's experience of entering the township
The soldier experienced great unease and wariness in himself and from others. His own sense of caution and trepidation added to the feelings of anger, frustration and pain emanating from the area. He felt the decay, destitution, squalor and poverty around him. The area was seen as harsh, barren and deadly. He experienced the environment as oppressive, destructive and dangerous, and himself as being foreign in it yet enclosed by its squalor and darkness. He was aware of feeling anger building up in the township and poised to erupt.

The soldier was aware of negative responses from residents and this added to his feeling of foreboding. He experienced a sense of the macabre, a strangeness and unreality. This was because his actions conflicted with his sense of the familiarity of the surroundings. He saw housewives shopping, children playing, shops whose names he recognised, and streets and houses where people live their everyday lives. These images triggered memories of his own life, and this created a tension. In addition, the soldier experienced the confusion of other conscripts as their expectations too differed from the reality they were experiencing.

The soldier's experience of authority

The soldier's experience of authority was multi-faceted and contained contradictory elements. On the one hand, he experienced confidence in and admiration for the morality of authority and its ability to assert control. He believed that authority at all levels sanctioned the violence and arbitrary brutal actions. The soldier accepted authority and discipline and felt that they must be obeyed. He did not hate authority itself. Thus he experienced distaste and consternation at the lack of control and viciousness of some soldiers. He had confidence in authority to control, guide and place boundaries to his own behaviour, as well as to any arbitrary actions others might engage in.

On the other hand, the soldier experienced bewilderment and anguish, coupled with great resentment and anger at taking orders, and tremendous hatred at being subjected to authority. He experienced a sense of captivity and powerlessness. He felt a sense of insignificance and regarded the army as voraciously taking from him. He experienced doubt and a lack of confidence in authority's ability to control. He did not believe their interpretation of his reality. This incorporated the feeling that he should not be engaged in war against fellow citizens; in fact, at moments he felt grudging admiration for the strength of the people opposing him. The soldier felt distanced from authority and engulfed by chaos, frenzy and confusion.

The soldier experienced resolution at two levels. He experienced a sense of gratefulness for authority placing boundaries to his emotional responses and allowing him to operate in an intellectually disciplined mode. This was coupled with an eventual excitement and sense of power when immersing himself in external discipline and handing over control of himself to authority. He experienced an acceptance as well of the arbitrariness of authority in its decision-making. At the same time, the soldier experienced anger and resentment towards authority for his situation.

The soldier's experience of violence and death

Death and violence in various forms pervaded the soldier's experience. He may have faced his own death, he may have witnessed the near-deaths of his victims and he may have participated in killing. The possibility of destruction, conflict and death engulfed his person.

It emerged in violent dreams in which he was dying, in a sense of tremendous loss because of his use of violence, and in his feeling brutalised and hurt.

The soldier experienced horror at seeing various forms of brutality. He suffered depression and guilt after observing the death of another human being. In addition, he experienced horror at the perception of war as a game and the eagerness for killing which others showed. The soldier felt surrounded by uncontrollable violence – aggressive, violent sounds filled his head, and he felt engulfed by the strength and potential violence of the structure he was involved in. He experienced a concomitant sense of foreboding and outrage at the destruction surrounding him.

The soldier responded in two ways. He attempted to distance himself from the engulfing brutality and expressed resignation at knowing he had changed in some way, as a result of the violence. He also felt horror and panic at the indifference to life and death expressed by township residents in their actions of self-sacrifice. To cope with a sense of the meaningless of death, the soldier intellectualised and dehumanised the deaths of others. In fact, he equated feeling with dying – to avoid dying he must stop feeling.

The soldier's experience of morality

The soldier experienced tremendous conflict and contradictions in relation to his experience of morality – his own and those of the authorities. He experienced himself on a number of levels: by responding in his usual caring way to other people's needs and pain; by denying other people's pain, in order to cope emotionally; and in feeling shock, anger, confusion, horror and guilt at the morality displayed by others which contradicted his expectations of them and which transgressed his moral boundaries and code of conduct.

He experienced horror at witnessing brutality and conflict, for his usual helping responses and the respect he would characteristically show were replaced with inaction. He may even have entered the violence as an active participant and experienced amusement at being involved in it. He may have witnessed torture, experiencing it in a voyeuristic, intellectually detached way. But, at the same time, he had confidence in authority's morality. He thus experienced great disturbances, for his own emotions contradicted this confidence. The soldier's experiences made him feel exposed and vulnerable as a human being, and he felt his own sense of morality destroyed, his sense of judgement diminishing; and his initial feeling of horror, felt so intensely, receding. He was now aware and angry that authority did, in fact, sanction violence, and that all moral boundaries were transgressed.

Yet at the same time, the soldier defensively denied the possibility of maintaining his usual moral principles in this situation. He consciously separated army and civilian life, and denied that anyone outside the situation could judge it.

The soldier's experience of separation from and relationship to reality

Engulfed by brutality and his horror of violent actions and torture, the soldier experienced himself and others on a number of seemingly contradictory levels. He experienced the other soldiers as vicious, violent and out of control, and he continually defined himself as separate from them and the brutality being meted out. This included maintaining rigid intellectual defences to understand and accept the dehumanisation of the 'enemy', distancing himself from the deaths of others, and trying to block out the noise of the horror surrounding him. It was coupled with an intense intellectual interest in the torture and death around him, and at points he experienced the humanity and pain, and connected emotionally with the 'enemy'. This caused tremendous conflict and guilt within him. Generally, the soldier was aware of rationalising his participation in violence, and felt uneasy and defensive about it. The consequent splitting of his intellect and his emotions laid the basis for the soldier experiencing himself as part of an abnormal, chaotic, unreal world. He sensed dislocation in meshing previously held beliefs with his present actions. Consequently, he experienced extreme loneliness, isolation and sadness. The sense of loss was all-pervading. He felt that part of his self was dying.

The soldier's awareness of having changed

The soldier experienced himself as emotionally distorted and battered. He was aware of feeling strange and different – previously adaptable, he now could not cope; previously enjoying life, he now no longer could. He experienced himself as having changed, on a number of seemingly contradictory levels. He was aware of being excessively and indiscriminately aggressive and brutal towards people around him. He experienced anger, hatred and resentment towards loved ones at home who were isolated from his experience. He experienced resentment and anger towards authority. He felt disdain and mistrust towards loving, intimate relationships. He experienced a great sense of desolation, misery and depression. And he experienced a sense of regret, but also resignation, at the changes he saw in himself.

The soldier's relationship to the future.

The soldier lived on a day-to-day basis. He did not think about the future – he felt it was destroyed and void. He experienced a sense of acceptance of hardship and the inevitability of things he disagreed with. A sense of meaninglessness permeated his being. He felt helpless to change the circumstances he was in and experienced resignation at the changes in himself. A sense of foreboding about the future dominated.

Conclusion

We see in these descriptions of the soldiers' experiences many of the themes that Lifton and Gault describe: the centrality of death; incredible anger which emerges in uncontrollable violence; the need to generalise the idea of the 'enemy' to cope with brutalising and killing them; the existence of a state of 'moral inversion'; and a sense of loss, meaning-lessness, and pessimism about the future.

This parallel does not imply that the civil war in South Africa is similar in all respects to the war in Vietnam. At a psychological level, however, certain general material situations, in this case a war experience, bring about particular psychological conditions. For this reason 'war trauma' has been incorporated in DSM III in the category of post-traumatic stress disorder (PTSD).

This is also the theoretical direction currently being taken by military psychologists and psychiatrists in the SADF. In the first symposium held on 'Stress in South Africa' (19–20 June 1986), hosted by the SADF, it was emphasised that research is necessary to 'identify specific emotional stresses which may be unnecessary, and by adequate prepara-tion perhaps the consequences of PTSD might be decreased' (King, 1986). It was noted, too, that basic training and border duty account for the majority of military stresses. Military psychologists argued that precipitating and predisposing factors need to be itemised, so that the young man at risk 'can be employed appropriately to avoid exposure to severe military hardships, for benefit of both the serviceman and the organisation'. Clearly, the psychological well-being of soldiers is of concern to the SADF, as it is to any army in the world which maintains young men in the field of battle.

7 The South African Defence Force in Namibia

TONY WEAVER

The history of Namibia is one of great violence committed by occupying powers against its inhabitants. Over the past decade, as popular resistance in Namibia has grown and the armed struggle of SWAPO escalated, South Africa has dramatically stepped up its security presence. Over 100 000 South African-controlled troops have been stationed in the country, most of them in the north, and Pretoria has spent more than R3 million a day maintaining the illegal occupation (*Cape Times*, 4.1.1985).

The occupation has had a devastating impact on the Namibian people. The lives of thousands have been severely disrupted through forced removals, the destruction of peasant agriculture, and security force atrocities and military action. Over 10 000 Namibians, about 1 per cent of the total population, have been killed, and over 100 000, or 10 per cent of the population, have been forced to flee the country. Almost 80 per cent of the people live under martial law, and 50 per cent under direct SADF rule. In addition, South African aggression has extended deep into Angola, with equally traumatic effects on the people of that country.

This chapter examines the role of the SADF in Namibia. It considers the development of armed struggle, the intensification of conflict after the independence of Angola in 1975, and the effects of the military occupation. It should be noted, however, that the South African Defence Act severely restricts what can be published about the activities of its security forces, and that, as US Senator Hiram Johnson said in 1917, 'the first casualty when war comes is the truth'.

The development of armed struggle

The current war in Namibia pales into insignificance against the early wars of resistance against the German rulers: 64 870 of some 80 000 Hereros and 10 220 of some 20 000 Namas were exterminated; 9 680 died in concentration camps, 1 030 of them on the notorious Shark Island prison off Lüderitz (Drechsler, 1980: 213–14).

The history of those early wars is integral to the guerilla war being fought today. There is a powerful strand of resistance which, according to Pastor Witbooi, 'is not dependent on weapons, but on the will and strength of the people. If you have the people behind you, that is more powerful than any weapon.' Speaking at a 'Heroes Day' commemoration in Gibeon in 1987, Pastor Witbooi, vice-president of SWAPO and grandson of a famous guerilla leader, said: 'the struggle we are waging today is only a continuation of the struggle of our fathers. We do not want war, but we have to resist. Our grandfathers died struggling for freedom and independence.' (Weaver, 1987b: 79)

On 18 July 1966, the International Court of Justice announced that it could not rule either way on the disputed territory of South West Africa. The news was jubilantly received in Pretoria and in white Namibia. The principal liberation movement, the South West Africa People's Organisation (later to become SWAPO of Namibia) responded with its now famous Dar es Salaam Declaration: 'We have no alternative but to rise in arms and bring about our own liberation. The supreme test must be faced and we must at once begin to cross the many rivers of blood on our march towards freedom.' (Katjavivi, 1988: 59)

SWAPO, along with other national liberation movements in colonial Africa, had been preparing for some time for the eventuality of having to resort to armed struggle. It sent its first group of 200 recruits to Egypt for military training in 1962, but the first guerillas only entered Namibia in August 1965. At that time, the northern region was still a relative wilderness farmed by Ovambo-speaking peasants, with little infrastructure in the main areas and none at all in the more remote parts. The first SWAPO military base was established at Ongulumbashe, today a major centre of SADF control (Katjavivi, 1988: 60).

It took South Africa until May the following year to realise that SWAPO fighters were active in the north, and the first battle between the two forces took place on 26 August 1966. Helicopter-borne South African forces attacked Ongulumbashe, killing two guerillas and capturing 27 others. South Africa claimed at the time that it had 'wiped out' the camp (Weaver 1987a: 240).

The early years of the war saw relatively little involvement by the South African Defence Force. SWAPO concentrated as much on political mobilisation among the peasantry in the Ovambo, Kavango and Caprivi regions as it did on developing its armed struggle. This was in accordance with the strategy developed by Tobias H. Hainyeko, first military commander of what was to become the People's Liberation Army of Namibia (PLAN). Hainyeko stated: 'Our guerilla warfare will first start from the weak point – that is the countryside – where the development of means of transportation for the enemy is too weak to enable them to mobilise their forces. In these areas the enemy forces could face some logistical problems.' (Katjavivi, 1988: 60)

The period from 1970 to 1974 was one of intense political mobilisation by SWAPO and its allies in the broad progressive movement. In 1971–2 a national strike by 20 000 contract workers in Windhoek led to a significant reform of the migrant labour system. 1972 also saw a mass uprising among the peasantry in the Ovambo-speaking region, as activists expelled from the mines and industry during the strike returned and embarked on political work on behalf of SWAPO. The subsequent 'rural revolt' in the north was brutally suppressed by the South African forces.

In 1972 the SADF was deployed for the first time in the north on a large scale, when it became clear that the South African Police were unable to cope with the rising tide of resistance.

The intensification of conflict

Against this backdrop of an emerging militance in the liberation movement, and a concomitant growth in the strength of the guerilla forces, critical changes that were to influence Namibia decisively were taking place to the north. No single historical process has had as important an effect on the development of the Namibian armed struggle as the 1974 coup in Portugal by the Armed Forces Movement, and the subsequent independence of Angola.

Prior to independence, any attempted incursion into Namibia by PLAN guerillas involved enormous risks and dedication. According to one field commander, Rahimisa Kahimise,

We had to walk a long distance from Zambia through Angola. Some of our people also died in Angola and some missions could not reach Namibia, because they had to fight through Angola . . . the battles we were involved in, most of them were in Angola with the Portuguese . . . but even the South African soldiers were also involved in Angola, and really we worked hard, because by then we had to train new recruits and we also had to fight to get food as we had to walk long distances, and then we had to try and get transport; also after a battle, then you must have more ammunition. . . . I could say by the time we crossed into Namibia we were a bit tired, but a bit more experienced. (Katjavivi, 1988: 85)

Former guerillas speak of the incredible hardships endured in simply getting through to the Ovambo and Kavango regions. Carrying packs which weighed up to 70 kg (all arms and ammunition were carried on the back), they had to dodge not only South African patrols, but a network of highly paid informers. A successful tip-off to the military or police would earn more in hard cash than the average peasant could hope to earn in a year's hard labour.

The liberation of Angola consequently represented a critical new phase in the Namibian war. It meant that PLAN guerillas now had a direct route from Angola into their homeland; they were able to establish a semi-permanent presence within Namibia; and, in later years, they had the backing of a powerful, although not always well-motivated and well-organised, revolutionary army – the combined Angolan and Cuban forces.

Most important, PLAN and SWAPO were able to open a 'second front' in an area which hitherto they had only penetrated in sporadic skirmishes – the Ovambo region, where half the population of Namibia lives and from where the vast majority of guerillas were drawn. The guerillas now had direct access to areas where they could find shelter and support from families and friends, and assume civilian identities with an ease which frustrated the South African forces and elicited a brutal response.

South Africa's first attempt to regain the lost ground they had once enjoyed through military and political cooperation with the Portuguese colonial regime was to invade Angola in 1975. Hopelessly extended beyond their logistical capacity, and faced with increasing numbers of relatively well-trained Cuban troops, the South Africans were eventually forced to withdraw from Angola, claiming they were 'victorious'. This writer, speaking from personal experience as a conscript involved in the 1975 invasion, can testify to the chaotic circumstances of the withdrawal and the ultimately futile attempt to seize control of the Angolan hinterland.

South Africa, and the South African Defence Force, have consistently attempted to glamorise and glorify even their worst defeats and failures. The 1975 debacle was blamed on the failure of the United States to deliver promised material and moral support, while South Africa continued to claim its forces were on the verge of victory.

While other significant developments in the war took place in the years 1975 to 1978, perhaps the landmark event both in propaganda terms and as an example of South African military aggression occurred on 4 May 1978. The 'Cassinga Raid' is best described first of all by an apologist for the military. According to Hilton Hamann:

Perhaps the Parabats' finest moment came in May, 1977 [sic] in an operation code-named Reindeer. The plan was to drop a combined force of national service and citizen force paratroopers onto a Swapo regional headquarters at Cassinga, some 250 km behind enemy lines. Known as Moscow, the base contained 1 300 men, heavily armed with an array of heavy machine guns, rocket launchers and small arms. . . . Despite the heavy enemy fire, all the Parabats landed safely and the battle started. The South Africans were armed particularly lightly when compared with Swapo – the heaviest weapon was a 60-mm patrol mortar and a number of RPG-7s. By 4 p.m. it was all over, and over 1 000 terrorists lay dead and the base was totally destroyed with the loss of three 'bats' . . . there is little doubt this country's Parabats have in a very short space of time built a proud reputation. 'One thing is sure,' said Commandant (Herbie) Pos, 'the enemy's wall of honour has a hell of a lot more names than ours.' (*Scope*, 23.9.1988)

This is the conventional South African wisdom about the Cassinga Raid. Hamann neglects to mention that the real facts are in serious dispute. Reports from various sources indicate that Cassinga was a military training camp, but was situated alongside several Namibian refugee camps. Figures differ as to exactly how many Namibians died: some sources say over 1 000; others say 900; still others 600 or more. The most accurate and commonly accepted figure is 315 adults and 298 children killed.

The number of children killed gives the lie to South African claims of a 'major blow' against SWAPO. SWAPO has long acknowledged that women combatants play a major role in their struggle, although it declared that many of the women killed in the raid were civilian refugees, teachers and nurses. A group of Western foreign correspondents who visited Cassinga five days after the raid reported a scene of horror:

Foreign journalists saw an open mass grave packed with the decomposing bodies of 460 people whom Angolan authorities said were 'massacred' by South African troops last week. The dozen foreign correspondents flown to Cassinga yesterday by the Angolan authorities could make out the brightly coloured dresses of a large number of women among the dead, said to be South West African refugees killed in the air and ground attack. Angolan authorities described the attack, which Pretoria said was aimed at a Swapo guerrilla centre, as 'genocide'. Another 122 bodies of South West African refugees were buried in a separate trench. Swapo officials said many other refugees – the town had a total population of 3 068 – had fled into the bush where they had probably been killed by South African paratroops. (*Rand Daily Mail,* 10.5.1978)

Legal indemnity

The Cassinga Raid had a curious sequel six years later in the Windhoek Supreme Court. South African troops had taken an estimated 200 people prisoner in the raid. The prisoners were 'processed' in the Ovambo region (several later alleged physical abuse and torture), and then interned in the Mariental prison camp in the south of Namibia. On 5 March 1984, lawyers acting for the internees filed papers in the Supreme Court seeking to declare their continued internment illegal and to secure their release. On 27 April, South African Minister of Justice Kobie Coetsee issued a certificate under Section 103 ter of the South African Defence Act, banning the court case from proceeding. The Bar Council of SWA observed in a statement that as far as they knew, this was the first time such a certificate had ever been issued. Section 103 ter gives the State President the power to authorise the Minister of Justice to issue a certificate banning court proceedings against SADF members if he is satisfied that their activities were 'done in good faith' for the 'purposes of or in connection with the prevention or suppression of terrorism in an operational area', and that 'it is in the national interest that the proceedings shall not continue' (Defence Act, No. 44 of 1957. The Act also stipulates that 'no court shall have the power to review, set aside or declare to be void or otherwise question the validity of [the] certificate'; and that the state 'shall not be obliged to furnish any reasons' for issuing it. While the legal wrangle continued, the state released all the Mariental internees, claiming that it had intended doing this anyway as they were 'no longer a threat to law and order' (press statement from Administrator-General's office, 25 May 1984).

There have been two other well-publicised trials banned under Section 103 ter (although there may well have been others not reported). On 30 November 1986, a senior SWAPO member and former Robben Island prisoner, Immanuel Shifidi, was stabbed to death when 50 armed members of the SADF's 101 Battalion at Ondangwa allegedly attacked a SWAPO rally in Windhoek. Six SADF members, including a private, a corporal, a lieutenant, a commandant and two colonels, were charged with murder. On 22 March 1988, a certificate was issued by President P. W. Botha banning the case because it was 'not in the national interest' that it proceed, and because the soldiers' actions were performed 'in good faith'.

On 28 November 1985, a patrol of SADF soldiers arrived at a homestead at Onengali in the Ovambo region where a migrant worker, Frans Uapota, was visiting his wife and family. The soldiers allegedly ordered everyone to lie on their stomachs, and began kicking and beating them. A witness said Uapota was blindfolded, kicked, beaten and hit with rifle butts, then strangled with rope. Four soldiers were charged with murder by the Attorney-General of South West Africa. President P. W. Botha again banned proceedings, for the same reasons cited in the Shifidi case. Sydney Kentridge SC, arguing in an appeal against the banning, said: 'Nobody could honestly believe that a group of armed soldiers was acting in good faith when they battered the skull of a 45-year-old man of slight build, broke his neck, partially strangled him with a rope, broke nine of his ribs and ruptured his spleen' (*Weekly Mail*, 2.9.1988).

In both the Shifidi and Uapota cases, the Windhoek Supreme Court has invalidated the presidential certificates.

The SWA Territory Force

A key factor in the evolution of the war, and a factor which will have enormous influence on post-independence reconstruction, was the formation in 1980 of the 'indigenous' South West Africa Territory Force. SWATF now numbers over 24 000 Namibian conscripts, recruits and permanent force members. Niddrie (1988: 11) claims that SWATF lost as many as 300 men in the 1987–8 battle for Cuito Cuanavale in Angola, and South African military spokespersons are frequently quoted as saying that SWATF has become their frontline force against SWAPO. Niddrie reports that 'this disproportion reportedly led to several mutinies among black troops, many of them complaining at having to don UNITA uniforms and fight (armed only with rifles) against the increasingly sophisticated Angolan forces' (1988: 12).

The universal conscription which applies in law to all races in Namibia is not evenly enforced. Conscription is not applied in the Kavango and Ovambo regions, on the grounds that the military have 'enough volunteers'. This is partly true – the starting salary for a recruit without rank is in the region of R800 a month, vastly higher than the income of a migrant labourer on the mines or the cash income of a peasant farmer. The main reason for not applying conscription in these areas however is the high level of support for SWAPO, and the danger that SWATF would provide military training for potential SWAPO guerillas.

For the purposes of this chapter, no distinction is made between SWATF and the SADF. Their functions and modes of operation are almost identical, and they routinely combine during operations. To the civilian population of the north, they are one and the same: the *omakakunya*, literally 'bone-pickers' or 'blood-suckers'.

Military occupation

It is in the Ovambo and Kavango regions that the war is most concentrated and where the SADF has its main presence. It is there that the civilian peasantry are caught in the crossfire and bear the brunt of South Africa's occupation of their country. The SADF recorded just under 500 'incidents' between their troops and guerillas there in 1987. Today, the northern war zones resemble an endless string of military fortifications. While it is illegal in terms of the Defence Act to give precise details of military emplacements, in broad descriptive terms it can be said that it is impossible to travel in the north without passing endless convoys of military vehicles. The major military centres are surrounded by sandbag and earth-wall perimeters topped with blade wire; machine-gun nests are strategically placed at all vantage points; and sophisticated anti-aircraft weaponry rings the bases, an evident counter to the rapid advance of Angolan and Cuban forces in 1988 and their reported achievement of air power superiority.

White civil servants and civilians in Oshakati, Ondangwa, Rundu and other key war-zone towns live behind heavily fortified perimeter fences; each house has its own bomb shelter, and no white ventures outside the 'white town' after dark. This prompted Archbishop Desmond Tutu to remark in 1988: 'you see what this war has done, it has even made prisoners of those who claim they are here to protect the people' (interview, May 1988).

In short, the Ovambo and Kavango regions, which together are home to more than half of Namibia's population, are under total military occupation and subjugation. All infrastructural developments are dictated by military priorities. The tarred roads in the Ovambo region lead in two main directions – west to the Ruacana border with Angola, and north to the Oshikango border with Angola. Their purpose is clear: not the conveying of agricultural produce, but the rapid deployment of military vehicles. The same applies to the main tarred road through Kavango, which is a south–north artery for the rapid movement of military forces from the massive Grootfontein base to Rundu, one of the major staging points for sorties into Angola.

The most significant dislocation of the lives of the peasantry wrought by the military presence has been in the partial destruction of peasant agriculture. In the mid-1970s in the Ovambo and Kavango regions, a systematic programme of forced removals was embarked upon to develop 'free-fire' zones of a kilometre or more wide where any person moving could be shot on sight. The logic was to create a buffer zone where guerillas would be separated from the peasant homesteads, and to allow for more effective monitoring of the border with Angola. Kiljunen claims that along this border strip, 'a very poisonous plant, Mexican sisal, was planted in the area. This plant can give a very deep cut which turns septic, and infection spreads through the body of a victim causing death.' (1981: 164)

Peasant agriculture in the north is a precarious business. In the flat Ovambo flood plain, a higher-than-average rainfall permits a limited form of grain cultivation. The staple food is *mahangu*, pearly millet. But the soil is not rich; in most areas it is little better than pure sand, lacking in adequate mineral and organic nutrients and tending to become waterlogged in the rainy season. Cultivation of *mahangu* is labour-intensive, and critical to its success is a high degree of farming skill to manage the complicated planting and harvesting seasonal cycle (see, for example, Moorsom, 1982: 45–50).

All the members of the extended peasant families participate in the various stages of production. In two critical stages, the early summer sowing and the autumn harvesting, this peaks to frantic spells of intensive labour. But the war has taken its toll. Large numbers of men have left the region, either to join PLAN or to seek a living wage as migrant labourers in the south. And at peak periods it is necessary to harvest through the night, something which is forbidden under the curfew regulations, and physically dangerous in the extreme.

With a delicate topsoil and precarious crops, the *mahangu* fields are obvious targets for retribution by the military. Those documenting human rights violations in Namibia have received routine accounts of security force actions in which *mahangu* fields are destroyed by burning the crops or driving heavy vehicles through them. This is done in retaliation for peasants failing to report the presence of guerillas, aiding guerillas, or simply living in areas where guerillas are known to be active.

The forced removals of the mid-1970s impacted seriously on the lives of the peasantry. They effectively split the Ovambo people, who have long lived on both sides of the border, preventing them from coming and going as they pleased, dividing families and in many instances destroying economic units. Pressure put on peasant farmers to move close to the main centres of military occupation 'effectively rendered many people, who had previously been farmers or cattle herders, destitute and dependent on the army' (Konig, 1983: 12).

In Kavango, the partial destruction of the peasant economy was even more starkly war-related. Along the Kavango River, 'field cultivation, chiefly of millet, is located on the terraces along the sides of the narrow valley (up to 10 km wide) while cattle are pastured alternately along the wet season streams *(omuramba)* of the sandveld to the south and by the banks of the river itself once the seasonal floodwaters have receded' (Moorsom, 1982: 49).

In the mid-1970s, as the SADF formed its free-fire zones, the military ordered the peasant farmers to move inland to prevent them providing food and shelter to guerillas. Entire communities were moved to less fertile inland areas. But by late 1982, when the SADF had established a string of bases along the river, they realised a fatal flaw: guerillas now had a secure network of peasant villages inland where they were assured of shelter and aid. As a member of the notorious police COIN unit, Koevoet, testified in 1984: 'Kavango is rotten with Swapo'.

So an operation began in order to move everybody, including some who had previously lived away from the river, back within easy surveillance of the military. Resistance to the removals was allegedly met with brutal torture. According to Paulus Sinoka, a peasant farmer from Kagunie:

In January 1983, the soldiers came to my kraal and they said, 'We see you have not moved to the river.' My three daughters were at that time staying with me, home from school for holidays. The soldiers then said to me, 'Where do these three girls come from?', and I replied that they are my daughters. The soldiers then said, 'You are giving your daughters as whores for Swapo', and they began beating me . . . one soldier held my arms, and one my legs. A white soldier took a stick as thick as my leg and began beating me on my back. I screamed. They said I had given food and drink to Swapo. I cried that I did not. I lost track of time, but it was a long time that they beat me. They saw I was getting weak, and left me . . . then questioned me again about the Swapos . . . they beat me again. After the soldiers had left, my daughters said, 'Papa, we are scared, we will not come here to Kagunie anymore because of the fear.' So I moved to the river. (Personal interview; see also Weaver, 1987a: 243–6)

In the Ovambo region, the forced removals and the pressures of living in vulnerable rural areas have resulted in a mushrooming triangular settlement some 35 km long and 20 km wide between Ondangwa and Oshakati. In squalid, mainly shanty-town conditions live close to 250 000 former peasants, almost a quarter of the total population of Namibia.

Many of those who moved there now survive through informal-sector activity, with the burgeoning 'cuca shop' trade being one of the main economic lifelines. Cuca shops are the ubiquitous pubs which form one of the mainstays of urban social life, being relatively safe places to socialise. Official statistics have it that there are over 6 000 licensed cuca shops in the north: in conversation officials freely admit there are well over double this number.

A doctor at the Oshakati State Hospital believes that alcohol abuse is probably the largest problem facing health authorities in the region. With the breakdown in the social fabric resulting from the forced removals and enforced crowding, a host of problems has arisen from alcohol abuse: violent crime (murder, assault and rape being the most common), spiralling venereal disease rates ('imported' by the troops), and increasing prostitution to support alcoholic addiction among women.

The doctor added: 'At the moment we are treating between 10 and 15 cases a month of women raped by members of the security forces. We treat civilians all the time, probably most of our cases, who are war victims – alcoholism, veneral disease, rape. These are all war diseases. Where will it end? Even if the war ends tomorrow, pray to God that it does, there are so many people walking around with guns, there are the men who have been in the camps in Angola, there is so much brutalisation. How can peace ever really return?' (Weaver, 1988: 8).

Another major effect of the forced removals has been a spiralling disease rate. With such a large concentration of people in extremely squalid conditions, primary health care operative in the region can only be a holding operation, particularly when the summer rainy season comes. Bubonic plague, malaria, tuberculosis, typhoid and venereal disease have reached epidemic proportions. With a dusk-to-dawn curfew in force, it is illegal, and often fatal, for civilians to travel after dark to seek medical help. However, by informal agreement, the curfew is not strictly applied between Oshakati and Ongwediva, an area about 20 km wide, where most of the civilians live.

Former SWA Attorney-General, Don Brunette, has given a graphic description of the extent to which law and order have deteriorated in the north under the SADF occupation.

We try our best to apply civil law in Ovambo, but it is no easy task. The circumstances are troubled and the mental frame of the people has become such that almost everyone carries a gun, many of them illegal. After a few drinks at a cuca shop, there is shooting, murder and rape. The psychological effect of the war is such that life has become cheap. Still, I can say that the most serious cases are nevertheless brought to court, but there is quite possibly a body or two under the bush which we don't know about, as recent civil cases before the courts have shown. We can, for example, also not apply the Inquests Law effectively. It is just impossible to remove the bodies of terrorists in the terrible heat from the dangerous areas to a hospital for an inquest. We have about 480 to 500 inquests a year in which the magistrate finds the death was caused by unknown people, terrorists or landmines. (*Beeld*, 31.8.1983)

In this atmosphere of casual brutality, the SADF appears to have abandoned its 'hearts and minds' campaign of the late 1970s and early 1980s. Extensive efforts were made then to win over the civilian population through the establishment of civic organisations, the co-option of health and educational services, and rewards for information leading to the arrest or killing of guerillas.

In its place has come a strategy of violence against civilians which the military constantly denies, but which has been extensively documented by human rights campaigners. Oswald Shivute, secretary to the Ovambo Legislative Assembly, claims that between 1982 and 1988, 'we have had 916 atrocity cases reported to us. We have brought most of these to the attention of the authorities. So far as I know, there have been five prosecutions. The people are scared to go to the police. They say, "How can we report this to the police when it is the same police and army who have done these things to us?" ' (Weaver, 1988: 8)

From January to August 1988, Shivute monitored over 200 allegations of atrocities and physical violence against the civilian population by the security forces. These ranged from allegations of destruction of *mahangu* fields, to rape, assault, torture and murder. During every trip made through the war zones between 1983 and 1988, this writer has heard similar allegations coming from a wide variety of people. The Windhoek weekly newspaper, *The Namibian*, carries several reports of human rights violations by the military in almost every edition.

The military presence has, not surprisingly, ensured that the northern regions have become fertile ground for political mass mobilisation. In March 1988, the siting of military bases near secondary schools, clinics and community centres sparked off a schools boycott which eventually spread throughout the country, involving over 40 000 scholars and students. They were protesting against the frequency with which schools, and particularly hostels, were hit in the crossfire between guerillas and the SADF. Some student leaders also alleged that the SADF deliberately fired into the schools as a form of punishment for resistance. As the boycott spread, the National Union of Namibian Workers called a one-day national strike in support of the youth. An estimated 100 000 workers responded, and even the government admitted that as many as 50 000 workers had joined the strike (Niddrie, 1988: 9).

The plight of the !Kung and Ju/Wasi

Of increasing concern to anthropologists and development workers is the extensive penetration of 'Bushman' society by the SADF. The effect of this militarisation has been extensively documented by Marshall, Gordon and others.

After the Portuguese coup and the subsequent invasion of Angola by South Africa in 1975, large numbers of !Kung 'Bushmen', who had been employed by the Portuguese armed forces as combatants and trackers, fled south. The SADF recruited them into 31 Battalion at Camp Omega in the Caprivi, which later became 201 Battalion. The !Kung are mainly employed as trackers, and have, with the high salaries offered, 'unwittingly become mercenaries' in international law (Gordon, 1984).

By 1981, Camp Omega housed 850 soldiers, 900 women and 1 500 children – half the estimated population of western Caprivi.

This camp has all the classic characteristics of a total institution. All the menfolk are in the army; the children go to a military school where they are taught Afrikaans, the lingua franca of the army; while the wives of the officers arrange activities to keep Bushmen women occupied. In addition, all widows and pensioners receive R25 a month plus food, rations and housing. (Gordon, 1984: 19)

Gordon and other anthropologists point out that besides the dislocation and destruction of an entire culture which this assimilation has accelerated, the question has to be asked, 'What happens after independence?' The !Kung not only will have no occupation other than that of soldier, but potentially face the wrath of a nation they have fought against and helped subjugate.

In general, army officers, however, appear to see the extinction of the Bushmen as inevitable, and argue that their programme is aimed at smoothing the way for the assimilation of the Bushmen into the emergent black rural-proletarian culture. Very little attention appears to have been given to what will happen after the army leaves, as it one day surely will. (Gordon, 1984: 22)

A similar situation pertains in eastern Bushmanland, where the last remnants of the Namibian San people, the Ju/Wasi, number approximately 2 300. They are confined to an area of about 17 750 square kilometres, whereas before the establishment of the 'Bushman' bantustan some 1 250 people had lived as hunters and gatherers over an area of at least 45 000 square kilometres (Marshall and Ritchie, 1984).

According to Marshall and Ritchie and the present writer's own research in the area, more than 600 Ju/Wa men have been recruited into the SADF–SWATF. They receive wages in excess of R600 a month. This sudden influx of cash into a traditional hunter–gatherer and emerging pastoralist society has had significant negative effects. Alcohol abuse and the spread of venereal disease have escalated, especially in the areas around the administrative capital of Tsumkwe, where up to half the population live in government housing.

A significant 'back to the land' movement has been initiated by the Ju/Wa San Bushman Development Foundation and the Ju/Wa Farmers'

Union. By late 1988 an estimated half the Ju/Wasi had returned to traditional hunting areas. But the pull of the military is still strong, and it is significant that in most of the villages very few younger men are in evidence.

Like the !Kung at Camp Omega, the fate of the 'Bushmen' soldiers could be precarious in a post-independence Namibia. However, SWAPO's former UN representative, Theo-Ben Gurirab, is on record as saying:

It is really tragic that South Africa has to go so low as to use these people who are not conscious of what they are doing. Since [the trackers] always walk in front of patrolling soldiers, in most cases they received the punishment meant for the racist soldiers. Their population is small, our concern is that they may be eliminated. (Gordon, 1984: 43)

These are but some of the many strands of the war in Namibia. The long-term psychological and social consequences alone will require massive rehabilitation programmes by a post-independence government. The legacy of South Africa's military occupation of their country is one which will not quickly be forgotten or forgiven by the people of Namibia.

It remains to be seen, however, what lessons the South African government has learnt from the occupation. It has not been able to resolve the conflict in Namibia through force of arms. Its repressive rule and massive military presence have intensified rather than eliminated popular resistance and the armed struggle. At the cost of thousands of lives and millions of rand, Pretoria has succeeded only in delaying the inevitable independence of Namibia.

8 The SADF's covert war against Mozambique

ROBERT DAVIES

It is well known that Mozambique is a country at war. The Frelimo government has faced an armed insurgency virtually since the moment of independence in June 1975. The war in Mozambique became particularly intense in the 1980s. According to the latest available official estimates, by April 1988 the war had cost 100 000 lives and led to the displacement of 1,8 million people inside and outside the country. The damage to the economy caused by the war as well as by South African 'economic aggression' is estimated to have totalled US$6 000 million by the end of 1986, equivalent to twice the country's external debt and 60 times the value of its exports in 1987 (CENE–DPCCN, 1988: 5–6).

The conflict in Mozambique is intended by those who are responsible for it to be seen as a 'civil war' between the Frelimo government and an indigenous 'anti-communist resistance movement', known as the MNR (Mozambique National Resistance movement) or by its Portuguese acronym, Renamo. It is, in fact, an undeclared, low-intensity, covert war waged by the South African Defence Force through surrogate forces. The SADF's war in Mozambique has served as a pilot project for similar operations against other neighbouring states. The experience gained in utilising surrogate forces in Mozambique and other neighbouring states has also undoubtedly influenced and informed the deployment of vigilante squads against democratic organisations inside South Africa. The domestic equivalent of calling covert aggression against neighbouring states 'civil war' has been to describe vigilante assaults as 'black-on-black violence'. In both cases the ultimate controlling role of the apartheid state is concealed; the deployment of force is cheap in terms of both direct SADF casualties and resources; and the level of violence and brutality can be raised at a lower diplomatic and ideological cost than would be the case if the state's regular security forces were directly involved. There has, indeed, even been a documented case where MNR bandits in camps in South Africa were sent into action against members of the Northern Transvaal Youth Congress (Notrayoc) in Venda in 1986 – on this occasion they styled themselves *Abafana bakaBotha* (sons of Botha) (*Weekly Mail*, 24–29.4.1987).

This chapter examines some aspects of the SADF's covert war in

Mozambique. It begins by documenting what is known from publicly available sources about the MNR and the form of SADF involvement in that war. It then attempts to place this action in the context of Pretoria's overall regional policy in various phases. Finally it examines some of the contradictions of covert military action in Mozambique that have become apparent.

SADF involvement with Renamo

No serious observer can now doubt that the so-called MNR or Renamo was created as a fifth column by the intelligence services of the illegal Rhodesian regime. This has been described in some detail in the autobiography of Ken Flower, the former head of the Rhodesian Central Intelligence Organisation, who was the officer directly responsible for this project. The MNR was formed in March 1974 as a 'pseudo-terrorist' squad consciously modelled on the *flechas*, recruited by the Portuguese in Angola in the 1960s (Flower, 1987: 300–2).

It is also common knowledge that shortly before Zimbabwean independence, control of the MNR bandits was handed over to the SADF (Flower, 1987: 262, 273). SADF support for the MNR in the period prior to the signing of the Nkomati Accord in March 1984 has indeed been publicly acknowledged by senior members of the Pretoria government. Foreign Minister R. F. Botha admitted in a speech in the House of Assembly in April 1985: 'There was a time when we helped to train Renamo and assisted it. There was such a time. . . . They [Renamo] approached us for assistance and we realised that it would further the aims of South Africa to help them.' (House of Assembly Debates, 25.4.1985, col. 4214)

Some details of SADF involvement with Renamo during this period have now emerged (*Weekly Mail*, 27.11–3.12.1987; *Moto*, 61, December 1987–January 1988; *Southscan*, 2.12.1987; *AIM Information Bulletin*, 141, April 1988). Direct operational responsibility fell to a Directorate of Special Tasks (DST) operating under the Chief of Staff (Intelligence). The DST was commanded by a Colonel (now Brigadier) Cornelius (or Charles) van Niekerk. The project of supporting armed banditry in Mozambique, which served as a pilot for similar actions in other countries, was codenamed 'Operation Mila'. The DST operated out of the Zanza building in Proes Street, Pretoria. It recruited or press-ganged Mozambicans who were 'illegally' in South Africa in search of work into the ranks of Renamo and provided them with a rudimentary military training before sending them on missions in Mozambique. Initially training took place at a base at Potgietersrus (closed in 1983 for security reasons) and later at what has remained the main base at Phalaborwa. The DST also organised the air-dropping of supplies, sometimes using airforce planes and sometimes those of a front company, Frama Intertrading. From Phalaborwa communications were maintained both with bandit groups operating inside Mozambique and with MNR officials in Lisbon. Propaganda radio broadcasts were transmitted under the name 'Radio Free Africa'.

The 'Gorongosa documents' (1985) discovered after the Mozambican army captured former MNR headquarters in August 1985, show beyond any possible doubt that this support continued until June 1985, despite the signing in March 1984 of the Nkomati Accord between South Africa and Mozambique. Article 3 of the Nkomati Accord bound the signatories 'not [to] allow their respective territories, territorial waters or airspace to be used as a base, thoroughfare, or in any other way by another state, government, foreign military forces, organisations or individuals which plan or prepare to commit acts of violence, terrorism and aggression against the territorial integrity or political independence of the other, or may threaten the security of its inhabitants' (Nkomati Accord, 1984: 2). The 'Gorongosa documents', an internal record of MNR activities, nevertheless noted instances in which arms, communications equipment, medical supplies, and material to produce propaganda were made available by the SADF to the armed bandits. They showed that the SADF had organised transport for MNR leaders to and from Gorongosa.

The 'Gorongosa documents' also indicated that SADF officers continued to play a leadership role in the MNR in the sense of determining the military strategy the bandits should follow. Instances are recorded where SADF officers told the bandits that in order to conserve ammunition they should avoid contacts with the Mozambican armed forces and concentrate on economic (soft) targets. Moreover, the documents showed that SADF involvement in these activities reached right to the highest echelons of its command. Colonel Van Niekerk was named as the direct liaison officer, but the extracts mention meetings with or messages from *inter alia* both the former and current chiefs of the SADF, Generals Constand Viljoen and J. J. Geldenhuys respectively; Lieutenant-General P. J. van der Westhuizen, then Chief of Staff (Intelligence); Lieutenant-General A. J. (Kat) Liebenberg, then General Officer Commanding Special Forces and now Chief of the Army; Brigadier Van Tonder, now Chief of Staff (Intelligence) with the rank of Lieutenant-General; and Colonel Greyling, also of Military Intelligence. Mention was also made of a Major Phillips, who had a key role in directing MNR operations out of Malawi.

Since Gorongosa, evidence of different types has emerged which, taken together, provides an overwhelming *prima facie* case of continuing SADF involvement with armed banditry in Mozambique. There have been:

(1) Accounts by local residents of air and sea drops of supplies to bandits in the Manhiça and Impaputo districts of Maputo province (*Noticias*, 26.10.1985); in the vicinity of Ressano Garcia in Maputo

province (*Noticias*, 22.9.1986); off the coast of Sofala province 30 miles south of Beira (*AIM despatch*, 8.7.1987).

(2) Testimonies by captured bandits and those surrendering under the government's amnesty programme about recruitment while in South African Police custody (Jorge Valoi in *Noticias*, 5.11.1985) and by SADF personnel in Malawi (*Weekly Mail*, 4.3.1988); about membership of a special commando unit sent to plant bombs in Maputo and Matola (South African passport holder George Alerson in *AIM despatch*, 22.6.1987); about air and sea drops of supplies (by two unnamed children and a youth in *Noticias*, 22.9.1987; by former MNR sector commander, Modesto Sixpence, in *Noticias*, 10.2.1988 and 14.5.1988; by Fernando Tepo and Eduardo Manuel in *Noticias*, 23.3.1988; by Paulo Oliveira in *Noticias*, 24.3.1988; and by Ian Grey in *Noticias*, 28.3.1988); and about SADF personnel operating with bandits in bases in Mozambique (by Abilio Jangane in *Noticias*, 2.3.1988; and by Louis Tomas in *Noticias*, 9.4.1988).

Mozambican military communiques have also referred to:

(3) infiltrations of bandits across the South African border around the time of the Homoine massacre in July 1987, in which over 400 people died (*Guardian*, 15.6.1987 and 22.7.1987); the Manjacaze massacre in August 1987 in which 72 were killed (*Guardian*, 13.8.1987; *AIM despatch*, 18.8.1987); the Taninga massacres of over 250 bus passengers in October and November 1987 (*Domingo*, 1.11.1987); and on other occasions (*Noticias*, 11.10.1986, 25.2.1987 and 18.5.1987).

(4) There have been violations of Mozambican airspace (*Noticias*, 16.11.1987 and 24.11.1987).

(5) There have been also operations conducted by units with specialist skills or hit-and-run teams returning to South Africa against railway bridges and powerlines (*Noticias*, 7.12.1985, 11.2.1986 and 17.10.1987); against civilians using beaches in Maputo city (*Noticias*, 10.2.1986); and against ANC members resident in Mozambique (*AIM despatch*, 30.5.1987; *Noticias*, 8.4.1988 and 6.5.1988).

All of this had been complemented by the testimony of former MNR Western European spokesman, Paulo Oliveira, who defected in October 1987. Oliveira, who spoke to the press in Maputo in March 1988 (*AIM Bulletin*, 141, April 1988), essentially confirmed that the SADF support network for the MNR bandits remained intact up to the time of his defection. According to Oliveira the main base continued to be located at Phalaborwa. Charles van Niekerk (promoted to Brigadier) remained in overall operational command, while a Colonel Grobbelaar was in charge of logistical support. This support came from the barracks of the 7th South African Infantry regiment. Oliveira also said that training was provided by No. 5 Reconnaissance (Recce) Commando and that SAAF Dakotas were used to drop supplies to bandits in Mozambique. Other sources have suggested that members of Special Forces command (the 'operational arm' of Military Intelligence) and No. 5 Recce Commando have from time to time travelled to Mozambique to conduct sophisticated sabotage operations beyond the capacity of bandit squads. 31 Battalion, based at Duku Duku, airforce units based at Louis Trichardt and Hoedspruit, and some commando units are also thought to have been involved (*Africa Confidential*, 28, 24, 2.12.1987).

Covert war in the context of Pretoria's regional strategy

The deployment of surrogate forces has not been the only form of South African aggression against Mozambique. There has also been economic action, including the cutback on and eventual banning of new migrant labour recruitment, and the restriction of South African traffic passing through the port of Maputo. In addition, there were until 1984 a number of direct, acknowledged SADF raids into Mozambique. Together these actions (of which the deployment of surrogate forces has been the most persistent and damaging) constitute what is generally known as the policy of destabilisation (Davies and O'Meara, 1985; Hanlon, 1986; Johnson and Martin, 1986).

The resort to such a policy has to be seen in the first instance against the background of the profound and dramatic change in the balance of forces in the southern African region brought about by the collapse of the Portuguese African empire and the subsequent independence of Mozambique and Angola under governments formed by the liberation movements Frelimo and the MPLA respectively. This fundamentally undermined the basis on which South Africa's entire regional strategy had up to this point been constructed. Until the mid-1970s, Pretoria had been able to rely on the existence of a ring of colonially ruled 'buffer states' to ensure that the impact of the gathering liberation struggle in southern Africa remained largely confined to regions far distant from its own borders, and that regional territories continued to serve South African capitalism as labour reserves, markets, and suppliers of specific services such as transport.

The initial response of the Vorster government to the new situation created by the fall of Portuguese colonialism was vacillating and somewhat incoherent (Geldenhuys, 1984; Davies and O'Meara, 1985). Its half-hearted détente initiative, launched in an attempt to win allies or at least neutralise potential adversaries within the Organisation of African Unity, collapsed in 1976, partly as a result of the debacle surrounding the first major SADF invasion of Angola and partly in the wake of the brutal response to the Soweto uprising. Two years of virtual stagnation followed during which no important regional policy initiatives were taken.

The administration of P. W. Botha thus came to power, in September 1978, in the context of an acute crisis on the regional as well as the domestic plane of struggle. The Botha government represented a new alliance within the dominant classes between the top military commanders and monopoly capital. On coming to power, the new regime set about reorganising and reformulating both domestic and regional strategy in accordance with its well-known 'total strategy' doctrine. At the level of regional strategy, the vague notion of establishing a 'constellation of southern African states' (Consas), which had first been put forward by Vorster in 1974, was substantially developed and defined as the ultimate objective of regional strategy. The overall aim of the Consas strategy was to create a South African-led alliance of 'moderate states of southern Africa' united against a common 'Marxist onslaught' in circumstances in which they could not rely on the unqualified and unconditional support of the Western powers. Since apartheid policies were recognised as a barrier to the immediate establishment of formalised alliances with neighbouring states, preparatory action to generate a 'counter-ideology to Marxism' in the region was deemed essential.

The promotion of joint economic projects with neighbouring states was to be one of two main prongs in a new regional offensive. The other was the luring of regional states into 'non-aggression pacts'. Through such action on the economic and security fronts, ties with neighbouring states were to be deepened and the objective basis created for what Foreign Minister Pik Botha described as 'a common approach in the security field, the economic field and even the political field' (quoted in Geldenhuys and Venter, 1979: 54).

In addition to its direct impact on the regional plane, the promotion of Consas was intended to lead to the *de facto* international recognition of South Africa as the 'regional power'. This would bring about a general acknowledgement that southern Africa was a sphere of South African influence, and in turn this would reduce Pretoria's international isolation.

Achieving these and other more immediate goals of regional policy – such as ensuring neighbouring states would withhold support from liberation movements, maintain and deepen economic ties with South Africa, and modify the level of criticism of apartheid (Geldenhuys, 1981) – was seen as requiring the application of a 'sophisticated' mix of economic, political–diplomatic and military tactics. There were to be both incentives and disincentives, but the touted formula of that time specified that the appropriate mix should be 80 per cent political–economic–diplomatic and only 20 per cent military action.

In practice, however, after an initial abortive attempt from 1978 to 1980 to launch Consas, Pretoria fell back on aggression as the main instrument of its regional policy. Consas received a severe blow when Zimbabwe (which Pretoria had been expecting to become an ally after being brought to internationally recognised independence under a Muzorewa–Smith regime) became independent instead under a Zanu-

PF government. The Consas scheme suffered a further setback when all the independent states of the region associated themselves with the Southern African Development Coordination Conference (SADCC), whose central objective was to reduce the level of economic dependence of member states particularly, but not only, on South Africa.

These reverses to Pretoria's efforts to remould regional relations precipitated a second phase of South African action in the region lasting roughly from mid-1980 until the end of 1981. This period saw the application of destabilisation tactics in a fairly generalised and indiscriminate manner. Direct military action or the threat of such action was applied against a number of regional states. This was also the period in which surrogate force activity — by UNITA in Angola, the 'Lesotho Liberation Army' (LLA) in Lesotho, and MNR in Mozambique – became a serious menace. At the same time, the first major attempts were made to apply economic techniques of coercion.

This phase of generalised destabilisation gave way to a third phase lasting from the early part of 1982 until the signing of the Nkomati Accord in March 1984. This can be described as a phase of intensified and more selective destabilisation. During it, some attempt appears to have been made by Pretoria to categorise regional states and direct different tactics towards them. On one hand, the more conservative states, such as Swaziland and Malawi, were seen as potential collaborators. These were offered a range of economic and other 'incentives' to encourage them to 'cooperate' with South Africa. On the other hand, there were those states seen either as the most vulnerable or as Pretoria's principal adversaries in the region. States in this category included Lesotho, Angola and Mozambique.

As far as Mozambique was concerned, the country provided political support to the ANC and allowed its members to reside in the country (although bases as such were never established). It was an influential member of the alliance of frontline states, and one of the prime movers behind SADCC. Its ports and railways offered the only realistic alternative to continued dependence on South African transport facilities for many of the SADCC states. It maintained friendly relations with socialist countries, and was itself ruled by a party committed to bringing about a process of socialist transformation. It thus represented a barrier to a number of Pretoria's regional policy objectives, as well as posed a direct ideological challenge and potential alternative to apartheid capitalism.

With the turn to destabilisation tactics, Mozambique was rapidly singled out as a prime target. It was subjected to a number of direct attacks by SADF units – the first being the raid against ANC residences in Matola in January 1981. Members of the SADF were also implicated in clandestine acts of sabotage against strategic transport installations – in one such attack an SADF lieutenant, Alan Gingles, was killed by his own bomb (Johnson and Martin, 1986: 22). At the same time a number of 'economic disincentives' were applied against the country. For example, a partial economic boycott was imposed against the port of Maputo, and South African traffic in 1983 fell to half that of 1982 and only 16 per cent of the level of 1973 (Mozambique, National Planning Commission, 1984: 30).

The principal vehicle of South African destabilisation was, however, its sponsorship of the MNR. MNR action increased after the movement was taken over by the SADF in 1980, and escalated rapidly during 1982 and 1983. Official sources estimate that by the end of 1983, 140 villages, 840 schools, 900 rural shops and over 200 public health installations had been destroyed. The total cost of this destruction was put at US$3,8 billion (Mozambique, National Planning Commission, 1984: 38).

As indicated earlier, the SADF's involvement with the MNR during this period has now been acknowledged by senior state officials even though it was strenuously denied at the time. What is more controversial is the continuation of this involvement despite the signing in March 1984 of the Nkomati Accord. As evidence of continued support for armed banditry in Mozambique from within South Africa began to mount despite the signing of the Accord, one hypothesis which emerged was that this was the action of 'rogue' elements within the military acting without the authorisation either of the government or of the SADF command. This has been belied by the 'Gorongosa documents' which, as indicated earlier, showed tht the level of involvement or knowledge reached to the highest echelons of the SADF hierarchy.

Another hypothesis advanced was that the Nkomati Accord had never been accepted by the SADF and that it was thrust on the military by civilian politicians. How to respond to it had accordingly been a matter of disagreement and struggle between different forces within the state and wider ruling class. On one side stood the Ministry of Foreign Affairs (supported by 'economic interests') favouring an approach relying on diplomacy and economic leverage. On the other side was the SADF, wedded to 'quick fix' military solutions. There is more substance to this hypothesis than to the first. It does seem that both the initial idea and first draft of the Nkomati Accord were put forward by the Mozambican side (Johnson and Martin, 1986: 26–7). In the discussions which preceded it, Pretoria's negotiators had concentrated on demands for the complete removal of the 'ANC presence' from Mozambique, and access to the country by South African capital. The insistence on the need for a comprehensive security pact (implying obligations on both sides) does seem, initially, to have caught Pretoria somewhat off guard. In addition, the 'Gorongosa documents' do confirm that Foreign Minister Botha was mistrusted by military personnel. He was not briefed about the visit to Gorongosa of his own Deputy Minister, Louis Nel; military personnel were quoted in the documents describing him as a 'traitor', a 'Soviet nark' and a stooge of Chester Crocker; and conversations he held with the MNR delegation just before October 1984 were bugged by the SADF.

However, while acknowledging all this, it is necessary to avoid the kind of oversimplifying which tends to reduce the explanation of continued destabilisation entirely to the dominance of military 'hawks' over Foreign Affairs 'doves'. In the first place, such explanations exaggerate the differences, which have always existed and continue to exist within clear limits. The Foreign Ministry accepts the basic goal of establishing Pretoria's regional hegemony as well as the other shorter-term objectives defined by 'total strategy'. Moreover, it does not totally reject military action as one of the means of achieving these goals. One of the main tasks performed by Botha as Foreign Minister over the years has thus been to threaten and justify various forms of military action against neighbouring states. In the last analysis, the differences between Foreign Affairs and the military are differences of tactics or nuance. They are about the precise mix of military aggression and economic and diplomatic action, and not over whether military and economic aggression should be applied.

Secondly, it is necessary to locate any analysis of struggle between advocates of different options within the state in the context of a prior analysis of the objective conditions and constraints on particular options created by the evolving struggle between the state and its adversaries on both the regional and domestic planes. Space does not permit any extensive development of this point here (see Davies, 1987 and 1987a). Briefly, it is clear that while Mozambique signed the Nkomati Accord in the hope of reducing the level of conflict in the region and establishing a pattern of regional relations based on the norms of international law, Pretoria's strategists saw the Accord in a wholly different light. For them it was a tactical device to advance specific objectives defined in the stalled Consas initiative. More precisely, and partly with the benefit of hindsight, it appears that Pretoria's strategists hoped that through Nkomati they could: achieve a reduction in the level of armed struggle and mass action inside South Africa (by depriving the ANC of its alleged bases in Mozambique); broker a 'power-sharing' settlement which would place the MNR in a subordinate but influential role in government in Mozambique; pressure other regional states into signing security pacts as a first step towards a generalised acceptance of Pretoria's hegemony in the region; and significantly reduce the level of South Africa's international isolation based on *de facto* acknowledgement of its position as the 'regional power' and the gateway for foreign investment throughout the region.

It has been suggested elsewhere (Davies, 1987a) that Pretoria's failure to capitalise on the Nkomati Accord in these ways at the same time as the struggle inside South Africa itself was advancing, were major factors behind the steady drift back towards escalating and less concealed (if not openly acknowledged) destabilisation. This became particularly evident in the period after the SADF raid against oil installations in the Cabinda province of Angola in May 1985. In these circumstances, Pretoria's strategists increasingly saw themselves as having little to gain by attempting to put forward an (in fact tarnished) image of peaceful intent in the region. It suited them instead to project an image of ruthless, unassailable strength.

The experience of the post-Nkomati period has, nevertheless, revealed much about military influence over foreign policy formulation and militarisation in general. The response of the Botha government to the publication of the 'Gorongosa documents' was particularly instructive. None of the officers named, who included the former and current chiefs of the SADF and the current chief of the army, was in any way disciplined. On the contrary many were subsequently promoted, while P. W. Botha went out of his way to defend the then Chief of the SADF, General Viljoen. A commentator wrote at the time:

> The deep trust which binds President Botha to General Viljoen and the Minister of Defence, Magnus Malan, can fairly be compared with the relationship that bound Mr John Vorster with General Hendrik van den Bergh. . . . Military Intelligence has assumed under President Botha the same behind-the-scenes influence on policy, and has therefore acquired something of the same sinister reputation that BOSS had under Vorster. (Ken Owen, *Sunday Times*, 13.10.1985)

Contradictions of Pretoria's covert war in Mozambique

There can be no doubt that the SADF's covert war in Mozambique through Renamo has been relatively cheap and, at one level, a success. At the cost of very few SADF lives and comparatively little in terms of material resources, great damage has been inflicted on the economy and social fabric of Mozambique. Mozambique has been prevented from achieving its potential as a functioning alternative to apartheid capitalism, and many of the specific gains of the Mozambican revolution (in health and education in particular) have been undermined. According to the latest available figures, about a third of the health network (including 700 health posts) and 2 049 rural primary schools have been destroyed or rendered inoperative by bandit action (CENE–DPCCN, 1988: 36–7).

At the same time, however, Pretoria's resort to covert war has had contradictory effects at the political, ideological and diplomatic levels. These have become increasingly evident in more recent times. The turn to destabilisation in the first place derived from Pretoria's chronic inability to produce a viable political strategy to advance its regional ambitions. The original aim of Consas was to win allies. In the last analysis its failure was due not so much to the particular tactics applied, but to the nature of the strategic objective sought – acceptance by independent states of the hegemonic ambitions in the region of a racist minority government. The voluntary cooperation of independent states in such a project was never a viable proposition and, as indicated earlier, it was the failure to achieve this which led South Africa to fall back on aggression, with covert military action as the principal instrument of this assault. The turn to this option, and the fact that Pretoria has been seen to have continued to pursue it despite having signed a formal 'non-aggression' accord, have undermined its credibility in the region even further.

So, too, has the extreme brutality of the MNR assault. There is general unanimity among observers that Pretoria never at any time had any serious intention of trying to replace Frelimo with the MNR. Attempting to do so was recognised at a fairly early point as being too risky and costly for Pretoria. Even if the MNR had been able to overthrow the Frelimo government, Pretoria would then have been left trying to sustain an unrecognised puppet regime in charge of a war-torn country, undoubtedly facing a challenge from Frelimo. Pretoria's unwillingness to take on such a burden was spelt out in discussions between a South African delegation (including both R. F. Botha and General Constand Viljoen) and the MNR late in 1984. The 'Gorongosa documents' record the South African side telling the MNR that they should seek a cease-fire as a step towards 'power sharing' because the Mozambican government 'is recognised internationally and you are not. The RSA does not have money to help Renamo recuperate the economy if it wins the war.' (Gorongosa documents, 1985: 'Desk Diary' entry under page headed 'Week 39 September 1984', translated by author)

As the prospect of forcing even 'power sharing' on the Frelimo government increasingly receded as a realistic possibility, the overall objective of the MNR assault appears to have been downgraded to keeping the country in a state of permanent crisis and attempting to render it ungovernable.

The fact that the MNR is neither an indigenous political movement nor seen even by its sponsors as an alternative government has shaped the way it has conducted itself on the ground. It has never produced a coherent political programme nor, in practice, sought seriously to mobilise positive support among the people in areas in which it operates. This has been confirmed in a report commissioned by the US State Department based on interviews with nearly 200 randomly selected refugees in 42 different locations in Mozambique and neighbouring countries (Gersony, 1988: 25). The report noted: 'There are virtually no reports of attempts to win the loyalty – or even neutrality – of the villagers. The refugees report virtually no effort by Renamo to explain to the civilians the purpose of the insurgency, its proposed program or its aspirations.'

Instead, the bandits have relied on terrorism and intimidation in their relationship with the people. Their basic *modus operandi* is described in the Gersony report. Although they are supplied with arms by the SADF, they depend on local people to provide them with food and forced labour (mainly to transport supplies). Since there is little positive enthusiasm among local people, these demands are asserted through coercion. According to Gersony, the MNR divide the zones in which they operate into 'tax areas' (where people are compelled to provide food and make available 'a young girl or married woman for sex'), 'control areas' (where forced recruitment and forced labour practices are common), and 'destruction areas' (where indiscriminate slaughters are perpetrated). The effect of the presence of the MNR in any area is to inflict misery on the local people. Gersony's 200 informants witnessed 600 murders – by shooting, knife or axe or bayonet killings, burning alive, beating to death, asphyxiation, starvation and drowning (1988: 21). Some 91 per cent of those interviewed had 'very negative' and a further 5 per cent 'somewhat negative' perceptions of the MNR, compared to 7 per cent 'very negative' and 10 per cent 'somewhat negative' perceptions of Frelimo government troops (1988: 23).

The widespread reliance on such terrorist tactics has greatly undercut not only domestic but also whatever international legitimacy the bandit assault might have mobilised. Despite the fact that the basic technique of 'covert war' was undoubtedly partly modelled on the 'Reagan doctrine' of supporting 'anti-communist' insurgencies against 'left-wing' governments, the brutality of the MNR assault, in the context of active international diplomacy by the Mozambican government, has led even the US administration to distance itself from it. At an emergency aid donors' conference held in Maputo in April 1988, a Deputy Assistant Secretary of State, Roy Stacy, accused the MNR of 'one of the most brutal holocausts against ordinary human beings since World War Two' (quoted in *Citizen*, 3.5.1988).

The passing of a law at the end of 1987 offering an amnesty to bandits surrendering to the Mozambican authorities, as well as the relative success of a number of Frelimo military operations in 1988, seems to have caused some considerable disarray within the ranks of the MNR – both externally and on the ground in Mozambique. Some 911 former bandits had surrendered by the third week of April 1988 (*Noticias*, 21.4.1988); a former senior MNR official (Paulo Oliveira) defected in March 1988; and there have been murders of others (Mateus Lopes and João Ataide in Malawi in December 1987 and former secretary general, Evo Fernandes, in Lisbon in April 1988).

All of this will clearly have some impact on the process of diplomatic activity which began to take shape in April 1988 and was continuing at the time of writing (June 1988). While the main focus of the current 'super-power'-sponsored effort to seek a 'political solution' to conflicts in the region is on Angola and Namibia, Mozambique–South Africa relations and the question of continued South African support for armed banditry have also received attention. Mozambique will clearly enter any new negotiating process with some political and ideological leverage. It remains to be seen whether this can be consolidated into effective pressure on Pretoria to curtail or limit its support for the MNR, or whether, as in the past, this support will simply be reorganised and concealed in new ways. The experience to date suggests that it would be prudent to treat any claims by Pretoria of peaceful intentions towards its neighbours with grave reservations. The setbacks suffered by the SADF in Angola in 1987–8 may be forcing Pretoria to move into a phase of attempting to deploy more diplomatic and economic action in its struggle to achieve its hegemonic goals in the region, but ultimately the conclusion repeatedly asserted by the frontline states remains valid – lasting peace in southern Africa depends on the elimination of apartheid, the root cause of instability and violence throughout the region.

9 The South African Defence Force in Angola
JEREMY GREST

This chapter examines the role of the South African Defence Force (SADF) in Angola. The SADF intervention in this country has been much greater and more sustained than in any other in the region. The SADF invaded Angola in 1975 and, on being forced to withdraw, rearmed and reorganised one of the defeated wings of the nationalist movement – the National Union for the Total Independence of Angola (UNITA) – into an effective weapon of destabilisation against the government of the Popular Movement for the Liberation of Angola (MPLA). The SADF also waged a conventional war of high intensity against Angola and occupied large parts of southern Angola almost continuously from 1980 to 1988.

The SADF intervened in 1975 to counter the MPLA's dominance of the decolonisation process and to place in power a regime more favourably disposed to Pretoria and the West. Having failed in its immediate objectives, it set about neutralising the perceived threat to its interests from the multiracial, Marxist MPLA, which had come to power with Cuban and Soviet aid and was committed to providing material support to the ANC and SWAPO.

Angola's economic power as an oil producer is of immense strategic significance in the region, and has been important in shaping Pretoria's aggressive stance since 1975 (Hanlon, 1986: 153–4). Angola is the only oil producer in the region and under peaceful conditions would be a major supplier to the Southern African Development Coordination Conference (SADCC) states, which aim to lessen their economic dependence on South Africa. A client regime in Angola would provide Pretoria with an invaluable buffer against oil sanctions. Oil revenues potentially provide Angola with the means to embark upon an industrialisation programme as well as insulate the country to some extent from South African economic pressures. Because Pretoria has not been able to apply the same range of economic sanctions as in the case of other neighbouring countries, it has resorted to a military strategy against Angola. For the MPLA, oil revenues have been a lifeline in the defence against Pretoria's aggression.

Pretoria was encouraged to intervene in 1975 by the United States. In effect, South African and American pressure pushed the MPLA into a

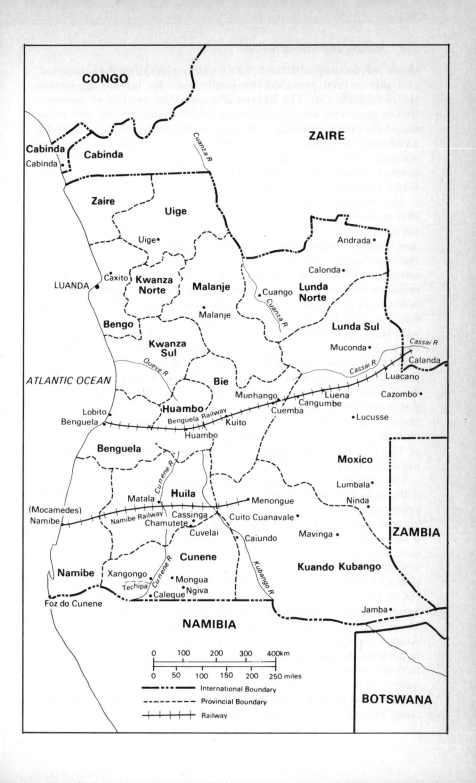

closer relationship with the Soviet Union and its allies than intended,
and this in turn provided the justification for further aggression
(Hanlon, 1986: 154). The Reagan administration's policy of 'constructive engagement' after 1980 licensed SADF destabilisation and introduced the policy of 'linkage'. In terms of this policy, the United States
and South Africa were not prepared to allow Namibian independence
without a prior withdrawal of Cuban troops from Angola. The MPLA,
however, could not contemplate any such withdrawal as long as the
SADF continued to menace Angola.

The effects of Pretoria's undeclared war have been felt at every level
of Angolan society: from conscription of young men to the thousands of
paraplegics and amputees, the war ophanages, camps for the displaced
and widows, food shortages, malnutrition and hardship. The United
Nations Children's Fund (Unicef) estimated that war-induced famine
killed 100 000 Angolans between 1980 and 1985, and that over 50 000
children died each year as a direct result of the war, leaving Angola
with one of the highest infant mortality rates in the world (ECC, 1988:
6.2). Food production has been disrupted in war-affected areas, along
with basic health services. The Red Cross estimated that Angola had
the highest national proportion of war-disabled in the world, 80 per
cent being women and children, many of whom were victims of anti-
personnel mines placed by UNITA in fields. According to the Red
Cross there are 30 000 civilian amputees in Angola. Official estimates
put at 690 000 the number of people displaced by the war, out of a total
population of 8,73 million. The Angolan government, in conjunction
with the United Nations, estimated war damage between 1975 and 1985
at US$17 billion, the equivalent of almost fifteen years of current
export earnings (ECC, 1988: 6.2).

The costs of Pretoria's war have been high for South Africa too. It is
difficult to give exact numbers of South African troops killed. SADF
press releases in June 1988 gave the casualty figure for Angola and the
'operational area' for the previous six months as 69 (ECC, 1988: 6.2).
The SADF did not announce the death of any black troops or members
of its 'special forces'. Angolan government figures were much higher; it
estimated the number of SADF and South West Africa Territory Force
(SWATF) deaths between November 1987 and April 1988 at about 400
(ECC, 1988: 6.2). The Angolan war was estimated by Dr Jammine of
Econometrix to cost South Africa R5 million a day, or R4 billion a year.
He said: 'If the government is to spend billions a year fighting a war in
Angola, the spectre looms of increased inflation, higher interest rates,
hyperinflation and an ever weakening economy. If we could put an end
to that [Angolan] expenditure we could cut present income taxes by a
quarter and create much economic growth' (*Weekend Argus*, 2.7.1988).

The SADF in Angola has been one actor, albeit a powerful one, in a
complex matrix of forces operating at different levels: from the local

through to the national, regional and international plane. It is beyond the scope of this chapter to provide a detailed analysis which accounts comprehensively for the mosaic of interactions of all the principal actors and social forces at these levels. However, it is important to locate the SADF clearly in the Angolan equation in order to understand how South African military power was inserted into an unstable balance of forces in an attempt to alter decisively that balance at a crucial juncture in Angola's history. It is necessary to trace how subsequent South African strategy worked on widening the internal social contradictions which had been created by Angola's uneven colonial development.

The approach adopted in this chapter is broadly historical. The first section outlines the major social forces involved in national liberation politics, and briefly discusses the South African invasion in 1975 in the context of the decolonisation conflict of 1974–6. After the invasion was checked by the MPLA, reinforced by Cuban troops, the SADF withdrew and began to rearm and redeploy UNITA. The next section considers the development of SADF strategy in southern Angola and the continued war against the MPLA government. The third section deals with the period after the Lusaka Agreement of 1984, which saw an escalation of conflict in Angola, culminating in the major battles of late 1987. The final section covers these battles and the shift in the military balance against South Africa which forced Pretoria to the negotiating table.

National liberation politics, decolonisation and the South African intervention 1974–6

South African military involvement in Angola grew out of the forward defence strategy elaborated in the 1960s in response to the development of armed nationalist challenges to Portuguese colonialism and the illegal settler government in Southern Rhodesia. Pretoria sought to maintain a protective shield of white-ruled states on its periphery in order to bolster apartheid and hamper externally based insurgency. Angola's strategic significance for Pretoria at that time lay mainly in its shared border with Namibia, straddled by Cuanhama people from whom the South West African People's Organization (SWAPO) gained support.

The SADF became actively involved in the Angolan war of liberation five years after its outbreak in 1961, when SWAPO's first insurgents were encountered in Namibia, having infiltrated from Portuguese Angola. Helicopter squadrons began cross-border patrols from bases in Namibia, and two years later the SADF established an air base at Cuito Cuanavale in south-east Angola. From there the SADF carried out reconnaissance and transport operations against both SWAPO and Angolan guerilla forces (Cawthra, 1986: 114).

In the late 1960s South Africa became jointly involved with Portugal in the development of the Kunene hydro-electricity and irrigation scheme designed to foster white settlement in southern Angola and to provide water and power for northern Namibia. In addition the ports of Luanda and Lobito were of strategic concern to South Africa, as was the Benguela railway, a lifeline which connected Zambia and Zaire (regarded by South Africa as two potential détente partners) with the sea.

By the early 1970s the progress of the guerilla wars in the Portuguese colonies had become a source of concern to Pretoria. Only in Angola was the war in any way under control. The nationalist movement was divided into three competing groups, each of which was a coalition of specific regional, cultural and class interests emerging out of a social formation which had undergone significant changes in the late colonial period.[1] The first group, the FNLA, originally drew on a northern, Bakongo peasant base, with significant support from coffee-growers increasingly displaced by immigrant Portuguese from the 1950s. The movement was led by an emigré petite bourgeoisie in the Belgian Congo. Socially conservative, it failed to broaden its base following the northern uprisings of 1961, and limited its armed activities to sporadic forays from across the Zairean border. The FNLA leaders established close links with Zaire's rulers and through them gained the patronage of the United States government, which viewed the movement as an anti-communist counter to the MPLA. Much of the FNLA's energy was directed towards denying its rival, the MPLA, access to bases in Zaire.

The MPLA developed its main support in the urban areas of the central colonial society among the petite bourgeoisie of mixed race and *assimilado* background and the recently urbanised working class. Its top leadership was predominantly urban-based, intellectual, progressive, and anti-imperialist in orientation. It looked principally to the Soviet Union and its allies for support in its anti-colonial struggle. It managed to develop only a fragile base in the peasantry restricted to the rural hinterland of Luanda and the south-east of Angola. The movement's spread into the central highlands in the early 1970s had been contained by Portuguese social-action programmes coupled with counter-insurgency tactics. The MPLA was also beset by factionalism. In 1973 three groups contended for power in a debilitating struggle which seriously compromised the movement's ability to prosecute a guerilla war.

The third group, UNITA, was created in 1966 by Jonas Savimbi as a result of his dissatisfaction with the FNLA in which he had held a key foreign affairs position. Not being powerful enough to displace the FNLA leader, Holden Roberto, he resigned in 1964 and made contact with the MPLA. He was unable to reach agreement with them on the position he would occupy, and in 1966 he entered Moxico province with a small group of supporters and established UNITA (Somerville, 1986: 36). Savimbi then set about constructing a multi-ethnic alliance of Angola's peripheral rural societies – in essence, the failed FNLA project of the 1960s. Militarily UNITA was the weakest of the three movements, and this contributed to its collaborating with the Portuguese in the early 1970s in a context where all the movements were expending at least as much energy against each other as they were in fighting the Portuguese.[2]

Pretoria kept a close watch on developments in the Portuguese colonies, and was alarmed by the April 1974 coup in Lisbon and its possible implications. The SADF intervention in 1975 has to be seen in the light of Pretoria's assessment of the international situation and of the balance of forces in Angola itself.[3] In the wake of America's withdrawal from Vietnam, and the fall of Richard Nixon as a result of the Watergate scandal, American interventionism in Angola was channelled through CIA-sponsored covert activities in support of alliances made with the FNLA and its Zairean patrons in the 1960s. The State Department under Henry Kissinger encouraged South Africa to intervene as a proxy force with its own agenda (Gavshon, 1981: 243–8).

Pretoria had been in contact with the FNLA and UNITA from July 1975 when they had canvassed support for their struggle against the MPLA. There was also covert diplomatic support from Zaire, Zambia and the Ivory Coast for South African assistance to prevent an MPLA victory in the fighting which broke out between July and September 1974.

Portugal's policy towards Angolan independence reflected struggles within the Portuguese armed forces movement. General Spinola argued that Angola was not ready for independence and began secret negotiations with the FNLA, UNITA and the Chipenda faction of the MPLA. These negotiations were aimed at cementing alliances with the settler population, isolating the MPLA and steering Angola on a path of gradual decolonisation. Following Spinola's overthrow in September 1974 and the advent of successively more radical governments in Portugal, an all-party conference at Alvor agreed in January 1975 to the formation of a transitional government with representatives of all three movements. Independence Day was set for 11 November 1975.

The Alvor Accord provided for elections as a test of popular support prior to independence, but these never took place as the Accord broke down irreparably and fighting between the movements became generalised. Of crucial importance in the decolonisation process was that no single broadly based populist, multi-class and multi-ethnic movement had emerged in Angola by 1974 to dominate the anti-colonial struggle and lay down terms for decolonisation (as had occurred, for example, with FRELIMO in Mozambique). The resulting contest between the movements took on a military character. The

FNLA, although potentially the smallest of the three movements electorally in terms of its regional support base, was militarily the largest and best-equipped nationalist grouping. It adopted an extremely aggressive military posture towards the MPLA from the outset. The MPLA with only a regional support base could not be certain of confrontation with the FNLA, that they should proceed to crush UNITA militarily as well before it became too powerful a force politically. The MPLA with its own regional support base could not be certain of dominating an electoral struggle with the other two movements, especially in view of the indications that UNITA was effectively mobilising support from a broad spectrum of colonial society, including significant settler elements (Heimer, 1979: 65–71).

The SADF intervention in Angola from August 1975 was aimed at keeping the MPLA from power and preventing a movement of socialist orientation, sympathetic to the ANC and SWAPO, from gaining control over a country of great strategic importance and economic potential in southern Africa.[4] Having crossed the border and taken up positions around the Ruacana hydro-electric station, the SADF began sending in supplies to UNITA and setting up training camps in August and September, with CIA encouragement (Hanlon, 1986: 156–7).

The heavy battles began in October. In the north, President Mobutu committed his Zairean troops to help the FNLA take Luanda, from which it has been ejected by the MPLA, before Independence Day. The SADF committed some long-range artillery to shell Luanda from 9 November. On 10 November the joint FNLA and Zairean column launched its attack on Luanda but was routed because the first Cuban reinforcements, urgently requested by the MPLA when the scale of the SADF invasion became apparent, had arrived two days before and deployed heavy weaponry shipped in earlier (Hanlon, 1986: 156).

In the south the SADF moved up the coast in October, driving the MPLA forces back rapidly. By 15 November the SADF column had moved 700 km north and was only 200 km from Luanda. The SADF troops – mostly conscripts – were issued with green Portuguese-style uniforms and instructed to say they were mercenaries. The arrival of the first Cuban troops on the southern front prevented any further advance of the column. The SADF sent in two further armoured columns in November and December which concentrated on consolidating control over the Benguela railway line and setting up FNLA and UNITA administrations in the captured towns. On 23 November they announced the formation of a joint government, the Democratic Republic of Angola, but within a month there was fighting between the two movements in several towns.

Cuban reinforcements began arriving in large numbers in December and January in response to MPLA appeals for assistance. Further SADF advance became impossible without substantial reinforcement, and an escalation of the war would have generated serious diplomatic consequences since Angola was by then formally independent. The South African role in the fighting had become public knowledge and this served to tip the balance of opinion at the OAU in favour of recognising the MPLA as the legitimate government. In addition the CIA undercover operation was also exposed, and the US Congress took offence at not having been informed and banned further expenditure of military funds in Angola.

Pretoria's diplomatic isolation and the greatly increased potential costs of further involvement were important considerations leading to the SADF withdrawal in mid-January 1976. Pretoria had overestimated the fighting capacity of its allies and underestimated the willingness of Cuba and the Soviet Union to intervene decisively to prevent the defeat of the MPLA. What is more, the South African government had misread the international diplomatic situation and did not receive the support it had anticipated once its own involvement was known. The net result was a serious set-back for South African and American policy, and a victory for 'socialist internationalism'.

Rebuilding UNITA and destabilising Angola

As the SADF retreated before the advancing Cuban and MPLA forces, it destroyed much of the remaining infrastructure, blowing up hundreds of road bridges, including 50 major ones, and causing an estimated damage of $6,7 billion (Hanlon, 1986: 157). UNITA was expelled from the main towns in which it had been installed during the invasions, and both MPLA and UNITA supporters were killed by their respective opponents as territory was ceded and captured. Part of UNITA's forces withdrew with the SADF to Namibia, whilst other units retreated into the central highlands and began a guerilla war which effectively disrupted food production and trade in Angola's 'bread basket' for the next three years. Several hundred thousand peasants in Bié and Huambo fled their homes and followed UNITA into the bush.

There was a serious economic crisis in Angola following the MPLA victory. Most of the settlers left, withdrawing their skills, and many *mestizo* (mixed race) and African collaborators departed in their wake. The vital transport network collapsed as vehicles were driven over the border or sabotaged. The rapid social promotion that followed the exodus of the settlers and their allies, and the state interventionist economic strategy of the MPLA, led to the growth of a bureaucratic apparatus which constituted a strong right-wing in the new government.

The government in Luanda was distinctly fragile during the crucial first few years of its rule. A 1977 coup attempt indicated severe tensions within the ruling stratum of the MPLA (Wolfers and Bergerol, 1983; Birmingham, 1978). Internal problems within the MPLA, its continued urban orientation, excessive statism, and the breakdown of rural production and exchange networks, all worked to delay the development of a coherent strategy to win over key areas of Angola where the party had never had a base. The political division between the MPLA and both UNITA and the FNLA reflected the history of Angola's uneven development and the contradiction between the central urban society and the peripheral rural societies. Through its military support for UNITA, Pretoria was able to work on this tension and strengthen its effects.

With the end of the conventional war in February 1976, the SADF established a line of new bases along the Angola–Namibia border and began to rearm and reorganise the remnants of the FNLA and UNITA groups which had retreated with it. The FNLA soldiers were largely incorporated directly into 32 Battalion of the SADF. Portuguese mercenaries and ex-colonial remnants were also brought into the SADF. UNITA was maintained as a separate movement and attempts were made to contact the UNITA groups in central Angola (Cawthra, 1986: 148).

In the period 1976–80 South African support for UNITA was maintained, but at a lower level than previously. The Benguela railway became UNITA's chief strategic target, and successive attacks effectively kept the line closed. UNITA, from having been an early ally of SWAPO's, now became involved in armed clashes with it as alliances were cemented on both sides of the Angolan conflict. The counter-insurgency tactics of the MPLA army, FAPLA, seemed to be making little progress against UNITA, which was also active in the south, seizing small towns and holding them for brief periods (*Africa Contemporary Record*, 10: B506). The unresolved Namibian issue led to repeated cross-border raids by the SADF against SWAPO bases. In May 1978 over 600 Namibians were massacred and 1 000 wounded in a strike against a SWAPO transit camp at Cassinga (Soggot, 1986: 231).

However, by mid-1979 the situation in Angola had begun to improve for the MPLA. Relations with the West were better, the party was more coherent, and FAPLA offensives had crippled UNITA militarily.[5] In the central highlands tens of thousands of destitute UNITA followers began to return to their homes as the prospect of victory receded and demoralisation set in. The Benguela railway was opened to international traffic for the first time since 1975 (Hanlon, 1986: 158).

From 1979 there was also a build-up in direct SADF action in Angola. P. W. Botha's accession to the premiership marked the beginning of a much more aggressive military posture in the region. Bombing raids were carried out in the south and there were helicopter-borne sabotage raids. The attacks were aimed at economic targets, and SAAF air superiority enabled the systematic destruction of the civilian infrastructure to proceed. South African aggression was meant to alarm

Western investors who were showing growing interest in joint ventures with the MPLA government, divert Angolan budget resources from reconstruction to defence, and generally weaken MPLA resolve to support SWAPO.

The SADF also stepped up its support for UNITA as a weapon against the MPLA. The Reagan administration's policy of constructive engagement effectively licensed the SADF to wage an undeclared war against Angola. A pattern in the fighting began to emerge: where FAPLA sweeps threatened to destroy UNITA militarily, the SADF would intervene to neutralise FAPLA and draw its troops away from UNITA.

By 1980 FAPLA was confident enough to deal with SADF raids unassisted by Cuban troops, but the latter's planned withdrawal was halted by increased SADF aggression. The Cubans were largely deployed in behind-the-lines back-up tasks, although Savimbi often claimed they were being used against UNITA. In April–May 1980 the SADF launched a series of raids on villages in the Cunene and Cuando Cubango provinces. In June it launched Operation Smokeshell – a full-scale invasion of parts of these provinces, involving larger forces than those deployed in 1975. In September it captured and destroyed Mavinga in central Cuando Cubango, and set up a forward base for UNITA there (Hanlon, 1986: 162).

From the beginning of 1981 there was a state of permanent war in southern Angola. In Operation Protea over 5 000 SADF troops moved into Cunene province and occupied the main towns for several weeks. They were halted by FAPLA in fierce fighting but the SAAF inflicted severe damage in the attack. The SADF cleared a buffer zone in southern Cunene and enabled UNITA to move in behind it. It became clear, too, that 32 Battalion had been operating inside Angola for the previous two years, its attacks being passed off by both Savimbi and South Africa as UNITA work. UNITA itself engaged in urban terrorism in the main centres, including Luanda, Benguela, Lubango and Namibe (Moçâmedes).

The SADF effectively occupied over 40 000 square kilometres of Cunene province from 1981 to 1984, clearing a space for UNITA which had been on the point of collapse earlier, and attacking economic targets of strategic importance. The SADF consistently claimed its attacks were to neutralise SWAPO insurgency. While some of its actions were directed at the Namibians, most were intended either to cause Angola economic damage or to assist UNITA with the eventual aim of installing it in Luanda. Under the SADF umbrella UNITA was able to spread its operations through central and southern Angola, and was also active in the north.

Operation Askari was launched in December 1983. The SADF sent 10 000 troops into Cunene province, supported by Mirage and Impala fighter-bombers. The invasion was ostensibly a pre-emptive strike at SWAPO bases in Angola. However, it also coincided with a move to push UNITA into the north of Angola, and served to draw FAPLA into battle in the south whilst this was happening.

On the strength of satellite reconnaissance of the SADF build-up for Askari, the USSR issued a warning that if the South Africans pushed beyond a certain point, the rules of engagement would be altered and the SADF would face Cuban forces directly. The South African ambassador to the UN was told that any further escalation would be matched by the Soviet Union, and that the MPLA would be given whatever support it needed to stay in power. It seems as though there were debates in Pretoria over how to proceed. Generals Malan (Minister of Defence) and Van der Westhuizen (Military Intelligence) wanted to go all the way to Luanda. General Geldenhuys, head of the SADF, and P. W. Botha ruled out this option as unachievable (Bridgland, 1986: 424).

In fact the SADF failed even in its modified objectives. The bulk of the SWAPO force was able to withdraw northwards out of range. The SADF could not capture the important provincial military headquarters at Lubango, and could not eliminate the new Soviet-supplied air defence system between Namibe and Cuito Cuanavale because the SAAF lacked the technology to baffle the sophisticated radar-guided missile systems. A final factor was that FAPLA fought back more strongly than anticipated. In a major battle for Cuvelai, 200 km inside Angola, two SADF troop carriers were destroyed with the loss of 21 lives. Back home this event drew unfavourable comment about deaths on distant battlefields and the lack of information with which to evaluate such operations.

From Lusaka to Cuito Cuanavale

On 16 February 1984 Angola and South Africa signed the Lusaka Accord, a limited ceasefire agreement. The Angolan internal economy had been almost totally disrupted by the war: damage amounted to tens of millions of dollars, and military action by the SADF and UNITA had displaced over 600 000 people (Hanlon, 1986: 160). It also suited South Africa to negotiate: the government was being pressed to do so by American officials anxious to produce evidence that 'constructive engagement' was working, and the Accord was in keeping with South Africa's attempts to rehabilitate its image in the West and to project itself as a regional power. There were also clear military reasons for South Africa wanting a stand-off: the SADF had met with unexpected setbacks during Operation Askari and needed time to regroup.

The Lusaka Accord provided for the withdrawal of South African troops from a zone in the south of Angola corresponding roughly with Cunene province. The phased withdrawal was to be complete by the end of March, and a Joint Monitoring Commission was created to oversee the process. The Accord provided that no 'outside forces' (UNITA or SWAPO) were to move into the area vacated by the SADF, but it was vague on the position of those groups already there. The Accord also said nothing about what should happen when the withdrawal was complete. It excluded Cuando Cubango in the south-east of Angola where UNITA's main bases lay, because South Africa refused to discuss its support for UNITA at the ceasefire talks.

The ceasefire agreement was supposed to be part of broader diplomatic efforts to resolve the deadlock on Namibian independence in terms of UN Security Council Resolution 435 of 1978. American and South African insistence on linking a Namibian settlement to a Cuban troop withdrawal from Angola made any prospect of lasting peace a distant one. The South African withdrawal began, and by May 1984 they had abandoned the capital of Cunene province which they had occupied since August 1981. At that point they stopped, and held on to a 40-km buffer strip up to the Namibian border. The Foreign Ministry announced that the withdrawal had been halted 'pending a response from Luanda on key issues'.[6] The South African government felt confident enough in the wake of the Nkomati Accord and the European tours of P. W. and Pik Botha to attempt to win further concessions from an Angolan government weakened by war. The Angolans continued to negotiate with South African and American delegations following the halted SADF withdrawal, so as to keep the diplomatic process alive.[9]

The manoeuvring following the Lusaka Accord indicated that the linkage of a Cuban withdrawal to a Namibian settlement remained a prime tactic of both the South Africans and the Americans, effectively making the ending of South Africa's illegal occupation of Namibia dependent upon an outcome in Angola favourable to their interests. The South Africans added the new element of the inclusion of UNITA in any political solution in Angola. In July the US Senate repealed the Clark Amendment of 1976 which had prevented further US military aid to UNITA, thus paving the way for more direct assistance to the movement. At that point Angola suspended further contacts with the State Department in protest.

In August 1985, FAPLA, re-equipped and with better organisation and an improved airforce, launched a successful offensive against UNITA, and threatened to capture its southern headquarters at Mavinga. The South Africans responded by sending in troops, armoured cars and the SAAF. Savimbi denied any South African involvement in the large-scale encounter which ended in a FAPLA retreat after taking heavy losses in lives and equipment. However, it was an open secret that the SADF had saved UNITA from an extremely threatening situation, and in late September General Malan admitted publicly for the first time that UNITA received aid from South Africa of 'a material, humanitarian and moral nature'. In October P. W. Botha argued that his government could hardly sit still in the face of an escalation in the level of Soviet weaponry being employed in Angola (Bridgland 1985: 445–6). Publicly, UNITA was being held up as an anti-Marxist people's movement standing for Western values.

South Africa's diplomatic posture on withdrawal was badly blown by the Cabinda sabotage incident of 21 May 1985. A commando unit sent in to blow up Gulf Oil installations in the north of Angola was surprised by FAPLA, and two men were killed and one captured. Captain Wynand du Toit, the captured SADF officer, gave details of the unit's instructions and his own involvement in previous operations; he confirmed that the SADF undertook specialised sabotage operations, which were then attributed to UNITA as evidence of its military capabilities.[7] The incident destroyed South Africa's post-Lusaka and Nkomati peace-making image, undermined the credibility of constructive engagement, threw doubt on previous UNITA military claims, and highlighted the vulnerability to sabotage of the Angolan oil industry as the mainstay of FAPLA's war effort.

A new phase began in the southern African conflict around the latter part of 1985. The Namibian question had been stalemated since early in the year, and the Western Contact Group had ended its activities. The FAPLA offensive had crystallised the US debate on Savimbi, and by the end of January 1986 he was in Washington being given promises of further aid and meeting Reagan himself. The way was open for further military escalation.

Throughout 1986 there were repeated offensives, retreats and counter-offensives by UNITA, SADF and FAPLA forces. UNITA, operating through Zaire and Zambia and equipped with new weapons from the US, intensified its attacks in the north. It disrupted diamond production, attacked the Benguela railway line and engaged in large-scale hostage-taking to win publicity. The SADF launched strikes at Xangongo and Cuito Cuanavale, and sabotaged ships and oil storage tanks.

In January 1987 the SADF pointed to a new Angolan air power and warned against any challenge to its own air superiority. This was a recognition of the increasing effectiveness of a change in FAPLA strategy which aimed at countering South African air power and cutting off UNITA's supply lines, rather than attempting to inflict military defeat on UNITA. The new strategy was based on the erection of a major defensive line across the south of Angola, and on matching the SADF in conventional war. Having been re-equipped by the Soviet Union and its allies, FAPLA began to concentrate 90 per cent of its resources in the south against the SADF and only 10 per cent against UNITA (*Africa Confidential*, 28, 11).

In a counterstroke to the Angolan defensive posture in the south, the

US stepped up its aid to UNITA through the disused Kamina air base in Zaire. It became clear that the frontline states had failed to persuade President Mobutu not to allow Zaire to be used for this purpose: he was reported to be actively encouraging the US to take over the Kamina base and it was alleged that Israel was training UNITA in Zaire. UNITA spread its operations in northern Angola, clearly benefiting from the increase of US aid. The Angolans viewed this development seriously enough to resume contact with the US, abandoned in mid-1985.

The Angolan government initiated an intense diplomatic effort in the second half of 1987 aimed at gaining membership of the IMF and Western support for plans to revitalise the economy through aid and foreign investment. Angola's foreign debt stood at US$4 billion in 1986, and its economy had been badly affected by oil-price drops and UNITA attacks on the diamond fields in the north-east (*Africa Contemporary Record*, 24, 8).

The costs of the war in financial terms were running very high. Angolan defence expenditure more than doubled between 1982 and 1985, from US$502 million to $1,147 million. By 1985 some 43,7 per cent of government revenue was spent on defence. The war was using up over half the foreign exchange available for imports (Economist Intelligence Unit, 1987: 34–7). Half the urban population faced acute food shortages, and there were an estimated 690 000 rural dwellers in the cities displaced from the devastated southern region. The flow of food from the countryside to the towns had virtually halted because of a lack of transport, the disruption of communications and the collapse of marketing structures (*Africa Research Bulletin*, 24, 8).

Cuito Cuanavale: The battle for Angola

In September 1987 FAPLA launched a major offensive against UNITA, deploying large numbers of men and much sophisticated war material. The offensive aimed to capture the town of Mavinga in order to complete Angola's southern air-defence system and enable its airforce to attack UNITA supply lines to its headquarters at Jamba. Once again the SADF came to Savimbi's rescue, and effectively repulsed the attack through the deployment of 32 Battalion and combat aircraft.

The battle over Mavinga indicated the limits of SADF power, however. South African casualties were high – perhaps as many as 230 dead, and at least three aircraft lost. The Angolans claimed to have downed at least twelve aircraft (*Africa Confidential*, 28, 23). It was clear that the SADF could not afford to lose a single engagement. UNITA itself sustained heavy losses during the FAPLA offensive, and was no match in conventional warfare.

Having won the battle of Mavinga, the SADF turned towards Cuito Cuanavale where the Angolans have an air base and radar defences as an important link in their southern network. From there they are able to monitor both UNITA and the Namibian border. The SADF besieged Cuito Cuanavale in November, but was unable to project its air power over the town and had to rely instead on long-range artillery. UNITA claimed Cuito Cuanavale had fallen in late January, but FAPLA remained in control and the SADF offensive became bogged down. An SADF analysis in January concluded that a combined UNITA–SADF infantry attack could have taken Cuito Cuanavale, but that losses would have been unacceptably high (around 300 white troops, 2 000 Namibian soldiers and unspecified numbers of UNITA troops) (*Africa Confidential*, 29, 7).

In March 1988 the SADF launched a tank attack on Cuito Cuanavale instead, which nearly overran FAPLA's defence perimeter before being repulsed with losses. While Cuito Cuanavale was under siege the SADF launched UNITA towards the Benguela railway line, where it took Munhango, and then moved east to Cuemba where it met strong FAPLA resistance and was repulsed. The aim was to capture the towns on the line, and to declare an alternative government for UNITA based on territory held in Cuando Cubango and Moxico provinces. Had the gambit succeeded it would have been easier for the South Africans to argue for the necessity of a government of national unity in Angola as part of any peace process (*WIP*, 54: 7). Having failed to take Cuito Cuanavale, and to set up a credible alternative UNITA government in south-eastern Angola, the SADF lost the strategic initiative.

Cuban reinforcements arrived in Angola and moved rapidly southwards with FAPLA and SWAPO forces, coming within kilometres of the Namibian border in June. The combined force of 11 000 troops set up sophisticated radar and anti-aircraft equipment, and began building an airstrip capable of launching MiGs deep into Namibia. The move was designed to halt further SADF attempts to recreate the UNITA government option and to raise substantially the costs for South Africa of further intervention in southern Angola. In addition, SWAPO was reinstated in areas the SADF had spent ten years trying to keep clear of insurgents. Undoubtedly the arrival of Cuban reinforcements, bringing the total force up to around 50 000, and the sweep towards the frontier, concentrated Pretoria's thinking on strategic options for the future. The SADF's loss of air superiority and the growing domestic opposition to the increasing loss of life helped tip the balance in favour of peace talks.

A series of meetings to discuss peace began in London in early May, attended by representatives from Angola, Cuba and South Africa, and presided over by the US Assistant Secretary for African Affairs, Chester Crocker. Further talks took place later in May in Brazzaville, and in Cairo in June, where the teams were upgraded to foreign minister level. The international conjuncture had clearly changed in favour of a settlement of Angolan and Namibian issues. Crocker wanted an outcome favourable to the Reagan administration before it left office in January 1989. The Soviet Union was in the process of reviewing its regional commitments in the context of improved relations with the West. Although not directly represented at the Cairo talks, high-level Soviet representatives were on hand to facilitate discussions. UNITA was excluded from the talks. With the SADF's failure to locate Savimbi in Cuando Cubango and Moxico, it became more difficult to argue for UNITA's inclusion, and Crocker's view, that it unnecessarily complicated the peace agenda, prevailed.

Fighting broke out again immediately after the Cairo talks. In response to long-range bombardment of Angolan and Cuban positions at Techipa and the launching of a probe by the SADF, the joint Angolan and Cuban forces retaliated by bombing SADF positions at Calueque. As a strategic move the episode backfired badly on the SADF. Twelve white recruits were killed, causing further loss of morale and reinforcing the reality of South Africa's loss of domination both in the air and on the ground. Unconfirmed reports that a sizeable SADF force was pinned down inside Angola and facing annihilation or surrender highlighted the considerations compelling South Africa to remain at the negotiating table or face an unacceptable military setback (BBC, 8.8.1988).

The talks continued in New York in July, and at Geneva in early August agreement was reached on a ceasefire, effective from 8 August 1988. At these and subsequent talks, agreement was also reached on the withdrawal of South African and Cuban troops from Angola, and the implementation of Security Council Resolution 435 in Namibia. As of writing, the process of transition to Namibian independence is due to begin on 1 April 1989.

Conclusion

After thirteen years of war, a ceasefire has been called in the conflict between South Africa and Angola. The 1984 limited ceasefire did not hold because in the final instance South Africa felt able to continue to pursue its strategic goals through military means. In 1988 the balance of forces in the conflict shifted to a point where the military and financial costs for South Africa of continued intervention in Angola became unacceptable. The high-technology battles fought in southern Angola in 1987–8, culminating in the SADF attempt to take Cuito Cuanavale, were the largest ever fought on the African continent. South Africa was forced to negotiate in order to extricate itself from a position that was becoming increasingly dangerous to maintain.

The SADF withdrawal will leave behind a legacy of destruction that will take many years to overcome. The impact of the war on Angolan society has been incalculable. To the total loss of life and limb and displacement of population should be added the effects of direct damage to the infrastructure from attack, the disruption of economic activity, and the diversion of scarce manpower and material resources to military use.

However, whilst it appears that a resolution of the Namibian question is in sight, it is premature to anticipate the end of the war in the region. There are signs that the Americans are trying to unlink UNITA's fate from the Namibian settlement by moving its headquarters away from Jamba in the south-east and relocating them in Zaire. Without rear bases in Namibia for training and resupply it would be virtually impossible for UNITA to maintain its war with the MPLA. Relocation of UNITA in Zaire would provide a base from which the economically important diamond fields of the north-east and the coffee-growing areas of the north can be harassed. Furthermore, it would serve to help unlock UNITA from South African patronage which is politically embarrassing for both the movement itself and the US administration. Relocation of UNITA would also open up the alarming prospect for the MPLA of a war on two fronts, should the South Africans decide that further concessions could be won by maintaining a low-level war in the south-east. It is conceivable that a new phase of the struggle could open, once the Namibian issue is settled, in which UNITA based in the north seeks to win a place for itself in a government of national unity sponsored by the US, Zaire and Pretoria.

UNITA's future is uncertain at present. It hinges largely on the support of the Bush administration and its attitude towards the Angolan government, which has never been formally recognised by the United States. UNITA is probably capable of indefinitely maintaining a low-level war, which would serve as an irritant to the MPLA but not significantly threaten its control. As matters are viewed from Luanda, no compromise with UNITA is possible while Savimbi remains at its head. However, national reconciliation is seen as vital to repair the damage of war and begin the interrupted process of incorporating Angola's peripheral societies into the central political structures of the nation.

PART TWO
Militarisation and political power

10 State power in the 1980s: from 'total strategy' to 'counter-revolutionary warfare'

MARK SWILLING & MARK PHILLIPS

The 1980s in South Africa have been about reform, repression and resistance. But what are the connections between these processes? What impact have black resistance and the structural crises of apartheid had on state strategy? What has been the relationship between reform and repression? What role have the military and the security establishment played in formulating and implementing state strategy?

To answer these questions we shall refer to three arenas of political power: the state, political society and civil society.[1] The state comprises the fundamental institutions of public power: the executive, administration, judiciary, police, military and intelligence organs. Political society consists of the formal vehicles of competition for state power: parliaments, local councils, parties, fronts, alliances and coalitions. Civil society is built around the innumerable collectivities in and through which people organise their social lives: clubs, sports associations, ratepayers' organisations, reading groups, civic associations, recreational networks, churches, cultural organisations, street committees, women's groups, and so on.[2] In democratic societies ordinary people can express their political aspirations through the institutions of political society. When, however, authoritarian states restrict democratic processes, then disempowered people tend to turn to social movements built within civil society to express their political demands. This strong foundation may then provide the basis for the expression of demands in political society.

In this chapter it is argued that 'total strategy' – the state's response to the social movements of the mid-1970s – partially restructured the citizenry's access to political society. It promoted new forms of partial inclusion of the unenfranchised into the formal, officially sanctioned institutions of political society. This reformist impulse was formulated primarily by the security establishment. It failed when the consequences of apartheid policies triggered new social movements in civil society in the early 1980s. Articulating their interests chiefly through a national front in political society – the United Democratic Front (UDF) – these social movements rapidly mounted a challenge to state power. In response, the government declared a partial state of emergency in mid-1985. Elements within the state attempted to extend the reform programme beyond its original parameters to dowse the flames of resistance with 'more concessions'. When these measures failed to achieve their objective, a national state of emergency was declared and the security establishment implemented a new and more penetrating repressive–reform strategy. This 'counter-revolutionary warfare' strategy aimed at reconstituting the fundamental bases of civil society *prior* to altering the rules of political society. The new strategy, therefore, starts from the assumption that 'total strategy' failed because it left civil society intact. Learning from experiences in Latin America and south-east Asia, the security establishment is currently attempting to unite the state and political society around a long-term programme whose goal is to restructure social hierarchies 'from below'.

Soweto 1976 and the reorganisation of the state

The manufacturing boom of the 1960s resulted in the rapid urbanisation of blacks in 'white' South Africa and the growth of a large black industrial working class. Apartheid policies, however, dictated that African workers would be denied opportunities for skills acquisition, as well as permanent or adequate housing, services and urban infrastructures. The onset of recession from the early 1970s effectively restricted the creation of new jobs, while the collapse of rural economies exacerbated the process and problems of urbanisation. Deteriorating and increasingly overcrowded urban environments, the poor overall performance of the national economy, a discriminatory educational system and a newly assertive Black Consciousness movement combined to form an explosive mix by the mid-1970s.

The 1976 Soweto uprising, following black strike action in the early 1970s and the defeat of the SADF invasion of Angola in 1975, exposed and heightened these long-term structural contradictions in the economy, cities, rural areas and the political system. In turn these stresses became foci of state strategy and ruling-class reforms over the next decade.[3]

Within the state there were important differences of opinion on how to respond to the deepening post-Soweto crisis. The military, under the leadership of Minister of Defence P. W. Botha, was highly critical of the laissez-faire practices of the Vorster administration. The latter was characterised by empire-building, uncoordinated departmental action, internecine conflicts within the security establishment, and the absence of an overarching strategic plan. The military's solution to these problems was the formulation of 'total strategy', which was presented publicly for the first time in the 1977 Defence White Paper.

'Total strategy' was defined as involving the coordination 'with all the means available to the state' of the military, economic, psychological, political, sociological, diplomatic, cultural and ideological fields of state activity. It was further argued that South Africa was the target of a 'total onslaught', and therefore required a 'total strategy' capable of combining effective security measures with reformist policies aimed at removing the grievances that revolutionaries could exploit. The military were able to win support for these arguments from *verligte* elements in the National Party and key sectors of English and Afrikaner capital. By proposing that defence is more than a military matter, the military were also laying claim to their right to have a say in all public policy-making.

Having outmanoeuvred the *verkrampte* element in the National Party through the Muldergate scandal, P. W. Botha became prime minister in 1978. The new political–business–security alliance was now in a position to implement its programme. Botha immediately embarked upon a three-phase 'rationalisation programme' to reorganise the state (Geldenhuys and Kotze, 1983). The first and most important phase involved the dramatic reorganisation of the pinnacle of state power. Four fundamental changes were made: four 'planning branches' to deal with security, economic policy, and social and constitutional affairs were established in the Prime Minister's Office; a cabinet secretariat was created for the first time to coordinate cabinet meetings and affairs; the twenty *ad hoc* cabinet committees that had existed under the Vorster administration were replaced by four permanent cabinet committees to deal respectively with constitutional, economic, social and security issues; and the fourth of these committees, the State Security Council (SSC), was transformed into the key decision-making body in the state.

The second phase involved cutting down the number of state departments from 39 to 22. In the process, a new mega-department was created in August 1982, namely the Department of Constitutional Development and Planning under Minister Chris Heunis.

The third phase involved the ongoing process of rationalising areas of authority. The most important example of this was the way the old 'Native Affairs' empire was dismantled. By 1985 the Department of Cooperation and Development (as the empire was last known) seemed virtually defunct. The administration of blacks was now spread across various departments, and the Department of Constitutional Development and Planning emerged as the real power-centre involved in managing black affairs. Its responsibilities were no longer defined in purely racial terms, however. By 1985 it controlled a wide range of multiracial structures including local authorities, Regional Services Councils, the Council for the Coordination of Local Government Affairs, Provincial Executive Committees, and Regional Development Advisory Committees. It also concerned itself with policy related to homeland consolidation, group areas and urbanisation.

The most significant and outstanding feature of P. W. Botha's reorganisation effort was the central role given to the security establishment. In a rare public lecture in 1980, General Magnus Malan elaborated his understanding of the 'total national strategy', and pointed to the SSC and its substructures as the key organs involved in executing this strategy (Malan, 1980).

Tightly tied to the Office of the Prime Minister, the security establishment became, in effect, the institutional apparatus through which Botha consolidated his hold on state power. The security establishment at this time consisted of the following (Grundy, 1986: 41–8): the Department of Defence and the South African Defence Force (SADF); the intelligence services; the intellectual community based (mainly) at Afrikaans universities in organisations like the Institute for Strategic Studies at the University of Pretoria and in private concerns such as the Terrorism Research Centre; Armscor; and the South African Police.

Power was centralised in the executive; lines of command were clarified and institutionalised; the Office of the Prime Minister became the centre of organisational gravity; and the security establishment developed into the primary coordinating and binding force within the state.

The raison d'être of the SSC is 'security', defined so as to include economic, political, constitutional, ideological and welfare issues. The SSC embodies, therefore, what Stepan calls the 'new professionalism'. Referring to Latin America, but with direct relevance to South Africa, Stepan defines this military credo as follows:

Instead of increasing functional specialisation, the military began to train their officers to acquire expertise in internal security matters that were defined as embracing all aspects of social, economic and political life. Instead of the gap between the military and political spheres widening, the new professionalism led to a belief that there was a fundamental interrelationship between the two spheres, with the military playing a key role in interpreting and dealing with domestic political problems owing to its greater technical and professional skills in handling internal security issues. (Stepan, 1988: 137)

To pull a state together into an efficient machine capable of synchronised action is a complex and difficult task. But as in many Latin American countries, the security establishment in South Africa comes closer than any other institution in the state to having the skill and capability to do this because of its internally tight hierarchy of command and its substantial resources that are mobile and deployable. In short, what has taken place is a militarisation of the state and politicisation of the military.

To argue that the security establishment became dominant in the state does not mean that it or any one of its component parts (such as the military) became the government. In reality, what emerged was a dual state that rested on a hybrid of party government based on the parliamentary process, and a militarised state rooted in the security establishment. Furthermore, the politicised security establishment operated on the assumption that although it had the right to formulate state strategy and control 'order functions', reformist and welfare functions were required, by definition, to be carried out by 'the civilians'. Hence the critical and central importance given to the Department of Constitutional Development and Planning. Minister Heunis was presented, in the words of one official, with 'a mandate to carry out reform'. This explicit secondment of responsibility for reform was consistent with the military's view of 'civil–military relations'. According to a restricted document: 'There is always a temptation to let the military direct the entire process but this must be resisted by all means. Giving the soldier authority over the civilian would contradict the major characteristics of this type of war, i.e. that it is a political war.' (Fraser, n.d.: 21)

In short, Botha built around himself a tripartite partnership between the government, the security establishment and the Department of Constitutional Development and Planning. It was this unique partnership of power that formulated, managed and attempted to implement 'total strategy'. While the government kept alive the 'sham of democracy', the security establishment took overall control of strategy and decision-making in the state, and the Department of Constitutional Development and Planning operationalised the reform side of the 'total strategy' formula.

Total strategy re-making political society

Two conceptual frameworks underpinned 'total strategy' thinking: British and French counter-insurgency theory and conservative American political science. The basic strategic objective was to modify the access points to officially sanctioned institutions of political society so that certain sectors of the oppressed could compete to a limited extent for economic resources and public power. Two theorists in particular were influential, Harvard Professor Sam Huntington and French military strategist André Beaufre.

On the basis of the conceptual approach provided by Huntington and Beaufre, and a critique of the problems of the Vorster administration, 'total strategy' planners identified four areas of 'reform'. These were the legalisation of black trade unions according to the recommendations of the Wiehahn Commission; the recognition of the permanence of urban blacks in line with the recommendations of the Riekert Commission; the formulation of a new constitution that brought Indians and coloureds into parliament as junior partners; and the introduction of a new regional development policy to coordinate industrial development planning on the basis of de-politicised regional boundaries rather than racially determined constitutional divisions.

These reforms were premised on specific perceptions of South Africa's social reality. The Riekert Commission assumed, for instance, that bantustans could be retained but that, in response to the unrest of 1976–7, 'urban blacks' must be recognised as permanent members of the cities and towns. Once 'urban rights' had been conceded by the Riekert Commission, then a range of other complementary rights necessarily followed: rights to form trade unions, to purchase property, to sell labour on a 'free urban labour market' without a contract, and to trade. The municipal franchise was seen as the ultimate embodiment of the new 'urban identity'. Blacks were given, for the first time ever, fully autonomous municipal institutions – the black local authorities – with extensive urban powers (such as the allocation of housing and trading sites).

However, the new urban policy created several critical problems that soon contributed to black protest. Firstly, because the policy aimed to create a privileged elite of 'urban insiders' divorced from the impoverished rural masses, it required an intensification of influx control – hence the proposed Orderly Movement and Settlement of Black Persons Bill of 1982 (Hindson, 1987). Secondly, the black local authorities, as a form of local political self-government, were designed to be financially self-sufficient but were excluded by the Group Areas Act from access to rateable commercial and industrial property. Thirdly, because the access of Africans to higher forms of political representation was limited to the bantustans, the overall adequacy and legitimacy of state constitutional reform were severely called into question.

The constitutional reforms were premised on the consociational theory that 'group identities' in multicultural societies must be protected but that structures for 'co-determination' and 'joint decision-making' must be created. The result was a new 'consociational contract' for whites, coloureds and Indians in the form of the tricameral parliament.

As far as the majority African population was concerned, the new regional development policy that was elaborated rested on the principle of 'economic interdependence and political independence', or what the Buthelezi Commission called the 'soft-borders approach'. Bantustans would proceed to independence and then enter into an inter-state agreement to form a 'confederation of southern African states'.

In summary, 'total strategy' may have left many fundamentals of apartheid intact (such as bantustans, influx control and the constitutional exclusion of Africans from central government), but it did introduce significant modifications to some basic institutions of political society. These institutions regulated access to three social arenas: the city, the factory and government. In reality, however, what the white minority was prepared to concede in the early 1980s fell far short of what the black majority was prepared to accept.

In the end 'total strategy' failed because its idealistic intentions were thwarted by a sustained period of black resistance. This resistance exacerbated and brought to the fore the key structural contradictions which the 'total strategy' reforms had failed to address.

Social movements and the rise of civil society

The centralisation of state power under the auspices of the security establishment and the subsequent top-down reorganisation of political society could not be directly countered by the black majority. The oppressed and exploited communities and classes faced sophisticated state power, an increasingly monopolised capitalism and a mass communications system entirely controlled by the state or monopoly capital. Except for the trade unions, the new access points to formal political institutions created by 'reform' offered meagre quantities of power.

Reform was consequently resisted by social movements created and built within the fabric of civil society. Disempowered and alienated, ordinary people organised what was closest to them and hence where they were strongest – the workplace, the community, the sports club, the church, the school, the street and the home. Embedded in generations of culture and informal networks, these institutions became the well-springs of social movements that expressed the aspirations, interests and values of the oppressed groups and classes. Combining rich idealism and deep rage with long traditions of resistance, these reactive challenges from below blew the fuses of 'total strategy'. In one sense the social movements succeeded in making reform unworkable. They won hegemony in black civil society: they 'won the hearts and minds of the people'. They also succeeded in thrusting their challenge into the terrain of political society, thus challenging the state's desire to exclude them from contesting political power.

The labour movement helped undo the 'rural–urban' divide. It organised migrant workers and urban proletarians into single industrial trade-union organisations committed to joint wage demands, thereby undercutting the state's intention to create two entirely separate labour markets – one urban and privileged and the other rural and cheap (Webster, 1988).

Another crucial aspect of the reform package – the local government system which was supposed to bind the new urban system together – was soon in ruins. Because the state insisted that community councils should raise their own finance for development, councillors were forced to increase rent and service charges. The increases triggered a nation-wide popular rebellion that began in the Vaal townships in September 1984 and spread across the country. By mid-1985 most black local authorities had collapsed because of mass resignations or because councillors had been killed by residents. The root cause of the rebellion was the fact that the local franchise was not tied to a programme of granting full political rights to blacks. This facilitated the emergence

through local community organisations of national political organisations – like the United Democratic Front – committed to the total
dismantling of apartheid and the creation of a non-racial democracy.
The new labour dispensation also failed to achieve its objectives.
When the unions challenged the legislation because migrants were
excluded from the right to join unions, the state backed down and
extended the definition of 'employee' to include migrant workers. The
'consociational contract' likewise foundered on the rocks of popular
resistance expressed through the boycott of the tricameral parliamentary
elections in 1984. The confederal schema also began to come apart at
the seams. The steady political and fiscal decline of 'model' bantustans
like Ciskei, Transkei and Bophuthatswana made it abundantly clear
that separate development and the grand vision of a confederation of
states was turning into a nightmare.

   In short, by aiming to widen the access points to political society,
'total strategy' inadvertently created spaces for initiating and deepening
popular mobilisation and organisation. Through the granting of
industrial rights, unions were spawned that challenged relations in the
factories, cities and political society. Opening up the urban political
system generated urban movements that politicised civil society and
destroyed the cornerstones of the new urban policy as enunciated by
the Riekert Commission. And constitutional reform provided the focus
for national organisation and resistance on a scale not seen since the
1950s. All these manifestations of resistance and opposition short-
circuited key state strategies and prepared the way for new ones.
Intense struggles were fought within the state during 1985–6 over what
was to replace the failed policies of 'total strategy'.

Divisions within the state and the struggle to regain control
   Proceeding from the assumption that further concessions would
satisfy black demands and legitimise state strategies, political reformers
in the state responded to black resistance by extending the reform
programme. There were five critical moments in the extension of this
programme. In November 1984, Minister Heunis announced that black
local authorities were to be incorporated into the proposed Regional
Services Councils. In May 1985 National Party MP Stoffel van der
Merwe published a pamphlet entitled . . . *And What About the Blacks?*,
which argued that the homelands policy was a failure. In September
1985, P. W. Botha announced that citizenship would be restored to all
Africans residing permanently in 'white' South Africa. Moreover, Botha
conceded that the tricameral parliament was not the final solution, but
merely one step in an 'evolutionary process'. And in September 1985
the President's Council published its report on urbanisation; from this
issued the December 1985 statement by Minister Heunis that blacks
would be given freehold property rights, and the Abolition of Influx

Control Act of 1986.

All these extensions of the reform programme were *ad hoc* responses to the deepening crisis and to pressure from political movements, business organisations, the international community and trade unions. What is important about these shifts is that they unintentionally undid existing policy positions without being coupled to a coherent set of alternatives.[4] The security establishment believed that the confusion caused by these reactive proposals of the reformers was contributing to rising levels of unrest, and that state policy was therefore urgently in need of rationalisation within a new strategic matrix. Convinced that it was directly threatened with imminent revolution, the state turned to the 'counter-revolutionary warfare' strategies of the military to resolve the general crisis of legitimacy and apartheid rule.

Up until April–May 1986, the reform initiative within the state lay in the hands of an influential group located largely in Minister Heunis's Department of Constitutional Development and Planning (but also to some extent in the Departments of Manpower, Finance and Foreign Affairs and in the National Party itself). However, as the so-called 'revolutionary climate' intensified, the top echelons of the state came to rely increasingly on security strategists for advice, policy proposals and direct repressive power. Popular protest, therefore, produced two responses within the state. There were the political reformers who believed it was possible to extend the reform programme and widen the access points to political society, and there were the securocrats straining to implement a counter-revolutionary programme.

In April–May 1986 divisions within the state emerged at a public level. Whereas P. W. Botha and the security establishment were at this time referring to 'city-states' and independence for bantustans, and defending the detention of political leaders, Heunis and the political reformers were extending reforms and supporting negotiations between senior government officials and UDF leaders around the country.

The collapse of the Eminent Persons Group (EPG) initiative after the SADF bombing of the capitals of the frontline states in May marked a decisive break between the political reformers and hard-line securocrats. Significantly, whereas Botha had previously stated that the 'suspension' of violence by the ANC was a sufficient precondition for negotiations, he subsequently argued that the 'renunciation' of violence was necessary. When the EPG indicated the ANC would accept the former, Botha and the military were struck with the sudden realisation that they had to make a choice: release Nelson Mandela and negotiate a transfer of power from a position of weakness; or re-establish control by crushing resistance in civil society, outlawing it in political society, creating new social relations and promoting 'new' black leaders. In choosing the latter option, the state put in train a counter-revolutionary strategy which involved the imposition of the national state of emergency and the full-scale activation of the National Security Management System (NSMS) at local and regional level. The security police and the military assured the State Security Council that township protest, 'people's power' and popular support for the ANC could be eliminated by applying a sufficient degree of force in a relatively short space of time. This would restore the state's 'position of strength' and refute the claim that 'the state had lost the initiative to the people'.

The decision to scuttle the EPG and regain the initiative was taken largely by an inner power elite of 'Cold War warriors' that surrounded P. W. Botha. They did not share Police Commissioner Johan Coetzee's 'soft repression' strategies that emphasised limited coercion and espionage to control low-intensity conflict. Instead, this group, which included Major-General Charles Lloyd (SSC secretary), Major-General J. van der Merwe (head of the Security Branch of the SAP) and Major-General Bert Wandrag (head of counter-insurgency in the SAP), redefined the problem. Borrowing heavily from 'counter-revolutionary warfare' theory as developed and applied in Malaysia, Algeria and South America, they argued: 'A governing power can defeat any revolutionary movement if it adapts the revolutionary strategy and principles and applies them in reverse. [The purpose is] to defeat the revolutionaries with their own weapons on their own battlefield.' (*The art of counter-revolutionary warfare,* unsourced document circulated in government circles)

By mid-1986 their position had won out against the political reformists in the Department of Constitutional Development and Planning, and the 'soft war' strategists like Coetzee. According to a general in the State Security Council, 'The impetus is no longer just from the military. It's now accepted by the civilians. It took a bit of education. But they learned very quickly after 1984.' (Personal interview)

This decision to fight the battle directly through state institutions required the 'unified effort' of soldiers, policemen, politicians and bureaucrats. Securocrats are fond of quoting General Templer, one-time governor of colonial Malaysia: 'Any idea that the business of normal government and the business of the Emergency are two separate entities should be killed for good and all. The two activities are completely and utterly inter-related.' (*The art of counter-revolutionary warfare:* 23) What emerged was a highly centralised bureaucratic-cum-military structure with the power and ability to coordinate the implementation of both security and political policies. This was not a coup d'état. Political society and the dual state remained largely intact even though the NSMS took direct responsibility for the formulation and implementation of all strategies 'with the common objective of winning the war'. (*The art of counter-revolutionary warfare:* 69)

Presiding over this dual state is the State President's Office.

Representing in both real and symbolic terms the twinning of political government and coercive rule under a single command, the President's Office directly controls the Ministries of Information and Privatisation, the National Intelligence Service, the NSMS through the State Security Council, the National Priorities Committee, parliament and the National Party.

WHAM: re-making civil society in the state's image

The counter-revolutionary theory that informed state strategy is based on the desire to 'win hearts and minds' – the so-called WHAM programme. The fundamental difference between 'total strategy' and the WHAM programme is that the latter is no longer concerned primarily with restructuring the access points to political society. Instead, the emphasis falls on recasting the foundations of civil society so that political access points can at some future date be restructured in a way that does not threaten the system as a whole. Realising that it was resistance from below that limited the effectiveness of 'total strategy', the state has now turned to strategies aimed at radically reshaping the moral, cultural, religious, political and material underpinnings of civil society in the black townships. This shift from grand visions of reform from above to building up new foundations from below is the single most significant feature of current strategic thinking in the state. Although the objective of dividing, neutralising and containing black opposition still stands, the means to achieving it have changed.

The idealism of Beaufre has been replaced by the Machiavellian materialism of Colonel John J. McCuen, a US army officer whose work, *The art of counter-revolutionary war*, has been widely read in security circles. McCuen identifies four stages of revolutionary warfare: the organisational, terrorist, guerilla and mobile warfare stages. The task of the state is to 'determine which phase you are in – then use the direction of that phase and turn it back on itself' (Major-General G. Meiring, *Southern Africa Record*, 1985). In South Africa this has involved the elaboration of a series of counter-guerilla, counter-terror, and counter-organisational tactics. McCuen gives very precise and specific instructions on how different techniques and tactics should be implemented. For example, he refers to the need for 'special constables', 'co-option of leaders', 'formation of counter-guerilla gangs', 'civil education', and 'the counter-organisation of classes, clubs, social, career, sport, education, medical, religious and military activities'. He also speaks of the need to build 'roads, dams, irrigation schemes, schools, churches, etc.'

Police COIN chief Major-General A. Wandrag (1985) summed up the objective of current strategies when he said: 'Drastic action must be taken to eliminate the underlying social and economic factors which have caused unhappiness in the population. The only way to render the enemy powerless is to nip revolution in the bud by ensuring there is no fertile soil in which the seeds of revolution can germinate.' This view was echoed by a high-ranking State Security Council official: 'We have studied counter-revolutionary tactics in Malaysia, Chile, El Salvador. We're using the same hearts-and-minds techniques here. First we neutralise the enemy, then we win over the people so they will reject the ANC.'

In a recent private speech (transcribed by a member of the audience), Major-General Lloyd, secretary of the State Security Council, observed that the counter-revolutionary strategy involved three things: the countering of planned subversion on all fronts; the 'elimination of the revolutionaries'; and the 'reform of the environment'. The underlying logic, according to Professor Willie Breytenbach of Stellenbosch University, is that 'where once there could be no security without reform, now there can be no reform without security' (1987).

The NSMS provides the structure of unified command that co-ordinates the implementation of this strategy. Although set up as part of the original 'total strategy' programme, prior to 1985–6 the officials in the NSMS 'were just keeping the seats warm' (interview with ex-official from Dept of Constitutional Development). When the moment came to activate the system during the state of emergency, to quote an ex-security policeman, 'all we needed to do was hit the switch' (*Newsweek*, 20 June 1986).

The lifeblood of the NSMS is the network of more than 500 national, regional, district and local Joint Management Centres (JMCs). These bring together military, police and civilian officials usually under the chairmanship of the ranking military officer. It is claimed by some officials that access to the State President's Office can be obtained from any level in the JMC within hours. The JMC interfaces with the public through Community Liaison Forums, and with business through the Joint Liaison Forums and Defence Manpower Liaison Committees (Demalcoms).

The concrete counter-revolutionary strategies pursued by the state since 1986 illustrate the dual security and welfare objectives. The repressive or 'hard war' measures include the following: press restrictions, mass detentions, vigilante and death squad activities, forced removals, banning or restricting organisations and activists, rent boycott evictions, and security force harassment.

In short, the JMCs are using their power to rip communities apart, remove their leaders and put together the pieces in the state's image. These repressive measures are complemented by the 'reformist' dimension of state strategy. Some of these reforms were articulated by the political reformists before 1986, but they have since been appropriated and recast by the 'counter-revolutionary warfare' strategists. Referred to by security planners as 'soft war' or 'welfare' measures, they include:

(1) *infrastructural upgrading.* Some 34 'oilspots' or key target areas have been identified for special attention and a further 200 townships have been earmarked for upgrading projects. The Directorate of Urbanisation in the Department of Constitutional Development and Planning hopes to acquire R16 billion from the proceeds of privatisation to spend on socio-economic upgrading. This will be used to complement private-sector initiatives from groups such as the South African Housing Trust and the Urban Foundation.

(2) *housing development.* By way of special grants through the South African Housing Trust and National Housing Commission, the state, in conjunction with the private sector, is embarking on the most extensive housing-construction programme since the 1950s.

(3) *local government reform.* Some corrupt local authorities have been dismissed, and Regional Services Councils have been introduced because townships are no longer expected to pay for themselves.

(4) *scrapping of influx control.* Millions of people who were previously excluded from the right to reside in urban areas may now do so on condition they have access to employment and 'approved accommodation'.

(5) *legitimation of state structures.* This involves massive expenditure on propaganda through radio, TV and pamphlets to persuade people to pay rent, service charges and bus fares. In addition, this propaganda boosts the image of the security forces. Black 'moderates' – front-men for 'counter-organisations' like United Christian Reconciliation Party, Ama-Afrika, and Operation Advance and Upgrade – receive extensive TV and radio coverage and have been given resources to form new political parties. Complementing these strategies is a massive propaganda campaign designed to criminalise popular organisations.

(6) *populist cooption in squatter camps.* Emulating their counterparts in Latin America, JMC officials have realised that squatter camps provide invaluable opportunities for cooption. By granting local populist 'warlords', like Johnson Ngxobongwana in Crossroads, control over the allocation of resources (including employment), and by providing basic urban services, it is possible to buy cooperation.

(7) *the 'National Council'.* To carry through to higher levels of government the inclusion of Africans that has already taken place at RSC level, a National Council is being formed. Its brief is to hammer out a post-tricameral constitution within the framework of what Van Zyl Slabbert has called a 'multiracial autocracy'.

(8) *'Bothanomics'.* This may mean a repressive version of inward industrialisation based on wage freezes, de-regulation, uncontrolled regional–metropolitan labour markets and reckless privatisation.

In short, the state is making important concessions but on its own terms and while popular leaders are in jail. The concessions are responses to bitter struggle: they include the provision of housing and better services, financial support for local government, and some form of political representation at central government level. The form of representation, however, falls short of majoritarian democracy. When asked by *Leadership SA* whether the state of emergency was 'an attempt to crush the notion that black government is a possibility', Stoffel van der Merwe's answer was an unambiguous 'yes' (April 1988).

The counter-revolutionary strategy assumes that resistance is a product of grievances exploited by revolutionaries. It follows that if the revolutionaries are annihilated, the worst grievances addressed, and communities re-organised under trustworthy leaders supported by the security forces, then the ultimate political questions will disappear. As one general put it, 'what is more important to the masses in the natural situation without revolutionary instigation is the economic and the social . . . and the government is working towards giving them *in these fields* a better life' (interview with SSC member).

The state's public instrument of counter-organisation is a class of accommodating black leaders who, it is hoped, will be prepared to support actively the government in return for increased privilege and power. The long-term objective is 'to get a sufficient number of prominent leaders to participate so that eventually those who still lust after revolution will become as irrelevant in South Africa as they are in the US or Britain' (Stoffel van der Merwe, *Leadership SA*, April 1988).

Conclusion

By 1986 the state had realised that the attention given to 'political society' by the reform-oriented policies of the early 1980s was not a sufficiently 'total' strategy to deal with the tensions and contradictions of apartheid. The slogan of the early 1980s – 'there can be no security without reform' – has been turned on its head. Under the current state of emergency the approach adopted is that there can be 'no reform without security'. Beyond this, though, and equally important, has been the redefining of the very concept of reform. No longer does it refer primarily to the search for a political compromise on the issue of black political rights. Reform has been transformed from a top-down political process into a bottom-up restructuring programme of intervention into and reconstitution of the very fabric of 'civil society'. 'Taking out' revolutionaries and 'counter-organising' communities so that they become bulwarks against popular pressure form the essence of the strategy.

The likelihood of this strategy succeeding is the subject of extensive debate in all circles. Several considerations stand out that suggest it will not succeed in transforming black compliance into real consent.

Firstly, the current strategy denies the absolute necessity of resolving the 'national question' – the exclusion of blacks, and Africans in particular, from political power. Counter-revolutionary strategies implemented elsewhere in the world may have defeated communist insurgency on occasion but have never succeeded in preventing decolonisation.

Secondly, the government and state have no unifying political framework to rival either liberal democracy or the national democratic programme of the main liberation movement.

Thirdly, unlike counter-revolutionary regimes in South and Central America, the state cannot rely on international support.

Fourthly, there is no evidence that the economy will achieve the 5–7 per cent growth rate that Professor Jan Lombard argued (1988) is required to make the welfare component of the strategy work. There is in fact increasing evidence that sanctions and political conflict have forced the economy into a trap of long-term low growth.

Fifthly, the success of the two-day stayaway during the May 1987 white elections and the three-day stayaway in June 1988 suggests that black militancy and support for popular organisations remain high despite repressive state actions. Now that organisations are increasingly being forced underground, they may well become more effective and powerful in the long run.

Moreover, a strategy which criminalises peaceful opposition destroys the middle ground it so desperately requires so as to make constitutional reform work. Hence the importance of black moderate rejection of the National Council and the adoption of the Freedom Charter by the Cape Teachers' Professional Association.

Lastly, there is a real possibility of a 'white Thermidor' if the Conservative Party wins a general election. This highlights the contradictions faced by a state trying to reform a multiracial society while remaining rooted in a white power-base.

In the final analysis what the state has achieved is a defeat averted, not a victory won.

11 South Africa's National Management System

JAMES SELFE

It is often claimed in political analyses of South Africa, particularly by commentators far removed from its shores, that the 'apartheid regime' is on the point of imminent collapse. Despite the fact that these five-minutes-to-midnight prophets have been confidently predicting such a cataclysm since Sharpeville, the regime continues to survive and at times even prosper.

The apocalyptic analyses have been based on seemingly compelling factors, such as the regime's lack of legitimacy, its unpopular policies, the numerical preponderance of its subject people, the worsening international climate, and so on. These are factors which in less resilient polities would have tended to indicate imminent collapse. However, such commentaries have tended to underestimate the impressive and sophisticated bureaucratic structures developed since P. W. Botha became head of government. The express purpose of these structures is to retain white minority control, despite its manifest weaknesses. This chapter chronicles the growth of these structures, outlines their functions and ramifications, and assesses their effectiveness and durability for the future.

The growth of the National Management System

The bureaucratic structures did not originate merely at Mr Botha's whim. They developed as a carefully and deliberately conceived counter-revolutionary strategy. In the 1960s and early 1970s, prior to Botha's premiership, it was assumed that the simple expedient of divide and rule plus a safe buffer of politically compliant neighbouring states would satisfy the twin goals of keeping guerillas at a distance without, and containing any popular resistance within.

Both these confident assumptions were shattered during the 1970s: the durability of the buffer states by the coup d'état in Portugal in 1974 and the subsequent independence of Angola and Mozambique, and the quiescence of the black population by the 1976 Soweto uprising. As these events unfolded, it became increasingly clear to the more perceptive members of the ruling elite that the old formulae for securing white minority rule were no longer viable. A new, more durable and sophisticated form of domination was required to guarantee white rule in the fundamentally altered regional and domestic circumstances.

Significantly, most of the proponents of such a changed system were drawn – at least initially – from the officer cadres of the armed forces. Studies of revolutionary wars, undertaken in the course of their professional training, had persuaded many of them that South Africa was experiencing the first stages of a classic revolutionary war. In order to win this war, political adaptations would have to be made. They argued, in the now familiar adage, that a successful counter-revolutionary war was only 20 per cent military, and 80 per cent political, economic, social and psychological.

These officers were fortunate to have as their political head a man who was receptive to this type of thinking. From the early 1970s onwards, and in ever more polished form, Minister of Defence P. W. Botha began to propagate this concept in his speeches and writings, particularly in the biennial Defence White Papers.

According to this view, South Africa faced a 'total onslaught' from revolutionary forces that was highly integrated and multi-faceted in nature; thus an equally comprehensive and multi-faceted state response had to be devised and put into operation. The response was named 'total (national) strategy'.

Botha's idea of 'total strategy' had, and still has, at least four components. The first was a reform package aimed at resolving some of the structural contradictions of apartheid which had emerged in the mid-1970s, and at defusing black resistance which had emerged as a result. The second was using the concept of 'reform' to involve sectors in the South African society previously hostile or lukewarm to the NP government (such as business and sections of the press) in combating the 'total onslaught'. The third was the development of a much more sophisticated repressive strategy than grand apartheid had been, coopting a class of 'insiders' and using it as a buffer against the frustrations of the vast mass of 'outsiders'. The last was the reorganisation and rationalisation of the state to ensure a more coordinated and state-wide approach to formulating strategy.

The problem was that Botha, as Minister of Defence, was not in a position to insist on the operationalisation of the total strategy, and he could for some time do little more than plan and lobby for the creation of structures that would give practical expression to his views. Once having been elected prime minister he moved swiftly, and the National Security Management System was inaugurated on 16 August 1979.

The structure of the National (Security) Management System

The NMS can best be described as a militarised bureaucracy, which operates in tandem with the regular civil service to promote the coordination of state security action. It has been continually refined since its inception, and currently comprises five elements:

1. The Cabinet is in formal command and control of the system, but appears to have extensively delegated responsibility for the management of security-related issues to one of its sub-committees, the State Security Council (SSC). There is an ongoing debate as to whether the Cabinet or the State Security Council actually 'runs' the country. Because of the SSC's political prestige accorded by its chairman (the State President) and members, the sophisticated and sensitive nature of its deliberations, and the sheer volume of work of the Cabinet, it is unlikely that the Cabinet ever does more than rubber-stamp SSC recommendations. However, recommendations which have overtly domestic political implications for the white electorate have been known to be rejected by the Cabinet.

2. The State Security Council is one of four permanent Cabinet sub-committees, created by rationalising the 19 or so *ad hoc* committees which existed under the Vorster administration. The SSC differs from other Cabinet committees in at least three significant respects: it is the only committee whose membership and functions are laid down in statute, it is chaired by the State President, and it is served by a permanent secretariat. These features tend to suggest that the SSC occupies a more prestigious position than the other committees.

Apart from the President, the other members of the SSC are the senior ministers of the Republic, the Ministers of Defence, Law and Order, Justice and Foreign Affairs, and the civil service heads of these departments, and the National Intelligence Service (NIS). The statute that set up the SSC empowers the Council to coopt other members on a permanent or *ad hoc* basis. In 1984, P. W. Botha stated that he had coopted the Ministers of Constitutional Development and Planning, Cooperation and Development, and Finance on a permanent basis. Other ministers are evidently permitted to attend meetings of the SSC if they wish to raise matters of significance.

The SSC meets approximately once a fortnight to consider suggestions as to how the 'revolutionary onslaught' can most effectively be counteracted by coordinated state activity. The recommendations of the SSC are then submitted for approval to the full Cabinet, which usually meets the next day.

The SSC is the body that *de facto* and in terms of statute shapes total strategy. However, it rarely determines the details of such strategy because of the volume of work of its members. The details are determined by the secretariat and the Interdepartmental Committees (IDCs), whose role and functions are considered below.

3. The Working Committee of the SSC forms the next level in the apparatus, consisting of all the official (i.e. civil service) members of the SSC, under chairmanship of the SSC secretary. It acts as a type of management committee for the SSC, determining its agendas, and acting as a link between the SSC and the Secretariat.

4. The next level, the Secretariat, constitutes an extremely important and significant element in the system. Consisting of approximately 80 officials on secondment from other departments of state, the Secretariat is divided into four branches, dealing respectively with administration, strategic communication, the coordinated interpretation of intelligence, and the formulation of strategic plans. The Secretariat is staffed overwhelmingly by members of the NIS, but has representatives from the Defence Force, the police, the prisons service and the Departments of Foreign Affairs, Justice, and Constitutional Development. In 1984, nearly 90 per cent of the Secretariat officials were drawn from the security establishment (that is, members of the SADF, SAP, NIS and prisons service).

From a political perspective, the activities of the administration branch are of little relevance, but the roles of the other three branches are extremely significant. The National Intelligence Interpretation Branch consists of the four line departments concerned with intelligence gathering – the Department of Foreign Affairs, the Military Intelligence section of the SADF, the Security Branch of the police and the NIS. It ensures that there is coordination between these departments, and brings an interdisciplinary approach to intelligence evaluation. It has effectively ended the empire-building that was a feature of this state function while General Van den Bergh, the former head of the Bureau for State Security, was in charge under the Vorster administration.

The Strategic Communications Branch ensures that the activities of the NMS are portrayed in the best possible light, and monitors what is perceived to be 'revolutionary disinformation'. It has strong institutional links with the public relations sections of the security forces, as well as (in the recent past) the Department of Home Affairs in its action against the alternative media.

It is the Strategy Branch which is ultimately responsible for the construction of total strategies to counteract manifestations of the 'total onslaught'. This branch does not, however, determine strategies unilaterally – total strategies are by definition intended to coordinate the activities of more than one government department. Before making recommendations up the line, the Secretariat will frequently request an Interdepartmental Committee (IDC) to consider whether the resources or expertise of more than one government department should be brought to bear in a coordinated fashion against the perceived threat.

5. There are 13 Interdepartmental Committees, covering matters which are directly or indirectly the concern of more than one government department. Should a national security problem require the coordinated activity of a number of departments, the problem will be referred to one or more of the IDCs for consideration and for recommendations, which are then fed back through the Strategy Branch

to the SSC.

6. These five elements all operate on central government level, effectively from Pretoria. But the perceived 'revolutionary onslaught' needs also to be counteracted on a local and regional level. For this reason, the NMS has regional and local coordination committees, known as Joint Management Centres (JMCs). Their task is to oversee the implementation of total strategies at the local level, as well as to supply intelligence on local conditions and grievances for communication up the line.

There are eleven JMCs countrywide, at present corresponding to the ten SADF command boundaries plus Walvis Bay. The JMCs are chaired by a senior civil servant, usually a senior officer in the SADF or SAP, and consist of some 60 regional representatives of all the government institutions in the particular area.

The JMCs are divided into committees which correspond to the branches at Secretariat level. A Joint Intelligence Committee evaluates intelligence gathered on a local level either to take appropriate local action or for communication up the line or both. A Communication Committee performs local public relations for the JMC. Finally, a Constitutional, Social and Economic Committee coordinates the provision of state welfare and upgrading functions at the local level.

The JMCs meet in full plenary session relatively rarely; most of the work is done by the committees, and the essential day-to-day management is the responsibility of an executive consisting of the chairmen of the committees and the chairman of the JMC itself.

Beneath the JMC are some 60 sub-JMCs and approximately 350 mini-JMCs. They, too, are divided into the same committees, although the smaller the JMC, the less formal their modus operandi and more flexible their membership tend to be: only on sub-JMC and mini-JMC level may non-official members be invited to participate.

In 1986, a further element, whose formal status is still unclear, was added to the system. This is the National Joint Management Centre, operating on central government level under the chairmanship of the Deputy Minister of Law and Order. This body apparently coordinates the activities of the JMCs countrywide, and provides a ready nexus between the largely bureaucratic staffs of the local JMCs and the politicians entrusted with security matters.

The workings of the system

Within the formal structure, the NMS can construct and give effect to externally or internally directed total strategies. Moreover, it provides a grassroots organisation, allowing for an assessment of the implementation of total strategies internally, as well as for the gathering of local intelligence.

Typically, a total strategy will originate as a result of intelligence evaluated by the National Intelligence Interpretation Branch. An analysis of the threat or perceived threat will be fed either directly to the SSC or to the Strategy Branch for comment prior to submission to the SSC. Should the SSC decide that action is required, the Strategy Branch will be required to evolve an appropriate counteractive strategy. In doing so, it may refer the matter to one or more appropriate IDC for suggestions. Once a strategy or mix of strategies has been determined, the Strategy Branch will refer the matter to the SSC and Cabinet for approval or adaptation. Once approval has been given, the implementation will be coordinated by the JMCs – if internal – or by line departments, such as the Department of Foreign Affairs or the SADF, if external.

The JMCs are in turn able to report back on the effectiveness of the strategy, and their Joint Intelligence Committees are able to inform the National Intelligence Interpretation Branch whether particular occurrences are merely local grievances, requiring local action, or whether these form part of a wider mosaic requiring a total, country-wide, counteractive strategy.

Viewed cynically, the overall task of the NMS is to recreate the conditions which pertained prior to the Portuguese coup in 1974: a buffer of politically compliant states to the north, and a quiescent internal population. The former is achieved by a mixture of diplomatic, economic and military action; in short, the carrot-and-stick approach implicit in the policy of destabilisation. In pursuing the second objective, the NMS is charged with the responsibility of containing and, if possible, eradicating altogether the 'revolutionary onslaught'. As was noted at the outset, the security planners accept that pure security action will not achieve anything more than temporary stability. More durable solutions require political, economic and social reforms and adaptations.

Accordingly, the NMS operates in a welfare mode as well as a security mode, and is able to convert from one to the other with ease. Because of this flexibility, the NMS can adapt itself to changed circumstances quickly and effortlessly.

The planners in the NMS appear to accept (somewhat uncritically) the belief that it is the goal of the 'revolutionary organisations' to make the country 'ungovernable'. In dealing with this threat, the NMS defines two stages of counteraction. The NMS's task in situations of unrest, similar to that experienced during 1985–6, is, firstly and urgently, to restore stability. Stability means the ability of local authorities to deliver essential services to communities, if necessary under escort. In restoring stability, the NMS is acting primarily in the security mode, which is characterised by police activity, restrictions, detentions and so on. Once stability has been achieved the NMS moves towards restoring normality, again defined as the ability of the local authorities to provide services on a normal basis. In order to move from stability to normality, the NMS operates primarily in the welfare mode. The reasoning behind this is that the 'revolutionary onslaught' will have nothing upon which to mobilise support if the population is properly housed, educated and employed – in short, if the leading 'agitators' are detained or neutralised and the masses are content.

Expressed differently, the NMS can, by a judicious mix of security action and socio-economic upliftment, raise the cost of confronting the state whilst simultaneously enhancing the benefits of cooperating with it. Needless to say, in the welfare mode the NMS ensures a similar degree of departmental coordination in providing upliftment services – normally involving the Departments of Education, Manpower, Health and so on – as it does in coordinating security matters. It also needs to be stressed that the two modes are not mutually exclusive; in the security mode, upliftment services can and do take place, while in the welfare mode, the security activities do not disappear.

By and large, problems tend to be solved on the lowest level where this is possible – by pooling resources and by the logical and coordinated deployment of men and materials. Where a problem cannot be solved locally – either because of the political implications or because of practical difficulties – reference can be made to the higher levels in the system. The system ensures a high level of inter-departmental cooperation and cuts a great deal of red tape.

Expressed in this way, the NMS can be seen as simply a way of making government more efficient and responsive. There can be no doubt that many of the officials who serve in the system see themselves as a new breed of quasi-missionaries, undoing the wrongs and correcting the injustices which have been caused by forty years of apartheid, and three hundred years of general neglect. Few, except the most cynical, can object to a government food parcel when the alternative is starvation, however culpable the same government may have been in exacerbating or even creating starvation in the first place.

However, in assessing the system, we need to look beyond its technical impressiveness and the undoubted dedication of individual officials, and consider instead the real motives which lie behind its operation. There is no doubt that the system is efficient and that, largely as a result of its sophistication, the heady talk of 'revolution around the corner' heard in the townships during the latter part of 1985, has been replaced by a more sober appraisal of the power of the state. The system has, in short, bought the regime breathing-space.

It would not, however, be true to say that the government intends to use this space to create a genuine democracy in South Africa, or even to lay the foundations for one. The task of the NMS is in large part concerned with bolstering the credibility and legitimacy of local apartheid structures. The NMS defines acceptable and unacceptable political behaviour, rewarding those who play the game and punishing those who want to play a different game. Those who do not wish to participate in, or advocate the boycott of, structures set up to give apartheid a hue of respectability, and even more so those who attempt to establish genuinely democratic structures, are severely harassed. In these circumstances, the NMS becomes a way not of counteracting 'Soviet expansionism', but of perpetuating apartheid rule.

The system and the future

What does the future hold for the NMS? One possibility is its disappearance. Some would argue that just as the Department of Bantu Development and the Bureau for State Security, respectively the favourite children of Verwoerd and Vorster, were eclipsed once they were no longer in office, so too will the NMS suffer demise when P. W. Botha retires or dies. However, there are several reasons why this is unlikely. Firstly, the NMS is not merely a state department which has been favoured by a particular head of government. It is an elaborate new coordinating structure whose activities span the entire central, second-tier and even municipal government bureaucracies. Secondly, no future (white) president could afford to alienate the security forces, which are the major driving force behind the system. Thirdly, unlike both Bantu Development and BOSS, the NMS is both efficient itself and also promotes general bureaucratic efficiency, an asset which no future head of government can afford to ignore.

The efficiency of the system is in a very large measure promoted by its flexibility and responsiveness to top-down instructions. This is because the system is mainly staffed by 'security force' officials, trained in the explicit and immediate carrying out of commands. The system is neither directly accountable nor responsive to elected bodies, far less to the wider public. In the government's view, the fight against the 'total onslaught' cannot be hampered or hindered by considerations of accountability or open debate. Moreover, the idea of the 'total onslaught' has gained primacy in the thought patterns of many officials, even those in non-security line departments. The unrest and the accompanying states of emergency have been a powerful socialising influence in achieving this. The premise underlying the system is consequently that the kind of efficiency required in counteracting the onslaught, and the requirements of democracy, are mutually incompatible.

The political process in South Africa has seen a conscious drift away from popular accountability towards indirectly elected and nominated quasi-legislative bodies. Thus, the functions of popularly elected third-tier authorities will gradually become the responsibility of indirectly elected Regional Services Councils. The white-elected Provincial Councils have already given way to nominated Executive Committees, and real decision-making power is increasingly moving away from parliament to an extra-parliamentary executive.

At the same time, a similar process is occurring within the NMS itself, as officials hitherto responsible to one minister who was in turn responsible to parliament, now find themselves responsible to amorphous and secret committees. Under these circumstances, it is often difficult to establish exactly which minister is responsible for the activities of NMS officials. Recent attempts to elicit information about the NMS by means of questions in parliament have demonstrated this tendency. This trend towards non-accountability is likely to become more marked in the future.

At the same time it is likely to be the case that the NMS will come to include a greater number of non-military personnel. Because non-military officials were drawn into the NMS in increasing numbers during the states of emergency, and because the welfare mode of the system typically involves officials in non-security departments, the officials in these departments are likely, in the course of time, to gain prominence within the system's structures. Although the State President refused in 1988 to divulge the names of JMC chairmen, it is understood that at least one JMC chairman is now drawn from a non-security line department. The JMCs themselves are evidently keen to change their areas of jurisdiction from military command boundaries to more rational ones, such as the economic development regions. As part of this process, sub-JMCs could then correspond to RSCs and the mini-JMCs to municipalities. This move would go some way towards demilitarising the JMC structure, and would also ensure a greater degree of cooperation and interaction on local government level. Finally, as if to consummate this change in emphasis, the NSMS is now referred to simply as the 'National Management System'.

An analysis of the system may suggest that the National Party government is secure in the short or even medium term, bolstered by a security management system which simultaneously coopts clients and cows critics within the country, and keeps in check guerilla insurgency on the borders. Yet there are weaknesses. Ironically, many of the weaknesses are the same as those pointed out by the five-minutes-to-midnight prophets. What differs is the time scale. The structural weaknesses of minority domination may cumulatively prove the undoing of the system in the longer term.

Firstly, the NMS is inordinately expensive. According to one source, R3,2 billion was spent in 1987/8 on upgrading 34 of the 'hottest' townships, and a further R16 billion has been earmarked for this purpose in a further 200 townships (Swilling, 1988) marked for special attention. Ultimately – inflation notwithstanding – there is a limit on the amount of taxation which can be imposed on what is a relatively small wealth-producing base. Furthermore, while there are undoubted savings which can be effected within the context of a siege economy, the government will eventually be faced by the classic dilemma of opting either for guns or for butter, but not both simultaneously.

Secondly, the South African government critically lacks legitimacy. What acceptability it does enjoy accrues from the majority of the whites, who see it as a vehicle for guaranteeing their continued survival, identity, prosperity and privilege. Should the government fail to deliver these, or should the costs outweigh perceived benefits, one might expect the white electorate to opt, in increasing numbers, for a right-wing alternative whose appeal is more simple and more direct. The perceived possibility of this occurring might induce the government to resort to cheaper, more basic, but ultimately less effective forms of repression.

Thirdly, the international context in which the South African government operates, and in terms of which it has to trade, continues to deteriorate markedly. While it tends to be true that in conditions of enforced protectionism most reasonably diversified economies enjoy a short-lived boom, the ultimate effect of a relatively comprehensive sanctions package is a shrinking productive base, increased unemployment and less state revenue.

Fourthly, sheer weight of numbers precludes the minority government from being able to rule effectively in the face of popular dissent. However effective the regime might be in coopting and intimidating black communities, the demographic imbalance in South Africa is so great as to suggest that ungovernability will occur, not necessarily as a coherent strategy of resistance, but more plausibly because there will simply not be sufficient manpower to exercise effective internal and external domination.

Moreover, the South African state is not dealing simply with vast numbers, but with a long history and deep tradition of organised mass resistance, through trade unions, civic associations and political organisations, which have withstood many periods of intense repression. It is ultimately organised resistance, fed by a natural disaffection with apartheid, that will be the undoing of the work of the NMS.

All these considerations cumulatively suggest a scenario for South Africa of degenerative collapse. In this view, the regime will become increasingly desperate and probably vicious, faced with a series of worsening and seemingly insoluble political dilemmas. While the NMS may have won breathing-space, it seems unlikely that the government will be able to deliver the type of political reform which would permanently win it the hearts and minds of the black majority.

12 The militarisation of urban controls: the security management system in Mamelodi, 1986–1988

ANDREW BORAINE

This chapter is a case study of the way in which the South African security forces have attempted to regain and establish control in Mamelodi, a black township that featured prominently in the nation-wide uprising between 1984 and 1986. Mamelodi, 17 kilometres east of Pretoria, is one of the 34 townships designated as 'oilspots' by officials of the Joint Management Centres (JMCs). This term, borrowed from American military strategists in Vietnam, refers to the establishment of 'strategic bases' from which the security forces believe they can 'regain control' over the black population (Swilling, 1988).

In November 1985, 13 Mamelodi residents were killed by the police during a protest against high rents. At the funerals following the 'Mamelodi massacre', a call was made on residents to boycott rents and join street committees. This received widespread support. Within a few months, a remarkable network of 'organs of people's power' stretched through 35 zones, under the leadership of the Mamelodi Civic Association (MCA).[1] In the first half of 1986, with the Mamelodi Town Council (MTC) severely weakened because of revenue shortages and political illegitimacy, the civic association began to assume increasing hegemony over the day-to-day events in Mamelodi.

During this time, Mamelodi residents attended meetings of the street and section committees, where they participated in discussions that ranged from conditions in Mamelodi to national political issues. Residents boycotted the Mamelodi police-station, and began to bring disputes to 'people's courts'. They participated in numerous stayaways from work, and conducted a consumer boycott of white shops in Pretoria. In the schools, students boycotted classes and applied in practice rudimentary concepts of 'people's education'.

Many of these 'alternative structures' were the first targets of the state crackdown on 12 June 1986, when a nationwide state of emergency was declared. The period of repression in Mamelodi was followed by a JMC-initiated strategy of 'upgrading' the physical and material conditions in Mamelodi that security officials believed had led to the resistance in the first place. These were identified as a lack of land, housing, infrastructure, services and facilities. Part of this strategy has also been to try to bolster the political and financial position of the town council in various ways, such as by attempting to end the rent boycott.

This case study is an attempt to take an analysis of current state strategy beyond the level of state structures and policy statements, and probe the large gap between the intention and the implementation of strategies. State strategies are more often than not diverse, contradictory and incoherent responses to pressures from below, rather than the result of uniform manipulation of the whole country and the unfolding logic of state planners. Just as the 'total strategy' of the early 1980s was often neither total nor strategic, current state strategies cannot be reduced to a single 'masterplan', but are constantly being shaped by the struggles of the oppressed classes and their organisations, and by struggles between different institutions within the state.

There are important political and strategic implications that can be drawn from these points. If analyses of state strategies do not go beyond an outline of the structures of the state and the ideological discourse of state policy-planners, then there is a strong tendency to regard the state as all-powerful, particularly in the current climate of repression. This leaves political initiative within the domain of the state, and reduces the ability of the oppressed to organise and resist.

At the same time, avoiding a 'doom and gloom' scenario should not lead to the opposite extreme. The repressive measures of the last two years are not the actions of a 'panic-stricken' state, as has been argued in some quarters. Current state strategies are not simply cosmetic or inconsequential. They *do* affect the terrain on which the forces of the opposition organise, the issues around which organisation is built, and the nature of class and political alliances.

The security forces in Mamelodi

The declaration of the second state of emergency in June 1986 was marked by dawn raids throughout Mamelodi, and the detention of over 200 activists. Those detained included civic and youth leadership, trade unionists, and membership of the section and street committees. A reward of R1 000 was offered for information leading to the apprehension of any 'comrade', a tactic designed to sow division between activists and residents.

Security force action against the residents of Mamelodi, including detentions, had of course begun long before the second state of emergency, even though the Pretoria townships had been excluded from the partial state of emergency declared on 21 July 1985. However, June 1986 marked the start of a systematic attempt to crush all forms of progressive organisation.

A permanent army camp was established on the hill near the water reservoir, overlooking the whole of Mamelodi East.[2] Army patrols, in Casspirs and on foot, together with roadblocks at the three main entrances to Mamelodi, sought to pre-empt and contain all political activity. During the 'June 16' stayaway which followed the imposition of the state of emergency (and which was supported by 90 per cent of all black residents in Pretoria), telephone lines to all the townships, including Mamelodi, were suddenly 'out of order' (*Pretoria News,* 16, 17, 20.6.1986). Security forces patrolled Mamelodi from helicopters and dropped pamphlets urging residents to go to work.

All gatherings including funerals were banned.[3] Many youths were picked up at random off the streets by the SADF, beaten, and then handed over to the security police for 'processing'. Those that were known to be politically involved were then detained under the emergency regulations; the rest were sent home. Sections of Mamelodi were cordoned off at random, and searched house by house. Even the possession of a 'political' tee-shirt was sufficient to guarantee detention. A civic member described the conduct of the SADF on such raids: 'When they raid, they are as brutal as the police. Whenever they go and raid an activist, they go as if they are raiding Angola, because they come with tanks and everything. For instance, with me, they came with a tank, and pointed it at my shack.' (Interview, February 1988)

This comparison with 'border' duty was certainly not lost on the SADF itself. In a visit to the Mamelodi East SADF base in December 1987, the Deputy Minister of Defence, Mr Willie Breytenbach, told troops that their presence in Mamelodi 'was just as important as the presence of troops in Namibia and Angola' (*Pretoria News,* 19.12.1987).

Although the rate of detentions slowed after the first three months of the state of emergency, and many activists were released after six to twelve months, the state has continued to apply pressure through selective detentions. In October 1987, six Black Consciousness activists in Pretoria, including the Mamelodi branch chairperson of Azapo, Denis Ndlovu, were detained. In March 1988, youth activists in the Pretoria townships, including Mike Seloane, general secretary of the Mamelodi Youth Organisation, were detained (*Argus,* 5.10.1987; *Weekly Mail,* 18–24.3.1988).

One of the main tasks of the state of emergency, as perceived by the security forces, has been to try to destroy the street and section committees, as well as the people's courts. Civic members admit that for a long time it has been very difficult to retain a high level of support in various sections of Mamelodi:

People were scared off. There had been a high level of mobilisation, without necessarily having an in-depth politicisation of people. People thought that by continuing as street-committee members, they would be taken away. What the army would do is to get into a street, and ask, 'Wie is die straat kommandant hier? [Who is the street commander here?], who is a comrade here?' (Interview, February 1988)

Another area targeted by the security forces was the schools. Under the state of emergency, students have had to study with members of the SADF sitting in their classrooms, with some soldiers even being appointed as teachers in the Standard 6 classes (*Pretoria News*, 22.8.1986; interview, Mamelodi Civic Association, February 1988).

The state has also attempted to strengthen the local security forces in Mamelodi with the introduction of 243 municipal police, known locally as 'greenbeans'.[4] In addition to the municipal police, the conventional police forces in Mamelodi (numbering 300) have been strengthened by the introduction of a new mobile police station and additional personnel (*Cape Times*, 27.7.1986).

By September 1986, the state had regained sufficient control over Mamelodi to be able to take reporters on a tour in an SAP bus to show that 'all was quiet' (*Pretoria News*, 30.9.1986). The guide for the tour was SADF Captain 'Bossie' Boshoff, a key security official based in Mamelodi. Reporters were welcomed by Bennett Ndlazi, now back in charge as 'mayor' of Mamelodi.

Principles of the National Security Management System

The public relations tour for the press could probably be said to mark the end of what Adriaan Vlok, Minister of Law and Order, has identified as the first of three steps in current security-force strategy: 'You have to address the security situation; secondly, you have to address grievances and bring good government to the ordinary people and, thirdly, you have to address the political situation' (*Leadership SA*, 6, 1, 1987: 28).

The National Security Management System (NSMS) is not a recent phenomenon in South Africa, and can be traced back to the development of a general strategy of counter-insurgency by SADF officers from the early 1970s.[5] The structures of the NSMS were technically in place from 1979. However, it was their ability to respond to the uprisings of 1984–6 that enabled NSMS officials and structures to begin to play a pre-eminent role within the state and in the management of conflict at national, regional and local levels.

The current counter-revolutionary strategy that has been formulated by security officials hinges on the recognition that many of the grievances that sparked the township uprisings were real. Military strategists maintain that social welfare programmes could gain the confidence of the majority of people, and simultaneously provide opportunities for collecting intelligence on political activists. This emphasis on 'welfare' in addition to security action was spelt out in a paper by Major-General A. J. Wandrag, deputy commissioner of the SAP in charge of riot control:

The outcome of this struggle will not be determined by weapons alone. If this had been the case, I would not have any fears, because the communists are bent on avoiding military confrontation. They prefer to foment domestic grievance – real as well as imagined – and to instigate the country's inhabitants to full-scale insurrection and revolution. The only way to render the enemy powerless is to nip revolution in the bud, by ensuring that there is no fertile soil in which the seeds of the revolution can germinate. (Wandrag, 1985)

A State Security Council general was more direct about the reasons for the upgrading and welfare programmes: 'These people have their aspirations of course, but they are really concerned about bread and butter issues – housing, schools, motor cars, "the good life". And if you want their support, you can *buy* it.' (*Newsweek*, 20.6.1988)

The National Security Management System in Mamelodi

Mamelodi has been included under the Pretoria regional JMC, whose boundaries coincide with those of the Northern Transvaal command of the SADF. The Pretoria JMC has the task of supervising both security (known in NSMS terminology as 'hard war') and welfare ('soft war') functions.

The 'welfare' side of the Pretoria JMC is divided into the communications committee (KOM-kom), run by the Bureau for Information and responsible for the creation and management of information; and the constitutional, economic and social committees (SEM-kom), staffed by high-ranking personnel from all the relevant government departments. The SEM-kom has a number of defined tasks. These include the countering of economic resistance (defined as consumer boycotts, strikes, stayaways and industrial sabotage) and social resistance (defined as alternative education, youth and women's organisations, and liberation theology).

The communications committee distributes a variety of forms of media, containing information and propaganda on various government initiatives. This committee also manufactures media designed to look like items produced by anti-apartheid organisations, but containing a different message in order to try to sow confusion and disunity.[6] For example, pamphlets appeared in Pretoria in September 1986, ostensibly produced by the 'Pretoria Consumer Boycott Committee', but calling for a two-week stayaway from work (*Star*, 19.9.1986). A strategy involving a stayaway of this length was unlikely to have been adopted by activists in Pretoria because of the small chance of support from workers.

One of the first large projects of the communications committee was a film on Mamelodi which was shown on 'Network' on TV1 and TV2 in February 1987 (*Star*, 6.3.1987; *Cape Times*, 16.2.1987). The project was characterised by subterfuge from the start. The film was introduced as having been made by an independent film company called Alpine Productions on behalf of the SADF. The SABC claimed at the time that Alpine Productions was a company based in Zurich. However, newspaper reporters could find no trace of the company, either in Switzerland or in South Africa. It seems that this duplicity was a fairly clumsy attempt to give the film 'independent' status in order to pass it off as an objective assessment of life in a township under the state of emergency.

Another probable example of the work of the Pretoria JMC communications committee was the distribution of fake Cosatu pamphlets in Pretoria in October 1987. The pamphlets were closely modelled on posters put out by Cosatu's education department, and called on workers to attend a Cosatu 'intimidation' conference, where workers could learn 'how to necklace fellow workers who don't participate in strikes' (*Weekly Mail*, 23–29.10.1987).

The Pretoria regional JMC is linked to several decentralised structures, including a local management centre in the city centre of Pretoria, and mini-JMCs based in townships such as Mamelodi and Atteridgeville. An example of the work of the 'economic management system' is the close cooperation between the Pretoria Chamber of Commerce and the security forces. During the 1986 consumer boycott, Pretoria businessmen were asked in a confidential letter from the secretary of the Chamber of Commerce, Mr C. Viljoen, to pass on any information about the consumer boycott to the Chamber 'who are in constant contact with the police and security forces' (*Weekly Mail*, 2–8.5.1986). This information was intended to put the security forces in a better position to end the boycott.

The Pretoria regional JMC is also divided into a security and an intelligence committee. These receive daily reports from the surrounding townships. However, most of the security operations in Mamelodi are coordinated through a Joint Operations Centre (JOC) based in Mamelodi itself.

The Mamelodi Joint Operations Centre

The JOC, which falls under the command of the local police commander, Lieutenant-Colonel Lekganyane, is the central security body in Mamelodi, coordinating the activities of SADF troops, the local police, the security police, the riot police and the municipal police. These activities, the 'hard war' functions, include pre-emptive security action (detentions, arrests, roadblocks and patrols), intelligence-gathering operations, and the monitoring of all oppositional activities.

The intelligence and monitoring work is performed by the Joint Intelligence Committee (JIC), which is made up of members of the security police, military intelligence and the National Intelligence Service (NIS). One of the objectives of this committee is to collect information on all political, cultural, religious, sporting, welfare and business organisations in Mamelodi. The JIC also tries to monitor the whereabouts of all activists and community leaders in Mamelodi, as well as the identity of visitors to the township. For example, a visitor to Dr Nico Smith, the resident DRC dominee in Mamelodi, found her car surrounded by SADF Casspirs within a few minutes of parking outside his house. When questioned, it became clear that the soldiers had already established whom the car belonged to through their link to the Pretoria Traffic Department's central computer.

There are various other indications of the activities of the JOC (*Newsweek*, 20.6.1988). On one wall of the JOC offices, there is a map of Mamelodi, highlighting the houses and names of community leaders and activists known to the security forces. Another board gives a breakdown of all political, cultural, religious, sporting and economic bodies in Mamelodi, with a list of known office-bearers and times and venues of meetings. In June 1988, these included a meeting of the shareholders of the African Bank, a meeting of a branch of the National African Chamber of Commerce, and a Cosatu workshop.

Another wall of the JOC has examples of the various tee-shirts and slogans of community organisations (presumably for recognition purposes). A chart outlines the various 'signs of unrest' that will indicate to members of the security forces that oppositional activities are being planned (such as residents placing buckets of water outside their houses in anticipation of teargas).

The JOC thus combines both intelligence and security functions; that is, the collection of information on activities in Mamelodi (sometimes referred to as *'gatkruip operasies'*), which is processed by a committee that meets on a daily basis, and the removal of oppositional groupings. These groupings are defined in particular as the Mamelodi Civic Association, the Mamelodi Youth Organisation, as well as the street and section committees and the people's courts.

In a recent interview, a senior SADF general acknowledged that 'sometimes you have to take out the revolutionaries if they are controlling the people' (*Christian Science Monitor*, 11.5.1988). The State Security Council's officially distributed booklet, *The art of counter-revolutionary war*, is explicit on the need for the 'elimination' of political activists. It can be argued that this is what has been happening in Mamelodi. On 1 December 1986, Dr Ribeiro, a well-known medical practitioner and political activist in Mamelodi, and his wife, the sister of the late Dr Robert Sobukwe, were gunned down outside their house. A car, seen by witnesses in the immediate area just prior to and after the murders, was subsequently traced to the commanding officer of the Security Branch unit in Schoeman Street, Pretoria. No-one has been charged with responsibility for the murders (*Weekly Mail*, 5–11.12.1986).

In June 1988, the chairperson of the Mamelodi Civic Association, Peter Maluleka, was abducted from his home by unknown men. Police later confirmed that he had been detained. Maluleka has subsequently been charged with treason, along with 11 other Pretoria activists (*Weekly*

Mail, 13–19.1.1989). During the same month, the general secretary of the civic association, Stanza Bopape, was detained by security police. Subsequently, police informed his family that Bopape had 'escaped' from detention. He has not been seen since, and is feared to be dead.[7]

The information provided by the JIC is also used for the planning of upgrading activities in Mamelodi by the mini-JMC. Two SADF members of the JOC, Captain 'Bossie' Boshoff and Lt. Peter Gagiano, form the 'security' committee of the Mamelodi mini-JMC, and provide the intersection between the 'hard war' tactics of the JOC and the 'soft war' approach of the mini-JMC.

The Mamelodi mini-Joint Management Centre

The Mamelodi mini-JMC is chaired by Mr Wolmarans of the Department of Transport. It consists of committees that deal with 'communications', 'welfare' as well as 'security'. These committees meet in secret twice a month, once jointly and once separately. The mini-JMC has a total membership of about 30 people, including 8 representatives from the Mamelodi Town Council. These are the town clerk, the four chief executive officers, the social welfare officer, the sports liaison officer and the council's public relations officer. (These representatives, it should be said, are not councillors but paid officials of the councils. Four of them are white and four black.) The other members of the mini-JMC are drawn from various government departments (in particular those dealing with black education, constitutional affairs, transport, telecommunications, health and social welfare), as well as the security forces.

Constitutionally, JMCs (at any level) do not have any executive power. The JMC structure as a whole is meant to report to the secretary of the State Security Council, recommending action to be taken in relation to grievances in a particular township. The appropriate government department is then meant to act on the recommendations, drawing funds from the central Treasury if necessary.

According to Veleleni Mashumi of the Mamelodi Town Council, the mini-JMC is

nothing else but an *ad hoc* committee which identifies problems immediately. . . . The JMCs do not run the show here, they are only acting in an advisory capacity, and in a very helpful manner, in that because the representatives of the various departments are serving on the JMC, they know what the problems are. . . . It's just a group of people that are concerned, who want to see the standard of living upgraded in the black areas, and the chairman we have got is one of the best chairmen ever seen. (Interview, February 1988)

Mashumi claims that once a particular project has been identified, it is then referred to the town council for implementation. According to Mashumi, a number of current projects in Mamelodi, including building new houses, improving the road-network system, laying paving and building new schools, were all initiated by the mini-JMC.

The question arises as to whether the mini-JMC is really just a benevolent technical advisory group to the town council, as Mashumi claims, or a body that is in direct control of all development, upgrading and welfare in Mamelodi, operating in terms of a carefully planned counter-revolutionary strategy.

In a township like Alexandra, where there is still no black local authority, the mini-JMC is the actual body in control of the daily welfare and security operations. In Mamelodi, because the town council has been able to begin functioning again, there is clearly a form of 'relative autonomy' between the two structures. There is also a high level of cooperation between them. This is not surprising, as Seegers points out: 'For local government officials and politicians there are powerful incentives to participate in the JMC network: material benefits can be gained or "law and order restored". Indeed, local authorities, bogged down in red tape and hampered by insufficient funds, may well be awed by the speed and volume with which benefits are received.' (1988a: 134) And as Mashumi admits: 'All it [the mini-JMC] does is deal with practical situations. It then makes recommendations to the council. But because these recommendations are of such a profitable nature, the council invariably accepts them.'

One of the functions of the mini-JMC is to make sure that various government departments are contributing to these projects, by providing research, expertise and, in some cases, funding. Another function is to ensure that the town council is given the credit for the projects so as to bolster its authority and influence (this was particularly the case during the time of the October 1988 municipal elections). This is the main function of the 'communications' committee, which develops methods through which the town council can 'interact' with people. So far, this has been attempted mainly through the provision of sporting facilities to schools.

Operation Upgrade

A central task of the mini-JMC is to identify 'upgrading' projects in Mamelodi that could assist in re-establishing state and local authority control over the township. So far, plans have encompassed the development of infrastructure (the building of a highway through Mamelodi, the installation of traffic lights, the tarring of 160 km of roads, and the construction of storm-water drains and a pedestrian bridge), and the provision of new facilities and amenities (two post offices, a mobile police station, eight schools and new telephones). There are also numerous large housing projects, including the recently completed elite suburb of Mamelodi Gardens.

Certain of the projects of the mini-JMC have been self-consciously aimed at 'winning the hearts and minds' of some of the residents of Mamelodi. These have included the development of the R3,5 million Moretele Park, with five planned swimming pools and a cable-car link to the top of the Magaliesberg (*Pretoria News,* 12.11.1987).

Over the next twelve years, a development project on 2 000 hectares of land east of Mamelodi will be undertaken. It will include 10 000 houses, two business districts, a hospital, an old-age home and another stadium, and will potentially double the size of Mamelodi. In addition, a major overhaul of Mamelodi's electricity, water and sewerage systems is planned. There are also various schemes to provide residents with jobs, and to dismantle the migrant hostels and build family houses.

Financing development in Mamelodi

Together with the removal of progressive community organisations and their leaders, the central function of the mini-JMC has been to re-establish the power of the town council, and through it supervise large land, housing and development projects in Mamelodi. To do this it has had to try to overcome the long-standing fiscal and political weaknesses of the town council, made more severe by the rent boycott which has continued throughout the state of emergency.

As a result of the rent boycott, the Mamelodi Town Council has been faced with two diverse sets of pressures. Firstly, residents have continued to refuse to pay rents and service charges, either out of political choice or out of economic necessity. This has reduced funds available to the council. Secondly, authorities such as the Transvaal Provincial Administration, eager to see black local authorities financially more self-sufficient and in a position to pay their debts and contribute to the upgrading process, have urged the council to evict rent defaulters and raise rent and service charges.

In October 1987, the *Weekly Mail* announced that the authorities in Mamelodi had launched a campaign to break the two-year-old rent boycott (*Weekly Mail,* 16–22.10.1987). This involved council officials, accompanied by members of the SADF, urging residents to pay arrear rentals. In many cases, households were issued with eviction notices if arrears were not paid within one week. Other methods have been more devious, such as refusing to register a new-born baby unless a rent receipt can be produced (interview with Lucas Banda, February 1988).

Another means of attempting to end the rent boycott has been to promote home-ownership. Over the past two years, the number of home-owners in Mamelodi has risen substantially. This is in part the result of reductions in the cost of houses. In addition, the Transvaal Provincial Administration embarked on a marketing campaign to promote sales of houses in townships affected by the rent boycott (*Star,* 26.9.1987). This campaign involved 20 full-time sales representatives, and 24 SADF soldiers seconded to the TPA, attempting, in the words of

an SADF spokesperson, to 'contain the total onslaught' and 'help beat
the rent boycott' (*Sowetan*, 29.9.1987).

It is unclear whether the strategy of home-ownership will actually
help solve the rent boycott. As Friedman has pointed out, residents
who have bought their homes still pay high service charges, which are
not very different from those levied on tenants (*Weekly Mail*,
15–21.6.1988: 14).

Between 1986 and 1988, the Mamelodi Town Council spent R16
million on upgrading and development projects. This reflected
additional expenditure, over and above the projected budget amounts
during this period, which were used to purchase and maintain existing
services. If the various statements about future development projects
that have been issued by the town council are taken into consideration,
the council plans in the near future to raise and spend over R100
million on infrastructure and services, and another R315 million on
housing. This finance has been provided by a number of different
sources. Particular projects have been sponsored by government departments that are represented on the mini-JMC. The town council has also
benefited from 'bridging loans' provided by the Transvaal Provincial
Administration. Much of the new revenue for the upgrading of infrastructure has come from the Pretoria Regional Services Council. Other
projects have been developed through investment provided by the
South African Housing Trust, the Development Bank, various banks
and building societies, or coordinated by the Family Housing
Association of the Urban Foundation.

Assessing the NSMS strategy in Mamelodi

In Mamelodi, there are (as yet) no clear indications whether the new
strategies of 'addressing grievances' and 'bringing good government to
the people' have gone any way to providing a solution to the urban
crisis, or have been able to 'buy' political support from township
residents. There are, however, some general conclusions that can be
drawn.

The state of emergency and the operationalising of the NSMS in
Mamelodi have unquestionably affected opposition and resistance to
state policies. The Mamelodi Joint Operations Centre coordinates a
systematic and effective campaign against activists and community
leaders, and has intimidated many residents against becoming involved
in the civic association. The JOC has been able to assemble substantial
information on activists in Mamelodi, and can move swiftly to counter
oppositional activities through its centralised security networks.
Through the JOC, control has been regained over the day-to-day
administrative functions of the township. The Mamelodi mini-JMC
has been able to identify problems quickly, and put forward a
(relatively) coherent programme of upgrading.

This does not mean that the NSMS upgrading programmes are being implemented as intended. Apart from the question of whether the 'oilspot' technique can be extended successfully to other townships, it is apparent that while the JMCs can often identify problems, they cannot always 'deliver' the goods and services required. The reasons for this include tensions between the JMCs and various government departments that resent security interference in their functions; the inefficiency and corruptness of many of the black local authorities that the JMCs are required to work through; and a general lack of resources available for township upgrading.

A major weakness of the NSMS strategy is its deliberate coupling of repression with the upgrading programmes. What distinguishes the NSMS upgrading strategies of 1987–8 from the 'total strategy reforms' of the early 1980s is the perception of the need for systematic repression in order to bolster reform. Swilling in the present volume quotes Professor Willie Breytenbach of Stellenbosch University as saying that 'where once there could be no security without reform, now there can be no reform without security'. This means that in Mamelodi, the assassination of the Ribieros, the abduction and subsequent trial of Mamelodi Civic chairperson Peter Maluleka, and the 'disappearance' of the MCA's general secretary Stanza Bopape and two others, are 'necessary' components of the upgrading–reform strategies.

On one hand, this means that unlike the 'reform' period of the early 1980s, the current strategy affords fewer opportunities for oppositional forces to organise. On the other hand, most residents remain cynical of the upgrading programmes because they are seen to be connected with the actions of the security forces in the townships. As the editors of the *South African Review* point out, this exposes one of the contradictions in the state's current reform policy: 'The stability necessary for reform is impossible without repression, while repressive measures deepen the crisis to which reform is a response' (1987: xiv). This is borne out in a recent paper by De Villiers and Roux (1988), who point out how massive repression in the Eastern Cape region, while destroying many local community organisations, has alienated vast numbers of township residents from reform programmes.

A central weakness of the NSMS strategy is that it is unable to put forward a national political solution. Despite the state of emergency, support for certain mass actions has remained fairly constant. For example, most residents stayed away from work on 21 November 1986 (the anniversary of the 'Mamelodi massacre'), May Day 1987, and 16 June 1988. Community organisations such as the Mamelodi Civic Association and the Mamelodi Youth Organisation have continued to function, albeit at a fairly low level.

The effectiveness of the NSMS strategy in Mamelodi needs also to be assessed in terms of the current status of the town councils, and the issue of the affordability of houses. These will be considered in turn.

Propping up the town council
The state of emergency and the NSMS have greatly strengthened the position of the Mamelodi Town Council. Councillors are protected physically by the municipal police and the security forces, and have been provided with a coordinated political and economic back-up system in the form of the mini-JMC. The ability of the mini-JMC to gather information about local conditions, place this information at the disposal of the NSMS, identify areas where action needs to be taken, and then prod both government departments and the town council to respond, is probably the main strength of the structure.

Through government departments, the Transvaal Provincial Administration, and the Pretoria RSC, substantial revenues are being raised outside of Mamelodi and channelled to the town council. This process is being complemented by private investment programmes. The council still faces a partial rent boycott, and has been unable to make much progress in collecting arrears. However, because of external sources of revenue, the council no longer finds itself in as vulnerable a position as in the period following the November 1983 black local authority elections.

The town council is also able to disburse patronage in the form of houses, sites, jobs and business contracts. The council can switch off electricity to people's houses and threaten to evict them; it can also block access to halls for the purpose of holding meetings.

Mamelodi residents see visible evidence of the upgrading programmes taking place, including the completed Moretele Park, and the council receives good media coverage for any promises of further schemes. Completed housing projects, such as Mamelodi Gardens, are not only used by the council to show off its supposed effectiveness and power, but have also provided the council with a residential pocket of potentially conservative supporters.

Despite these obvious advantages, however, the town council did not attract any more support in the 1988 municipal elections than in the 1983 black local authority elections. One of the main reasons was that it is still widely perceived to be under 'white' control.

Notwithstanding the official acceptance of the need for redistributing financial resources in a limited way from white to black areas, the black local authorities are still supposed to be self-financing. While additional funds are being channelled from government departments and the Regional Services Councils for the purposes of upgrading or for constructing *new* infrastructure, the councils still rely on payments from residents for the consumption of *existing* services. This remains one of their central weaknesses. The continued pressure from the Provincial Administration on councils to raise rent and services charges, and evict those not paying rent or unable to pay arrears, means that councillors have little chance of winning widespread support.

While the town council now occupies a strong position compared with two years ago, it also has many promises and expectations to fulfil. This in the end could be its downfall. As one activist said:

after Mamelodi Gardens, everyone thought there would be something for the ordinary man who doesn't work for the government. And the people thought, let's play a waiting game for a year or two and see. All that has happened is that a few show houses have opened. . . . So this thing has started off again, it's boiling somewhere with the people, they are dissatisfied with the thing. Right now with the state of emergency, we cannot just go and stand in the street and tell the people again, look, to hell with everything. . . . But somewhere deep down, it's starting all over again. . . . If all those grievances are not entertained very soon, the people might go back to the stage of saying, '*Fok alles,* we have suffered, we have lost people, people have been killed, people have been detained, so we'll mess the whole thing up again.' Because the people have learned to be no more afraid.

Affordability of housing

If the town council is able to transform all the announcements made regarding housing in Mamelodi over the past three years into reality, a total of nearly 20 000 new houses will need to be constructed.

For most residents in Mamelodi, however, the prices of the housing units provided so far are still beyond their financial means. In 1985, 51,2 per cent of the potential African labour force in Pretoria was unemployed, and over one-third of all African households were living below the minimum effective level of income (Martins, 1986: 11). Figures for the Pretoria–Witwatersrand–Vereeniging area as a whole have shown that 72 per cent of township residents cannot afford a conventionally built house, 47 per cent cannot afford a minimum unit, and 34 per cent cannot afford the houses currently being provided, even with a first-time home-owner's subsidy (*Star,* 24.10.1987).

The inability of most African households to pay for housing exposes the weakness in the state's attempt to solve the housing crisis through privatisation and deregulation. There are signs that the black upper-income housing market has become saturated, and there are few indications that housing companies are willing to become involved in the construction of low-cost, low-profit housing projects. Financial institutions such as building societies continue to be reluctant to lend to low-income groups. Low-cost housing projects by non-profit companies such as the South African Housing Trust have not been able to achieve significant results so far (*Financial Mail,* 3.6.1988).

Conclusion

The point has been made that the state does not have sufficient resources to upgrade every township. This is true, but then it is not the state's intention to upgrade all areas on a mass scale. The current NSMS strategy is deliberately selective, designed to favour certain areas at the expense of others. This differential policy seeks to create fissures and cracks, making the formation of political alliances within townships and between different townships and even regions more difficult.

The upgrading programmes within various 'oilspot' townships should not be judged in terms of whether they can be reproduced sufficiently on a national scale at the present (they cannot). The question is rather whether, under a state of emergency over the next 10–20 years, sufficient resources can be generated to coopt a significant minority of black people.

The NSMS 'winning hearts and minds' (WHAM) strategy is not really aimed at a 'mass conversion' of the black population but rather at containment, control and neutralisation. Security officials, despite their rhetoric, do not really believe they can 'buy off' large sections of the black population. They are more concerned with using a selective upgrading approach to assist in the repression of oppositional groups and activists, and the cooption of conservative elites.

Current urbanisation trends indicate a growing gap between the traditional urban working class – located mainly within established urban townships – and the rapidly increasing masses of unemployed and unhoused, who live in informal settlements on the fringes of urban areas. Selective upgrading has specific implications in terms of the state's policy shift away from traditional influx control to controls *within* urban areas. Rather than trying to keep Africans out of the white-designated urban areas, the state is currently attempting to maintain control through a combination of selective allocation of resources to bolster conservative elites and vigilante forces, and repression of democratic community organisations. In this sense, the 'success' of state urban strategies can be seen not so much in the 'oilspot' upgrading of townships such as Alexandra and Mamelodi, but in the divide-and-control tactics used in squatter settlements such as Crossroads and Khayelitsha in the Western Cape.

13 The militarisation of the bantustans: control and contradictions

CAROLE COOPER

The last two decades have seen the increasing militarisation of the bantustans, with bantustan military forces being used by South Africa both against the perceived external enemy and to quell internal opposition to bantustan rule and apartheid in general. However, there is no simple relationship between the South African state, ruling bantustan elites and their military forces, and contradictions have emerged which have undermined the role that the state intended such elites and their armies to play. Firstly, the actions of the elites have, in a variety of ways, given rise to instability in the regions. Bantustan armies, in turn, have added to this instability, sometimes being used by the elites to further their own aims, and, at other times, acting independently against them. It is the intention of this chapter to examine these contradictions, and to review the development of the bantustan forces and the militarisation of the homelands.[1]

Political overview

The bantustans had their origin partly in the South African state's concern to maintain white power. It was envisaged that separate ethnic entities economically and politically independent of South Africa would act as a counter against the growing proletarianisation of blacks and their continuing demands for power in a unitary state. At the same time, however, the bantustans were to remain under Pretoria's ultimate control and act as its agents in defending South Africa against liberation forces, as well as in suppressing internal unrest. The growing militarisation of the South African state has not stopped at the borders of the bantustans – these areas have been part of the process of militarisation, and their security forces have formed an integral part of South Africa's security system.

Although the state has modified its homeland policy in the 1980s and appears to be looking increasingly towards a regional solution, the bantustans remain important as ethnically based entities forming a bulwark against rural black demands for power in a unitary state. Whatever the exact nature of the state's blueprint for regional government, its success will depend on its ability to create stability within these regions. Although envisaged by Pretoria as forming part of both its political and military structures, the effectiveness of the bantustans in playing this role has been thrown into question in a variety of ways. These will be examined later in the chapter.

The role envisaged by Pretoria for the bantustans has been undermined by a series of unintended side-effects. Pretoria has found itself caught in the dilemma of needing to keep these areas under its control and of having, in the interests of gaining acceptance for its political strategy, to maintain some semblance of the fiction that these areas are indeed 'independent'.

Bantustan military forces

The bantustan military forces can be seen as having two broad aims: to function as part of South Africa's defence system against insurgency, and to quell domestic unrest. After the Soweto uprising of 1976 the state embraced the theory of 'total strategy', which sought to contain attacks against the state while 'reforming' the apartheid system in order to satisfy certain popular demands.

The state's policy regarding the use of blacks in the armed forces has changed over time. Until the early 1960s National Party policy was that blacks would never be used in the armed forces. In 1970 the Minister of Defence stated that Africans would be employed in the army only as common labourers. By 1973, however, 21 Battalion – an urban-based battalion for Africans – had been established. This was followed by the creation of forces for the 'independent' bantustans as they took 'independence', regional forces from 1979 for the non-independent bantustans, and since 1978 the recruitment of Africans into the commandos, albeit on a segregated basis (Grundy, 1986: 23).

This change in policy was partly the result of staff shortages in the South African Defence Force, and its need, faced with increased guerilla warfare, to intensify counter-insurgency (COIN) operations. The Deputy Minister of Defence has said that blacks 'have to help us spread a geographic presence and maintain it'. The regional companies, he observed, 'fulfil the role of a military presence, the showing of the flag in a specific region' (Grundy, 1986: 75). An additional motive relates to the ideological importance of having a multiracial army in order to create the impression that blacks and whites are acting together against a common enemy. Finally, it has been argued elsewhere that blacks bear a 'disproportionate burden of combat (compared to their numbers in the SADF itself)' and thus are being used as a form of 'cannon fodder' (Grundy, 1986: 24).

Blacks are recruited in the armed forces on a voluntary basis. Legislation in all the 'independent' bantustans provides for conscription of all male citizens between the ages of 18 and 65, but has not been implemented (SAIRR, 1977: 339; 1986: 614; Defence Acts of the various bantustans). All bantustan forces are either permanent or auxiliary forces. The arming of blacks, but on a limited basis, points to a contradiction in Pretoria's thinking: on one hand it wants to arm blacks in the interests of white control, but on the other it does not want to arm too many.

At present the four 'independent' bantustans – Transkei, Bophuthatswana, Venda and Ciskei – all have their own forces, with five regional battalions (which form part of the SADF) having been established for the non-independent bantustans. These battalions (except one) are ethnically based and are designed to become homeland forces once the respective bantustans take 'independence'.

As a way of binding each force ideologically to the bantustan to which it is linked, and thus of fostering the bantustan system, ethnicity is stressed. Each force has its own uniform and badge which tie it to its ethnic background. Thus the Venda force's emblem of the spear, battle axe and the bow are traditional weapons of the Manenu, according to *Paratus,* and symbolise that the enemies of Venda can be engaged at various ranges (*Paratus,* November 1986: 19). Intense ethnicisation has been introduced in the Ndebele force (perhaps because its ethnic diversity makes it more vulnerable). The troops are encouraged to sing traditional songs during their routine duties, while the army buildings 'were built in harmony with Ndebele lifestyle' (*Paratus,* March 1986: 54).

The strength of the forces is impossible to determine accurately as information is not available. They seem to be relatively small and not well developed in terms of equipment, and must consequently be seen as forces of initial reaction rather than capable of containing any substantial offensive. A recent report said that the Transkei Defence Force (TDF) was 'less than 3 000' (Bell, 1988: 24). There were 1 000 troops under training in Venda in 1987; according to the officer commanding of the Venda Defence Force (VDF), Colonel P. Faure, the strength of the VDF should be some 2 400 by 1992, consisting of infantry and mobile reaction units (*Paratus,* December 1987: 34; Maré, 1982: 16). It was reported in *Paratus* that 1 000 soldiers under training took part in celebrations in 1987 of the seventh anniversary of the Bophuthatswana Defence Force (BDF), while a recent report put the strength of the BDF at 1 500 (*Paratus,* February 1987; *Weekly Mail,* 12.2.1988). Black forces in the SADF constitute about a third of the army and navy permanent force (Grundy, 1986: 24).

The budgets for these 'independent' forces are small but (apart from the Ciskei) growing steadily. Transkei's defence budget increased from R7,9m in 1982/3 to R40,7m in 1987/8, or 2,5 per cent of the total budget; that of Bophuthatswana from R10m in 1982/3 to R41m in 1987/8, or 2,7 per cent of the budget; the comparative figures for Venda are R19 800 in 1982/3 to R27,8m, or 5,6 per cent of the budget in 1987/8. The Ciskei's budget decreased from R31m in 1983/4 to R25,5m in 1987/8, or 3 per cent of the budget (SAIRR, various).

All bantustan troops receive their initial training in the SADF at 21 Battalion. This training is similar to that at the white infantry bases and also involves a counter-insurgency course. In addition, all the bantustans have their own training division which undertakes basic training. More specialised training is still undertaken in South Africa. Most bases also run educational courses enabling troops to improve their qualifications and thus apply for admission to the permanent force.

The forces are largely made up of an infantry battalion, which varies in size. All four 'independent' bantustans have an airforce unit, special COIN forces and intelligence services.

Control of the bantustan forces

While recognising the necessity for the creation of bantustan armies (both to fulfil the notion of 'independence' and for the manpower reasons mentioned earlier), Pretoria has perceived the danger that these nominally 'independent' armies present. In order to secure these armies as part of its defence system, Pretoria maintains control over them in a variety of ways.

Through the non-aggression pacts that it has signed with the four 'independent' bantustans, it ensures that such forces fall within its sphere of influence. These treaties contain two major elements: each party pledges not to resort to the use of armed force against the territorial sovereignty and political independence of the other, and not to allow its territory to be used as a base or thoroughfare by any state, government, organisation or person for military, subversive, or hostile actions or activities against the other party. It can be argued that the second condition leaves the way open for South Africa to intervene, as well as providing the basis for any of the bantustans under threat to call for help (as occurred in Bophuthatswana in February 1988) (Grundy, 1986: 84). In 1987, following hostilities between Ciskei and Transkei, the two bantustans and South Africa concluded a tripartite treaty along the same lines as the bi-lateral ones (*Eastern Province Herald*, 11.4.1987).

Elaborating on the basis for this military cooperation, the Defence White Paper of 1982 said: 'The SADF recognises the supportive capabilities of the Independent States and encourages their participation in an overall Southern African military treaty organization against a common enemy.'

The SADF has also exercised control through the secondment of white SADF officers to positions of authority within the bantustan forces. These officers generally fill the senior posts. There were, for instance, 44 SADF officers in the Ciskei until 1985, when Pretoria recalled them after the chief of the Ciskei force, Brigadier A. Nell, was suspended (SAIRR, 1985: 292). It was revealed in the aftermath of the Bophuthatswana coup in 1988 that there were 14 SADF officers and

NCOs seconded to the BDF (*Citizen*, 4.4.1988). All the bantustan forces have had, at one time or another, white heads, and at present the VDF is headed by Brigadier Steenkamp and the BDF by Major-General H. S. Turner, with Colonel S. van Loggerenberg destined to become the first chief of the KwaNdebele defence force (*Star*, 11.2.1988; *Paratus*, March 1986: 54). While the black heads of state have usually taken on the portfolio of Minister of Defence (though Bophuthatswana until the coup had an SADF officer, Brigadier Hennie Riekert, as its defence minister), it would seem that effective control of the forces lies with their white heads. The SADF and the bantustan administrations have said that they are training black officers to fill the higher positions, but this process is generally not well advanced. The exception is the Transkei, which has followed a programme of Africanisation in all spheres.

South African influence is also exerted through the training, specifically in counter-insurgency, which bantustan forces have received in South Africa, either at 21 Battalion or elsewhere. Through such training South Africa is able not only to pass on COIN skills but to exert an ideological influence over the bantustan forces. The rigorous selection procedure to which volunteers are subject, and the fact that there are usually far more applicants than places, allow the SADF to choose men whom it thinks will support its ideological position. High unemployment and financial security would seem to be the reasons for the high number of applicants.

Bantustans are also dependent on South Africa for supplies, the financing of the forces, and the provision of bases and military equipment. Weapons not supplied by South Africa have been provided by countries with whom it has a close relationship, thus minimising any threat to its military dominance in the region. For instance, it was reported in 1983 that Israel was to supply the Ciskei with military aid, special weapons, and help for a small airforce and pilot-training school. It subsequently trained about 15 pilots for the Ciskei's airborne division (SAIRR, 1984: 522).

Counter-insurgency and domestic unrest

The extent to which the 'independent' bantustan forces form part of South Africa's defence system is clear from the role they play in aiding the SADF in regional defence. Since 1982 South Africa has developed the concept of an 'area war' in response to the armed struggle of the African National Congress. The bantustans, both 'independent' and non-independent, fall under South Africa's area defence plan, although the integration of the 'independent' bantustans is not publicly acknowledged (*Transformation*, 6, 1988: 66). Referring to this system in 1982, the chief of the SADF, General Constand Viljoen, said:

They [the ANC] apparently do not have a border war in mind. They are going to fight an area war. . . . If we had to deal with this using the full-time force, the demands on the system would be too great. But we are going to deal with it by using Area Defence . . . people living in an area must be organised to defend themselves. They must be our first line of defence. Our full-time force must be a reaction force. The first line of defence will contain any terrorist threat and the better-equipped and trained reaction forces will deal with insurgents. (*Financial Mail*, 15.1.1982)

In terms of this plan South Africa is divided into 10 territorial regions, each bantustan force falling within one of these regions.

There have been numerous instances of bantustan forces working together with the SADF in action against guerillas, one of the more recent examples being in 1987 when Venda security forces cooperated with the South African security forces in killing two alleged insurgents north of Venda (*Sowetan*, 15.9.1987).

South Africa has also utilised the bantustans in its actions against governments in foreign countries. In 1984 Lesotho alleged that Transkei was being used as a base by the Lesotho Liberation Army (supported by the South African government), which was sending hit-and-run squads into Lesotho in an attempt to undermine the Lesotho government (SAIRR, 1984: 544).

Increasingly in the 1980s, particularly since the outbreak of widespread popular opposition to apartheid rule in 1984, both the SADF and bantustan forces have been used to assist the SA Police in containing unrest domestically. The various Defence Acts of the 'independent' bantustans allow their defence forces to be employed on police duties. To these laws have recently been added a series of provisions (applying to Ciskei, Lebowa, and KwaNdebele), that indemnify the administration and its representatives, including the security forces, against civil or criminal proceedings arising out of any actions done in 'good faith' for the purposes of 'maintaining law and order' during specified periods of unrest (SAIRR, 1986: 616).[2]

In their attempts to crush resistance in the bantustans, the army and the police have also been aided by vigilante groups. In some instances these groups are themselves of a paramilitary nature, such as the Green Berets in the Ciskei, which were allegedly organised by President Lennox Sebe's party (Haysom, 1983: 24). Such groups are usually linked, overtly or covertly, to members of the bantustan administration (*City Press*, 17.4.1988; SAIRR, 1986: 546 and 549).

In 1986 unrest in urban areas in 'white' South Africa spread to the bantustans. In Bophuthatswana, KwaNdebele, and Lebowa in particular, resistance reached intense levels, turning them, according to *Indicator South Africa*, into 'a new frontline in the struggle for South Africa' (SAIRR, 1986: 641). When the state of emergency was re-declared in June 1986, it was extended to cover them.

The SADF and bantustan forces have also been used extensively to support the police in attempting to quell resistance to forced removal by squatter communities. The most notorious example was in March 1986 when the BDF was involved in a joint raid with the police on the massive squatter community of Winterveld in Bophuthatswana. A crowd was fired on and 11 people were killed (SAIRR, 1986: 643). In a further raid on 31 August in Bophuthatswana, the police and the army combined repression with a 'winning hearts and mind' approach when they handed out food rations to the aged (SAIRR, 1986: 648).

In addition to their deployment inside South Africa, the bantustan forces have also seen service in the operational area in Namibia.

Winning hearts and minds

Apartheid military leaders have repeatedly claimed that warfare is 80 per cent social, psychological, and political and only 20 per cent military. The SADF has devoted considerable energy to social and political mobilisation to inhibit support for guerillas in rural areas. This has been attempted primarily through its civil action programme (CAP).

According to Major-General C. Lloyd: 'The basic aim of civic action, apart from assisting the black man in various fields, is to project an image of the soldier as a man of action who is nevertheless a friend of the black man and who is prepared to defend him. We want the NSM [national serviceman] to teach the black man whilst his rifle is standing in the corner of the class room.' (Evans, 1983a: 21)

The CAP in the bantustans involves the deployment of white SADF troops in such roles as teachers, doctors, and agriculturalists, and in specific tasks such as disaster relief. By providing services for which there is a shortage, they also bolster bantustan governments. A third function is that of intelligence gathering.

It has been estimated that there are at least 176 NSM teachers involved in the CAP in South Africa; the total of all NSM involved in the CAP is a lot higher than this (Evans, 1983a: 24). Most of them have been deployed in Bophuthatswana and KwaZulu (Evans, 1983a: 23). Responsibility for the CAP soldiers is shared by the military command under which they fall and the bantustan to which they are allotted. In the case of teachers in KwaZulu their salaries were shared by the command and the bantustan administration (Evans, 1983a: 22).

While it is difficult to gauge how successful the CAP programme has been in terms of 'winning hearts and minds', it seems that black communities which also experience the military in its repressive role would be unlikely to be won over by its civic action programme.

Youth and militarisation

Attempts to win the hearts and minds of the youth in the bantustans have taken a number of militarised forms. One is through holding youth camps, while a related phenomenon has been the formation of youth movements with a strong paramilitary character and linked to the ruling political parties. The main reason for the establishment of such groups and camps seems to be concern over the growing unemployment and radicalism of youth (the two are seen as being interlinked), and the need to harness that radicalism to the ends of the particular bantustan. The inculcation of discipline, loyalty to the bantustan, the fostering of an ethnic identity, and the acquisition of military and development skills are emphasised.

Youth movements have been set up in Ciskei and KwaZulu, while in other bantustans youth camps have been held with the same underlying purpose. In 1980 it was announced that an administration-sponsored paramilitary youth movement, Intsika Yesiswe (Pillar of the Nation), had been established in Ciskei. It was reported that Chief Sebe had decided to create the movement to counter the growing disillusionment of the youth with the rewards offered by the homeland system, to 'keep the wolf from the door', and to 'occupy our youth meaningfully and profitably for the whole year' (Evans, 1983: 23; SAIRR, 1980: 402).

In KwaZulu, the harnessing of the youth has taken place through both the Inkatha Youth Brigade, which has played a stormtrooper role in conflict against the 'comrades' in KwaZulu–Natal, and the Youth Service Corps (YSC). It has been argued elsewhere that this paramilitary corps was set up after the youth brigade failed to prevent pupils from participating in the schools boycott in 1980 (Maré and Hamilton, 1987: 187). In 1982 the Chief Minister of KwaZulu, Mangosuthu Buthelezi, said that the YSC structures would follow the lines of the Inkatha Youth Brigade, and would be formed into companies belonging to a regiment for a particular area.

During 1987 the Venda administration launched a 'youth adventure camp' at Maheni shooting range as a joint project of the VDF and the Venda Department of Education. The administration described the camp's objectives as being to educate the youth positively towards the VDF and the administration, to teach students to obey orders, to give lessons on defence tasks and on warfare, and to give youths target practice (*Weekly Mail*, 15.5.1987; *New Nation*, 19.11.1987).

The undermining of control

The formation of the bantustans has had some unintended, although perhaps predictable, effects. While Pretoria has attempted to draw the bantustans into its defence system, they have, paradoxically, undermined the system. Firstly, the creation of thousands of kilometres of new and fragmented borders, many adjacent or near to frontline states, has added to security problems. The weak bantustan armies are ill-equipped to protect these borders adequately.

In addition to this, the bantustans have increasingly become sources of instability. Some bantustan leaders are reluctant to accept un-equivocally Pretoria's control, especially where it relates to security issues. For instance, not all bantustan leaders have welcomed the role played by the SADF in suppressing unrest. The Chief Minister of KaNgwane, Mr Enos Mabusa, questioned the need for SADF troops in the bantustan during unrest there in 1986, as they gave the 'false impression that KaNgwane is in a state of war'. He said that the army was not there at his invitation and that the police were capable of handling unrest (SAIRR, 1986: 654). The KwaZulu administration refused to cooperate in the establishment of 121 Battalion, and, as a result, manpower levels within it dropped after an initial growth. The refusal would seem to have little to do with an aversion to the establishment of a KwaZulu regional battalion *per se*, but rather with the fact that it is not under KwaZulu's control. In fact, in 1984 Chief Buthelezi said that a paramilitary wing of the police force, over which KwaZulu would have control, was likely to be established (Grundy, 1986: 76; SAIRR, 1984: 535).

Growing instability in the bantustans is also the result of the existence of power-hungry and corrupt elites, having a very small social base and intent on entrenching their power. The emergence of such elites has its origins in South Africa's determination to ensure the allegiance of the ruling groups within the bantustans. To this end the central state created structures of power based on the most conservative traditional element, the chiefs. The cooptation of the chiefs was assured by granting them greatly extended responsibilities and financial autonomy.

Apart from widespread popular opposition to bantustan rule, the crisis of bantustan administration has been deepened by a number of challenges from within the system. There have been struggles between sectors of the elite for more power, and challenges from sub-elites, in particular the armed forces, dissatisfied with corruption and their lack of access to power.[3] These challenges have manifested themselves in a series of coups and attempted coups.

Hunger for power underlay Charles Sebe's attempted coup against his brother, President Lennox Sebe, president of the Ciskei, in 1983. He was aided by the TDF (organised by the Selous Scouts), which was advancing the imperialist ambitions of Transkei's ruling Matanzima family to create one great Xhosaland by uniting Ciskei and Transkei. South African intelligence sources were a factor in scotching the coup attempt, but in 1986 the TDF managed to spring Charles Sebe from jail and whisk him off to safety in the Transkei. A second attempted coup, staged by the Selous Scouts against Lennox Sebe in 1987, also failed. Chief Lent Maqoma, a former Ciskei politician in exile in the Transkei, was to have taken over the government in the Ciskei.

In contrast, the recent coups in the Transkei and Bophuthatswana had their roots in the dissatisfaction of an important sub-elite, the armed forces, with the management of the bantustans.

The Transkei coup

In October 1987 the prime minister of Transkei, Chief George Matanzima, and nine of his cabinet ministers were forced to resign after a successful coup led by Brigadier Bantu Holomisa.

A number of factors led to Chief George's downfall. Firstly, under his rule, the corruption which was already endemic in the homeland deepened. Secondly, he exacerbated tensions within the region by alienating a section of the ruling elite, the Sicgau chiefs of east Pondoland, when he stripped his political opponent, Paramount Chief Sabata Dalindyebo, of his paramount chieftaincy. A third factor was Chief George's close relationship with the Selous Scouts, who had been training the TDF since 1980. In early April 1987 about 200 junior officers in the TDF arrested the Scout's leader, Major-General Ron Reid-Daly, and other white officers, and a total of 27 were then expelled from the Transkei. Holomisa was promoted to the rank of major-general and succeeded General Zondwa Mtirara as commander of the armed forces. Mtirara, who had supported the white advisers, resigned after the 'mutiny', saying that he feared for his life (*Eastern Province Herald*, 9.4.1987).

The national executive of the ruling Transkei National Independence Party (TNIP) elected Miss Stella Sicgau, daughter of the late Chief Botha Sicgau, as the new prime minister and leader of the party. On 30 December Miss Sicgau was deposed in a bloodless coup after only 86 days in office, on the grounds of alleged corruption. However, there were other reports that the real reason was because she had said she would detain Holomisa.

Holomisa declared martial law and suspended Transkei's constitution. He banned all political activity and said that the country would be run by an interim administration comprising a military council and an appointed council of ministers. Describing the military takeover as an interim measure until a general election could be held, he asked the South African government not to interfere (*Eastern Province Herald*, 31.12.1987).

Bophuthatswana coup

On 10 February 1988 Radio Bophuthatswana announced that President Lucas Mangope of Bophuthatswana had been deposed in a military coup and that the army had handed power to the leader of the opposition Progressive People's Party (PPP), Mr Rocky Malebane-Metsing. Between 85 and 90 members of the BDF and the National Guard arrested President Mangope, most of his cabinet and 14 SADF seconded officers, and held them captive in Mmabatho's Independence

Stadium. Fifteen hours later the coup was smashed by a 34-man strong SADF force in armoured vehicles and helicopters. The SADF moved in after a decision by the State President, P. W. Botha, following an urgent meeting of the State Security Council. It was believed that Bophuthatswana's foreign minister, Mr S. Rathebe, who had sought refuge in the South African embassy in Mmabatho, had telephoned Pretoria to ask it to intervene. It was announced shortly after the coup that an 'element' of the SADF force would remain in Bophuthatswana, but was not intended to be a permanent presence (*Citizen*, 11.2.1988).

Mr Metsing escaped and later surfaced in Zambia, where he denied he had been behind the coup, claiming that the first he knew of it was when soldiers had fetched him from his home to be sworn in as the new president (*Sunday Tribune*, 27.3.1988).

In March the government disbanded the National Guard. It had been formed in 1986 with the sole intention of protecting dignitaries and buildings. About 250 of the 600-strong force, which received six weeks' training, were based at Mmabatho at the time of the coup.

In April, in what was seen to be a direct outcome of the coup, Brigadier Hennie Riekert, Minister of Defence, resigned. Riekert admitted that the country's intelligence forces had been taken completely by surprise, and that the defence force had failed to take any action in the 15 hours that the coup had lasted before it was crushed (*Citizen*, 20.4.1988).

Comparison of the coups

The coups are significant for the way in which they highlighted weaknesses in bantustan administration and the position of the military in bantustan power relations.

One of the key reasons given by both forces for the respective coups was the widespread corruption in the bantustans. Corruption in Transkei had come to light through the findings of a commission of inquiry into the Department of Works and Energy, which alleged that the Matanzima brothers had defrauded the government of at least R42m. On seizing power, Holomisa expanded the terms of reference of a second commission of inquiry into the Department of Commerce, Industries and Tourism, which had also revealed corrupt dealings by George Matanzima. Widespread corruption was also cited by dissatisfied forces in Bophuthatswana as one of the prime reasons for the coup, especially the dealings between Mangope and Mr Shabtai Kalmanovitch, a Russian-born Israeli, who had ingratiated himself with Mangope and had been appointed the bantustan's trade representative in Israel. He had amassed a fortune in Bophuthatswana after securing two lucrative contracts – one to build a shopping centre in Garankuwa, and the second, which was given to him without tenders being called for, to build the Independence Stadium. In January he was arrested in

Israel on charges of spying for the KGB (*Sunday Star*, 14.2.1988).
The coups also point to dissatisfaction caused by Pretoria's policy of seconding white officers to senior positions in the bantustan armies. The black troops saw this control as blocking their chances of promotion and as racism. Giving reasons for the coup attempt, the BDF said that all senior posts in the force were held by whites seconded by South Africa, who were allegedly ill-treating soldiers, and that Mangope had given his son a commission in the BDF without his having received military training. Attempts by Mangope to brush off the coup as merely the work of the National Guard must be seen as a face-saving exercise. There is little doubt that the troops staging the coup had the support of the BDF, which did not intervene.

The role played by the Selous Scouts had also led to widespread dissatisfaction in the two bantustans. The Selous Scouts had been active in the Transkei since 1980. South Africa ceased its training of the TDF in 1978 when Kaiser Matanzima broke off diplomatic relations with South Africa over the latter's refusal to cede him East Griqualand. Relations were restored in 1980, and the Transkei, with South Africa's approval, brought in the Selous Scouts under Ron Reid-Daly, who was made chief of the defence force, to take over the training of the TDF. On his retirement as chief of the defence force in 1986, Reid-Daly and 22 other Selous Scouts stayed on officially as security advisers – 'but in fact as a private army loyal to George Matanzima personally' (*Transformation*, 6, 1988: 62). The Scouts had won the enmity of a group of TDF soldiers under Brigadier Holomisa, which had been critical of their role in the attempted Ciskei coup as well as of their presence and influence in general (*Sunday Tribune*, 12.4.1988). Malebane-Metsing mentioned the alleged secret employment of the Selous Scouts by Mangope after their expulsion from the Transkei as a reason for the coup in Bophuthatswana (*Sunday Tribune*, 27.3.1988).

The coups also point to the irregular practices of the ruling elite when faced with opposition from other elite groups, and the instability these power struggles have caused. The PPP, which has its power base in Bafokeng, long an area of opposition to Mangope and Malebane-Metsing's home, alleged that Mangope had rigged the 1987 elections (*Star*, 14.2.1988). These irregularities were put forward as another reason for the coup. In much the same way, the disaffection of the east Pondo-land chiefs was a challenge to the Matanzimas' rule, with claims that the Matanzima–Sicgau split reached into the military (*Transformation*, 6, 1988: 62).

While the coups point to serious instabilities within the bantustans, neither constituted a direct challenge to the concept of 'independence', however. Both had their origins in the dissatisfaction of a deprived sub-elite, the armed forces, which did not wish to do away with the bantustans, but rather wanted a share in the spoils.

It is difficult to gauge the extent of popular support for the coups. While there were reports of scenes of jubilation in Bophuthatswana, the situation in the Transkei seemed different, with crowds showing their support for the Matanzimas when they appeared to attend a meeting of the military council in Umtata (*Sunday Star,* 10.1.1988). However, it may be that there was support for the coup but that the populace was wary of showing this.

Pretoria's reaction to the coup underlines a number of features bearing on the nature of the relationship between the bantustans and the central state. It throws into sharp relief the continuing dependence of these areas on South Africa. The question to be asked is why South Africa chose to intervene in Bophuthatswana, thereby undermining the homeland's 'independence'. Why did it not follow the same path as in the Transkei coup?

Pretoria's own stated reasons bear scrutiny. These were that the Bophuthatswana coup was violent, while the Transkei's was not; the Bophuthatswana government asked South Africa to intervene, while Holomisa asked it not to (Malebane-Metsing did make such a request, however); in Transkei (as compared with Bophuthatswana) the coup leaders did not seek to replace the constitutional head of office (this is also not accurate, as Holomisa replaced the head with himself); and in Transkei there was no competing entity vying for power. While these may have played a part in South Africa's thinking, they cannot be taken as the real reasons.

A number of more complex reasons need to be considered. First there is the relatively greater strategic importance of Bophuthatswana, and the necessity of securing the Botswana border against insurgency. Second, with one coup having already occurred a few months earlier, South Africa's failure to intervene could have sparked off other coup attempts, thus increasing instability in the bantustans. A third factor relates to Pretoria's concern over the putative rulers. Although Malebane-Metsing cannot be seen as an opponent of 'independence', he is probably seen by Pretoria as having undesirable populist leanings. He was accused of being a member of the United Democratic Front and the ANC by bantustan MPs, and of being the 'prime mover' in unrest in the Odi–Moretele area in Bophuthatswana (*City Press,* 15.6.1987). Keeping control in the hands of Mangope, a friend of South Africa, and the only bantustan leader to win international support (albeit from small conservative groupings), was more important to Pretoria than a new government head, however zealously he might clean up corruption. The Matanzimas, on the other hand, had no international credibility, while Holomisa, who had received most of his training with the SADF and was one of the first blacks to undergo the staff and management course at the army college in Pretoria, must have seemed potentially more likely to maintain the bantustan status quo than Malebane-Metsing.

Conclusion

Bantustan armed forces have been used as part of South Africa's defence system both in its area defence against insurgents and in a COIN role within the bantustans. South Africa has attempted to maintain ultimate control over these forces with a view to harnessing them to its political and military ends. However, Pretoria has not always been able to maintain total control over the regional armies, and, by their very creation, has laid the way open for them to intervene in regional politics. In a period of growing regional instability, bantustan forces, or parts of these forces, have added to the instability by sometimes engaging in action designed to serve the corrupt and (in the case of the Matanzimas) imperialist ambitions of bantustan elites. At other times such as in the Bophuthatswana and Transkei coups, they have acted against such elites, both to gain increased power for themselves and with the professed aim of stamping out corruption.

Whatever its professed aims, the advent of a military government in the Transkei has extended the militarisation process within South Africa. Although Holomisa has said that he will bow out to a civilian government once order is restored, whether he will do so remains to be seen. In addition, if he is successful in his aims and succeeds in winning popular support, the example might not be lost on planners in Pretoria, who have already shown their anxiety about levels of corruption in the bantustans and the resulting instability. Pretoria might be willing to see the example repeated, and the militarisation process further extended.

The militaries within the bantustans, although weak in comparison with the SADF, have shown themselves to be capable of affecting regional events in significant ways. It would appear that because of their unpredictability, bantustans and their military forces form far from adequate structures for any future confederal or federal plan the South African state might have in mind for the regions, and may, in addition, constitute weak links in South Africa's overall defence system.

14 Vigilantes and the militarisation of South Africa
NICHOLAS HAYSOM

For township residents in many parts of South Africa, vigilante activity has become the most terrifying manifestation of a conflict-ridden and violent society. Since 1985 this phenomenon has claimed the lives of several hundred people, rendered thousands homeless, and in some regions created an acute refugee problem. The emergence and role of vigilante groups in South Africa's black areas since 1985 is an expression of the militarisation of South Africa. The violence accompanying their activities amounts to a low-intensity civil war, which appears on the surface to be conducted an arm's length away from an aggressive state. In fact, however, the state benefits in a variety of ways from the conflict it covertly encourages or sponsors.

As other commentators have noted, there is a strong parallel between vigilante violence in South Africa and that in El Salvador and the Philippines. In those countries vigilante assassinations have become a central element of the mode of repression adopted by the governing regimes (Diokno, 1988; Prendes, 1988). Modern counter-insurgency theory lays stress on 'total war', which incorporates the concept of 'winning hearts and minds'. The need to destroy popular movements without appearing to be directly waging war on the populace is the dilemma that has led to the 'low-intensity' civil wars of Central America, the vigilante movements of the Philippines and South Africa, and the destabilisation of the frontline states in southern Africa. The logic of this theory involves the clandestine creation of surrogate armed forces, which appear to emerge spontaneously from the 'people' themselves. It is then claimed that the Contras, UNITA, or the Philippine vigilante groupings are an expression of popular support, or popular rebellion, as the case may be. The truth, though, lies elsewhere.

Vigilantes
This chapter is more concerned to record the patterns and implications of vigilante activities in South Africa than to provide specific details of each vigilante group. A full survey of these groups can be found elsewhere (Haysom, 1986; Lawyers Committee for Human Rights, 1987; Catholic Institute for International Relations, 1988b; Aitcheson, 1988). In South Africa the term 'vigilantes' denotes violent,

organised and conservative groups operating within black communities. Although they receive no official recognition, they are politically directed in the sense that they act to neutralise individuals and organisations opposed to the apartheid state and its institutions. These features, and the fact that the groups allegedly enjoy varying degrees of police support, are what links the A-Team, Phakatis, Mabangalala, Amadoda, Witdoeke, Amabutho, Mbokotho and the Green Berets.

Although the composition and operation of these groups varies from region to region, the face of the vigilante phenomenon is well illustrated by the following random but representative incidents I have described elsewhere (Haysom, 1986).

In April–May 1985 a vigilante grouping calling themselves the Phakatis emerged in Thabong township in the Orange Free State. The group, openly using the facilities of the municipal authority, embarked on a campaign of indiscriminate assaults on youths whom they believed were involved in a school boycott. One night they apprehended a boy on the streets, David Mabenyane, and whipped him so severely that he died. After whipping the boy, and while he was still alive, they dropped him at the local police station.

During August 1985 armed gangs of Amabutho took to searching houses in Umlazi, Natal, claiming they were looking for United Democratic Front 'troublemakers'. Mr B. M., a UDF supporter, was at home one night when the Amabutho arrived at his house, surrounded it and set it alight. His brother attempted to flee with his infant niece but was shot in the head. His elder sister was also shot as she tried to escape the flames. B. M. recognised one of the armed men as a local member of the KwaZulu homeland legislature.

In 1985 the KwaNdebele homeland leader, Simon Skosana, launched a vigilante organisation called Mbokotho. On 1 January 1986 a large group of Mbokotho vigilantes abducted over 400 men from the Moutse district, which was resisting the jurisdiction of the KwaNdebele homeland authorities, and took them to a community hall in the capital of KwaNdebele. There they were ordered to strip and were severely beaten for several hours before being released. The prime minister of KwaNdebele supervised the assaults. Some of the victims identified their assailants to the police that very day when they were being escorted back to Moutse. Police have not as yet apprehended any of the assailants.

A more recent example is that described in the *Monitor* (June 1988: 46). In Kwanobuhle, a township bordering on Uitenhage in the Eastern Cape, a vigilante group calling itself Ama-Afrika emerged in the latter part of 1986. On 4 January 1987 a mob marched through the township destroying the houses of 14 activists and killing two persons. The people responsible for the chaos that reigned for more than 12 hours were led by the Ama-Afrika. Most of them live in the newer section of

Kwanobuhle, known as Khayelitsha. All the houses they attacked were in the area now known as Old Kwanobuhle, and in particular in the very oldest section, 'Angola', where many members of UDF-affiliated organisations lived.

One of the most disturbing aspects of the day's events was that the Kwanobuhle municipal police and the South African Police apparently made little effort to curtail the violence and destruction. Indeed, the rampage appears to have been pre-arranged on the understanding that the destruction and assaults would be perpetrated by the vigilantes with the police monitoring the events to ensure the safety and success of the Ama-Afrika. The police also used the opportunity to take more detainees.

Since the emergence of vigilante groupings in 1985 the media and the Bureau of Information have persisted in referring to all incidents of vigilante violence under the label of 'black-on-black' conflict. This label has as much heuristic value as describing the Second World War as white-on-white violence. It serves in effect to obscure the emergence of a pattern of extra-legal violence by right-wing black groupings, and to hide the relationship between them and apartheid structures. Furthermore, the label implicitly suggests that the conflict in the townships can be understood in terms of a racial propensity for tribal or internecine strife.

The emergence of vigilantes

Vigilantes are not an entirely new phenomenon in South Africa. For example, vigilantes supervised by the Ciskeian authorities terrorised the inhabitants of Mdantsane during the course of a bus boycott from June to October 1983 (Lakob, 1984; Haysom, 1983). However, 1985 saw a sudden proliferation of such groups in the bantustans as well as the emergence of their more complex urban counterparts.

In 1986 a survey of 13 communities which had experienced vigilante violence revealed a distinct pattern (Haysom, 1986). The communities examined in the survey included Crossroads, Ashton and KTC (Western Cape), Queenstown and Fort Beaufort (Eastern Cape), Huhudi (Northern Cape), Thabong (Orange Free State), Umlazi, Inanda and Lamontville (Natal), Leandra, Moutse and Ekangala (Eastern Transvaal), and Soweto (Transvaal). Subsequent studies have confirmed this pattern (CIIR, 1988b: 67–163).

The first feature of this pattern was that nationwide vigilante activity in the form of violence against members of anti-apartheid organisations commenced in 1985. As the political crisis in South Africa deepened in the mid-1980s, and as the crisis of control over black areas extended geographically, so did the incidence of vigilante activity.

Secondly, the composition of both the vigilante leadership and the victim groups was broadly the same in all regions. The target groups were those perceived to be resisting apartheid institutions – whether students campaigning against 'Bantu education', community leaders creating alternative local structures, or communities resisting the juris-diction of homeland authorities. Vigilante leadership in the bantustans was comprised mostly of functionaries in the homeland governments (including chiefs), and in the urban areas of members of the state and local state organs (police and community councillors) or members of an 'embryonic middle-class with an interest in stability and a natural inclination to conservatism' (Seekings, 1985: 27).

The third feature in the pattern of violence was that the vigilantes appeared to enjoy police support, operating brazenly as if there were no legal constraints on their extra-legal violence.

It cannot be firmly proven that all vigilante groups received overt sanction or direct support from the security forces, although they allegedly did in areas such as Crossroads, Kwanobuhle and Queenstown (CIIR, 1988a: 10–14). However, the security forces' reluctance to curb vigilante activity and failure to intervene in township conflict allowed the vigilantes a substantial advantage over other groups. The effect on anti-apartheid organisations and residents was much the same whether the police actively sanctioned and supported the vigilantes or merely appeared incapable of curbing or reluctant to curb their activities. This was particularly the case where the vigilante group had access to fire-arms. The police's passivity while a vigilante gang killed community leader Mayise in Leandra (Transvaal), or while an impi of Inkatha supporters marched into Lamontville (Natal), or as Mbokotho leaders pursued an intensive regional campaign of intimidation in KwaNdebele, must be contrasted with their vigorous dispersal of UDF gatherings and prosecution of members of anti-apartheid organisations and trade unions. When the victim communities or organisations attempted physical contest with the vigilantes, police intervention was perceived as supportive of the vigilantes.

The vigilantes' use of township council facilities (notably in Thabong and Ashton) and resources provided by homeland governments (in KwaNdebele and Ciskei) demonstrated further support for vigilante activities by the authorities. This does not mean that the widespread emergence of right-wing groups can be shown to have been centrally orchestrated. But a copy of minutes of a meeting between a senior police officer and black traders in the Vaal Triangle area on 13 November 1985 suggests that police attitudes could have prompted the formation of vigilante groups in some areas. At this meeting the police officer offered to arm the traders and encouraged them to form 'a self-protection organisation' (Haysom, 1986: 8–9). It should also be mentioned that it is nearly impossible for a black South African to acquire a gun licence without police approval. However, in Natal many of the vigilante warlords openly carry firearms, and recently a security policeman was

seen acquiring from a sportshop six guns registered in the name of
Inkatha members.

Leandra represents a typical case-study illustrating all the elements
of the new vigilantism. In Leandra, a black township on the East Rand,
the residents had been involved in a grassroots campaign to improve
their living conditions in order to prevent a threatened forced removal.
To this end they had formed an alternative civic structure to the
officially approved municipal council. By late 1985 the organisational
strength of the Leandra Action Committee (LAC) was such that the
authorities were compelled to negotiate with one of its leaders, Chief
Ampie Mayise, rather than with the officially recognised black
councillors. Shortly thereafter vigilantes began brazenly attacking
members of the LAC. The attacks culminated in a mob assault on Chief
Mayise's house on 11 January 1986, during which Mayise was hacked to
death. A policeman alerted to the attack by Mayise's call for assistance
to the nearby police station was ordered not to intervene. Shortly thereafter youths in the township were forced to flee the area for fear of their
lives, and the LAC collapsed. No-one has been prosecuted for the
killing of Mayise. Throughout the period of violence the police are
alleged to have openly sided with the vigilantes, and have even been
accused of arming one of them (Haysom, 1986: 32–46). The police did
however raid a church sanctuary in Johannesburg and detain LAC
youths who had taken refuge there.

Why vigilantes?

A description of vigilante activities does not answer two most
important questions: why did vigilantism come to the fore as a form of
repression against popular organisations, and why did vigilantes
emerge only in 1985?

To understand why vigilantes made their appearance in 1985 we
must examine briefly the intensity and scale of the political crisis of
apartheid during 1984–6. Black urban councils and municipal advisory
bodies had in the course of the reform process been delegated increasing
executive functions in the administration of black townships. As
pressure on the government to provide for meaningful political
participation by blacks increased, the state proposed that such participation take place through structures built upon these black councils, now
known as community councils. The political crisis South Africa faced
in 1985 and continues to face is founded on the refusal of blacks to
accept these inadequate alternatives to full political participation.

In 1984 the United Democratic Front and other organisations
launched a nationwide campaign of opposition to the exclusion of
Africans from the franchise in the new constitution and the partial
cooption of coloureds and Indians. The opposition was also directed at
what came to be known as the 'Koornhof Bills', which were intended to

refashion some of the institutions of apartheid. In particular, the bills sought to bolster the community councils and fortify the legislative grid which separated homeland residents from their urban counterparts. The campaign was undoubtedly successful as evidenced by the very low percentage polls in the Indian and coloured elections for the new tricameral parliament, and in the elections for community councillors in African areas. One of the consequences of the campaign was a rapid politicisation of black communities.

At the same time, the economic climate in South Africa began to deteriorate as a recession developed and unemployment reached extremely high levels. In the urban areas, short-sighted parsimony by the authorities responsible for black local government brought pressure on the community councils to become self-financing. When the community councils attempted to impose increases in rentals and service charges in order to meet their budgets, a number of civic associations began to orchestrate protests against these bodies, which were perceived to be corrupt and self-serving. The protests took the form of marches, attacks on the councillors, and a rents boycott which involved up to 300 000 persons and cost the state over R188 million (*Sunday Tribune*, 31.8.1986).

Late in 1984, school pupils commenced a nationwide campaign against inadequate education, and were confronted with an authoritarian approach to their representations. A school boycott spread throughout the country so that by the end of the year even areas in the bantustans had been affected.

This confluence of political and economic forces generated widespread protest in the townships in the Vaal Triangle area from September 1984. As the school and township protests gathered momentum, a pattern of conflict emerged that was to be tragically measured by a daily death-rate. Protests would lead to confrontations with the police, which would be followed by acts of arson and damage to property. At the funerals of the victims of these confrontations, police would again confront the mourners. The result was a self-perpetuating spiral of violence. In late 1984, one of the largest stayaways in South African history took place when 800 000 trade-union members responded to the call of township residents and schoolchildren complaining of inferior schooling, inadequate township conditions and police brutality. While the issues were initially bread-and-butter ones, the frustration and resentment of township residents became increasingly directed at the community councillors and black policemen, persons believed to be profiting from their participation in administering apartheid.

The existing administrative structures collapsed in the majority of urban areas in the Transvaal and in the Eastern Cape. By 1985 only 5 of the 38 black local authorities could operate effectively, and community councillors and policemen who had not resigned were being housed, for their own safety, outside the black townships (SAIRR, 1985: 89). In order to reconstitute and bolster government institutions, particularly the community councils, the police were strengthened by additional personnel from the South African Defence Force. Regular security force patrols confirmed township residents' fears that they were under siege by an occupying army. Clashes between security forces and township residents mounted and finally in July 1985 the government declared a state of emergency.

In the homelands, resistance to the bantustan authorities began to emerge in discrete pockets. The homelands could not be isolated from the rebellion which had spread throughout South Africa. Moreover, the homeland regimes are particularly brittle and undemocratic, dependent on authoritarian rule by chiefs and government agencies.

It is in the context of this crisis of control in black areas and the failure of the police to restore 'order' that we should understand the emergence of vigilantes. By mid-1985 it became apparent that the state's initial response to the civil rebellion – 'maximum force' policing – was failing. That grizzly index of 'unrest', the daily death-rate, had not been affected by the proclamation of the state of emergency. Moreover the policing methods had further politicised the black community and created a degree of social cohesion amongst township residents. What was needed was an additional disorganising strategy. Vigilante groups were specifically suited for such a purpose, for a variety of reasons.

Firstly, the South African Police and South African Defence Force were constrained by potential publicity and hindered by legal considerations in perpetrating the deliberate terror and violence deemed necessary to combat popular organisations.

Secondly, however brutal the vigilante groups, by purporting to act under the banner of 'restoring law and order' they could justify their actions, elicit at least some support from the police and, in certain cases, play on a broad sense of disgruntlement with the disruption caused by the unrest (particularly where vanguard youth groups had acted undemocratically in imposing community boycotts). Three groups – black policemen, traders and community councillors – naturally allied themselves with the need to restore 'law and order'. For example the mayor of Thabong, explaining his support for vigilante activity to local businessmen, stated: 'Under the guidance of council members, patrols were organised and inspired by the old axiom "spare the rod and spoil the child". All meetings of potential stone throwers and arsonists were broken up with no more violence than the energetic use of sjamboks [whips] and the result has been most satisfying.' (*Sunday Star*, 9.6.1985) Black policemen, when requested by residents to curb vigilante activity, frequently responded with comments such as, 'You come here when you are in trouble, but you forget that you broke our houses.'

Thirdly, the security forces could not coerce support for community councils and could not administer the townships themselves. A Soweto councillor clearly expressed the council's frustration with conventional responses to township opposition in a speech to a Sofasonke party rally. He stated that he had asked the government to allow councillors to avenge attacks on their homes, and to embark on full-scale vigilante activities aimed at rooting out *abo siyayinova* (troublemakers) in the townships. 'Hopes that security forces would bring peace were a pipe dream,' he said (Seekings, 1985: 28). Furthermore, unlike the random and indiscriminate violence which took place when the police confronted popular organisations, vigilante terror was more accurately targeted on the leaders of oppositional organisations. The terror came from within the community, thus rupturing community confidence and cohesion. When leaders were systematically assaulted or killed and the police appeared unwilling or unable to stop this, it became almost impossible for popular organisations to function in the open. In such cases, it was not only vigilante interests that were served but also those of the authorities which the popular organisations challenged. Vigilantes in magisterial districts not covered by the 1985 state of emergency disrupted civic and youth organisations to a greater extent than did the detentions and actions of the security forces in townships under emergency regulations.

Fourthly, vigilantes are cheap. Lennox Sebe, prime minister of Ciskei, rationalised the formation of the Green Berets in his bantustan by saying that the vigilantes were acting as low-cost police auxiliaries. In this sense the vigilante phenomenon represented a Reaganomic tendency in one of South Africa's 'growth industries' – the privatisation of repression.

Fifthly, as its proponents argue, privatisation has ideological benefits. Vigilante violence, reported locally and internationally as 'black-on-black' violence, seemed to justify the security force presence in the townships on the ground that the residents are susceptible to internecine strife. More important, organised opposition to the state was destroyed without the intervention or presence of the security forces, and without the same public outrage that would follow brutalities committed by them.

Finally, cowed and disorganised communities gave rise to a political vacuum which could be filled by community councils or homeland political parties, and allowed these bodies to impose their will on the communities. This was so particularly for communities that, without access to direct political power, had to rely on collective organisation as one of their only sources of strength.

Communities that were victims of vigilante action were faced with a dilemma as to how they could best resist attack. Should they go on the offensive and commit a pre-emptive violent assault on the vigilantes? There is no doubt that they would, in such an event, face the full might of the very law-and-order machinery which had failed to protect them. Furthermore, vigilantes were in most cases better armed, and defence against them could prove fatal. Just how effective the vigilantes were, and how difficult it was to oppose them, can be seen in the cases of Crossroads and Edenvale.

In January 1986 vigilantes, calling themselves 'Witdoeke', emerged in four squatter camps near Cape Town referred to here as Crossroads and KTC. The communities, numbering nearly 70 000 persons, had been engaged for several years in a struggle with the authorities over their right to live in these settlements. They had persisted in their campaign despite detentions, threats and intrigue by the authorities. Vigilantes tore through the camps in May and June, destroying and burning houses and driving the inhabitants out. Inhabitants of the squatter camps have described the attacks, which started on 17 May, claiming that police assisted the Witdoeke by breaking up groups of resisting residents and clearing the way for Witdoeke to penetrate the camp. Police stood by and watched the blatantly illegal destruction of property and the assaults. They intervened whenever the Witdoeke were under attack. Witdoeke also took 'prisoners' and tortured them without police intervention (Lawyers Committee for Human Rights, 1987; CIIR, 1988b: 69–82; Phillips, 1988). In the attacks, 53 people were killed and 7 000 shacks demolished. In several weeks vigilantes accomplished what the state had failed to do in ten years. The 70 000 refugees were compelled to seek refuge in other townships, including the government-designated option, Khayelitsha.

The Edendale valley near Pietermaritzburg has since 1987 become the site of the bloodiest and most violent clashes in Natal between residents who are supporters of Inkatha and those who are not.

In a series of attacks and counter-attacks between pro- and anti-Inkatha groups between September 1987 and March 1988, 528 people were killed (Aitcheson, 1988: 16–19). This figure comprises nearly two-thirds of the persons killed nationwide in 'unrest-related events' in this period. In other words, vigilante violence and counter-vigilante violence in Pietermaritzburg have formed the single most important cause of death under the present state of emergency.

The background to the conflict in the region dates back to 1984. That year saw the formation of UDF-affiliated youth groups; this was followed by the first attacks on Inkatha opponents. In 1985 the United Workers' Union of South Africa was formed as the trade-union wing of Inkatha and soon thereafter attacks commenced on its rival, Cosatu, and its members. In December 1985 in nearby Howick, a mob led by nine Inkatha members dragged three Cosatu worker leaders out of a car and killed them. A stayaway called by the UDF and Cosatu on 5 and

6 May 1987 was 90 per cent successful, and Inkatha, fearing it was losing ground, commenced a recruitment drive. UDF and Cosatu claimed that this drive was accompanied by threats of violence and actual violence. In Vulindlela all residents were ordered to join Inkatha by 4 October 1987. This coercion was met with the increasing resistance. In January 1988, when Inkatha members are alleged to have mounted another attack, the monthly death-rate reached 161. The Inkatha 'warlords' who engaged in these acts of violence had little or no state action taken against them. When charged with murder they have been immediately released on bail. On the other hand over 1 076 UDF or Cosatu members were detained as against a handful of Inkatha members, according to one analyst (Merrit, 1988).

In an attempt to halt the warlords, ten Supreme Court interdicts were brought by a legal team acting for Cosatu. The interdicts have had only a limited impact. Four applicants or witnesses to these legal proceedings have been killed or executed, and none of the assailants has been prosecuted to date (late 1988). Many township residents feel that legal proceedings expose persons to violent retaliation, and afford little protection. Indeed the situation had become so serious by August 1988 that the lawyers were questioning whether the courts could really protect those who sought its assistance. For example, Johannes Mthembu and his four sons, living in Imbali near Pietermaritzburg, had clashed with local Inkatha personalities in late 1987. Mthembu brought interdict proceedings in January 1988 after a clash in which one of his sons, Elphas, was shot. After service of the court papers one of the Inkatha leaders cited in the interdict arrived at Mthembu's house. After an incident two other sons, Smallridge and Simon, were shot, and one of them died. In July 1988, shortly before the case was due to re-open, Mthembu's fourth son, Ernest, was shot dead when he opened the front door of his house. The family has had to leave the area and seek refugee assistance (*Natal Witness,* 5.7.1988). Court papers have also alleged instances where the security forces appeared to be sympathetic to Inkatha's activities. In a mob attack on the Ashton township outside Pietermaritzburg by persons who had attended a rally addressed by Inkatha leaders, the police were said in court papers to have stood by when victims were assaulted and killed.

From vigilantes to community guards

A trend which has caused concern amongst human rights activists and victim communities alike is the induction of vigilantes into the state's formal law-and-order machinery. The incorporation of many of the Queenstown vigilantes into the Queenstown Commando is one such example. A more prevalent form of this process is taking place through the recruitment of community guards, a form of municipal police under the control of the community councillors. It has already been reported that erstwhile vigilantes in Ashton and Thabong have made application to join the community guards. Minister Chris Heunis stated in 1986 that R26 million had been allocated that year for the training of 5 000 guards (*Work in Progress,* 29, 1986: 40). At a recent passing-out parade, he remarked that community guards would have the task of looking after law and order in the townships. He said that they should expect to be unpopular and that they may well come under the same hostility as has been directed at black police and community councillors.

The black municipal police ('Greenflies') and police auxiliaries (*'kits-konstabels'*) have made a special contribution to converting the mood of the townships from one of protest to fear. Human rights groups from the Eastern Cape and the Transvaal report numerous incidents in which the municipal police have assumed the methods of the vigilantes. Complaints include torture, beatings, thefts and forcible evictions. As such, the municipal police's responsibilities seem to have less to do with crime prevention and more with political pacification (Black Sash, 1988). At the same time, the Greenflies' increased involvement with the policing of the townships has gone hand in hand with a withdrawal of the security forces from the areas. Moreover, there has been little or no attempt by the authorities to curb the illegal activities of these forces despite the intense resentment of ordinary residents (Black Sash, 1988: 7; CIIR, 1988b: 31–66).

The community guards may well strengthen the hands of the community councillors in administering a reluctant and captive 'electorate'. However, black municipal authorities are vicariously liable in law for the actions of the guards should they perform their duties in the same fashion as have the vigilantes, and it can be expected that vigilante activities will still continue alongside such formal agencies.

Vigilantes and repression

It remains to place the vigilante phenomenon within the overall state strategy of repression and reform, and the current imperative to reconstitute a black politics dependent on and amenable to Nationalist government policies.

The vigilantes have become part of a multi-faceted strategy to create a moderate black politics. Vigilantism operates in tandem with other repressive practices. As an editorial in the *South African Journal on Human Rights* (1987: 145–6) points out:

The state of emergency provides a legal regime for the pacification and administration of the townships.

The mass detention of leaders and members of popular organisations and the intense police control over the freedom of assembly and expression results in organisational stasis in black areas.

Vigilantes are used to attack surviving popular organisations, and then the vigilantes together with municipal councillors and their police, *kitskonstabels,* or organisations such as Mbokotho, take charge of the townships. Activists returning to the area are isolated and victimised.

Upon this platform black local authorities are given both the financial and policing resources to administer or upgrade the area. Here, the joint management councils, convened and chaired by members of the SADF, play a crucial role in co-ordinating resources so as to win the 'hearts and minds' of township residents.

This strategy has been powerfully effective in some townships such as Alexandra in Johannesburg. Paradoxically, the very withdrawal of troops and police from the townships and their replacement by vigilantes, municipal police, planners and engineers is directly in line with the increasing militarisation of civil society. For greater importance is being laid by the state and security establishment on the manipulative but invisible role of the military in coordinating a total or comprehensive strategy involving economic, political, psychological and social factors. The logic of modern counter-insurgency theory requires that the opposition be destroyed without alienating township residents and without the security forces being seen as directly involved in a war on the masses. However, the prospect of this comprehensive strategy actually winning the 'hearts and minds' of township residents is remote. The vigilantes have not been able to create popular support for their politics. Instead they have created communities which are either sullenly cowed or violently vengeful.

PART THREE
Militarisation and the economy

15 The private sector and the security establishment

KATE PHILIP

With P. W. Botha's rise to power, 'total strategy' became the framework for an overarching state-wide political strategy. Central to that strategy was the argument that the war in South Africa is only 20 per cent military, and 80 per cent social, economic and political. This equation provided the basis on which the military legitimised its increasing involvement in the social, political and economic spheres of state decision-making, coordinated through the State Security Council.

With the imposition of the state of emergency in 1985, the military consolidated its 'creeping coup' by operationalising the structures of the National Security Management System at regional and local levels. This decisively entrenched military involvement and hegemony in internal security, defined in practice as the maintenance of control at all levels of society.

Within this context, resolving the country's economic crisis has been high on the state's list of strategic priorities. This is not a new development, but it has acquired an added urgency: the reformist thrust of the 'national security' strategy hinges on material upliftment schemes for black communities, that are in turn contingent on an economic upswing, and on the private sector's participation in the process.

As a result, security strategists have clearly targeted the private sector for their attentions, and have embarked upon a range of strategies both to win their support, and to draw them into the implementation of the state's social and economic programmes.

Although the private sector has not formulated a clear response to these initiatives, an increasing number of interfaces have been developing between the private sector and the security apparatuses at national, regional and local levels. These interfaces hold out the promise of economic advantage for the private sector, but their net effect is to reinforce state strategy politically and to implicate the private sector more deeply in the political maintenance of apartheid.

Before we look at some of the key interfaces that have developed at national, regional and local levels, it is necessary to contextualise this process by reviewing the political relationship between capital and the state since P. W. Botha came to power; and, secondly, by analysing the response of capital to the issue of security in the context of the states of emergency.

Capital and the state – a marriage of convenience

The rise to power of P. W. Botha signalled a shift in hegemony within the National Party, and the rise of a new alliance of social forces within Afrikanerdom. It did not merely signify the rise of the military in the corridors of power, but also reflected a shift in the class base of the party, with the emergence of Afrikaner capital as a powerful lobby. Botha's track record as Minister of Defence ensured him political support from these quarters. South Africa's military strategists, under the influence of Cold War ideology, were increasingly projecting themselves as the defenders of free enterprise, and asserting that 'military strength is inseparable from economic strength' (General Magnus Malan, quoted in Grundy, 1986: 67). The military advocates of 'total strategy' were also starting to formulate a reform package that would win black hearts and minds and ensure the long-term survival of free enterprise.

One of the Botha government's first priorities was to win support for 'total strategy' from the private sector, and from monopoly capital in particular. The Carlton Conference held in 1979 was intended to be the catalyst for this process. For a while, the private sector basked in Botha's flattery. Harry Oppenheimer declared the Carlton Conference to be the start of a 'new era'. Business leaders welcomed the new 'rationality' of the National Party, which seemed to be prepared to sacrifice some of the holy cows of Afrikaner nationalism in the interests of profit maximisation and social stability. A string of state commissions – particularly Wiehahn, Riekert, and De Lange – gave the private sector increasing faith in Botha's reform intentions; and the Nkomati Accord of 1984 held out the promise of new markets in southern Africa.

This honeymoon phase in the relationship between capital and the Botha government reached its height with the introduction of the new constitution in 1984. Its implementation, however, marked the turning point in their relationship. Far from defusing apartheid's time-bomb of social conflict, the new constitution detonated it.

In the early stages of the township uprisings that began in late 1984, most sectors of the business community hedged their bets. The *Financial Mail* defended the occupation of the troops in the townships and denied that this signified civil war, although it was concerned at the adverse effects on both political and investor confidence. But, it reassured its readership, there was really no cause for alarm: 'No-one except the ANC is demanding political rights tomorrow' (*Financial Mail*, 12.10.1984).

As the uprisings intensified, business confidence in the government's ability to handle the situation waned. Capital itself became a target for mass action, stayaways, consumer boycotts and limpet mines, and as a result its representatives became increasingly anxious to distance themselves from the government politically, and to distance capitalism from apartheid. Zac de Beer of Anglo American voiced the growing concern that unless concerted action was taken, 'the baby of free enterprise would be thrown out with the bathwater of apartheid'.

For some business leaders, capitalism stood wrongly accused of being party to South Africa's political and economic injustices. For others, the long-term survival of capitalism demanded a little more historical honesty: 'An economic system which historically has denied the majority of participants a share of the opportunities which are assumed to be inherent in the system cannot hope to survive unless that system itself is instrumental in effecting a redistribution of power, opportunities and wealth' (Mike Sinclair, United States–South Africa Leadership Exchange Programme, quoted in *Financial Mail*, 23.11.1984).

Social responsibility programmes mushroomed, business leaders became increasingly vocal in their opposition to apartheid, and a group of leading businessmen visited the ANC in Lusaka. These moves reflected the changing mood – and the changing prognosis for the future – in the business community. In less than a year, organised business had shifted from unprecedented support for the Nationalist government to a position in which a *Financial Mail* editorial claimed that business was on the verge of mutiny because of the slow pace of reform: 'Not in modern times in this country have businessmen been so united in their condemnation of government and its social and economic policies' (*Financial Mail*, 18.1.1985). Yet as Murray Hofmeyr, chair of the Johannesburg Chamber of Industries, aptly put it: 'The complete rejection of apartheid by all shades of business reflects the moral repugnance of many, but the commercial realism of even more' (*Leadership SA*, 7, 2, 1988).

Three years into the states of emergency, a pall of quiescent silence has fallen over most sectors of the business community. Initial moral outrage at the state of emergency has waned, and the clampdown has provided the space for a return to 'business as usual' – and a strong resistance to the politicisation of industrial relations.

The business community's response to the Labour Relations bills of 1987–8 showed its true colours. The state made no bones about its intention to use the legislation to crush the labour movement, yet a representative of organised business estimated that 'probably well over 80% of our members are basically in favour of the State's position of taking a harder line against organised labour' (*Leadership SA*, 7, 2, 1988).

This overt support for the bills and tacit support for the maintenance of the state of emergency have come from sectors of organised business that continue to assert their opposition to apartheid; but it is an opposition that goes hand in hand with support for 'strong security'. The issue of security constitutes a key contradiction for those sectors of capital which are trying to project an anti-apartheid profile; and they face a fundamental and irreconcilable dilemma in this regard.

In any capitalist society, private property rights and the ground rules of the free enterprise system are protected by law, and in the final instance by the police and the army. Where capitalist relations form the accepted framework in a broadly consensual democratic society, the armed forces are rarely called out to protect the interests of capital in a direct way. In bourgeois democracies, politics and economics are ostensibly separate. The lack of direct coercion is one of the hallmarks of the system.

In South Africa, the system of free enterprise is also guaranteed by the state. But the state is not bourgeois democratic in nature; and the form taken by capitalist relations is not based on a bourgeois democratic consensus, but rather on a history of political conquest and coercion – and of resistance. In this process, many of the cornerstones of apartheid have at the same time constituted the basis of class control. The 1913 Land Act, the pass laws, migrant labour, the hostel system, the bantu-stans, Bantu Education, housing controls and other aspects of apartheid have shaped capitalism in South Africa on terms that have been highly profitable for capital. They have been premised on a lack of political rights for black South Africans, and have always had to be enforced through coercion.

As a result, the links between national oppression and economic exploitation have been articulated through decades of resistance, and resistance on the factory floor has long been part of the broader political struggle. Where this struggle has impacted on capital's control of the factory floor or on its profitability, the private sector has relied on the coercive power of the apartheid state to reassert control. The wave of resistance in the mid-1980s included intense conflict in the factories, with factory occupations, strikes, sit-ins, stayaways, and sabotage of equipment. While capital tried to distance itself from apartheid, its response to these actions was hostile. Thus, capital has relied on state repression to maintain its profitability, and to create the space for its own long-term agenda of reform.

While capital's use of the security forces is evidence of its reliance on the state to maintain conditions of profitability, it tells us nothing about direct collusion at the level of strategic planning and policy-making. The following sections examine the nature of this collusion around issues of security at national, regional and local levels.

Collaboration at national level

At a national level, there has been a range of institutional linkages between the military and the private sector. The Defence Advisory Council for instance, which was set up in 1973 to deal with armaments

206 *Militarisation and economy*

production, included representatives from Anglo American, Barlow Rand, Tongaat and SA Breweries; it was disbanded in 1982, and partially replaced by the Defence Manpower Liaison Committee. The Defence Research and Development Council links specialists in the private sector with military research needs; and the Economic Advisory Committee also addresses strategic economic issues. Many of these institutional links feed into the development of an overall strategy of self-sufficiency for the South African economy, which is seen as a key strategic necessity.

In this regard, the links between Armscor and the private sector are critical, with more and more industries tied into armaments planning and production through highly lucrative Armscor contracts. Graeme Simpson investigates the reciprocal nature of this relationship elsewhere in this book. He argues that while capital relies on a strong and well-equipped military machine to preserve a political order conducive to capital accumulation, the military relies heavily on the private sector to secure components and technology essential to boosting its fighting capacity. The Armscor connection implicates the private sector deeply in the economics of defending apartheid, and constitutes the most far-reaching and direct connection between the private sector and the military.

It is not just those companies with Armscor contracts that are involved in security collaboration at this level. Laws such as the National Key Points Act of 1980, the Atomic Energy Act as amended, the National Supplies Procurement Act as amended, and the Petroleum Products Amendment Act, among others, have resulted in the growing militarisation of the private sector, and require private firms to maintain secrecy about their production levels, sources of supply, trading partners, and so on (Grundy, 1986: 69). These laws apply as much to subsidiaries of foreign multinationals as to local companies.

At present, collaboration between capital and the state is facilitated by the fact that the two are increasingly in agreement over the direction of national economic policy. During the township uprisings of the mid-1980s, the private sector was scathingly critical of the government's incompetent economic policies and inability to overcome the economic crisis. However, under the states of emergency there has been a growing rapprochement between capital and the state over such issues as privatisation, deregulation and inward industrialisation.

In addition, the threat of sanctions is of mutual concern. If sanctions are implemented effectively, many companies are banking on being able to bust them. This demands the expertise and resources of the state – and in particular, of its information and security apparatuses. Sanctions-busting is by definition a covert affair, and has thus far been spearheaded by Armscor in its efforts to evade the arms boycott.

The threat of sanctions, coupled with the dismal performance of

South African manufacturing capital on international markets, has meant that both capital and the state have shifted their focus away from an export-led economic recovery in the short term. Instead, 'inward industrialisation' has come to be presented as the panacea for solving the problems of capital accumulation: 'given what will obviously be continuing difficulties on the foreign trade front, it is largely to inward industrialisation that we shall have to look as the locomotive of economic growth, although of course by no means neglecting exports or import replacement' (Kent Durr, Deputy Minister of the Budget and Works, SA Megatrends Conference, 27 July 1988).[1]

The state argues that deregulation, as well as the provision and privatisation of township housing, will 'kickstart' the inward industrialisation cycle, generating an economic upswing with ripple effects on consumer demand throughout the economy. This economic strategy has won widespread support within the private sector. It also dovetails neatly with the upgrading programmes of the National Security Management System (NSMS), which provides a framework for the private sector to participate in this strategy at a regional level.

The National Security Management System

The strategies of the National Security Management System are still based on the logic that the war in South Africa is only 20 per cent military, and 80 per cent economic, social and political. Thus while its aim is to 'eliminate the revolutionaries' and smash popular democratic organisation, this is intended to create the space within which a new hegemony can be built in the townships – a hegemony of moderate forces, prepared to accept the timetable of the state's reformist initiatives within the framework of a free enterprise future.

The NSMS strategy is based on an analysis that ascribes the origins of the township uprisings to the ANC's ability to 'manipulate' material grievances of black communities. Thus the first priority of the state is to remove these material grievances. As Major-General Wandrag, head of counter-insurgency in the SAP, explained: 'The only way to render the enemy powerless is to nip revolution in the bud, by ensuring that there is no fertile soil in which the seeds of revolution can germinate' (*ISSUP Review*, October 1985: 15).

The upgrading strategy is thus intended to impact on both the economic and political crisis. However, a major limitation of the strategy is that even if the NSMS only targets 'oilspot' townships for treatment, the state simply does not have the financial resources to upgrade them on the scale necessary to have much effect.

This is one reason for the state's attempts to draw the private sector into the process. A key aspect of this thrust is the privatisation of the provision of housing. Both the private sector and the state see home-ownership as the thin edge of the wedge in developing stable urban black communities with a stake in private property and therefore, it is hoped, in the free enterprise system. However, there is a fatal flaw in the privatisation strategy. It is premised on exactly the same logic that helped precipitate the 1984 uprisings, in that the intention is to recoup the expenditure on both housing and township infrastructure from township residents – this time through the costs of buying a house, rather than through rents and rates. At the same time, the only kind of housing profitable for the private sector to build is of a standard way above what the average township dweller can afford. When this constraint is coupled with the current consensus in both the private sector and the state that an economic upswing requires higher productivity and lower wages, the scene is once again set for disaster.

Nor does it seem likely that the privatisation of housing will achieve its other stated aim, which is to depoliticise this issue, particularly if SADF soldiers continue to be deployed to assist in the sale of houses. A spokesman for the SADF explained their participation on the basis that black housing is one of the areas that needs to be addressed as a matter of urgency in order to counter the 'total onslaught'. The sale of houses would also help to break the rent boycott, he said (*Star*, 19.9.1987).

The move towards the privatisation of township housing and development has changed the nature of private sector involvement in the townships. For example, at the height of the township uprisings, the state used every means at its disposal to draw the private sector into its attempts to break the rent boycott. In April 1986, the Black Local Authorities Amendment Bill contained a stop-order clause that would enable management to deduct rents from wages. The clause was withdrawn in the face of strong opposition from capital; an Assocom circular on rent boycotts in July 1986 urged its members: 'Do not become directly involved with the local town council over the collection of rents and service charges' (Boraine, 1988). It was clear that to do so would once again tarnish the image of capital as a 'lackey of apartheid'.

At present, however, if township residents are unable or unwilling to meet their bond repayments, the onus of sending the debt-collectors around or of evicting residents will fall on the building societies or housing contractors. Thus, far from depoliticising the sphere of housing, privatisation has the potential to politicise the role of those sectors of capital involved.

The private sector's involvement in upgrading does not necessarily reflect a political conspiracy between capital and the Joint Management Centres, those substructures of the NSMS that are dominated by the security forces. However, it does give those sectors of capital that would like a slice of the multi-million-rand development contracts a vested interest in helping conceptualise township development strategies, and a direct interest in the maintenance of 'law and order' in the townships. Both these interests may predispose sectors of capital to take up the gilt-edged invitations to participate on the JMCs' community liaison forums.

It is at this level that representatives of capital – in both their individual and company capacities – are being drawn into behind-the-scenes consultations with the welfare wings of the JMCs. At this level, too, the NSMS is attempting to harness the skills and resources of the private sector behind its upgrading strategies and in the long term, it hopes, behind the reform agenda of which these strategies are part.

It is difficult to ascertain how much success the NSMS is having in involving the private sector. Sufficient initiatives have been exposed to indicate that concerted efforts are being made. The nature of these efforts can be illustrated by looking at the community liaison forum in Port Elizabeth.

In Port Elizabeth, the community liaison forum defines its role as 'representative of *the private sector* drawn from *all population groups*'. The objectives of the forum are listed as follows:

a. *Main Objective:* To assist in restoring and maintaining peace and normality amongst all the people within the district of Port Elizabeth.
b. To identify grievances and problem areas timeously and to use the Forum's own resources and ability to rectify them whenever possible.
c. To create understanding and co-operation, through communication, between authorities and the private sector.
d. To assist the authorities with the necessary advice and expertise whenever necessary.
e. To act as a direct link between the private sector and the authorities to ensure effective action. (*Memorandum on Formation of Liaison Forum* issued by the Port Elizabeth mini-JMC)

The 27 members of the forum who represent the private sector include people from the Master Builders' Association, Assocom, the Midland Chamber of Industries, the Port Elizabeth Chamber of Commerce, the Small Business Development Corporation, the Afrikaanse Sakekamer, the NGK, and a range of others.

The first project of the community liaison forum is to construct a major sports and cultural complex at Kwadwesi, a new 'prestige neighbourhood' near Port Elizabeth. In motivating for the sports centre, the JMC memorandum says: 'The current lull in the unrest situation has created a vacuum, with youth searching for both their identity and direction. Thus, at the moment, an *opportunity exists* to harness their energies and guide their creative abilities and talents in the right directions.' The memorandum concludes: '*Kwadwesi Stadium Complex* to be identified by Joint Management Committee as a *top priority* in bringing stability and normality back to the metropole's townships; fostering a healthy alternative to unrest, thereby restoring the social fabric in these areas.'

Building a sports stadium in a 'prestige neighbourhood' has little chance of overcoming the acute economic and political crisis in Port Elizabeth. But the memorandum does highlight the ways in which the private sector is being wooed to participate in such strategies. Building a sports stadium may seem a rather innocuous activity for the private sector; but the key point is that two years ago, many of the bodies now represented on the forum were trying desperately to build relationships and credibility with United Democratic Front affiliates, and were meeting with them to discuss the kind of upgrading needed in the townships. Such initiatives took place with the support of mass-based organisations, or not at all. Today, JMC upgrading strategies are part of a broader process of disempowering people, and of boosting the undemocratic local black authority structures that were so decisively rejected in popular struggle before the state of emergency. Regardless of whether a sports stadium is needed in Kwadwesi or not, the participation of the private sector in such a project implicates them in this process.

But the involvement of the private sector in the conceptualisation and implementation of NSMS upgrading strategies is not only occurring through the community liaison forums of the JMCs; it is also taking place through the Defence Manpower Liaison Committees (Demalcoms).

The Defence Manpower Liaison Committees

The brain drain has long been of concern to capital, in the context of an acute skilled manpower shortage. The skills shortage and the allocation of manpower have also received attention from military strategists. 'In many ways the efficient use of manpower is the most crucial element in defence programming,' argued Professor J. C. van Zyl (*ISSUP Review*, April 1979). He called for a strategy in which 'those sub-groups of labour likely to cause the least disruption of production processes are called up first.' The failure to use such criteria could lead to untold disaster, for example, in the sphere of labour relations. 'If, for example, white supervisors in a particular factory should all be called up, the effect on the black labour force employed in that factory is at least problematical and could be disastrous if their loyalty to the defence effort is suspect.'

Until 1982, manpower utilisation strategies were the responsibility of the Defence Advisory Council; this body was then replaced by the Defence Manpower Liaison Committee, whose task was to 'promote communication and mutual understanding between the SADF and Commerce and Industry with regard to a common source of Manpower' (1982 Defence White Paper). In addition to the Chiefs of Staff personnel from the four arms of the Defence Force, the Defence Manpower Liaison Committee includes representatives from 21 employer bodies. In January 1984, *Paratus* disclosed that the Demalcom was involved in planning the massive increase in conscription put forward in the Defence Amendment Act of 1982. This included drawing up guidelines for employers of national servicemen, encouraging them to make up the difference between company salaries and national servicemen's pay. It has been estimated that most private companies currently do this, and that one-fifth continue to pay full salaries. However, there is no legal obligation on them to do so.

Eight Demalcoms have been set up at provincial level to establish forums for the SADF, commerce and industry to discuss 'the commodity of manpower – which commerce and industry need, and so does the SADF' (interview with Colonel Chris du Toit, chair of the Johannesburg Demalcom, August 1988). In May 1987, the provincial Demalcoms were supplemented by regional structures. The Witwatersrand Demalcom has since branched into seven smaller bodies, which include the Johannesburg Demalcom. The Johannesburg Demalcom has representatives from the SADF's Witwatersrand Command, the Randburg Commando, the Johannesburg Chamber of Commerce, the Johannesburg City Council, the Randburg Town Council and Chamber of Commerce, the Transvaal Chamber of Industries, the Security Association of South Africa, the Engineers' Association of South Africa, the Institute of Bankers, the Anglo American Corporation, and others (*Business Day,* 16.7.1987). Colonel Du Toit, chair of the Johannesburg Demalcom, says that invitations have also been sent to township local authorities, the University of the Witwatersrand and the Rand Afrikaanse Universiteit – but they have not yet responded.

The Johannesburg Demalcom used to be based at Wits Command, but is now housed in the Assocom offices. Colonel Du Toit says it was decided that a 'civilian' should chair the Demalcom to counter allegations that it is run by the military. 'It's an open forum, and it's not for security purposes – it's not to gather security information.'

The Demalcoms have kept a low public profile, but they constitute an increasingly key interface between organised capital and the Defence Force. One aspect of their role is to facilitate the reintegration of ex-servicemen in the economy: 'The SADF has servicemen coming out of tours of duty, and we know which industry needs people, and so these ex-servicemen can be routed into the private sector.' At the same time: 'The business sector is in the know of people that are unemployed or redundant, and the SADF may have jobs for such people in the development side of things – such as in Alex[andra] township. So if they know of a core of building industry people that are unemployed, and we know of such projects that are on the go – the relationship can be meaningful to both.'

The Demalcoms do not regard their role as being confined to the regulation of manpower needs and army call-ups. They also see themselves playing a role in relation to labour issues and unrest in general. Colonel Du Toit explains:

We put everything under the hat of labour. The brain drain, labour unrest, stayaways – so, for example, we would go to the organised sector and say, 'You can expect trouble on the following days' – say, for example, on the 16th (that's a bad day to pick!) – to give them time to adjust, and pre-empt unnecessary hardship and firings, by giving clear guidelines to workers. It could be a small business – he doesn't read the papers, he's not aware – so by warning him, he can buy stock early, make sure his salesmen aren't on the road, and so on.

The Demalcoms are also linked in directly to township upgrading strategies. 'We know about projects that are taking place in the townships, and so we are able to channel private sector involvement there,' Colonel Du Toit said. He used Alexandra township as an example:'We are involved in getting contracts to people to develop housing, improve roads, and so on.' The presence of municipal councils on the Demalcoms facilitates this process. 'We believe that from our side, we will identify the most serious improvements and developments that need to be done in the townships, and then identify where the funds will be allocated from.' The support of the private sector is given in the form of 'allowing us to use the expertise and knowledge that they have so much of. The idea is not to look for funds from them, because that's not on, but to get them to appreciate that we need their expertise.'

One way of getting such expertise is by conscripting it, and some skilled conscripts have been called up and placed in ostensibly civilian positions where their skills are needed. 'So for example, the army is involved in Alex, then they would call up an engineer, and say to him, "You are going to work in Alex for such-and-such a company." I'm not going to say a name. Then the army would use his technical skill in this way. In the building trade, this approach has been very successful. These guys don't wear uniforms, they just work in the company, and they are credited with their call-ups.'

There is not much publicity about this development, Colonel Du Toit said, because the SADF does not want to create the impression that all skilled conscripts can expect civilian jobs. Yet the brain drain has clearly forced the SADF to be flexible about the placement of people with key skills. 'The last thing the army want to be seen as is dogmatic, because we appreciate that the economy is what we live on, not the army, and we need to be aware of and sensitive to the needs of qualified people.'

Colonel Du Toit was adamant that there is no contact between the Demalcoms and the JMCs, and he welcomed the opportunity to correct the 'misunderstanding' that had arisen when *Business Day* quoted him as saying that the Demalcoms send their minutes to the JMCs. However, from his description of the role of the Demalcoms in upgrading, there must necessarily be a close working relationship between them and the welfare wings of the JMCs – in fact, it is hard to draw a clear line between their respective roles. If the Demalcoms are working hand in hand with the JMCs, then this is another key way in which organised capital is being drawn into state upgrading strategies.

Barricading the factories

Growing fears of sabotage attacks on factories, labour unrest and uprisings in nearby townships have led many companies to seek greater on-site security at their factories, and increased liaison with local security forces.

For companies defined as 'national key points', certain levels of factory security are now mandatory. The 1980 National Key Points Act enables the National Key Points Committee in any region to designate a factory a 'national key point', and to determine minimum security standards on site. Brigadier P. J. Schalkwyk, Director of National Key Points, defines an NKP as 'any place or area that is of such national importance that its loss, damage, disruption, or immobilisation may prejudice the Republic, or any place or area which the Minister [of Defence] considers necessary or expedient for the safety of the Republic or in the public interest' (Jackson, 1987: 37).

The management at a factory designated a national key point is required to meet certain security requirements at its own expense. Despite some initial opposition, it was reported soon after the implementation of the Act that management at 85 per cent of 633 national key points were cooperating fully.

Management at national key points is also required to set up joint planning committees to monitor security. The committees may include the following: a chief security officer, an SADF commander responsible for the NKP, a financial manager, a personnel manager, the local fire chief, a local SAP representative, a civil defence member, and a security consultant. According to Brigadier Schalkwyk, the 'Police or the SA Defence Force are not security specialists and will not advise an owner on what security steps he should take. We always recommend that he appoints a good security consultant. If not, the key point will be either insecure or an over-kill situation is achieved resulting in unnecessary costs.' (Jackson, 1987: 44)

As a *Financial Mail* headline pointed out, the National Key Points Act set the private security industry on course for 'a multi-million rand bonanza'. By 1983, the security industry had an annual turnover of R1 000 million, comprised over 500 companies, and employed a quarter of a million people.

The burgeoning security industry has increasingly become part of the security establishment in South Africa. The Security Association of South Africa is represented on the Demalcoms, and in Cape Town certain security firms have been helping the JMCs set up 'liaison links' between companies in certain areas. In Bishop Lavis, a coloured township in Cape Town, the JMC has encouraged companies to organise themselves into six zones; Pritchards Security has radio links with these companies, and is also in radio contact with the Bishop Lavis police station. The aim is to 'co-ordinate the resources in the area, human, financial and technical, into one effective unit that can react to any form of emergency' (*Weekly Mail*, 28.8.1986). The scheme also involves training staff in first-aid and pistol shooting. A Pritchards Security spokesperson denied that the scheme was designed for unrest situations, but said that there is a 'fine line' between civil unrest and other types of emergency.

In 1987, a conference of 'top persons in the security family' was held to discuss 'the interface between the Public and Private Sector security fraternities' (Jackson, 1987: Foreword). All speakers emphasised the desirability of a high degree of integration between the security forces and the private sector. Major-General Wandrag urged that private security officers should become part of intelligence-gathering networks. The role of private security companies in dealing with labour unrest was also discussed. There was a call for security officers to be given a correct understanding of how to deal with 'these emotional problems', and to be trained in diplomacy (Jackson, 1987: 69).

When it comes to the role of private security in industrial relations, the mines have the longest track record, as well as the largest private army in the country.

Mine security: privatising repression

At the large mining house Gold Fields, mine security has its own armoury of 6 000 shotguns, has patented its own rubber bullet, and runs a mine-security training camp where security personnel from other mining houses are trained. In a confidential report leaked to the National Union of Mineworkers (NUM) by a former Gold Fields employee, details of mine security's role were spelt out. The service is designed to cater for the following: prevention and detection of crime; protection of company assets; control of vulnerable and vital areas; screening of personnel; combating labour unrest; combating subversive activities; training, supervision and administration of the security force; and liaison at a local level with the SADF, SAP, and civil defence.

Each mine has a team of security personnel to suit the requirements of that particular mine. The strength of the team varies from one white security officer and 20 blacks, to 20 white security officers and 200 blacks. In addition to their regular and routine security functions, selected personnel on each mine are specially trained and equipped to form riot control teams. These teams consist of a mobile element in anti-riot vehicles; an assault team using riot dogs; and a support team equipped with special protective clothing and capable of delivering tear-smoke.

From the perspective of mineworkers, the distinction between mine security and the state security forces is blurred by the fact that the former not only use the same hardware as the latter, but also use similar methods. According to a worker from Anglo's Western Deep Levels mine where workers fought bitter battles with mine security during the 1987 mineworkers' strike, 'The boers [mine security] have guns, pistols, sjamboks, teargas, Hippos [personnel carriers] and dogs. They have all the dangerous weapons which they may turn on us at any time.'

During the strike, the NUM negotiated with management at Western Deep that workers would stay in the hostel area, where the union would be in charge. Workers had locked themselves into the compound, and the shaft steward chair had the key to the main gates. One afternoon, six green Hippos from Western Deep Levels security and six white Hippos from another mine arrived at the gates. Management assured the shaft committees that there was no cause for alarm, and so workers, who had gathered at the gates, turned back to continue with a meeting.

As we turned back, those boers rammed the gate with the Hippos, broke it open, and rode into the hostel. They said over their loudspeakers, 'Now we are taking control, no-one is going to control again, you are too late with your controlling.' They told us to go to our rooms, and then they just started to attack us with their dangerous weapons, shooting at us, without even giving us five minutes, using teargas, rubber bullets, and pistols with proper bullets. When we were in our rooms, they turned off the water, and they stopped food from coming in.

At nine o' clock that night, they told us to come out, we are going to work now. They shot teargas into the rooms, and chased us out with batons, and forced us to stand in a line. Then they forced us into the lifts at gunpoint, and we were faced with no choice but to go underground, all the shifts at once, and also the surface workers, forced down underground at gunpoint. (Interview with mineworker)

Since the 1987 mineworkers' strike, repression on the mines has intensified. 'Mine management has declared a state of emergency on the mines,' says NUM general secretary, Cyril Ramaphosa. A recent report on repression at Anglo American mines highlighted the extent of this (NUM, 1988). On many mines, roadblocks are manned at the entrances, and union meetings are banned on mine property or their agendas have to be approved by management. Meetings are videoed, and workers are banned from distributing union literature without management's permission. A pamphlet commemorating the Kinross mine disaster, which blamed Anglo management for continued use of polyurethane foam despite international safety warnings, was banned for distribution on Anglo mines on Kinross Memorial Day in 1988. Mine security has the right to enter and search hostels without a warrant or prior authorisation, further infringing workers' limited privacy. Mine security has also its own *impimpis* (informers). At Gold Fields, their reports are compiled into briefings for the industrial relations department, which uses them to monitor union activities.

By training and equipping private armies, the mines have been able to fine-tune their control; but in the process, they have taken on the role and powers of the state in the eyes of workers.

Conclusion

The states of emergency have made possible a return to 'business as usual' for capital in South Africa. Despite the vocal opposition to apartheid expressed at the height of the township uprisings in the mid-1980s, political acquiescence has now become the dominant trend in business. The states of emergency have renewed business confidence in the state's ability to keep the lid on resistance in the short term, and capital is settling in for a long, slow process of reform, entailing as little disruption of capital accumulation as possible.

There are of course those within the private sector who remain convinced of the need for a democratic South Africa to be established as soon as possible, and who oppose the state of emergency and the repression of democratic organisations. They are at best what businessman Christo Nel defines as a 'creative minority', and at present there is little doubt that they are fighting a losing battle against a springtide of business conservatism.

The repression of democratic organisations, detentions, assassinations and the rule of vigilante squads in the townships have all been effectively obscured by the media's portrayal of a return to 'law and order'. The Bureau of Information has successfully established itself as the source of news of township unrest, and it has become all too easy for the business community – and for most white South Africans – to believe that the security clampdown has achieved a degree of normality. This has been illustrated by the extent to which the PFP – in its self-appointed role as the party of business – made 'strong security' its rallying cry in the October 1988 municipal elections.

This tacit backing for the state of emergency provides the framework within which the private sector is engaging with the security forces at the range of levels discussed above. In many cases, such engagement is entered into because it serves certain relatively narrow economic interests for the sectors of capital involved. But it remains a choice with political effects. In sum, the state has a coherent strategy of drawing the private sector into the conception and implementation of its national security strategy, and into the defence of apartheid. The private sector has not articulated a clear response to this; but in practice it is increasingly collaborating with the state in its security strategies. The net effect is to reinforce state strategy, and to implicate capital all the more deeply in the maintenance of apartheid.

16 The politics and economics of the armaments industry in South Africa

GRAEME SIMPSON

In August 1986, J. G. J. van Vuuren, chief executive of Armscor, when interviewed about his upbringing and the background to his involvement in the armaments industry in South Africa, commented: 'My childhood was one of clay-pellet fights with the coloured boys and growing up with my parents' interests' (*Finansies en Tegniek,* 12.9.1986).[1]

Were it not for the brutal nature of National Party rule for most of the 50 years since Van Vuuren's birth, the apparent continuity in his life would almost be humorous. Today, however, the struggle with 'die bruin seuns' is over the fundamentals of political and economic power in South Africa. The tools of Van Vuuren's trade include some of the most sophisticated weaponry currently available, and the interests which he is entrusted to protect are those of 'the survival of the free enterprise system' in South Africa and the very security of the apartheid state.

The above quotation provides an apt introduction to this chapter, which attempts to map out briefly the integration of the political and economic features of the developing armaments industry in South Africa.

A military–industrial complex?

Armscor, and the armaments industry in general, present one of the central points of interface between the security establishment and the business community in South Africa. The strategic importance of the industry in the context of the international arms embargo and of mass resistance to apartheid is self-evident. The aspiration to develop a fully self-sufficient, technologically sophisticated arms production capability in South Africa has also placed Armscor at the cutting edge of technological research and development within South African industry.

This latter feature has been built on an interdependent relationship between Armscor and the private sector. Indeed, key Armscor personnel, including Piet Marais (chairman) and Van Vuuren, boast that Armscor has acted as a model of successful 'privatisation' over the past twenty years or so. They argue that the 'privatisation' of the arms industry is of fundamental importance in developing its self-sufficiency in the face of international embargoes. These views are reflected in the recommendations of the Geldenhuys Committee of Investigation into the Future Planning of the South African Defence Force and Related Armscor Matters. On the issue of self-sufficiency:

The arms embargo against the RSA is currently implemented by the international community to such an extent that it is not envisaged that Armscor will be able to import any weapons systems in the future. . . . The armaments industry is a national asset to the RSA, and its survival is of critical importance. In the current situation, the most cardinal aspect is to ensure self-sufficiency, and the concern is to preserve the expertise of contractors. (Defence White Paper, 1986: 8–9)

Two paragraphs further on, the committee mapped out Armscor's particular approach to the issue of privatisation:

The Committee accepts the fact that privatisation is indicative of a broad spectrum of measures aimed at reducing the State's share of the economy. The method employed by Armscor to promote privatisation is to encourage provisioning by the private sector, contracting out and industrial leasing. In addition, no facilities are created if they already exist in the private sector. (*Ibid.:* 9)

The existence of this 'privatised' armaments production capacity has prompted writers such as Ratcliffe and Frankel to describe the South African system as a 'military-industrial complex' of one sort or another (Frankel, 1984: 82–95; Ratcliffe, 1983). Their analyses identify the development of mutually dependent relationships between business and the military, characterised by the infusion of the strategic concerns of the security establishment within the South African economy as a whole.[2]

This 'militarisation of the South African economy' was not merely a strategic necessity in a hostile international environment. However obvious, it nonetheless bears stating that the rise of militarism and, indeed, the expansion of arms production in South Africa were responses to internal social, political and economic crises. Furthermore, within this military–industrial collusion, the representatives of capital are also political actors with an agenda of their own.

The responses of business people to the crises have seldom been consistent and have varied from a willingness to engage in discussions with representatives of democratic black organisations, to active support for the most severe repressive measures adopted by the Nationalist government. Nevertheless, business's primary concern is to secure the conditions for the survival of the free enterprise system in South Africa. It consequently places a high premium on 'political stability'.

In this respect one factor remains constant: ultimately, the military represents the last line of defence against the liberation struggle. This means that in spite of the oft-quoted anti-apartheid rhetoric coming from some sectors of the business community, it remains fundamentally in their interests to ensure that the military capacity of the apartheid state remains intact.

It therefore comes as no great revelation to demonstrate the active involvement of leading South African industrial corporations in the building of a local armaments industry over the last twenty years. However, the extent to which one can talk of the existence of a 'military–industrial complex' is a slightly more complex issue. Smith and Smith suggest: 'The military–industrial complex . . . functions on the basis of a structural pairing that inevitably develops into mutual interests' (Smith and Smith, 1983: 74). They go on to assert that this 'structural pairing' is based on two shared, central politico-strategic assumptions. Firstly, there is the assumption that national self-sufficiency in arms production is a requirement of state policy and security; secondly, that the development of advanced technology will service industry and the military simultaneously. In short, the relationship is a reciprocal one in which security priorities are married to the economic strategies of capital. This remains to be demonstrated in the South African case.

The short-term economic benefits for business from its involvement in contract work for Armscor are undoubtedly substantial. It seems to be a universal characteristic of the armaments industry that market prices for armaments-related industrial products tend to be inflated. This is due in part to the fact that either strategic concerns, or profit subsidising, takes precedence over short-term cost-effectiveness. As McKenzie argues:

In military industry, design and innovation is focused on the product alone. Its destructiveness, speed, accuracy, or whatever, is the key criterion. That is what the buyer wants. . . . How the product is to be produced, and what it costs to produce it, are strictly secondary considerations. Indeed, [often] . . . the interest of the producing firm actually lies in coming up with a product that is more difficult and more expensive to produce. (McKenzie, 1983: 41)

This is compounded by the fact that there is no 'free market' in the trade of arms. Despite the growing number of arms purchasers, particularly in the Third World, the arms market remains largely controlled by governments which act as both buyers and sellers (McKenzie, 1983: 42). The result is a further inflation of market prices for armaments-related products.

According to Van Vuuren, the economic benefits to the business community through investment in the armaments sector go well beyond their short-term profit potential. In particular, Van Vuuren notes the developmental potential inherent in the arms industry's brand of privatisation. Furthermore, in a climate of paranoia about the potential effects of sanctions, he also points to the lessons that can be learned by all sectors of South African industry from Armscor's success in breaking the arms embargo (*Finansies en Tegniek*, 12.9.1986 and 30.1.1987).

In this vein, Van Vuuren argues that the armaments industry offers the potential for solving some of the structural limitations on growth in the national economy. This view is based on the calculated beneficial effects for manufacturing industry as a whole, as a result of the development of locally produced high technology in the armaments sector.

Referring to the industrial utility of high technology developed in the US space programme, Van Vuuren claims that domestic technological breakthroughs in the armaments industry are already having the same sort of developmental economic effects. He even asserts that the armaments sector, through its self-sufficiency programme, offers the potential to break the dependence of South African manufacturers on foreign technology. He argues that in this way South African manufacturers could avoid the restrictive licensing agreements which tend to accompany technology transfers and which prohibit competition between the lessor and the lessee of such high technology. On this basis he claims that the armaments industry can offer South African manufacturers the potential capacity to break into foreign export markets with products which are unique, if not always necessarily cheaper.

Van Vuuren places the development of the armaments industry at the heart of an export-led programme of economic recovery. Should there prove to be any realistic possibility of such a scenario occurring, it would substantially affect our analysis of the nature and extent of the militarisation of South African capitalism.

By the end of this chapter, through tracing the development of the arms industry and some of its constraints, we hope to make some evaluation of Van Vuuren's case. In particular, it will be possible to assess the extent to which the relationship between capital and the military is a truly reciprocal one, servicing not only the technological requirements of the SADF but the economic strategies of the business community as well.

A brief history of Armscor and armaments production in South Africa

The genesis of an armaments industry in South Africa can be traced back to the production of munitions during the Second World War in order to supplement the Allied war effort. In the course of the war the industry expanded rapidly, producing 50 million rounds of ammunition a year and employing 12 000 people in six factories countrywide (Frankel, 1984: 84; and Ratcliffe, 1983: 72–3).

Predictably, at the end of the war the industry shrank fast, most factories either closing down or going into 'civilian production'. Nonetheless, in 1940 an advisory committee on Defence Force requirements was set up to investigate available resources for armaments production. In 1949, this committee was transformed into the Board of Defence Resources, responsible to the Minister of Defence for advice on all matters concerning the country's armaments potential.

In 1951 the Munitions Production Board was established as a sub-division of the Department of Defence. Two years later the Department of Defence set up the first rifle-manufacturing plant. It was from the turn of the decade, however, that the armaments industry really took off in South Africa. On the political front, the development of the arms industry and the form which this took reflect the state's response to a preceding period of intense popular struggle. The mass resistance of the 1950s, culminating in the massacre at Sharpeville on 21 March 1960, the banning of the ANC and PAC and, as a consequence, the launch of organised armed resistance to Nationalist rule, provided the political backdrop to the post-war renaissance of the South African armaments industry.

At a strategic level, with the establishment of the Republic in 1961 and simultaneously the first hints of international arms sanctions against South Africa, the Munitions Production Board was immediately expanded. Despite an initial outflow of capital after the Sharpeville massacre, the early 1960s saw the beginnings of one of the most sustained boom periods in the history of the South African economy. In particular, the rapid expansion of the manufacturing sector provided the economic and financial underpinning for the development of a domestic armaments production capacity. The early 1960s therefore signalled the beginning of a significant shift in emphasis from the importation of arms to the procurement of arms technologies necessary to support local production (Frankel, 1984: 82). By 1965, 120 licences for the local manufacture of military equipment were negotiated with a wide range of foreign sources (Leonard, 1983: 140).

In 1963 the National Institute for Rocket Research was established at the CSIR and it immediately undertook the development of a ground-to-air missile system with radar support (Ratcliffe, 1983: 74; *Sunday Times*, 27.10.1963). With a view to furthering this programme, local scientists were recruited and sent overseas to study the principles and techniques of missile construction. This missile programme was jointly financed by the South African and French governments, and the missiles were developed with the assistance of a French electrical engineering concern – Thomson CSF (Ratcliffe: 74).

The development of a local armaments manufacturing capability depended on the acquisition of skills and technical know-how, as well as on the creation of the necessary industrial infrastructure. The future of the fledgling industry required access to and local development of the appropriate high technology. In the long term, this demanded substantial investment in the research and development of such technology, whilst in the shorter term it required both training of technicians and securing access to imported technology and licensing arrangements.

In 1964 the Armaments Production Board was established under the Armaments Act No. 87 of 1964. Its immediate objective was to extend ammunition production and its attendant infrastructures. Three years later, in August 1967, the UN Security Council passed its first resolution calling on all states to stop the supply of arms to South Africa. In 1968, when the objective of laying the infrastructural foundations had been sufficiently realised, the Board's name was changed to the Armaments Board under the Armaments Development and Production Act of 1968, and its activities were substantially expanded to include control of production, procurement and supply of armaments in the broadest sense. In the same year, Armaments Development and Production Corporation (Armscor) was established as a fully fledged state enterprise and took over the previously government-controlled munition factories as subsidiary companies.

The objects and tasks of Armscor as defined by the Armaments Development and Production Act of 1968 are to

> promote and co-ordinate the development, manufacture, standardisation, maintenance, acquisition, or supply of armaments by collaborating with, or assisting or rendering services to, or utilising the services of, any person, body or institution or any department of the state. . . . To develop, manufacture, service, repair and maintain, on its own account or as the representative of any other person to buy, sell, import or export and through advertising or otherwise, to promote the sale of, armaments, including armaments required for export or firearms, ammunition or pyrotechnical products required for supply to members of the public. . . . (Armaments Development and Production Act, No. 57 of 1968)

The Act did stipulate that all purchases of armaments by the Board had to be approved by the Treasury. However, this inhibiting measure was discarded in 1974 (Ratcliffe, 1983: 75).

By 1977 it was clear that the procurement of armaments and the control of armaments production would best be served by one body. As a result, under the Armaments Development and Production Act of 1977, the Armaments Board was amalgamated with the Armaments Development and Production Corporation to form the new Armscor.

It is no coincidence that this occurred in the same year that the Security Council imposed a mandatory arms embargo on South Africa. By the time the arms embargo was imposed, and less than a year after the brutal suppression of the 1976 Soweto uprising, a centralised and administratively efficient armaments infrastructure was in place under the autonomous control of the Ministry of Defence.

The strategic imperatives which lay at the root of Armscor's development have resulted in the corporation's activities being shrouded in secrecy. This is even true of the central Armscor structures. The Armscor board is appointed by the State President and is responsible to the Minister of Defence. It includes the Chief of the SADF and the

Director-General of Finance. The rest of the board members are primarily drawn from the private finance, manufacturing and commercial sectors. The names of the directors of Armscor are not made public for security reasons. Very little information is available on the structure of the enterprise, resulting in some disagreement among writers over even the most basic facts.

Both Ratcliffe and Frankel, writing in 1983 and 1984 respectively, suggest that Armscor has twelve nationalised subsidiary companies directly under its auspices (Frankel, 1984: 84; Ratcliffe, 1983: 77). Grundy, writing in 1988, suggests that there are only nine (1988: 45). What is clear is that Armscor's assets increased from R200 million in 1974, to R1,3 billion in 1984 and approximately R1,7 billion in 1987/8 (Frankel, 1984: 83; Grundy, 1988: 45; Ratcliffe, 1983: 77). The corporation presently employs 23 000 people within its immediate subsidiaries – down from 29 000 in 1984 – and supports at least a further 100 000 jobs in the private sector (1986 Defence White Paper; Grundy, 1988: 45).

There is further uncertainty about the exact extent of Armscor's contractual relationships with private sector companies. Armscor's chief executive refers to 975 companies supplying Armscor directly. This implies a much larger number of sub-contractors (*Business Day*, 21.9.1987). Ratcliffe suggests that in 1983 Armscor was distributing work to over 1 200 private industry contractors and sub-contractors, and that at least 400 companies were dependent on Armscor contracts for their survival (Ratcliffe, 1983: 77). Grundy estimates that the corporation presently has around 3 000 private sub-contractors (Grundy, 1988: 45).

There is little disagreement about the fact that Armscor has been highly successful in developing its production capabilities in the past decade or so. The corporation's turnover for 1987/8 is estimated at over R3 billion (*Leadership SA*, 1988: 137). The Economist Intelligence Unit (EIU) reports that Armscor now produces at least 4 000 items and only imports 5 per cent of its requirements, as compared to 70 per cent before the arms boycott began (EIU Country Report, 2, 1988: 14). Grundy claims that today around 15 per cent of the defence budget is spent on material imports (1988: 46). These figures are not officially made available by Armscor and it is therefore difficult to distinguish between the facts of the matter and political propaganda.

Perhaps even more significant is the growth of the armaments industry into the largest manufacturing exporter in the country. Armscor exports to at least 23 countries worldwide, and exports in 1988 were expected to realise 60 per cent of the corporation's turnover (*Leadership SA*, 1988: 137; EIU Country Report, 2, 1988: 14).

Today Armscor boasts a particularly impressive arsenal of locally designed and produced weapons. These include the G-5 and G-6

155-mm Howitzers, a 127-mm multiple rocket-launcher, frequency-hopping radio equipment, the Buffel mine-protected armoured personnel carrier, the CB-470 cluster bomb, the V3 air-to-air missile with a 'unique slaved target acquisition system', as well as various light- and heavy-duty infantry weapons, mines and armoured cars (Heitman, 1988).

Frankel summarises this impressive record: 'in the fifteen years of its existence Armscor has proved an almost unattenuated success – in developing the South African arms industry to a high degree of self-sufficiency in the face of international sanctions and, of no lesser importance for domestic politics, in locking together the military, government and economic elite into a tight tripartite network in support of Apartheid policy' (Frankel, 1984: 82).

However, the exact nature of Armscor's proclaimed self-sufficiency needs to be more closely analysed. Richard Leonard has examined several of Armscor's claimed technological achievements, and argues that they are all dependent on circumvention of the embargo regulations. From the lowly Ratel armoured personnel carrier, which he implies is a copy of the French Berliet VXB, to the 127-mm truck-mounted multiple rocket-launcher, which he says has some remarkable similarities to the Taiwanese Working Bee 6 system, Leonard questions the extent of Armscor's proclaimed self-sufficiency (Leonard, 1983: 141–6). Other examples are the much-vaunted G-5 and G-6 155-mm Howitzers mentioned above. A close examination reveals that the technology required to develop the weapons was supplied in the form of shells, gun barrels, technicians and testing equipment by the Space Research Corporation of Canada and the United States. This was done in a large-scale violation of the arms embargo between 1976 and 1978 (Leonard, 1983: 141). The G-5 was produced by Cementation Engineering, a South African subsidiary of Trafalgar House, which is a large British conglomerate. Cementation is formally involved in the manufacture of mining equipment. Special lathes for producing the G-5 shells were imported from CIT Alcatel of France, and equipment for filling the shells from Rheinmetall of West Germany (Leonard, 1983: 141–2).

The extent of the industry's self-sufficiency seems to have been overstated. In particular, Armscor's technological independence is based largely on the involvement of private-sector companies, which facilitate access to vital technology by acting as conduits for US and Western European multinational corporations.

Armscor and the private sector

From the early days of arms production in South Africa, the concern of armaments producers was to encourage the active involvement of the private sector in producing armaments and related technology and

components. Thus, prominent figures in the arms industry have argued that 'privatisation' is not a new strategy, but has always been pursued as a priority by Armscor.

The process of integrating security and business interests was, however, not left to chance. On one hand, the material benefits involved for the private sector were great. Cost-effectiveness being of less significance than strategic considerations, it was viewed from the outset as essential to give business a material stake in the expansion and upgrading of the armaments sector.

On the other hand, legislative measures were introduced to ensure that some degree of security was observed by the business community. These measures included the Atomic Energy Act as amended in 1978, the Petroleum Products Amendment Act of 1977, and the National Supplies Procurement Act of 1970 as amended in 1979. The last-mentioned Act provides the Minister of Defence with the power to order any company or individual to produce or supply any goods or services required in the defence of the country. Under the Act it is also illegal to disclose 'any information in relation to the acquisition, supply, marketing, import, export, development, manufacture, maintenance or repair of, or research in connection with, armaments'. It is not surprising that these Acts were introduced or amended only a short period after the adoption of Security Council Resolution 418, which imposed the mandatory arms embargo on South Africa.

Furthermore, the state's approach to integrating the interests of the business community with those of the arms-producing sector was also an ideological one – captured in the alluring concept of 'total onslaught–total strategy'. This ideological appeal did not by any means consistently guarantee business support for the security concerns of the government. However, if apartheid policies were regarded by many business leaders as reprehensible or undesirable, this did not at any stage compromise their contribution to the military and security concerns of the state as expressed in the needs of Armscor.

The developing relationship between the security establishment and the business community had two main objectives: to foster industrial input into the armaments sector whilst at the same time infusing the whole of industry with the ideological and material concerns of the military.

As has been noted, the achievements attained in armaments production have been impressive. Yet despite this there is still some doubt as to the extent to which they represent the attainment of military self-sufficiency through import-substitution. It appears as if local corporations, rather than producing and upgrading armaments technology, are acting as conduits through which this technology is smuggled into the country via links with multinational corporations. This is best demonstrated by considering the example of the leading local industrial supplier of Armscor, Barlow Rand.

The Barlow Rand experience

Barlow Rand is the biggest industrial corporation in the country and one of the largest South African monopolies. The corporation presents itself as an enlightened opponent of apartheid, and its chairman A. M. Rosholt regularly expounds business's role in bringing about meaningful change in South Africa. Yet despite this 'liberal' image, the corporation is a major contributor in the production of technology and armaments fundamental to the repressive capacity of the apartheid state.

Thomas Barlow and Sons began as a British textiles producer, and at the beginning of the century established itself in South Africa as an importer and distributor of electrical supplies. Following the economic boom of the 1960s, Barlows entered the mining sector through the take-over of Rand Mines in 1971. In the following year P. W. Botha, then Minister of Defence, established the Defence Advisory Council to discuss broad policy issues. Invited to sit on the first council were the Chief of the SADF, his retired predecessor, the chairman of Armscor, and two industrialists – Wim de Villiers, chairman of General Mining (Gencor) and C. S. ('Punch') Barlow, chairman of Barlows. One of Gencor's subsidiary companies to this day is Sandrock Austral, a manufacturer of French-licensed armoured cars. Barlow's presence on the council at that stage seemed to have no such logical connection.

However, by 1977 the connections had become somewhat clearer. Barlows had already become involved in the limited distribution of electronic components from the 1960s. The corporation began to supply the SADF through Barlows Electronics Ltd, which from 1965 secretly became one of the two chief electronics suppliers to the SADF (*Rand Daily Mail*, 21.2.1985). This included a contract to supply the army with locally assembled Thomson-CSF radios from France (*Jane's Defence Weekly*, 4, 9, 1983: 830).

In 1977 Barlow Rand bought the C. J. Fuchs group, best known in South Africa as a manufacturer of household appliances. Soon thereafter they bought a 50 per cent stake in the British-owned giant, General Electric Company (South Africa). Included in this deal was Marconi South Africa, a major supplier of radar and communications equipment to the SADF. Less than a year after these acquisitions, Barlows established Barlab, a training research and design facility in electronics at the University of Pretoria. By the end of 1980, Barlows employed about 4 000 people in its electronics division, with a turnover of R120 million. 1980 also saw Barlows launch into the computer sector by buying a 51 per cent stake in Perseus, local agent of the US giant, Data General (Barlow Rand Annual Report, 1980). The head of the Barlows electronics division during this period was Johan Maree. In 1979,

Maree was seconded by Barlows for three years to serve as the Armscor chief executive.

In 1980, with P. W. Botha's rise to power, the old Defence Advisory Council was replaced by an enlarged Defence Advisory Board to which 13 of the biggest names in South African industry were appointed. Included were the new Barlows chief executive, A. M. Rosholt, and two other members of the Barlows board, R. Goss (managing director of South African Breweries) and F. Cronje (chairman of Nedbank) (*Paratus,* June 1980).

In 1983 Barlows embarked on a major restructuring process. Reunert, a Barlows subsidiary in property and the motor industry, was stripped of all its assets and the corporate shell was used to group together all of Barlows' high technology operations. Reunert was subdivided into four groups: Reunert Informations Systems (computers and control systems), Reunert Technology Systems (Reutech), GEC (electrical engineering), and a mechanical division (later to be sold to allow Reunert to concentrate on the electrical and electronic fields) (*Financial Mail,* 31.8.1984).

Within four years Reutech became one of the most important suppliers of military electronics in South Africa. It is made up of five companies which, despite adverse publicity, continue to operate primarily within the sphere of the South African armaments industry. The companies include:

– Fuchs Electronics, which produces a wide range of radios including frequency-hopping versions. It also manufactures the electronic fuses for most of the bombs, mortars and rockets in SADF service (*Armed Forces,* March 1986).

– Barcom, which produces the Z66, the standard area-defence radio, linking white farmers throughout the rural areas with their local commando unit. Barcom is also active at the high-tech end of the market, most probably in electronic warfare equipment (*Armed Forces,* March 1985).

– ESD, which appears to be an amalgamation of Barlows Electronics and Marconi (still apparently half-owned by its British parent company, GEC).

When Marconi (UK) updated the S247 radars of the SA Air Force's northern air-defence sector in 1983, it was through ESD that the equipment was channelled (*Observer,* 24.4.1983). ESD is involved in 'avionics, weapon electronics, digital systems, electronic warfare, radar systems and radio communications systems' (*Paratus* Suppl., Nov. 1982). ESD was also responsible for completion of the SADF's 'large telecommunication network'.

Little is known of Reutech's other two companies, Aserma and OMC Engineering. In 1983, OMC, operating in Kempton Park with a workforce of over one thousand, dismissed a senior executive because he was unable to obtain an upgraded security clearance from the SADF. The new clearance was required because OMC work was reclassified from 'confidential' to 'secret priority' (*Sunday Times*, 21.8.1983).

Why Barlows was chosen to be the standard-bearer of high-tech private sector cooperation with the military is not entirely clear. But the fact that Barlows, despite having no manufacturing experience whatsoever in these fields, was an active distributor of electronic components, could well be a pointer. The Reunert group lies at the centre of a web of connections with international business on which the South African electronics industry is completely dependent. Components, designs, test equipment and a variety of other essential elements flow into the country relatively unhindered. Since the 'disinvestment' of IBM in 1987, Reutech has also been able to establish itself as an important conduit in the field of computer technology. A survey of Armscor weapons systems published in the Geneva-based *International Defence Review* highlighted a Reutech product, the AS80 Artillery Fire Control System, supposedly designed by ESD for use with the SADF's G-5 Howitzers. *Defence Review* claimed that the computer components were all of US origin, and an Armscor spokesperson was quoted as saying that getting the components 'was not a problem' (3, 1983: 270).

In 1985, Barcom won a South African award for the design of a synchronisation processor – a microprocessor for frequency-hopping communications. Despite the boasts of local self-sufficiency and import-substitution, the chip was in fact designed 'in consultation' with AEI Henley's micro-electronics division. AEI Henley is a Reunert subsidiary, but it is still half-owned by its British parent, GEC. Telcor, another Reunert company, operates a range of distribution agencies for US and British electronics companies. On the computer side, Barlowdata represents amongst others Hitachi and US-based Data General. In a nutshell, Reunert is an amalgamation of subsidiaries and agencies of international companies. In the words of the Reunert managing director, 'Most local manufacture is merely assembly of imported parts' (*Financial Mail*, 21.6.1985).

This is by no means a comprehensive survey of Barlows' contribution to the South African armaments industry. Nonetheless, the Barlow Rand experience, as it is described here, casts some light on the claims of self-sufficiency in arms production in South Africa.

It is no secret that Armscor takes pride in its ability to break the arms embargo. Despite the high level of security involved, many cases of boycott-breaking have found their way into the commercial press and even into the courts in other countries. They include the establishment of clandestine foreign companies, bogus disinvestment schemes or management buy-outs, a range of other corporate manoeuvres, as well as straightforward smuggling.[3]

Conclusion

In the final analysis, the South African armaments industry remains technologically dependent. Where military technology is locally available, it is still largely based on the remodelling of licensed military hardware. Furthermore, there are some areas in which the Armscor arsenal is still severely lacking, most notably in the capacity to produce militarily competitive aircraft and naval vessels. This was graphically demonstrated in the scandal which emerged in 1986 as a result of the smuggling of submarine blueprints out of West Germany in a consular bag. It was alleged that top-ranking German politicians were involved in the affair, as well as top South African consular staff (*Beeld*, 27.11.1986 and 26.1.1987). Similarly, in the battles waged in Angola in 1987–8, the vulnerability of South Africa's dated Mirage and Cheetah fighter-aircraft exposed the urgency of developing an updated fighter which could match the latest Soviet or Cuban technology.

The implication seems to be that the South African armaments industry is still more of an assembly than a production enterprise. The fundamental technological dependency at this stage remains, if for no other reason than because of South Africa's undeveloped research and development capabilities. As a Third World economy, South Africa remains dependent on periodical rehiring of updated technology.

However, the South African oil-from-coal industry does provide an example of the local capacity to generate novel and strategically indispensable technological innovations. These seem not to be completely beyond the reach of the South African arms industry. In the sphere of arms production, the potential for growing independence and innovation should not be too easily dismissed. Where the know-how itself is lacking, there is the possibility of importing the necessary skills, as was rumoured to have taken place with regard to Israeli engineers working on the Lavi jet-fighter project (*Citizen*, 13.2.1988; *Business Day*, 13.12.1987).

There can be no doubt that, despite the long-term vulnerability of the armaments industry to effective international sanctions, at present Armscor is successfully able to supply the SADF with most of its immediate needs. In fact, the industry is having to cut back to avoid over-production.

Perhaps of even greater significance is the extent to which the South African arms industry has been able to cultivate an export market. Today Armscor can claim to be the biggest single exporter in the South African manufacturing industry (*Business Day*, 22.1.1988). In some senses this is less surprising than it may seem. The arms trade is a notoriously dirty business and South African arms, uniquely suited to Third World terrains, are extremely marketable by virtue of having been tried and tested. Fellow 'pariah states' in Latin America and the Middle East provide a willing and eager market for arms from South Africa (see

Vayrynen, 1980).

The successful cultivation of an export market in armaments has some bearing on the assertions of Van Vuuren, referred to at the beginning of this chapter, regarding the potential of the arms industry to lead economic growth and recovery in South Africa. Indeed, this 'spin-off benefit' for the rest of South African manufacturing is given considerable coverage in the 1986 Defence White Paper. Albeit in somewhat convoluted style, the White Paper argues that defence expenditure, through supplementing and renewing industrial production, as well as developing resources and industrial infrastructure, stimulates economic growth and provides both direct and indirect benefits to industrial economic activities in all sectors (Defence White Paper, 1986: 34–8). To the extent that this is true, it represents a central process in the developing militarisation of the South African economy.

The White Paper focuses on two primary 'spin-off' benefits resulting from investment in the armaments industry: the benefit of technology transfer to other sectors of the economy; and job creation and skills development in the wider labour force. While some examples of such technological 'spin-offs' are given in the 1986 White Paper, they are rather specialised and are largely limited to the field of electronics and the steel and metal industries. As both Kaldor, and Smith and Smith, point out, the more sophisticated the armaments themselves become, the less applicable the technology tends to be in other areas of the economy (Kaldor, 1982; Smith and Smith, 1983: 94–6).

It therefore remains to be said that the successes of the armaments industry rest on very insecure technological and ideological foundations. The capacity to cultivate an arms-export market of unique and cost-efficient products is not simply transferable to other sectors of the economy as are the technological benefits. South Africa's dependent economic status is not about to be altered, in spite of the Armscor propaganda.

There is considerable debate about the role of military expenditure in resolving crises in capitalist production, much of which revolves around the area of spin-off benefits. For the purposes of this chapter we can say that there is no indication that military rather than any other form of expenditure is necessary to foster economic growth. This is true of both the industry's capacity to create jobs (a dubious contention under any circumstances), and its capacity to generate technological innovation applicable in other sectors of industry.

On the contrary, there is every indication that military expenditure acts as a drain on national resources so desperately needed for improving the standard of living of the majority of South Africans. To the extent that this is true, it represents a disjuncture in the reciprocal relationship between the military and big business over often varying perceptions of what are appropriate economic solutions to the current crisis.

Ultimately, the very political and economic crisis which breathed life into the South African arms industry is simply being exacerbated by its development. The money spent on bullets and buckshot is drawn from the wealth-generating capacity of the South African working class. It is wealth unproductively spent and expended. Rather than generating growth, ever-increasing defence expenditure will contribute to escalating inflation, continued contraction in the growth potential and employment potential of the South African economy, and, inevitably, will play its part in intensifying political conflict and violent struggle in South Africa.

17 Apartheid's army and the arms embargo

WILLIAM COBBETT

On 4 May 1978, South African forces launched a combined air-and-ground attack on a SWAPO-run refugee camp in Angola, 150 miles north of the Namibian border. Its name was Kassinga. The Angolan government described what happened in the following manner: 'After the planes had fired rockets and dropped explosive and fragmentation bombs, as well as paralysing gases, the paratroopers landed on the terrain and during the six and a half hours that the attack lasted gave full vent to their basest instinct, indiscriminately massacring the terror-stricken population in cold blood' (Katjavivi, 1988: 110–11). The casualty figures were 612 Namibian refugees (comprising 147 men, 167 women and 298 children), 12 Angolan soldiers and 3 Angolan civilians killed; and 611 Namibian refugees, 63 Angolan soldiers and 15 Angolan civilians wounded. For their part, the South Africans continue to refer to the attack as a 'victory' over a SWAPO 'terrorist' camp (*Weekly Mail*, 13–19.5.1988).

Nearly a decade later, on 19 May 1986, South African Air Force jets attacked capital cities of the frontline states, thus effectively destroying any hopes attached to the diplomatic efforts of the Eminent Persons Group (EPG).

These selective examples serve to underline two points which are central to this chapter. First, proponents of international sanctions argue that it is the activities of the South African armed forces (and its surrogates) that provide the moral justification (and no small amount of vindication) for the arms embargo.

Second, and equally important, the continued ability of the SADF to carry out these types of operations points to the fact that the embargo can only be regarded as partially effective. It has not been able to keep apartheid's army inside South Africa's borders, nor has it been able to prevent the deployment of well-armed and systematic state violence against the people of South Africa.

This chapter begins with a short appraisal of the history of the arms embargo against South Africa. It then examines the ways in which the South African government has sought to cope with the embargo – through the development of a domestic arms industry, and through the covert procurement of arms from international sources, often with the assistance of sympathetic governments. This is followed by an assessment of the implementation of the embargo, with special attention paid to the roles of the Israeli and British governments. Finally, the arms embargo is assessed in the larger context of the debate around economic sanctions against South Africa.

These are of course issues surrounded by propaganda, deceit, claim and counter-claim. The growth of the domestic arms industry is proferred by the government as evidence of the 'failure' of the sanctions campaign to date, and thus, by implication, of any future sanctions efforts. Indeed, it claims that such has been the 'creative response' of South African talent and industry that the actual effect of the arms embargo has been entirely contradictory and thus undermined.

History of the arms embargo

On 7 August 1963, the United Nations Security Council recognised South Africa as 'a threat to the maintenance of international peace and security'. It called on all states 'to cease forthwith the sale and shipment of arms, ammunition and all types of military vehicles to South Africa'. The embargo was purely voluntary, however, and relied on the goodwill and integrity of member states for its effective implementation. South Africa's major arms suppliers – the United Kingdom and the USA – agreed to abide by the embargo, although they abstained on the UN vote. They nonetheless gave a very subjective definition to the terms of the boycott. They continued, for example, to allow the crucial supply of spare parts, radar and electronic equipment. Other loopholes were employed – the British government did not view the embargo as retrospectively affecting contracts to supply arms (Cawthra, 1986). Accordingly, in the period immediately after the imposition of the embargo, South Africa received Buccanneer and Canberra jet bombers, WASP helicopters, naval shells and other equipment. Additionally, the British government took no steps to disallow the purchase of British goods through third parties. South Africa was thereby able to equip its Impala jets with Rolls Royce engines purchased through Italy *(ibid.)*.

The existence and creation of British subsidiary companies in South Africa provided another crucial loophole. Marconi and EMI, for example, established electronic equipment subsidiaries in South Africa which produced goods for the military, British Leyland (SA) provided transport for the SADF, and ICI helped establish an explosives factory *(ibid.)*. The importance of these and many other companies' involvement lay both in the value of the capital and confidence they invested in post-Sharpeville South Africa, and in the way in which they facilitated the transfer of technology in contravention of the arms embargo.

Notwithstanding the efforts of sections of the British government and industry to circumvent the embargo, the South African government was unable to obtain replacements for its major weapons systems from Britain and the USA, and was forced to cast around for alternative suppliers. The gap was soon filled by France, Belgium and Italy. France, a permanent member of the Security Council, played a particularly significant role in arming apartheid by providing South Africa with its airforce's main strike capacity. During the 1960s and 1970s the French supplied or manufactured under licence inside South Africa, helicopters, transport aircraft, Mirage F1s and Mirage F11s. These jets were at the time amongst the most modern and sophisticated military jets available. Additionally, French companies supplied South Africa with missiles, armoured cars and submarines. Over the period 1960–83 France was the largest supplier of arms to South Africa.

Italy and Belgium were also important European suppliers of arms. A well-used method, before the arms embargo was made mandatory, was to enter into co-production and licensing agreements with firms inside South Africa. The supplying nation could then ingenuously claim that it was not actually exporting arms directly to South Africa. Such transfer of technology still occurs, although since 1977 arrangements have been shrouded in secrecy and thus increasingly difficult to monitor. These co-production and licensing arrangements were generally open and above board, at least to the extent to which it would be fatuous to deny that a certain company was producing or investing in South Africa. However, as will be discussed later, South Africa also engages in covert and illegal means of arming itself.

In 1970 UN Security Council Resolution 282 (paragraph 4) called on all states to strengthen the arms embargo. The United Kingdom, United States and France abstained on the motion. The arms embargo was still not binding on member states, and its effect was consequently limited. 'The arms embargo which was in force between 1963 and 1977, often questionably referred to as the "voluntary" arms embargo, failed to achieve its stated objective. It was openly flouted by France and Italy and covertly violated by several other states as well. Using Western and Israeli technology, South Africa has developed a domestic arms industry.' (International Maritime Organisation, 1986a: 3–4) Indeed, not only did the 1963 embargo fail, 'it was such a manifest fiasco that it led many observers, both sympathetic and hostile to the struggle against apartheid, to question the usefulness of sanctions against South Africa' *(ibid.).*

Subsequent events in South Africa established the conditions for more intense international pressure. In 1977 an international conference on the arms embargo was held in Lagos, Nigeria. It was attended by representatives from 112 countries, and laid the groundwork for the United Nations resolutions to follow.

On 2 November 1977, a draft resolution to impose both economic and arms sanctions against South Africa was defeated by the triple Western veto in the United Nations Security Council. The Western permanent members objected to economic sanctions and to the clause that 'the situation in South Africa constitutes a threat to the maintenance of international peace and security'. The 'situation' referred to was the immediate period after the SADF invasion of Angola, the killing of hundreds of schoolchildren in 1976–7, and the murder of Steve Biko. The UK, USA and France were prepared to accept a statement to the effect that the acquisition of arms by South Africa was a threat to peace. The arms embargo thus became mandatory in 1977, and binding on all members of the United Nations.

Arms procurement

In 1968 South Africa created two organisations designed to procure and to produce its arms – the Armaments Board and the Armaments Corporation. They were merged in 1977 as Armscor, clearly in response to the imposition of the mandatory arms embargo. Armscor has subsequently undergone enormous growth. The stimulus provided by the drive to produce and subsequently to export arms has led to the development of South Africa's own military–industrial complex. As has been documented elsewhere, the relationship between the military and the private sector has become increasingly close, at a political, security and economic level. 'To both civilian and military leadership Armscor is of inestimable strategic value in that it has played a crucial role in allowing South Africa to circumvent United Nations' sanctions and to reduce, if not necessarily to totally break, the country's previous almost total dependence on foreign sources of armaments' (Frankel, 1984: 85). South Africa now arms itself in a variety of ways, combining legal and covert methods (International Maritime Organisation, 1986b: 2).

Armscor and its many subsidiaries manufacture a limited number of armaments, often proudly proferred as examples of 'indigenous development' and 'South African' expertise. Although these arms are domestically produced, they are highly dependent on a significant input of foreign technology, either imported by the private sector or manufactured under licence by subsidiaries of foreign companies.

A range of arms is still being produced utilising technology resulting from agreements entered into before the arms embargo became mandatory in 1977.

Goods exported to South Africa sometimes fall into the vague 'dual purpose' category. The export of such goods is technically 'legal' as they are stated to be outside the scope of the arms embargo. However, much of the equipment is put to military and strategic use once inside South Africa.

Where South Africa cannot procure arms by the above methods, it may revert to covert action, smuggling arms, components and spares for military use. This has even extended to the involvement of the staff of military attaché sections of South Africa's embassies abroad. In Britain, for example, 'evidence was presented in Court of an invoice with an official Embassy stamp indicating that payment had been made for the supply of components for machine guns' *(ibid.)*.

Finally, a point often overlooked in relation to the arms embargo is that foreign technology is transferred by Armscor's ability to attract highly skilled foreign-contract technicians and scientists.

In a statement submitted to a closed session of a United Nations Security Council committee, the following covert methods were identified as being employed by South Africa in its procurement of arms: equipment is licensed for export to a third country and then en route redirected to South Africa; forged licences are used; equipment is falsely labelled; dummy companies are established in South Africa to front for Armscor; and private sector companies agree to act as 'conduits' for Armscor (statement by A. S. Minty to Security Council Committee on the Arms Embargo Against South Africa, 23.9.1983).

Taking all these methods together, the chairman of the World Campaign Against Military and Nuclear Collaboration with South Africa candidly stated in 1983: 'We have to admit that, despite the mandatory arms embargo, the South African regime has been able to acquire, through direct and indirect routes, and by covert and overt means, much of the equipment, technology and expertise needed for its military forces. . . . Whilst we do not suggest by any means that the mandatory arms embargo is a total failure, experience to date shows that its effect has been far less than was expected, not least by the original drafters of the resolution itself, namely the western members of the Security Council.' *(Ibid.)*

A major success for the South African government in this regard was a covert operation named 'Project Advokaat', which involved the establishment of a sophisticated electronic surveillance centre at Silvermine near Cape Town. It was set up in 1973 with equipment supplied by companies from, inter alia, West Germany, Britain, France, Holland, Denmark and the United States. The Silvermine centre is reputedly able to monitor maritime and air movements over half the globe. As such, 't provides cover for more than even the most fantastic threat conjured up in the minds of South Africa's propagandists. It forms part of an international surveillance network, linked with the Royal Navy in London, the United States naval base in Puerto Rico, Argentina, Portugal, and the French naval bases at Dakar (Senegal) and Madagascar (Cawthra, 1986: 91).

South Africa passes on information from Silvermine to other countries, for which service it obviously expects reciprocal treatment. In April 1976, the British (Labour) government's Ministry of Defence admitted that it was in direct contact with Silvermine. Silvermine is also used by the South African government in its attempts to ingratiate and integrate itself with Nato. Documents presented to the UN Security Council revealed that South Africa had been given access to Nato military communications equipment and spare parts, specifically for the monitoring equipment at Silvermine (Cawthra, 1986: 92).

In the last decade, several advanced British radar systems, intended for military use, have been supplied to South Africa. The Plessey AR3D system was shipped in April 1981. The British government conceded that the radar was to be used for military purposes, but claimed that it had a genuine civil application as well. In 1983–4, the British company GEC-Marconi supplied equipment for the modernisation of an air-surveillance radar system it had originally supplied to the South African Air Force. The British government used the same 'dual purpose' argument to justify the sale (International Maritime Organisation, 1986a: 15). This fatally undermines the Thatcher government's arguments against instituting wider sanctions against South Africa. The conventional argument deployed by the British government against mandatory economic sanctions – that they will 'hurt the very people we are trying to help' – cannot, by any stretch of the imagination, be used to support the supply of technology which will be harnessed to the service of the SAP and SADF.

More recently South Africa again openly evaded the arms embargo by acquiring a piece of high-tech military equipment, ostensibly for 'civilian use'. The equipment, called a multi-sensor platform, was developed by British Aerospace and Messerschmitt to track the behaviour of high-speed airborne objects (*Guardian*, 5.7.1988). The South African Department of Transport ordered three of the systems, one of which has been delivered. Export licences were granted by the British and German governments after South African assurances that the system would be used 'to track weather satellites'. However, the system had been bought by the British Ministry of Defence for target trials at Royal Aircraft Establishment ranges.

For all South Africa's claims to have responded to the arms embargo with its own technology and expertise, the fact remains that the overwhelming majority of armaments produced in South Africa are crucially dependent on the transfer of technology from abroad. Most of the arms which South Africa claims to have developed 'indigenously' – such as the G5 cannon in use in Angola – are in fact copies of arms produced elsewhere, to which South Africa has somehow gained access. The G-5 155-mm artillery gun provides an illuminating example of South Africa's 'achievements', especially as it has been consistently proferred as an example of 'South African' expertise. Armscor bought the G-5 and patents for its manufacture from the Canadian–American firm, Space Research Corporation, smuggled four of the guns and 60 000 shells into South Africa, and brought Space Research personnel to Pretoria to set up the manufacturing plant. Equipment for the plant was imported from France and West Germany. Additional examples of 'South African' arms which are in reality copies of foreign technology, notwithstanding their 'ethnic' names, are the Eland armoured car (French Panhard), the Ratel (Sibmas, Belgium), the Cactus missile (French Crotale), the Valkiri multiple rocket system (copy of a Taiwanese copy of a US system), and so on (International Maritime Organisation, 1986c: 5).

Self-sufficiency claims regarding the production of arms do not stand up to analysis. With the possible exception of ammunition, South African arms production is reliant on imported machinery, technology and components. This reliance has been indicated in a number of cases in recent years where arms smugglers have been caught attempting to secure vital components for the South African arms industry and spare parts for military equipment in SADF service. The limited domestic arms production facilities available have in all cases been established with assistance from overseas companies and governments. *(Ibid.)*

The 'Coventry Four': a case study in covert arms procurement

A recent case exposing the covert methods employed by South Africa in circumventing the arms embargo was the operation set up by four white South Africans – apparently employed by Armscor – who were to gain notoriety as the 'Coventry Four'. In 1984 the four were arrested in Britain, together with three Britons, and charged with acquiring missile components, spare parts for Buccanneer bombers, radar-jamming magnetrons, infra-red detectors and other military equipment. Customs officials in Britain believed that three of the accused were employees of Kentron, one of the many companies used by Armscor in its operations. 'Colonel' Hendrik Botha was in charge of administration and security, Stephanus de Jager was the company accountant and Jacobus la Grange was the technical expert. The fourth accused, William Meterlekamp, was managing director of McNay (Pty) Ltd, a company used by Kentron to bring in required military merchandise (*Coventry Evening Telegraph*, 9.7.1985).

A shipment of artillery elevating gears was seized at Birmingham International Airport in 1984, thus finally revealing the illegal manufacturing of arms and related equipment for South Africa that had been occurring in Coventry for almost a decade. The *Coventry Evening Telegraph*, which played a crucial investigative role in uncovering the illegal trade, reported that despite ludicrous attempts by managers and foremen to conceal their activities, the true nature of the work was 'an open secret' among the hundred or so Coventry employees of D. W. Salt and Hi-Tech Engineering Ltd. South African blueprints for mortar casings were distributed with the Afrikaans instructions blotted out clumsily with felt-tip pen. Skilled craftsmen were expected to believe that high-precision bullet dies were rollers or bobbins for sewing machines. The artillery gears – intercepted in a 3-ft square package at Birmingham Airport – were so sophisticated that they were manufactured in a special temperature-controlled room. The staff were told that they were parts for 'farm machinery'.

The smuggling ring was a complex international affair, and one which clearly demonstrated how easily (and profitably) a British company could aid Armscor and the SADF. According to the *Coventry Evening Telegraph* the technical expert, La Grange, would travel to the United States looking for suppliers for the required equipment. Once a suitable supplier had been found, a Devon (England) company – Fosse Way Securities – would place orders with the American manufacturer, effectively disguising the real destination of the goods. They would then be reshipped from the UK via West Germany and other European countries to South Africa. In a similar manner, the goods manufactured by D. W. Salt in Coventry would be shipped to McNay (Pty) Ltd in South Africa by means of a circuitous route.

As emerged in the trial, D. W. Salt had been dealing with South Africa since the mid-1970s. Previously, while an employee of another company, he had been sacked for the unauthorised manufacture and supply of ammunition dies, concealed as sewing-machine parts. Undeterred, he continued aiding South Africa militarily. When British Customs officials had gathered sufficient evidence to prosecute five companies and individuals, Salt included, the companies paid a fine of £193 000 to prevent the adverse publicity threatened by a court case. A year later Salt was instrumental in setting up Quad Engineering in South Africa as a factory to make detonators. He and his partner Gardiner, who was also convicted in the Coventry case, opened an agency in West Germany, GTT, through which they established contact with TBT Tiefbohr-Technik in Stuttgart, a subsidiary of the Swiss multinational Schweizerische Industrie-Gesellschaft (SIG) (*Guardian*, 10.7.1985). TBT, according to evidence presented at the trial of Salt and others, was used to manufacture gears for gunsights and to forward the parts to South Africa. Salt was given a ten-month jail sentence and fined £25 000. Astoundingly, Mr Justice Leonard granted the South Africans – the 'Coventry Four' – bail of £400 000, and accepted the assurances of the South African government that they would return to Britain to face charges. Once they were safely back in South Africa, the South African government used the occupation of the British consulate in Durban by some UDF leaders as an excuse for not allowing them to return to the UK.

Israel and apartheid

Arms trading between South Africa and Israel has a history nearly as long as that of the two states themselves. Israel sold Uzi submachine guns to South Africa in 1955, and Centurion tanks in 1962. In turn, South Africa helped Israel circumvent a French arms embargo during the Six Day War by supplying spare parts for her French fighter jets. The relationship reached a high point with the visit by Prime Minister Vorster to Israel in 1976 (conducted despite the strong objections of many Israelis concerned by Vorster's previous Nazi sympathies).

Besides being an increasingly important investor in South Africa, with many cheap-labour operations in the bantustans, Israel has had extensive military collaboration with the apartheid regime. The contact has extended to visits, in an 'unofficial' capacity, of Israeli military specialists, and close military links have been established between Israel and the Ciskei. In 1983, some 23 pilots for the Ciskeian 'Air Force' were trained in Israel, and Israeli mercenaries have been hired as personal bodyguards for Ciskei cabinet ministers and as advisers to the Ciskei Defence Force (Cawthra, 1986: 93).

It is reported that Israeli weapons in the service of the SADF include a 105-mm gun and modification package for Centurion tanks, Gabriel anti-ship missiles, anti-personnel mines, Mooney TX-1 military training aircraft for the Ciskeian Air Force, RPV pilotless reconnaissance aircraft, Reshef- and Aliyah-class fast-attack boats (assembled in South Africa), fire-control systems for the SADF's 155-mm nuclear-capability artillery, the Galil rifle (called the R4 by the SADF), and various other military electronic components. There are also unconfirmed reports that the SADF has acquired 36 Kfir fighter aircraft, Arava tactical troop-transport aircraft, Shafir air-to-air missiles, and Barak point-defence missile systems (Cawthra, 1986: 93). Recently, South Africa managed to recruit a number of Israeli engineers and technical experts working on Israel's fighter-aircraft project, Lavi, which had collapsed because of financial constraints in Israel. Israeli radar experts are also reported to have assisted in South Africa's attacks on Angola in 1987.

Israel has thus become a crucial partner for South Africa in its attempts to keep its weaponry and military technology up to date. The SADF will arguably be benefiting as well from the indirect transfer of sophisticated American technology, as the military and political links between the USA and Israel are extremely close. When one considers the extensive similarities of the South African and Israeli political situations, and of the response of the two states to internal opposition and external criticism, the extent of their economic, military and political links is understandable (Sahak, 1988). However, recent pressure on Israel by the United States – a direct result of anti-apartheid lobbying efforts – could force Tel Aviv to reduce its military dealings with Pretoria.

Sanctions

Despite the fact that the call for sanctions was made over a quarter of a century ago, the debate around the issue has only recently assumed a particular intensity. Advocates of sanctions state that, first and foremost, it is the policies of the South African government which have placed sanctions so firmly on the agenda. For all the apartheid regime's talk about the Western world's 'double standards', it is a demonstrable and quantifiable fact that South Africa's repressive internal and external activities have all served to increase international demands for telling action against Pretoria and its allies. The South African government and apartheid keep sanctions alive – the issue has no independent life.

At another level, it would be fair to concede South Africa's point that the West does employ double standards – although not for the reasons proferred by Pretoria, presenting itself as the 'whipping boy' of the Western democracies. In the period of its most violent activities, both internally and externally, South Africa has had the crucial advantage of right-wing governments in three key countries – the UK, USA and West Germany. South Africa has, moreover, been well aware of this fact in pursuing its policies, relatively secure in the knowledge that the back door of sanctions has been well covered by this trio, and especially by the Thatcher–Reagan veto on the Security Council.

Yet Britain and the United States have, indeed, called for support for sanctions – against states like Libya, Cuba, the USSR and Nicaragua. The double standards extend directly to the application of the arms embargo against South Africa. 'No Western country has adopted, with regard to South Africa, the criterion which underlies export controls to socialist states, namely whether commodities contribute to a state's strategic capability in a broader, especially technological, sense. Consequently, scores of highly sensitive commodities which Western and Japanese industry may not export to the socialist states are legally exported to South Africa.' (International Maritime Organisation, 1986: 15)

In 1983 these double standards were clearly revealed when the United States was deeply concerned about the diversion of an advanced US computer system to the Soviet Union, through Sweden, after the equipment had been cleared for export to South Africa. US law prohibited its sale to the USSR, but not to South Africa. The computer was the Vax 11/782, described by the US Department of Defense as a 'state-of-the-art computer' with 'heavy military value'. As Hanlon and Omond wryly commented, 'It is in fact so easy to sell military hardware to South Africa that one route for smuggling such items to the socialist bloc is to export them legally to South Africa first!' (1987: 271)

Conclusion

The arms embargo is crucially important in a number of ways. Of all the sanctions available to the international community, it is the one which its proponents find the easiest to justify, both morally and strategically. For this reason, it provides a very clear pointer to how other sanctions, especially those which are perceived as 'problematic' – such as mandatory economic sanctions – would be implemented, especially by South Africa's major trading partners.

Opponents of any form of sanctions claim that not only has the arms embargo failed to work, it has had the 'unintended consequence' of being instrumental in the creation of a burgeoning domestic arms economy in South Africa, to the extent that the country is now exporting arms. A close examination of the activities of the Western powers reveals a somewhat different conclusion – the arms embargo has not been fully implemented. With the exception of a few countries, such as some of the Scandinavian countries, it has been implemented in a very half-hearted manner in most cases, or knowingly circumvented in others. However, if one considers the political trends in the crucial countries – the UK, USA, Israel and West Germany – this conclusion should not be too surprising. The 1980s have seen in these countries, and most notably in Israel and the USA, the ever-increasing influence of the military and the right-wing in government.

The arms embargo will, however, remain an important part of international efforts in the struggle against apartheid. Notwithstanding the fact that the arms embargo has been imperfectly implemented, it has had a significant effect on South Africa in a number of ways. Firstly, the effect on the economy of South Africa, while unquantifiable, has been substantial. The decade-long G-5 project, for example, must have involved considerable strain on the economy. The economic strain imposed by arms procurement has been all the more sorely felt as the South African economy is under pressure from other quarters, largely as a result of apartheid measures. The circle of increasing costs has become a spiral. As South Africa's political situation worsens, so the perceived need for armaments increases. Much of the technology for these arms, however, has to be imported at inflated prices, and with a currency that has been severely weakened by the political crisis. The only way South Africa can finance this huge arms bill is to export its 'indigenously produced' arms – here, once again, it finds itself confronted by international efforts to prevent such sales.

Secondly, as events in Angola have recently demonstrated, South Africa's capacity to engage in conventional warfare has been considerably weakened by the arms embargo. The balance of forces in the region swung against South Africa when its ageing fighter planes were confronted by Angola's sophisticated MiGs and radar system. This development, as much as any other factor, explains South Africa's desire to extricate itself from the Angolan conflict.

The Angolan example should dispel many of the myths surrounding the 'ineffectiveness' of the arms embargo. The consequences of the embargo have had a significant impact on South Africa's aggressive policies in southern Africa, despite its claims to self-sufficiency in arms and despite the failure of its major trading partners to implement the embargo effectively. The defeat of South African aims in Angola vindicates the proponents of the arms embargo – it was they who have been shown to be on the side of peace.

18 Defence expenditure and arms procurement in South Africa[1]

SEAN ARCHER

Defence expenditure[2] evokes powerful emotions. For conservatives and nationalists this is the one form of economic activity by the capitalist state to be supported without qualms. Indeed, its expansion is urged and applauded whenever 'national security' is perceived, and presented in the political arena, as under threat. Conversely, the production and purchase of weaponry is seen as provocative and wasteful by many religious and political groups who make up a wider but less cohesive force in the debate about militarisation. Interestingly, similar lines of division appear to exist with their own peculiarities also within the socialist bloc countries.

In view of the symbolic role played by defence spending, an examination of its magnitude and significance is a venture onto difficult ground. The evidence available in all countries is deficient because of the purpose and nature of defence activity; this is compounded by the interest of governments in concealing information from potential antagonists and sometimes from their own populations, even in supposed models of accountable government like the UK.[3] South Africa is no exception. The interested researcher has to sift and cobble together those bits of information that are at hand; to suggest what seems likely or predictable by analogy with other countries more open and more studied; but principally to raise questions in anticipation that answers will be forthcoming in the future. This is a second-best procedure, but it reflects the infancy of peace research in South Africa.

This chapter sets out to examine four areas: the deficiencies in defence expenditure figures; defence spending in South Africa; the question of whether defence spending stimulates or retards economic growth; and the nature of arms procurement through production and trade.

Defence expenditure calculations

Why do we wish to measure spending on defence accurately? The principal economic reason is that it uses resources which might alternatively be employed in satisfying consumer demand, either directly through the provision of goods and services, or indirectly through the creation of new productive capacity for such provision in the future. From this perspective of opportunity cost, the deficiencies of defence expenditure figures are considered in this section.

A nettle that every researcher must grasp concerns what forces to count in addition to the accepted military categories of army, navy, airforce, intelligence and support services including reserves. Information sources like SIPRI (Stockholm International Peace Research Institute) and IISS (International Institute of Strategic Studies) allow for the inclusion of paramilitary forces and police, with stress laid upon the circumstances pertaining in each situation.

> The [world military expenditure] data . . . include . . . costs of paramilitary forces and police when judged to be trained and equipped for military operations (SIPRI, 1983: 175).
>
> Many countries maintain [paramilitary] organizations whose training and equipment goes beyond those required for civil police duties. . . . They may be usable in support, or in lieu, of regular military forces. Precise definitions . . . are not always possible, and some degree of latitude must be allowed. (IISS, 1987: 6)

An obvious difficulty is how to exercise judgement when testable information is absent, as in South Africa's 'operational areas' and where 'unrest-related' actions are filtered into public knowledge under state of emergency regulations. Such actions involve a large range of 'security force' units, from regular troops and other services' personnel to police, police reservists, *kitskonstabels,* local authority police and commando units. Reorganisation under the National Security Management System has blurred these distinctions even further, and coincidentally widened the scope of raising additional resources without public scrutiny.[4]

Another source of indeterminacy is military aid. Often it is not clear whether such grants appear in the published budgets of recipient countries under military headings, but they can comprise a significant proportion of defence spending: 40 per cent to Israel from the United States in 1980 is exceptional although it is matched elsewhere, as in Egypt (Rivlin, 1987: 107). South Africa may receive clandestine military aid; although this is not likely to represent a significant contribution to total spending, it may involve sophisticated items of weaponry or technology whose importance is not captured in rand terms. Conversely, there is stronger evidence for South Africa's being a source of military assistance, but the size of that component in general development aid to the 'self-governing' and 'national' states, and secret aid to regimes and armed movements elsewhere in the subcontinent, is unknown.

Other dimensions in which expenditure figures are incomplete in coverage or fail to reflect the true economic cost include, firstly, conscription and reserve duty. This diversion of manpower to the armed forces costs much more than the recorded pay levels of personnel while in service. There are no South African estimates, but in Israel by way of illustration the 'extra-budgetary manpower cost' as a share of GNP was measured to be 10,2 and 6,9 per cent in 1979 and 1980 (Rivlin, 1987: 107; 1983: 193). Similarly, one reason for France maintaining Europe's largest standing army in the past decade was 'that a conscript's *solde* [pay] was much lower than unemployment benefit' (*Guardian Weekly*, 18.9.1988).

Secondly, basic research, in contrast to research applied directly to a military purpose, is funded out of the state budget under non-defence heads but nevertheless can be crucial in the development of new weaponry. There seems to be no way of estimating this cost for South Africa, although it is said to take place (Grundy, 1986: 45). Thirdly, land for military end-use (bases, proving ranges, storage) is seldom ascribed a value equivalent to alternative use. Infrastructure is a separate but related category, because road networks, telecommunications, the siting of airports, harbours and other instances 'have in many cases also a strong bearing on a country's military capability [yet] it is not normal practice to define the costs of such activities as military expenditures' (Cars, 1987: 76). Strategic considerations have been believed for many years to apply locally, for example the location and size of Upington airport, tarred roads in remote areas, township design and the like.

Fourthly, subsidies earmarked for military activities are financed under non-military items, and stockpiles of strategic materials are purchased and interest is paid out of the civilian budget, as well as from extra-budgetary funds like fuel levies in South Africa. 'Such production . . . contributes strongly to a country's defence capacity. It is, therefore, a matter of opinion whether costs of stockpiling . . . ought to be regarded as military expenditure or not' (Cars, 1987: 76). And the category most problematic for the research-worker is where governments 'may not account for military spending at all and pay for it with export earnings that are never repatriated or entered into official trade accounts' (World Bank, 1988: 106). Information surfaces only with political changes, corruption scandals and leaks from outside the country concerned: Irangate is a classic case. It is possible therefore for Armscor's international trading activities to influence the resource flow into the defence sector without this being reflected in budgetary procedures. The fact of the matter is that funds can be effectively laundered by only the mildest bending of accounting rules in an atmosphere of patriotism and secrecy.

The final problem concerns prices. Partly the difficulty is one of method because there is no direct way of measuring a unit of military output or of military-use value: 'the only practical [price] series are those for military inputs. . . . The ultimate objective of military expenditure can be said to be national security: but of course this cannot be measured – and in any case it is also a function of the military expenditure of other countries. . . .' (Sköns, 1983: 197–8) This relationship between measurable inputs and unmeasurable outputs can be seen in Figure 1. Partly, too, the difficulty is that prices may vary considerably over transactions owing to political considerations, inflation, rates of exchange and the many variations on basic weapons. The general point is that a given nominal amount of defence expenditure can purchase widely differing quantities of military input. For instance, during the Gulf War, Iran is said to have paid '10 or 20 times the normal selling price of critical spare parts' (Klare, 1988: 18); and similarly, the prices of imported arms to South Africa are likely to be well above the world average owing to this country's isolation and the covert nature of its purchases. The opportunity cost – what could have been bought instead with the foreign exchange – would then be particularly high.

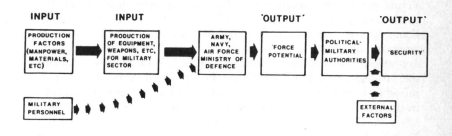

Figure 1: Defence sector input and output (Sköns, 1983: 197)

South African defence expenditure

Budget estimates are the principal source of information about defence expenditure in South Africa, although we know little about the individual components. Table 1 contains the categories destined unambiguously for defence purposes (if we accept the contention that part of police expenditure is properly classified as 'defence' under the circumstances current in South Africa). In Part A (the RSA budget), the constant price series show a marked rise in *real* resource use for defence over the budget years 1985 to 1988. We can express this in more than one way. The increased spending from 1985 is 19 per cent to 1987 and 26 per cent to 1988;[5] in other words, the growth rate after inflation is 8 per cent per annum. Further, the combined weight of these defence outlays within the total budget has increased by one to two percentage points, 16 to 17,7. In Part B (the SWA budget), the rise although lower is also unambiguous: in real terms about 18 per cent. Finally, as a proportion of GDP, the combined total of expenditure has also grown, but the period studied is too short to diagnose a trend.

It must be emphasised strongly that these figures are an incomplete measure on a number of counts. Firstly, regional, municipal and other local authority spending on security forces is funded at lower levels and through transfers from the centre that are difficult to monitor; for example Department of Manpower recruitment of municipal police (Seegers, 1988: 17). Secondly, other South West African expenditure includes sums with a probable defence purpose additional to those in Table 1, like infrastructural and communication projects in the public sector. Thirdly, the homeland budgets of Transkei, Bophuthatswana, Venda and Ciskei contain parallel outlays in some, possibly all, the defence categories identified in Table 1 but are not fully disclosed. Fourthly, the 'self-governing states' like KwaZulu spend significant amounts on police and paramilitary units. Finally, there are the mysterious extra-budgetary sources like the Central Energy Fund and the Strategic Fuel Fund which are in command of large resources raised by levy, loan or transfers from the Treasury. Defence suppliers in the shape of Armscor and the Atomic Energy Corporation (RSA, 1987: 16–17), and defence-related activities like stockpiling by the National Supplies Procurement Fund (RSA, 1985: 197), have received loans or grants from these funds in recent years.

With these gaps in mind, Table 2 lists the principal transfers from the central budget to other spending authorities on the premise that they are either known, or considered highly likely, to contain a defence component. These are extremely large sums: R8,25 billion in the current fiscal year (1988/9). In a complete accounting of resource use for defence, were the detail available the true total could consequently be greater by many millions of rands.

What we can deduce is that existing expenditure levels will remain burdensome, and become more so with continued deterioration in economic conditions. The current regime faces a form of scissors crisis, with static real GDP and rising defence needs simultaneously. If the scissor blades open further, the gap between what appears politically desirable and what is economically feasible will also widen. No government can tie itself to spend 'whatever is necessary for the defence of South Africa', but will be constrained to keep security outlays within boundaries set by normal budgetary considerations, even though this

Table 1: **Estimated defence expenditure, 1985–88 (R millions)**
A. **Allocations to defence in RSA budget**

	1985/6	1986/7	1987/8	1988/9
Defence	4 274	5 123	6 683	8 196
Police(a)	478	536	765	898
	(955)	(1 071)	(1 530)	(1 795)
Public works(b)	173	191	223	244
Secret service	95	169	198	221
Total expenditure				
Current prices	5 020	6 019	7 869	9 559
Constant prices	5 020	5 203	5 953	6 347
As % total budget	16,0	15,8	16,8	17,7

B. **Allocations to defence in SWA/Namibia budget**

	1985/6	1986/7	1987/8	1988/9
Defence	142	162	204	220
Police(a)	34	62	69	74
	(68)	(123)	(138)	(147)
National Intelligence	–	–	4,6	4,5
Total expenditure	176	224	278	299
RSA plus SWA defence expenditure as % GDP	4,9	4,9	5,3	5,7(c)

Notes:
(a) Given the paramilitary role of the police, half the total Police allocation (in brackets) is assumed to have a defence function.
(b) These are building and engineering projects for the defence force and police.
(c) All figures are planned expenditure (see also footnote 5), and 1988 GDP at factor cost is an estimate based on expenditure levels in the first two quarters.
Sources: RSA, 1985–1988; SWA, 1987, 1988; SA Reserve Bank, 1988.

Table 2: **Budget grants and transfers with presumed defence components, 1985–8**

	1985/6	1986/7	1987/8	1988/9
SWA/Namibia administration	1 487	1 366	1 433	1 178
TBVC countries				
Foreign aid	936	1 034	1 873	2 201
Budgetary aid	636	697	1 354	1 699
Tax compensation	175	192	212	270
Sub-total	1 747	1 923	3 460	4 170
Self-governing states development aid	1 888	2 403	3 030	4 075
Total	3 635	4 326	6 490	8 245

Note: SWA/Namibia and TBVC countries probably spend on all components of defence, the self-governing states on all except regular military forces.
Source: RSA, 1985–1988

brake may be obscured by the inflationary process.

Defence expenditure and economic growth

Is defence expenditure on balance stimulating or retarding in its economic effects? This question is clouded because the answers wanted are usually the firm opinions already held. Three aspects are considered here: the under-consumptionist proposition that defence spending acts as a desirable stabiliser in a capitalist economy; the claim about 'spin-off' from weapon procurement; and some explanations as to why the net effects upon economic growth are hard to pin down.

In 1950 a US government publication wrote: 'Business won't go to pot so long as war is a threat; so long as every alarm can step up spending, lending for defense at home and aid abroad; cold war is almost a guarantee against a bad depression' (Melman, 1986: 72). This view emerged from the apparent success of rearmament expenditure during the 1930s in mopping up unemployment, followed by the post-Second World War association of high defence spending with unprecedented growth and employment rates in mature market economies. While propagated principally by Marxists, it also complemented the orthodox interpretation of Keynesian thinking about the need for government spending, so-called 'pump-priming', when effective demand in the economy sagged below full employment levels. One inference drawn was that there thus existed formidable economic obstacles to the progress of disarmament.

Attractive in its simplicity, the under-consumptionist perspective has not survived empirical testing and the doctrinal upheavals in economics since the early 1970s. Within market economies as a group there is no clearcut association between high shares of military expenditure in national income, and high levels of per capita income and low unemployment rates. The plausibility of the perspective is undermined further by the stronger international linkages between these countries now than was the case in the 1930s, and hence effective demand in any single economy is powerfully influenced by trade. Defence expenditure furthermore turns out to be a rather blunt instrument of stabilisation because it can involve lengthy time-lags and because armaments production is generally less labour-intensive than other economic activities.

Hence critics (Kennedy, 1983), even sympathetic ones like Smith (1977), conclude that military expenditure's role in the present world has slipped out of the simple under-consumptionist frame. This may be due also to the permanent post-Second World War upsurge in public spending which characterises 'late capitalism'. In major countries government expenditure as a percentage of GDP rose on average from 12 per cent in 1913 to 27 per cent in 1950 and 45 per cent in 1981, with individual figures even higher: Netherlands 59, France 49 and Germany

48 per cent respectively (Maddison, 1984: 57).

The second question concerns the alleged spin-off for the civilian economy that comes from defence spending, with claims about the new processes and commodities flowing as by-products from investment in military-related research and development. The fields where such transfers may take place are those in which the technology is generic in nature, like aircraft, jet engines, computers, fibre optics, microcircuits, composite materials, metallurgy and nuclear power. Even 'Star Wars' research is claimed to throw light on problems like acid rain. Because the funds, provided by the state for 70–85 per cent of defence research and development, would not otherwise have been available, 'so the military programs should be seen as net additions to the civilian effort rather than as substitutes' (Reppy, 1985: 11).

Sceptics mount a number of criticisms of the spin-off claim, some factual and some analytical. One contention is that the more esoteric and advanced the military technology, the less likely will be its civilian applications: (1) it tends to yield elaborate, tailored output; (2) focused upon a narrow objective it inhibits other potential applications and interactions with possible non-defence users; (3) diffusion is restricted for fear that the fruits of research may reach adversaries; and (4) there is an emphasis on product innovation (new devices), rather than process innovation (new ways of producing existing devices). Another line of attack concerns the failure to consider opportunity cost in the spin-off debate. If the same investment in research and design were made in other ways and in other sectors, the innovation resulting is the true measure against which these benefits have to be compared (Brooks, 1986: 182–3). These inputs are moreover extremely skill- and knowledge-intensive: 'Currently, 70 per cent of government funding and about 30 per cent of total government and private spending on R & D are allotted to military projects. . . . For the post-war period as a whole, roughly 42 per cent of the United States' scientific workforce has been employed in military-related projects' (Reppy, 1985: 11).

In the South African case, the most recent Defence White Paper argues for spin-off mainly via the 'establishment of local skills and technology . . . [which] has given industry a tremendous technological boost [and,] by way of personnel turnover, the training offered by Armscor in the new technology permeates through to the private sector' (1986: 9). No independent evaluation of such claims is available, and while there may be truth in them it should be pointed out that the technological level in question is unlikely to be as advanced as in the major weapon-producing countries. Also, one study of poorer countries came to a sceptical view: 'the optimistic expectation, that the spin-off from arms industries will permeate to the rest of the economy, has failed completely [in less developed countries]' (Deger & Sen, 1987: 236).

Finally, the impact of defence spending on economic growth may be considerable given its size, but it is difficult to assess even qualitatively because contingent factors intervene. These factors include the phasing of the normal business cycle, the differing international trade dependence of individual countries, the changing internal mix of defence spending, the social context, and general strategic considerations. 'Overall, there does not appear to be any systematic relation between military expenditure and unemployment, inflation, or the balance of payments' (Smith, 1987: 464).

Research work on this question has proved difficult, firstly because we lack 'a baseline for comparison . . . we do not have any idea about what the economy would be like without any military spending' (Chan, 1985: 432). This is an exaggeration but it conveys the essence of the problem. Secondly, there are no adequate techniques for deciding on the causal direction when national income and the defence sector both grow or both decline together. Do politicians conceive national security to be a common good, more of which must be purchased as a country grows richer? Or does military spending push the expansion process via higher investment, technical change and the acquired skills of the labour force (Blackaby, 1983: 16)? Thirdly, discontinuities in the relationship are probable; that is, the direction and magnitude of the influence exerted by defence spending upon macro-economic activity, or vice versa, may change at different per capita income levels. Defence spending could initially be a stimulant, then a retardant and again a stimulant later during the growth process. The fourth reason for slow progress on this question may stem from the doctrinal upheavals in macro-economics during the past two decades. The Keynesian consensus that dominated for thirty years has disintegrated, so rival conceptions of an economy's stability properties now lead to rival views on state expenditure; hence there is no generally accepted framework for modelling the impact of defence spending on the growth process.

Despite these uncertainties, certain generalisations can be made with a bearing on South Africa. In so far as beneficial effects can be identified, they arise only in a deficient demand economy, and South Africa in recent times has been far removed from that condition. Then, concerning capital accumulation, in developed countries the trade-off or inverse relationship between shares of military expenditure and total investment in output seems to be high; that is, the defence sector expands at the expense of investment (Kennedy, 1983: 198; Smith, 1987: 464). Finally, armaments production is relatively capital-intensive, so that per unit of productive capacity the absorption of labour is lower than in the civilian economy. In a labour-surplus economy like South Africa this is a serious economic and social cost. Total employment in defence production according to the 1982 White Paper was 'almost 105 000 employees (Armscor subsidiaries 29 000 and private contractors

76 000) . . .' (1982: 25), which was 7,5 per cent of the total manufacturing labour force of 1,4 million at that time. These workers are likely to be relatively skilled, and in general the production and maintenance of weapon systems are a heavy drain on trained manpower: 'at the beginning of the 1970s an efficient armoured unit . . . required 150 trained mechanics for every 100 tanks and another 50 mechanics for every 100 armoured personnel carriers . . . these figures might have increased during the last decade and . . . [in developing countries] we estimate the requirement for trained mechanics to be at least 50 per cent higher' (Wulf, 1987a: 379).

To summarise, although there is the possibility of positive spin-off for technological practice within the civilian sector, the net effect of military spending is ambiguous. In the South African case we should recognise that, on balance, defence expenditure probably constrains sources of economic expansion like the volume of investment and pre-empts the use of labour skills up to the highest educational and occupational categories.

Armaments procurement through production and trade

The details of South Africa's weapon production are the subject of other chapters in this volume, so this section will concentrate upon more general considerations arising from international experience. Trends evidenced in recent efforts in the Third World to produce, sell and purchase armaments or armaments-making technology throw light on local activities, which we know so little about.

The age of mass armies that began with Napoleon and dominated warfare until early this century came to an end with mechanisation. As weapons became more lethal and more expensive, it was their supply rather than manpower which constrained the size of military establishments (Keegan, 1985: 15). Richer countries have come to see their strategic advantage to lie in the most sophisticated weaponry within their technological reach. To that end the 'investment' components of military budgets – research and development, procurement and military construction – have risen steadily, in the United States for instance to '48 per cent, up from 36 per cent in fiscal 1980, largely reflecting a strong commitment to new weapons' (Adams, 1986: 7).

A similar emphasis, spurred by efforts to design and produce complex weapon systems for self-sufficiency, can be discerned for some developing countries including South Africa: in the 'composition of the budget of the S.A. Defence Force . . . the percentage expenditure on capital equipment, that is renewal, has increased [in this decade]' (1986 Defence White Paper: 27). Other states with military ambitions, notably the oil exporters who have lesser balance of payments constraints, have relied upon trade sources.[6]

Since World War II four major developments have occurred in the defence industries in general. One is the increase in the costs of producing highly complex and technologically sophisticated weapons. The second is the greater degree of cooperation over arms production in the West. . . . The third is the dramatic expansion in the number of countries producing arms, especially in the Third World. And the fourth is a rapid increase in counter-trade, barter and offset practices in the transfer of arms. (IISS, 1987: 239)

All these trends can be seen in South Africa, but particularly the last two. Building up indigenous arms industries forms part of an 'import substitution industrialisation' (ISI) strategy which began in a serious way in South Africa in the mid-1920s. Sixty years later it would be surprising if there were not a diversified industrial structure, although serious problems face this sector currently (Archer, 1987). What South Africa has *not* succeeded in producing locally can be seen by a glance at the composition of its imports. The major categories of imports during the past three years are: chemicals and chemical products (10–11 per cent of total imports); machinery (27–31 per cent), including electrical machinery, machine tools and a vast array of other machines; vehicles and transport equipment (11–14 per cent); and unclassified (14–20 per cent), mainly oil, weapons and strategic materials (*Trends*, 1987, 1988). Together these account for 70 per cent of the annual import bill.

This composition pinpoints those industries still lacking for the indigenous production of weaponry, notably electronic equipment, precision machinery, engines, composite materials, scientific instruments and vehicle components. Their absence imposes major limitations on local self-sufficiency, despite South Africa's being one of only six developing countries (along with Argentina, Brazil, China, India and Israel) judged to possess by 1980 'across-the-board-capabilities' for producing all major weapons: aircraft, missiles, ships and armoured fighting vehicles (Neuman, 1984: 178).

Table 3: **South African manufacturing sector: industries relevant for armaments production** *(Percentage weight in physical volume of production)*

Basic iron and steel	10,4
Basic non-ferrous metals	3,1
Metal products	8,8
Machinery and equipment	6,6
Electrical machinery	5,3
Motor vehicles	5,0
Transport equipment	2,1
	41,3
Remaining industries (20)	58,7
	100,0

Source: CSS (1988: 4); also see Wulf (1987b: 367) and Deger & Sen (1987: 238) on 'potential defence capacity'

Table 4: **Arms production and production potential in developing countries (late 1970s)**

Country	Rank order of arms production (1)	Rank order of potential arms production (2)
Israel	1	12
India	2	1
Brazil	3	2
Yugoslavia	4	3
South Africa	5	4
Argentina	6	6
Taiwan	7	7
Korea (South)	8	8
Philippines	9	18
Turkey	10	9
Indonesia	11	23
Egypt	12	14
Korea (North)	13	—
Pakistan	14	24
Singapore	15	22
Iran	16	11
Colombia	17	19
Portugal	18	13
Greece	19	10
Peru	20	25
Thailand	21	20
Venezuela	22	17
Dominican Republic	23	—
Nigeria	24	27
Mexico	25	5
Malaysia	26	26
Burma	27	—
Chile	28	16
Saudi Arabia	29	28
Sudan	30	—
Zimbabwe	31	29
Libya	32	—

Source: Wulf, 1987a: 209

In the same vein, South Africa has been ranked along with another 31 developing countries according to actual and potential arms production. Seven industries are identified as 'relevant' for measuring the latter in terms (1) of their output, and (2) of their manpower base, being total employment in these industries along with the number of scientists, engineers and technicians involved in research and development economy-wide. What proportion of their output is for military end-use is not known, but Table 3 shows the weights of these industries within the manufacturing sector, in total a sizeable 41 per cent. Table 4 lists the rank orders which emerge, with South Africa fifth in actual and fourth in potential arms production out of 32 countries.

By now there is a considerable literature on the stylised facts of armaments production in the Third World.[7] Firstly, no single producer is able yet to produce a wholly indigenous system in the major categories (now five): aircraft, armour and artillery, missiles, warships, and guidance and radar systems. Some have produced prototypes, but for production and deployment all rely on one or other of licensing, co-production, refurbishing and upgrades, technical assistance, and the importation of sophisticated components. In other words, dependence on the major arms producers remains, whether openly or clandestinely (Neuman, 1984: 177). South Africa constructed

its domestic arms industry . . . step by step using foreign technology and components, while imports of advanced weapon systems, such as helicopters, fighter aircraft and fast patrol boats, continued. . . . South Africa still lacks the capability to design and build new and sophisticated weapon systems . . . the armed forces are pressing industry to design such weapons as helicopters and fighter aircraft [but] so far, these efforts have resulted in upgraded versions of weapons previously acquired abroad. (Brzoska & Ohlson, 1987: 26–7)

Secondly, the transfer of arms-making technology – blueprints, technical information and support, and design embodied in sample weapons, machines and components – has become a major feature of the trade in weaponry; furthermore, within the existing classifications of trade it is more difficult to monitor. Major buyers like Brazil have exerted leverage to obtain comprehensive transfers. By comparison, South Africa is at a disadvantage. While weapons and spares can change hands discreetly from time to time, the acquisition of technology is an extended learning process, needing collaboration on both sides to be successful.

Thirdly, weapons production takes place in an unusual cost environment: the state assumes the role of capitalist and entrepreneur, supplying all finance and absorbing all risks of failure. Contracts are usually on a cost-plus or full-reimbursement basis with little price discipline, resulting often in the production of baroque, 'gold-plated' weapons: 'the first four copies of [the American B-1 bomber] had a price that exceeded its equivalent weight in gold' (Melman, 1986: 76). This inefficiency is at least as great in Third World defence industries because the techniques employed, being more capital- and skill-intensive than the norm for the civilian sector, are therefore also less appropriate to the mix of resource inputs available in developing countries. There is no reason to believe that productive performance in South Africa's armaments sector is above the mean, but rather there is cause for concern that Armscor's monopoly (single seller) and monopsony (single buyer) power, coupled to its secrecy provisions, makes for an even less effective use of resources than the international norm.

Fourthly, a major constraint that applies to all new producers of arms, Israel being the outstanding exception, is the skills required for R & D and weapon design beyond the intermediate phases of competence. Further, there are scale factors: domestic defence forces are too small to provide an adequate market, national income is too low, and the industrial substructure is insufficiently diversified to support the needed innovation. For example, 'military technologies produced by Third World countries under licence in 1980 were, on average, designed and developed twenty-two years earlier' (Neuman, 1984: 179, 186). There is no evidence that South Africa is different in these respects.

On the trade route to procurement, major trends in the past decade are the proliferation of arms-supplying countries, growing trade in arms-production and modernisation technology, the surge in black market transactions, and the re-emergence of private dealers (Hartung, 1987: 33). Three tiers in the world market for weaponry are distinguishable: firstly, formal sales or transfers between governments, or from private sellers accredited by their home governments, on a wide spectrum of terms and conditions. Secondly, a grey market where greyness refers to 'the nature of the item being transferred, or in the character of the transaction, or both' (Klare, 1988: 19). In the present decade this category has expanded through an alleged 'sell first, ask questions later' policy under the Reagan regime (Hartung, 1987: 33), as well as from general pressures to reap scale economies by increasing turnover through the export of arms. Thirdly, there are clandestine or black market activities which are strictly illegal, either within the supplier country or by United Nations proclamation. No-one knows the dimensions of this trafficking but estimates are $5–10 billion, up to a third of all international arms transfers (Hartung, 1987: 33; Klare, 1988: 16). Accurate information about the trade in weaponry is consequently thin, an illustration of this being the range of published estimates of annual Israeli arms supplies to South Africa: $50 million (Hartung, 1987: 31), $100 million (Klare, 1988: 20), $300 million (SIPRI, 1987: 199).

We know little about South Africa's international arms dealing and we are prohibited from finding out more. That we import significant quantities, pay significant premiums above going prices, and sell to a range of buyers, are all plausible conjectures. For instance, South Africa is listed as supplying both sides in the Gulf War, selling over the past three years '300 000–400 000 155-mm artillery shells to Iran, probably in exchange for oil [as well as] spare parts for Iranian F-4 Phantom fighter aircraft' (SIPRI, 1987: 199). Recent newspaper reports quote sources from abroad, like *Jane's Defence Weekly* (London), asserting that Armscor is now 'the world's fifth-largest defence contractor with current orders of more than R9 billion . . . [having] exported R1,8 billion of armaments last year to 23 countries' (*Cape Times*, 18.5.1988; 21.1.1988). This seems exaggerated, an 'arms trade fact', although the local industry is claimed not to be as disadvantaged as it may seem in the context of the arms embargo: 'Despite political problems, Armscor's export organisation enjoys two major advantages over its competition: much of the equipment has been developed on the basis of operational experience, and all of it has been developed with the needs, problems and capabilities of a small defence force in mind' (Heitman, 1988: 16).

One clue to the value of arms imported lies in the 'Unclassified' category of South African imports. In 1986 this totalled R5,3 billion and since 1980 has averaged more than R4 billion per year, comprising between 20 and 30 per cent of total imports. We are not allowed to know its composition between oil, strategic materials and armaments, but to appreciate the orders of magnitude involved we should bear in mind the following. If in 1986 South Africa imported 70 million barrels of oil this would have cost R2,4 billion; if 100 million barrels then R3,3 billion,[8] leaving a balance of armaments and non-oil strategic stockpiles of R2–2,9 billion. Although speculative, this shows the large volume of resources allocated on a recurring basis to weapon procurements from abroad.

Conclusion
'An ebbing tide lowers all ships, with the notable exception of military ships.' In the past half-dozen years the South African GDP has either grown slowly or fallen while the level of real defence expenditure has increased. This has meant falling shares for other uses.[9] That the current regime in South Africa is not alone in the world in pursuing victory on the battlefield rather than grappling with underlying political and economic grievances is little comfort to us. A first task for peace researchers is to show the material cost in alternatives forgone of a war which cannot be won. A full accounting has yet to become available, but the estimates and qualitative judgements contained in this chapter are enough to show that the burden is heavy and increasing. In addition, South Africa's investment in organised and legitimated violence imposes great costs on her neighbours in the subcontinent, and ultimately is a serious threat to world peace.

A related question concerns the true meaning of 'national security'. What is apt to be forgotten is that it is not an end in itself: 'Its ultimate purpose must be to secure the independence and sovereignty of the national state, the freedom of its citizens and the means to develop economically, socially and culturally' (Thorsson, 1982: 41). Peace researchers should state clearly that the only rational and morally acceptable strategy to achieve such security is 'act in the way you wish others to act'. This embodies much besides altruism because it is perfectly compatible with the hard-headed pursuit of self- as well as national interest.

PART FOUR
Militarisation and culture

19 A 'battlefield of perceptions': state discourses on political violence, 1985–1988

DEBORAH POSEL

According to state ideologues, South Africa is experiencing a 'revolutionary onslaught' on a wide front. Part of this onslaught, the country is told, is an 'organised process of disinformation' (P. W. Botha, in *South African Digest (SAD)*, 27 September 1985) which presents an alternative perspective to the state's construal of prevailing political realities. Central to the state's 'counter-revolutionary strategy', therefore, is a strenuous ideological offensive in what the Bureau of Information has described as a 'battlefield of perceptions' (TV1 news, 5.45 p.m., 20 June 1986).

This chapter deals with one aspect of the state's ideological offensive – viz, depictions of political violence by and against the state, concentrated in the country's black townships in the period 1985 to 1988. The offensive had at least three aims. Firstly, state ideologues were intent on contesting the representation of township violence as 'a people's war' – a mass-based struggle, with an articulate and democratic leadership and a clear programme and strategy. This version of the escalation of violence post-1985 spurred local and international rejection of 'reform' as irrelevant to the wishes of the black majority. Secondly, the state had to rebut accusations of being a 'terrorist state', resorting to unjustifiably draconian measures to impose 'law and order'. Thirdly, state ideologues were desperate to dispute the white right-wing's portrayal of the violence as the mark of puny government, weakened by its commitment to 'reform'. The reassurance of strong government was also necessary to sustain business confidence in the country. In addition, white South Africans had to be made to feel safe about the state's proposals for some form of 'power-sharing' with blacks. To this end, state ideologues contested the right-wing verdict on the escalation of violence as 'a war on white South Africa' (TV1 news, 7 p.m., 31 October 1985), indicative of 'an irreconcilably polarised society' ('Newscomment', 4 November 1985), divided along racial lines. For 'power-sharing' to become a legitimate and persuasive option, the lines of political conflict had to be redefined in non-racial terms.

This chapter examines the content and effects of state discourses structured by this three-pronged ideological offensive, and identifies some of its involuntary pitfalls and contradictions. It is argued that the state failed to construct an ideological discourse which could simultaneously realise the three objectives outlined above. The images invoked to counter the idea of a 'people's war' by stripping township activists of their political purpose and identity, and which portrayed violence by the South African Defence Force and South African Police as defensive and reasonable action, also unwittingly drew on long-standing and deeply rooted white racist images and fears. At the heart of the state's discourse on political violence was a familiar white fear of the rampant black mob, a threat to the 'civilised order' which white society claims as its basis. Therefore, despite the state's efforts on other ideological fronts to *move away* from categorisations of political conflict in racial terms, its discourses on violence unintentionally recreated and reinforced exactly this perception. The result was to entrench white commitment to racial separatism 'by implicit reference to the nightmare possibilities of what would happen should the black crowd be allowed to get out of control' (Maughan Brown, 1984: 27).

The purpose of the state's discourse on violence was two-fold: it sought to explain why township residents resorted to violence, and to explain and justify the violence perpetrated by the SADF and SAP in the townships. This chapter shows that both objectives relied on a set of three principal symbols which, by repetitive association with news items on township violence, became apparently self-evident, short-hand explanations of state and township violence. The first part identifies these symbols and shows how they functioned as explanatory and justificatory devices. The second part examines why the symbols functioned in this way, by peeling away their various layers of meaning.

The study is essentially a content analysis of state discourses on violence.[1] It draws principally on television news coverage of violence as its main source,[2] partly because the visual medium is more powerful than the written word, and partly because television reaches a wider audience than any single written medium. The chapter does also draw on various government policy speeches, press statements and reports, and published pamphlets.

THE PRINCIPAL SYMBOLS OF TOWNSHIP VIOLENCE

One of the most immediately conspicuous features of television coverage of township violence was censorship. The state was anxious to prevent a mood of 'pessimism' or panic developing locally and abroad (*SAD*, 27 September 1985). In order to maintain the confidence of the white electorate, state ideologues were determined to convey the message that the SADF and SAP were always on top of the situation. News coverage of 'unrest' therefore studiously avoided giving it too high a profile – particularly since the introduction of the national state of emergency in June 1986. Thus, many violent clashes between township residents and the security forces were simply never reported.

Others were mentioned very briefly, without any visual coverage. In virtually all cases, the version of events presented was highly abbreviated, verbally and visually. It was in this process of condensing and curtailing information that three principal symbols for township violence emerged. During 1985–6 almost every newscast on violence made verbal or visual reference or both to the *crowd, stone-throwing* or *flames,* irrespective of the particular details or form of the violence in question. By repetition, these images and concepts became strongly associated with nearly all cases of violence perpetrated by township groups, and thus identified with the very idea of such violence itself. Moreover, implicit in this process of identification was a tacit explanation of why the violence had occurred, and a seemingly obvious rationale for violence by the SAP and SADF against township communities.

How were these visual and verbal shorthands established, and how did they function as a summary analysis of township violence and a legitimation of state violence? The following discussion considers each of the three symbols in turn.

The crowd

'Nine people died and almost 200 people were injured,' says the newsreader, while the screen shows shots of a crowd with raised fists (TV1 news, 8 p.m., 19 February 1985).

'Countrywide unrest cost the lives of 2 rioters last night,' is read out with accompanying footage of a crowd of about 30 encircling a burning object (TV1 news, 8 p.m., 14 April 1985).

In television news, viewers interpret the footage accompanying the verbal text as a visual confirmation or amplification of what is being said. Thus in both of the above examples, by a process of association, viewers were presented with an image of the crowd as though this self-evidently accounted for the injuries and deaths.

Some reports took this message one step further by drawing on the image of the crowd as an apparently exhaustive explanation and justification for police and army violence against township residents. For example, the 8 p.m. newscast on the police shootings at Langa, Uitenhage, on 21 March 1985, explained the day's events as simply the consequence of the fact that 'an unruly mob numbering several thousand . . . some armed with petrol bombs and other weapons, had encircled a small group of policemen'. No mention was made of the fact that the crowd was en route to a funeral, peacefully, and that the conflict was triggered when police shot dead a young boy on a bicycle who raised his fist in salute. Rather, the implicit message was that the mere presence of a large crowd was sufficient reason for the violence that ensued.

The same visual justification of state violence in the townships accompanied the announcement on television news of the introduction of the Internal Security Amendment Bill, on 22 May 1986. While viewers were told that the bill made provision for extended periods of detention of up to 180 days, they saw shots of crowds of youths shouting and burning vehicles and shacks. By implication, the mere existence of such militant crowds legitimised the new draconian measure.[3]

Stone-throwing

The creation of stone-throwing as a visual and verbal shorthand for township violence was quite explicit: 'stone-throwing' was defined as a category of 'unrest incident' in itself. Thus, television news coverage of violence in the Eastern Cape on 27 May 1985 summarised the problem as one of 'stone-throwing'. A resumé of 'unrest' in the news review programme Network on 3 February 1987 declared that 'the most dominant unrest incident by far has been stone-throwing'.

As with the symbol of the crowd, this ideological shorthand acquired explanatory and justificatory powers. Thus the above-mentioned account of violence in the Eastern Cape reported that police had discovered two dead bodies 'after stone-throwing and petrol bombs' – as though the fact of stone-throwing (and arson) was all the information relevant to an account of the two deaths. Perhaps the most striking illustration of this process of creating an apparently complete and unquestionable rationale for state violence was provided by one of the news reports on the hearings of the Kannemeyer Commission into the Langa shootings. The newsreader reported that a 15-year-old resident of Langa had given evidence of having been shot and then kicked by police while lying on the ground. The camera however was resolutely focused on two large stones, presented as an exhibit to the commission. The viewer saw the stones from several angles as the camera zoomed in and then out again. Visually, the substance of the youth's evidence and his version of what happened at Langa were overruled by the insistent image of the stones. The 'fact' of stone-throwing provided the authoritative verdict on the shootings (TV1 news, 8 p.m., 12 April 1985).

The account of the so-called 'Trojan horse incident' (when police hidden at the back of a truck opened fire on a crowd in Athlone in the Western Cape in October 1985) illustrated a similar process at work, in this case verbally. According to the television news of 17 October 1985,

police have defended their alleged ambush of stone-throwers in the area [Athlone] earlier this week in which three people were shot dead, as a necessary technique to protect people using public roads in the area. The police say the so-called ambush has been widely publicised and condemned by a variety of individuals and organisations both within South Africa and abroad. *They say the fact is that stone-throwing is rife in the area.* [My emphasis.]

In other words, the mere fact of stone-throwing was invoked – here explicitly – as justification in itself for the police ambush.[4]

Flames

Flames and billowing smoke were the images most frequently associated with reports on violence in the townships. For example, a report on 'more sporadic incidents of violence in the Eastern Cape' (TV1 news, 8 p.m., 12 April 1985) showed visual footage of burning tyres and burning buildings – as if these images epitomised the nature of the 'unrest'. A discussion of the problem of 'black terrorists who are murdering other blacks' was conducted against the visual backdrop of smouldering, burnt-out buildings – again suggesting that fire somehow symbolised the crux of the violence (TV1 news, 14 January 1985).

As a visual summary for violence perpetrated by township residents, the image of flames also provided a condensed rationale for police violence. For example, a television news report on the deaths of three residents of Kwanobuhle, on 24 March 1985, claimed that 'police had to shoot', while showing footage of flames and smoke engulfing a township house.[5] Similarly, brief mention of 'incidents of unrest . . . in several places' on TV1 news on 27 March 1985 was coupled with close-up shots of flames.[6]

Having become so firmly identified with the idea of township violence, the image of flames also functioned to usurp the verbal meaning of a newscast in much the same way as the image of stones did in the report on the Kannemeyer hearings. Thus, for example, a news report which mentioned that a young girl was wounded by birdshot as police dispersed a crowd in Soweto, showed footage of a fireman putting out a burning tyre (TV1 news, 8 p.m., 9 May 1985).

As can be seen from the examples selected, this set of symbols was developed during 1985 and early 1986, when news coverage of township violence (although censored) was more detailed than after the media restrictions were promulgated in the wake of the national state of emergency in June 1986. After June 1986, news reports were limited to sparse, vague mention on 'unrest incidents' in various parts of the country, with little or no visual footage. More comprehensive coverage of the 'unrest' took the form of resumé discussions in the programme *Network* after the news. The same set of symbols was used to provide the familiar economical and condensed series of explanations and justifications. For example, *Network* of 3 February 1987 presented a report on 'the latest on the security situation'. The bulk of the programme was devoted to a discussion with Kobus Neethling, of the Bureau for Information, who analysed various trends in copious statistical detail (discussed in the next section). This was preceded by a 'background report' which contained a re-run of the stock images; shots of flaming tyres, burning shacks and vehicles, crowds gathering, youths throwing petrol bombs and a car being stoned. By now well-established shorthands for township violence, these images were used as a comprehensive record of the nature of 'unrest' to date, and a seemingly incontrovertible vindication of the national state of emergency.

By repetition, the identification of township violence with the crowd, stone-throwing and flames came to seem obvious because the symbols seemed to speak for themselves. The implicit explanation and justification of police violence, as a response to the crowd, stone-throwing or flames, seemed similarly incontrovertible. However, when dealing with ideological discourses, the appearance of self-evidence is a tell-tale hallmark of an elaborate, if self-effacing, construction of a particular judgement and viewpoint. The next section therefore examines the values and judgements implicit in each of the three principal symbols, by exploring the ways in which their *meaning* was constructed. It looks first at the meaning of the three symbols singly, then in relation to each other, and finally in relation to other aspects of the state's discourse on violence. In accordance with semiotic principles, discovering the meaning of a 'sign' is a process of progressively widening its connotative field, defined in relation to that of other signs within the same or related discourses.

THE MEANING OF THE SYMBOLS

The crowd

To understand what the crowd signified, it is first necessary to identify what representations of the crowd were systematically omitted. In almost all cases, crowds were depicted as being without political purpose or direction. Visual footage of placards and slogans was usually excluded, or shown too quickly for their message to be read. It was a rare newscast which reported that 'several thousand people gathered at a mass meeting [at Mitchells Plain] to shout ANC slogans'. However, this admission of an articulated political position (even if reduced to slogans) was cancelled out visually by footage of a huge crowd, followed by a shot of a youth overturning a car (TV1 news, 7 p.m., 18 October 1985). Actions by the crowd were not seen to be responsive to leadership or the result of considered action. The crowd appeared as a huge sea of faces or bodies, unindividuated, with no visible structure or lines of authority. It seemed inchoate, uncontrolled, and unguided by rational purpose. Crowd violence was thus typically described as 'erupting' or 'breaking out' – explosive images which captured the crowd's seeming disorder and wanton energy. This metaphorical 'naturalisation' of the crowd ensured its ideological depoliticisation, symbolically stripping it of rational purpose or principles (Maughan Brown, 1984: 7).

For other reasons, too, images of the crowd were threatening and overwhelming – not simply because of the associated force and lack of control. Anxiety was also provoked by the sense of a seething collectivity, which swallowed up and engulfed the individual. This in turn spilled over into a fear of the 'primitive', as a mode of being in which individuality is extinguished by group identity.

Evocation of the 'primitive' sometimes took a different form, when the crowd was depicted as a tribal army or faction – fierce, ruthless and militant. The images of vigilantes, for example, often followed this pattern. Thus news coverage of the clashes between vigilantes and 'comrades' in Crossroads in June 1986 told the viewer of 'heavily armed vigilantes brandishing traditional weapons' (TV1 news, 8 p.m., 10 June 1986).

The image of an army or faction suggested some sense of structure and purpose. But this was tacitly identified with a predisposition towards violence. Thus the above image of the vigilantes was inherently aggressive, and symbolically linked their aggression with the use of 'traditional weapons', as if aggression was the hallmark of a more 'primitive' form of society. From preliminary research, it seems that a predisposition towards violence was also symbolically built into much of the television coverage of Inkatha's involvement in township conflict.[7] Here, a sense of the immanence of violence, as both a 'natural' tendency and 'primitive' cultural norm, was implicit in the image of Zulu impis as a vast, restless, homogeneous mass, clad in skins and carrying shields.[8]

In sum, whether the metaphor for the crowd was a tribal army or a destructive force of nature, the crowd was depicted as if violence, and the ensuing disorder, constituted its essence. This was why the mere image of the crowd could evoke an expectation of violence which is anarchic and destructive. Likewise in both sorts of cases, the images of the crowd connoted a sense of the 'primitive'.

Both sets of connotations – the crowd as 'primitive' and the crowd as 'mindless', destructive energy – were reinforced and extended by the symbols of stone-throwing and burning.

Stone-throwing

As an action of the crowd, stone-throwing was conveyed as similarly threatening, wanton and wild, evoking a sense of brute force. Doing battle by throwing stones also suggested savage and 'primitive' behaviour, as against more 'civilised' methods.

Flames

This was a powerful image of wild and destructive energy, ever threatening to get out of hand. It epitomised the disorder of the crowd. Thus, when P. W. Botha told the country on television that 'I am going to keep order in South Africa and no one is going to stop me keeping order', the viewer was shown shots of crowds in the midst of billowing smoke (TV1 news, 6 p.m., 23 March 1985). Furthermore, flames, as a natural force, helped to depoliticise the crowd: the message conveyed was that crowds, like flames, erupt spontaneously simply because they are crowds, driven by an inner force. Also, when combined with the symbol of the crowd – for example, when crowds were seen dancing around flames – the image of the flames was sacrificial, connoting a more 'primitive' form of society. In the case of reports of so-called 'necklacing' murders, which showed crowds gathered around a burning body, this evocation of the 'primitive' was verbally explicit. For example, a television report on 'intimidation' referred to 'necklacing' as a 'barbaric method of intimidation' and as 'unspeakable savagery' (TV1 news, 8 p.m., 14 April 1985).

Taken collectively, therefore, the symbols of the crowd, stone-throwing and fire strongly connoted disorder, destruction, unbridled energy, and the absence of reason or intelligent purpose. Furthermore, implicit in these images was the opposition between supposedly 'primitive' and 'civilised' behaviour. The significance of these symbolic oppositions was heightened and extended by the juxtaposition of the symbols of township violence with the images and accounts of the SAP–SADF's actions.

Representations of the SADF and SAP

The SADF and SAP were consistently presented on television in ways which evoked a sense of order, control and strength. Police and soldiers were rarely seen shouting or running. If they did run – when charging a crowd of township youth or university students, for example – the action seemed organised and strategic. When collections of police or soldiers were seen standing together, lines of command and an authority structure were usually clear. Likewise, when Casspirs were seen on the move, the image was one of slow, deliberate action, proceeding in military formation. The security forces were therefore presented as a different sort of collectivity from that of township residents: not simply a seething homogeneous mass in which individuality was obliterated, but rather an orderly, purposeful and controlled grouping.

Verbally too, television's account of security force actions stressed their restraint and orderliness. Except in the rare case when excesses were admitted, violence by the police or army was described as defensive, protective action. For example: 'police had to step in with rubber bullets and tear gas' (TV1 news, 8 p.m., 17 March 1985). 'Security forces were forced to make use of rifles and shotguns to disperse rioting crowds' (TV1 news, 25 July 1985). According to a police statement, 'in all incidents where people have died, police have acted in self-defence or defence of property' (TV1 news, 4 p.m., 10 July 1985).

These visual and verbal evocations of order, control and purposeful efficiency were strongly linked to the notion of 'civilised Western values'. This connotative linkage worked in two ways. Firstly, the actions of the SADF–SAP were often described in terms of rights, duties and obligations. SABC's Newscomment (on radio), for example, spoke of 'the obligation imposed on the authorities to take adequate steps for the protection of the moderate majority of black people. The security provided by the proper enforcement of law and order is the right of every citizen' (29 May 1986). The actions of the authorities were thus instantly contextualised with images of law, responsibility and fairness – all hallmarks of 'civilised Western norms' – and starkly contrasted with the apparent arbitrariness and wildness of crowd action. Whereas the image of the stone thrown by the crowd was presented as threatening, the image of the rifle in the hands of a soldier or policeman was not.

Secondly, the violence of the security forces was presented in scientific and technically neutral language and images, indicating the efficacy of the 'solution' it provided to the 'problem' of 'unrest'. In the Network resumés of 'the unrest situation' (mentioned earlier), Kobus Neethling of the Bureau for Information presented a rapid, baffling sequence of graphs showing how the state of emergency had brought down the number of deaths and 'unrest incidents' of various types, and how the rate of decrease fluctuated between certain periods and regions. The information was impossible to digest, since the graphs were flashed on the screen in quick succession. The point of the discussion was less to convey specific details than to create the impression of the SADF–SAP as a sophisticated, technocratic, problem-solving machine, whose effectiveness had been 'mathematically worked out' in the form of 'scientific trends' (Network, 3 February 1987).

The scientific language was also detached and clinical – wholly opposed to the representation of the crowd. The actions of the crowd were 'hot' and passionate – as suggested by the images of flames. Images of the crowd also connoted a strong sense of bodies and of physical energy and force. Members of the crowd were usually seen closely packed together, chanting, saluting or dancing in unison. The physical nature of the crowd was heightened by evocations of the pain inflicted by so-called 'black-on-black' violence. News reports spoke of 'burnt and mutilated bodies' (TV1 news, 8 p.m., 20 July 1985), and of people having been killed by 'sharp instruments and sticks' (TV1 news, 5.45 p.m., 21 May 1986). By contrast, attacks by the SADF–SAP were portrayed as if at a far greater remove. Images of the body and its pain were absent; the accounts were entirely depersonalised and sanitised. Thus, a Bureau for Information booklet on *The national state of emergency.* (1987) wrote of the decline, not in the number of deaths, but in the number of 'death incidents' (Bureau for Information, 1987: 8). Death was detached from the person and all associations of feelings and pain – it was merely an 'incident' in an impersonal 'trend' which was 'mathematically measurable'.

In sum then, the state's representation of violence perpetrated by the security forces used images and concepts which epitomised a 'civilised order' – symbolised both by the language of rights and duties, and by the restraint, expertise and neutral rationality embodied in scientific and technical language. These images and concepts were starkly opposed to those of destruction, disorder, mindless energy and 'primitiveness' which were attached to township violence. The overall message, therefore, was that the conflict between the crowd and the security forces was one between opposing value systems and ways of life – one 'civilised', 'advanced', rational and orderly, and the other 'uncivilised', 'backward' and unreasonable. The heat and anarchy in the images of the crowd, stone-throwing and flames fanned fears of the overthrow of the 'civilised' order; whereas the order and control associated with the images of the SADF–SAP established them as the custodians of 'civilisation'.

Racist images and fears

A further strand of meaning interwoven with the symbols of crowd, stone-throwing and flames concerned the way in which long-standing racist images and fears criss-crossed the 'civilised'–'primitive' and order–disorder axes of meaning. The crowd, in the sense in which we have identified it, was always black. A mass of white people – no matter how violent and unruly – was not presented in the same way. Consider, for example, the state's portrayal of the white right-wing movement, the Afrikaner Weerstandsbeweging (AWB). A television news report on a meeting of the NP in Pietersburg, which was violently disrupted by the AWB, showed AWB supporters crashing into the hall, and then switched to the face of their leader, Eugene Terre'Blanche, as he issued instructions. The lines of authority were clear; this was an unruly but not an inchoate group. Moreover, violent scuffles were seen to break out, but as an extension of heated arguments – suggesting that these were people with an intellectual purpose and strongly held beliefs. The newsreader then identified some participants in the brawl by name – immediately constituting the AWB as a heterogeneous group, in which individuality remained intact (TV1 news, 8 p.m., 22 May 1986). Finally, Terre'Blanche's image on television was not consistently fierce. A subsequent news programme, on 28 May 1986, filmed him addressing a meeting with hands clasped together – a mild, almost clerical image.

Such variations in television coverage reinforced the state's explicit verdict on right-wing violence: as aberrant, a perversion rather than a manifestation of the norm, and the outbursts of 'a few sick people' (P. W. Botha, in *Natal Mercury*, 23 April 1986). Botha described the AWB's actions in Pietersburg as 'atrocious behaviour' (TV1 news, 5.45 p.m., 23 May 1986) – suggesting that he expected better of them.

White left-wing revolutionaries were characterised in similar terms – as deviant or pathological personalities, perhaps the products of deprived upbringings. Moreover, their recourse to violence was portrayed as a decision borne of commitment to a particular political programme of action. In short, therefore, white extra-legal violence – be it on the left or right – was presented as abnormal and deviant, on one hand, and the product of strongly held political beliefs, on the other. This compares markedly with the depiction of black violence as a norm, an inevitable consequence of the mere presence of a crowd, and as mindless and unthinking.

Ironically, racist connotations in the representation of the black crowd were reinforced by the state's claim that the majority of black people are not 'agitators'. According to P. W. Botha, for example, 'most of them [black youth] are not communists. The master manipulators are the ones leading the others astray.' (*SAD*, 14 May 1986) The implication was that most blacks – and therefore the crowd as a phenomenon – were not intentionally or strategically revolutionary. Rather, the crowd was depicted as a mass of people whose emotions were whipped up by a small, cunning clique of 'agitators'. The 'agitators' provided the spark which lit the fire, and once the crowd 'erupted' into violence, it was uncontrollable, mindless and destructive. The underlying implication was that blacks – epitomised by the crowd – were dominated by their emotions rather than reason.

This racist message was reinforced by the assertion that most of the chief 'agitators' are white. The government of the Soviet Union was declared to be the chief mastermind; next in the chain of command was supposedly Joe Slovo, head of the South African Communist Party. The black 'agitators' merely took orders. Reason, here in the form of cunning and strategy, was once again principally the preserve of whites.

The contradictions in state discourses

Associations of blackness with the 'primitive' and with violence, and a concomitant fear of the unruly mob, are deeply entrenched in this country's ideological history. These associations and fears have been forged in different ways at different times, depending on the particular economic, political and social context. For example, Social Darwinism (the ideology of 'scientific racism', in terms of which blacks were 'proved' to occupy a lower rung than whites on the scale of evolutionary advancement) took root in South Africa as a result of the state's attempt to solve the problems of industrialisation in the early twentieth century (Dubow, 1987). Similarly, the fear of the *swart gevaar* or black peril, which became a central slogan in the 1948 election, was arguably the ideological response of the Afrikaner nationalist class alliance to the rapid acceleration of African urbanisation in the wake of the Second World War. The articulation of racist concepts and fears took a different turn in the

1960s, when the idea of African 'primitiveness' was reworked in terms of the notion of 'tribalism', as part of the state's efforts to legitimise its new bantustan policy. White fears of 'the black mob' have therefore been articulated in different ways, depending on the particular historical context and its configuration of dominant interests. Nevertheless, the persistence of these fears to the present day, notwithstanding their historically shifting material bases, is striking.

However, this ideological continuity is starkly at odds with other facets of current state discourses. Central to the description and justification of the state's reformist project has been the claim that the country is facing a 'total' or 'revolutionary' onslaught, against which 'reform' is said to be a rational and effective retaliation (Posel, 1987: 421–3). The scope of the 'onslaught' is supposedly wide-ranging – international, psychological, economic and emotional – and its agents ubiquitous. In each case, the origin and thrust of the 'onslaught' is said to be a 'communist' assault on 'democratic Western values'. The important feature of this ideological discourse, for the purpose of the present discussion, is its explicit effort to redefine the country's political problems in *non-racial* terms. P. W. Botha, for example, has claimed that 'strife in South Africa is between communists and democrats, not the black and white races' (*SAD*, 2 September 1986); and 'The struggle in South Africa is against radicalism' (*SAD*, 30 April 1986). Since the upsurge of black resistance to apartheid in the 1970s, the proponents of 'reform' have attempted to coopt support from 'moderate' blacks, touting the idea of political 'power-sharing' (although as yet ill-defined and ambiguous) as a necessary departure from the apartheid orthodoxy. Clearly, the legitimacy of this project, and the chances of its winning either black or white supporters, depend on the state's capacity to override starkly racial perceptions of the country's political conflict.

How do we explain the contradiction between these reformist ideological imperatives, and the reinforcement of long-standing racist images and fears by the state's representation of political violence? A full exploration of the issue is beyond the scope of the present chapter, but part of the answer lies perhaps with an argument made previously by the present writer (Posel, 1987: 419–43), that reformist state discourses are ill-equipped to displace the orthodox Verwoerdian representation of group identities and group relations made in racial and ethnic terms. This appears true also of the state's recent discourse on political violence. As has been shown, the depiction of state violence made some attempt to reconstitute group identities in non-racial terms, by redefining the lines of political division and conflict as between 'communists' and 'democrats', rather than between 'black' and 'white'. However, the ubiquitous, shifting scope of the 'onslaught', and the correspondingly wide and all-too-vague definition of what constitutes a 'communist', are self-defeating in this respect. If the 'communist enemy' is not easily and consistently identifiable, then the category is surely an ineffective basis for reconstituting group identities and relations. As a result, the old racial categories remain, together with their legacy of long-standing racist fears.

In conclusion, this chapter has argued that contemporary state discourses on violence must be understood in the context of the ideological offensive which the state is waging on several fronts. As information about violence has come to be carefully censored and controlled, state ideologues have set about constructing a symbology of violence, which provides a shorthand explanation for township violence and an implicit defence of violence perpetrated by the SADF–SAP. The chapter has also shown the limits to a purely instrumental understanding of these discourses. The symbols which contest the populist notion of a 'people's war', and which justify the violence of the security forces, also carry a racist overload which is at odds with other attempts by state ideologues to recast conflict in South Africa in non-racial terms.

20 Works of friction: current South African war literature

H.E. KOORNHOF

War, and more specifically the border war, has become an integral theme of current South African literature. Writers of every cultural and political persuasion are focusing on violence and confrontation, creating a myriad of contrasting perspectives on life and war in South Africa today. The sense of social fragmentation which emerges from and within these writings gives an indication of how the South African political reality has been internalised and personalised by individuals. This is true both of authors and of the characters they create. In these writings, termed 'border literature' *(grensliteratuur)*, a world view emerges which may be seen as reflecting, reinforcing, creating and deflecting from militarisation.

Generally the term 'border literature' is used by the media and literati to describe works of fiction written in the last decade or so, almost exclusively by young Afrikaner intellectuals who use the border war as the setting for their works. A remarkable aspect of border literature is that some of those writing about the war have never been in the army, and have never set foot on the border. Of course there are some notable exceptions, but by and large the genre consists of what may loosely be termed *avant garde* narratives, written by academics. When the entire body of border literature is examined, it becomes apparent that almost any work that deals with political conflict and violence in South Africa can be categorised as *grensliteratuur*.

The emergence of the category 'border literature' is itself an interesting development. It is indicative of a new[1] awareness of, and preoccupation with, the notion of borders. These 'borders' range from geographical to racial, cultural, and personal barriers; in short, the category has become a catchword indicating how social divisions are reinforced and emphasised as a result of political conflict. Writing about the 'South African experience' has become virtually synonymous with writing about war. A militarised, conflict-ridden consciousness seems to have created this category, as much as the works themselves.

Who are the writers of border literature?[2]
The category of border literature includes a variety of different strands. There are some Afrikaans writers of *grensliteratuur*, although

surprisingly few, who write unashamed eulogies of army life and the war that 'has to be waged against South Africa's enemies'.[3] War is seen by them as glorious, and the *dulce et decorum est pro patria mori* ethic prevails. Borders are there to be protected, and from within the laager everybody needs to fend off the 'evil forces of communism'.

White English writers in South Africa (Nadine Gordimer, John Milton, David Robbins, Peter Rule, Peter Wilhelm, and Anthony Ackerman, amongst others) have written about war in ways ranging from graphic pseudo-journalistic accounts[4] to explorations of fear and the moral dilemmas brought on by the trauma of killing and seeing people die. The emphasis is on the horror and futility of war.

Black writers who deal with war write mainly poetry lamenting the death of guerillas or describing the struggle which is waged as much in the townships as on the borders. Most of these works rely on a powerful symbolism and mythology relating to liberation and what is demanded by a sometimes reified and romanticised struggle. A strong moral stance informs these works.[5]

The most interesting aspect of border literature is the emergence of a group of young Afrikaner intellectuals writing short stories and novelettes about displacement, individual salvation and the need to survive both spiritually and physically. The development of this tradition of border literature, in which the majority of Afrikaans writers approach the subject of violent political conflict with irony, rejection and horror, is the major focus of this chapter.

Given that the nature of this work is modernistic and demands a certain measure of reader proficiency, it is clear that it is directed at a small audience of Afrikaner literati. The most prominent exponents of this genre are Etienne van Heerden, Alexander Strachan, Louis Kruger, George Weideman and Koos Prinsloo.

Although the setting or context is the war on the South African or Namibian borders, or the unrest in the country, the majority of these works explore issues separate from the war itself. Indeed, a substantial number take place away from any border, or on a border which is never named.

The border war is chosen because the violence of the situation provides the ideal framework for studying the kind of interaction where cultural and ideological shifts and schisms within groups take place. As with most war literature, political issues are ignored or seen as incidental.[6] But in contrast with most war literature, these works focus on group interactions and dynamics, and on existential doubts arising from the lack of a defined national or cultural identity. The writing explores not so much the war, but the breaking up of the previously monolithic Afrikaner ethnic identity in the face of the current political, military and moral crises in the country.

Early trends in border literature

The earliest overt *grensliteratuur* dates back to 1974, although a number of earlier works had already begun to explore similar issues. P. J. Haasbroek horrified Afrikaner readers and alerted them to the atrocities which he had apparently witnessed as a soldier. His works *Heupvuur* ('Shooting from the hip'), *Roofvis* ('Piranha') and *Skrikbewind* ('Reign of terror') contain sickening descriptions of the disembowelling of prisoners of war, the cold-blooded shooting of unsuspecting elderly people, the calculated torture of young men, and the accumulation of war trophies. He writes in a detached and aloof manner, devoid of any analysis, like a camera moving from scene to scene.

The intention of his works seems to have been to expose these activities, and to give utterance to his horror. No mention is ever made of the geographical and social context within which the action takes place. Although this may have been the result of self-censorship, the focus is very strongly on the senselessness of war and the dehumanisation that war produces. Haasbroek's writings have much in common with other literature on war which aims to shock.

In 1976 J. C. Steyn published an anthology of short stories entitled *Op pad na die grens* ('On the way to the border'), which has a predominantly philosophical tone. In this collection he questions whether war can ever achieve the political objectives for which it is waged. In the title story, for example, he uses the Anglo–Boer War as a case study, but leaves the issue unresolved.

In a later work entitled *Dagboek van 'n verraaier* ('Diary of a traitor') Steyn expresses the dilemma by juxtaposing the violence of war with structural violence. An Afrikaner academic commits treason against the establishment in order to bring about a new consciousness amongst young and receptive Afrikaners, when he makes his photographic material available for 'subversive purposes'. However, after he betrays one of his 'comrades' to the security police, and this person commits suicide, it appears that he becomes a state witness. The reason for these betrayals is that the character's attachment to his roots, traditions and language overrides his commitment to change.

Recent trends in border literature

Early examples of South African border literature were largely descriptive in nature. Their authors seem to have felt a need to explore their personal encounters with violence and death. Both earlier and some more recent writers appear to wish to distance themselves from their experience, or to come to terms with it, by describing their encounters in minute and graphic detail.

Especially in a society where the media is as heavily censored and restricted as it is in South Africa, the need must surely exist to share these dramatic experiences with others. In addition, the distortion in

the media of what happens on the border, or in situations of confrontation, must prompt some writers to want 'to set the record straight'. The
'record' which writers may want to set straight relates very specifically
to the hardships and suffering experienced by soldiers on the battlefield, which are minimised or ignored by the media so as not to destroy
morale; it does not relate to the actual dynamics of the conflict. Such
intentions have been expressly voiced by several South African writers,
notably Alexander Strachan in an interview with Marguerite Robinson.
Strachan said that he chose to write about the war because he 'wanted to
give an account of a world that I know, a world that few people know
about' (*Beeld*, 8.5.1985).

On the one level, these attempts to counteract censorship explain the
degree of anonymity in the works. The one feature almost all these
writings share is the lack of a defined context. Hardly ever is the border
named, or the geography explained, other than in terms of 'hostile
territory'. The enemy is usually nameless and, as often as not, even
their opponents are without identity. Even where the facts of war are
specified, or at least hinted at, a strong sense of unreality and anonymity
remains.

On another level, a substantial number of writers have not themselves had any personal encounter with 'the enemy' and have not been
in combat situations at all. The content of their work is drawn in fact
from the social conflict they experience, sense or read about in their
everyday lives. Much of the stress and insecurity of life in South Africa
is transposed into a war setting. These works may contain descriptions
of battle, but the emphasis is on philosophical questions about violence
and conflict. In sum, the writings of the last decade embody an attempt
to come to terms with living in a state of constant friction and permanent
tension. The political dimension of these tensions is subsumed by the
personal and individual toll that they exact.

What emerges from border novels is a sense of incoherence and
confusion. Neither 'total strategy' and 'counter-revolutionary warfare'
nor any other state response to the current political conflict has the
strategy' nor any other response to the current political conflict has the
slightest significance for those individuals caught up in activities which
alternately revolt and exhilarate them. These narratives do not only
signify the futility of war, but, far more specifically, convey an
unmistakable sense of political and moral disorientation.

Perhaps the clearest example in which this disorientation takes place
is Alexander Strachan's work, *'n Wêreld sonder grense* ('A world without
borders') (1984), where the leader of a special unit 'goes off the rails' and
refuses to return to base after the invasion of a SWAPO camp. His
erstwhile friend and comrade is sent either to persuade him to return
or to kill him. The disillusioned and warsick leader has his throat slit
by his former friend.

In the *grensromans* (border novels), groups or individuals are seen
groping helplessly at anything resembling the familiar as they cross
borders'), where the leader of a special unit 'goes off the rails' and
which they spend floundering in the vast bush of 'Africa'. They search
for whatever will root them in time and space. History and political
processes go by the board. All this entails a profound questioning of
previous values and of the means needed to survive, both physically
and spiritually.

This is particularly evident in the novel by Louis Kruger, *'n Basis
oorkant die grens* ('A base across the border'),[7] where a unit is sent across
the border on a special and secret mission. The mission turns out to be a
'lemon' (failure) and the leader is killed in battle. Initially the unit
decides to carry the corpse of the leader back across the border so that it
might have an honourable burial. However, as their situation
deteriorates and they are pursued by the enemy, run out of food, and
are caught in the rain, all but one of the unit decide to abandon the
corpse. The soldier who continues to carry the corpse eventually finds
himself among the enemy, but still miraculously manages to evade
them. He becomes desperately involved in trying to establish the
moral basis for his personal as well as military situation. The soldiers
are finally discovered by a South African helicopter, and brought to
safety. The narrator in this work is the corpse, who portrays the soldier
who carries him across the border, risking his life in this irrational
quest, with some irony, but as having done a brave and honourable
deed.

What border novels express in metaphorical terms is the erosion of
ideas (such as the grand design of apartheid) that have been accepted as
politically feasible in the past. In the story mentioned above the corpse
becomes a metaphor for the ideological baggage of the past, which has
to be lugged about at the risk of life and limb, until it can be given an
honourable burial.

Furthermore, the 'enemy' is not only found to have a 'human face', as
in conventional anti-war novels. In the *grensroman* there is a sudden,
shocking recognition that he is a fellow South African. As Elsa Joubert
points out, for many young white conscripts their first encounter with
black fellow South Africans on an equal footing occurs ironically when
they confront each other with guns (*Die Suid-Afrikaan*, May 1985: 45–6).

As if in response to this realisation, the writers contrive a situation in
which class and other social divisions are largely eliminated. They
seem to be suggesting that political resolution, whatever form it might
take, has to occur in a situation where South Africans recognise each
other's humanity (or mortality!) before all else.

Moreover, the novels explore shifting power relations and changing
dynamics within various military (or, metaphorically speaking,
'political') groupings. The context of war and crisis makes it possible

for writers to portray the forging of new alliances and the redundancy of old ones. It is important to note that these 'new alliances' are formed specifically within the boundaries of the army, or military units, and not with the 'enemy'. The implied suggestion is that change will arrive through the reorganisation of existing structures. The leadership of certain commanders can be rejected or lost, and therefore alternative leaders with different ideas and strategies need to be found.

'Boundaries' of behaviour and identity are extended or narrowed in these novels, as the needs of survival dictate. The war milieu allows writers to suspend ordinary civilian norms and conventions, and provides them with a context in which, without forfeiting credibility, they may describe actors behaving unconventionally. It consequently becomes possible to put forward new ideas of a national and cultural 'identity'. Survival necessitates the examination of previously inconceivable alliances and joint strategies. This 'regrouping' is often reflected in the decision of individuals to break away from their units. The decision does not come easily, and is often accompanied by a great degree of trauma and insecurity.

The writing seems to suggest that new political strategies and groupings are called for if white (and, more specifically, Afrikaans-speaking) South Africans wish to remain and survive in Africa. What is more, the notion of 'identity' needs to be reformulated in terms that are more in line with the political realities of present-day South Africa. Afrikaner nationalism, which was largely constructed around the symbolism generated by the Anglo–Boer War, is now being deconstructed and, to a lesser degree, reconstructed around another war – the border war. Some of the writings are filled with an anguished and rather tentative notion of a new, all-embracing South African cultural identity. It is 'anguished' because for Afrikaners it means the abandonment of Afrikaner nationalism and the historical and cultural heritage that comes with it, and 'tentative' because of the difficulties and fear of rejection in trying to cross cultural barriers and establish ties with other groups.

Women writers of border literature introduce a new angle on the subject, counterbalancing political and social conflict with interpersonal and sexual conflict. Authors like Jeanette Ferreira and Lettie Viljoen examine the personal relationships of women with men who are committed political activists, but who display blatant sexism and lack of commitment towards the women in their lives. 'War' in these novels is not only waged on the border or in the political arena, but also between the sexes. In Jeanette Ferreira's work especially, the implication is clear: the personal is political, and national liberation is not possible without addressing and resolving the issues of commitment in personal relationships first.

In her work, *Sitate vir 'n rewolusie* ('Citation for a revolution'), she explores this notion in describing the experience of a white female intellectual. She also uses the poignant situation of the wife of a black student activist who is first expelled from university and later killed, to expose the contradictions between personal and political relationships.

Lettie Viljoen in her work *Klaaglied vir Koos* ('Lament for Koos') describes the plight of a woman with a young child who is deserted by her husband when he joins a 'liberation' army. She experiences a double identity crisis, both as a woman in relation to her departed soldier-husband, and as an individual in a conflict-ridden and unjust society, where she continues to occupy a position of privilege despite her dire situation.

The language and structure of border literature

The overall sense created by the majority of border novels is one of nihilism, incoherence and suffering. Alternatively there exists a feeling of aloofness, and an overt attempt to be objective, giving a number of these narratives a 'journalistic' flavour. The only time either of these two styles changes is when actors are engaged in action or confrontation. Then the language becomes far more immediate, and there is a pronounced impression of 'being in the world', of cohesion and of praxis. It is as if the language itself wishes to suggest that the only way to deal with conflict is to confront it. The descriptions of battle, gruesome as they are, may be seen as metaphorical exhortations to deal with and resolve political problems.

In narratives where the overriding sense is that of nihilism and defeat, the sentences are often incomplete, lacking verbs, and constructed around single adjectives. A constant sense of being thwarted finds its way into sentences that are 'aborted' before a verb can complete the construction. The implication is that unless some form of engagement takes place, nothing can be accomplished.

Most border writings are short stories, or novelettes, or a series of incidents loosely connected by common actors. These works are about guerilla warfare, where short, fierce, isolated battles are fought, in unknown territory, by small groups. The single most prominent feature of guerilla warfare is the ambush. Individual, furtive action is part of guerilla strategy. Thus the writing is punctuated by short, sharp and often unexpected bursts of 'action', in amongst the vacuous, irrational or absent construction of the rest of the narrative. A substantial number of works are written as a continuum with moments of action within it. The reader is constantly being led into a narrative 'ambush', whereby he or she is brutally surprised by changes and shifts of perception, when action suddenly replaces the vacuousness.

Conclusion

South African authors are writing extensively about the conflict in their country at present. Whether they express their horror of war, laud the bravery of freedom fighters, or try to come to terms with the ideological components of that conflict through a symbolic examination of alternative strategies of survival, there is clearly a preoccupation with the turbulence manifest in present-day South African society.

This violent conflict consists of resistance to the state and the state's response to that resistance. The unrest in the townships, and the war on the borders, are both situations from which the average white South African is relatively sheltered.[8] From this protected position, with all the secrecy, uncertainty and ignorance it entails, has emerged the phenomenon of border literature. The literature wants either to 'tell it like it is' or otherwise to give expression to the vague and uneasy sense of constant violence that is prevalent in every South African's life.

The works which fall into the category of border literature are, in a certain sense, attempting to come to grips more with a militarised existence than with a state of actual war. It is a significant indication of the extent of the militarisation of South African society that dissident Afrikaans writers have found the army, and military conflict on the border, to be the most apposite context in which to explore political conflict and their perceptions of the dissolution of Afrikaner unity and hegemony.

21 Classrooms of war: The militarisation of white South African schooling

GAVIN EVANS

Once a week over 300 000 white South African youth leave their school uniforms at home and come to class in military browns. For an hour or more a week they will learn the basics of army drill, how to shoot and more advanced forms of 'military preparedness'. This school cadet programme is not an isolated anomaly in an otherwise military-free education system. It is complemented by a variety of other forms of activity whose prime purpose is to mould the consciousness of white pupils and to educate them to accept the national priorities of an increasingly militarised state. These activities include Youth Preparedness programmes, the veldschools in the Transvaal, civil defence exercises, school guidance programmes and more recently the 'emergency anti-terrorist plan' initiated by the Joint Management Centres.

While the subject of this chapter is the militarisation of white schooling, it is worth noting that white schools are by no means alone in experiencing the pervasive influence of the SADF. Within the black educational arena the SADF has played an extensive coercive role, patrolling schools and campuses, and attempting to prevent or contain student resistance. At times this has amounted to a permanent military presence – as was the case at the University of the North (Turfloop) in 1987–8.

Since the late 1970s the SADF has also played a 'hearts and minds' role in some black schools through the use of SADF teachers in township classrooms, holding youth camps at African and coloured schools, and through other aspects of its Civic Action Programme. While this role was severely curtailed during the 1984–6 uprising, there are signs of attempts to revive it in new forms in selected townships as part of the initiatives of the Joint Management Centres. Both the control and the 'hearts and minds' roles of the SADF have become major points of resistance for black students.

The SADF has also sought to increase its presence in the 'white' universities and colleges. In the early 1980s the English-language universities successfully resisted the SADF's attempts to set up University Military Units on campus, but these continue to exist at the Afrikaans and dual-medium (English and Afrikaans) campuses.

Students at these universities and colleges who have completed their initial military service have no option but to perform their army camps through these units. There has also been an increase in research attentive to the needs of the military at South African universities, despite efforts by some English-language universities to curtail or prevent this. Another important development has been the growth in the number of military- and security-related courses and research institutes, most of them linked to Afrikaans universities.

Within the arena of white schooling there are two essential roles which the military seeks to fulfil. The first is to ensure that white youth are able to adjust to the rigour of military life immediately on beginning their national service. The second is an ideological role, helping create an ethos whereby white youth accept the military's goals without challenge.

For the state, which depends largely on white support for the SADF for its survival, it is essential that each new generation of white subjects comes to accept the military's objectives as their own. And as the conflict in South Africa increases, and the corresponding role of the SADF grows with it, so the need for white consensus on 'security' issues becomes more and more vital. This need for consensus is particularly important with respect to white school pupils who are on the verge of being called up for an initial two years' military service. It is against this background that the growing role of the SADF in white schools should be seen.

Cadet programmes

The most overt and perhaps the most significant aspect of the militarisation of white schooling has been the expansion of the cadet programme. According to the SADF, cadets were introduced for three reasons:

(1) for the youth to develop a sense of responsibility and love for their country and national flag;

(2) to instil civil defence in the youth; and

(3) to train them in good citizenship as a forerunner to their National Service (*Paratus*, September 1980).

It is clear that both the ideological and the physical components of the programme are seen as important. As the SADF journal *Paratus* (July 1979) put it: 'The cadet system has brought new awareness amongst schoolboys of the nature of the onslaught against South Africa. They recognise and understand the threat and are highly motivated to undergo training.'

After flagging in the 1960s, cadet programmes received new emphasis in the mid-1970s after the SADF's invasion of Angola and the Soweto uprising. An inquiry initiated by the Minister of Defence identified the problem of the cadet system as being the lack of centralised coordination, as a result of which the SADF had 'no meaningful role in the development of the schoolgoing youth in South Africa' (*Uniform,* April 1980). From January 1976 the existing cadet programmes were drawn under the direct control of the SADF. By September 1978 *Paratus* felt confident enough to comment: 'Schools are rapidly approaching the state where the whole cadet programme will be completely integrated into the school system in general and to the needs of the SADF in particular' (September 1978). An inter-departmental cadet committee was set up, consisting of representatives from all the white education departments and the army.

The number of high-school students involved in cadet programmes grew rapidly. In 1975 there were 56 000 cadets in South Africa. This number rose to 154 000 in 1980, to 210 000 in 1983 and to a quarter of a million in 1987. The current figure is over 300 000 if girls and private schools participating in the programme are included (*Neusa News,* June 1987).

Since 1976 there has been greater emphasis on training teachers as cadet officers and on promoting student cadet leadership. The programme has also become more diversified. It is now closely coordinated with Youth Preparedness programmes offered as part of the general school syllabus, and at many schools the two have become one.

Topics presented in lectures at cadet training and cadet-leadership camps include 'the philosophy behind cadet training', 'the organisation of the SADF', 'civilian defence' and 'the nature of the threat against South Africa'. There is also instruction on various forms of warfare and military procedure, drill, shooting, fieldcraft, concealment, camouflage, field marches, tracking, survival and band practice.

In 1979 *Armed Forces* magazine noted that the 'new cadet' was beginning to make his appearance: 'issued with Browns, boots and webbing, it is difficult to tell them apart from the South African Defence Force . . . equipped with R1 rifles and full webbing they are able to present a very presentable display attack and I understand are even capable of working with helicopters' (*Armed Forces,* November 1979).

Some schools have even gone beyond official guidelines in their cadet programmes. At Grey High School in Port Elizabeth the cadet programme, headed until recently by a teacher who bore the rank of commandant, includes motor mechanics, map reading, camouflage and concealment, the dismantling of R1 rifles, section attacks, regular films and lectures on military activities, and annual camps involving intensive combat work.

Interviews conducted with cadet officers from 14 schools in the Cape Province and Transvaal in 1982 and 1983 showed a considerable variation in the way the programmes were implemented, with Afrikaans schools tending to be far more enthusiastic. There was also, however, a trend towards greater uniformity, those schools with low-key programmes being under pressure to upgrade. Greater emphasis has also been placed on inter-school competitions for cadets, bands and shooting.

The increasing emphasis on the integration of the political and military roles of the cadet programme can clearly be seen from the Cape Education Department's 1986 *Cadet Training Manual.* For Standard 6 pupils the various sections covered by the cadet syllabus include the following: the advantages of cadets; musketry and rifle-range procedure; drill, ceremonial and band training; saluting and compliments; radio communication procedure; intelligence and security; discipline and leadership; organisations in the SADF; internal services of a unit. In the first lesson, Standard 6 pupils are warned of the 'threat to peaceful co-existence and prosperity in South Africa', and learn that cadet training is the way to prepare themselves against this threat because young people have been 'selected as the target group for revolutionary attack'. According to the manual, the importance of drill lies in the fact that it leads to self-discipline, by which pupils will become 'proud of themselves as a human being'. They are also told that 'to be really disciplined . . . they must identify with the basic objectives of the cause for which the discipline is required', and that discipline requires 'loyalty to one's superiors and subordinates'.

Standard 6 boys learn it is absolutely necessary that information about 'actual and potential enemies' be gathered by them and reported to the cadet officer 'as soon as possible', because the enemy is desperate and 'aims to overthrow the present government and create a black majority government' (1986: 74). Pupils are also told that even though there 'may not be any visible signs of threat, the enemy is collecting information years before direct attack', and therefore cadets must constantly be on their guard so as not to become a 'source of information' to the enemy.

Much of the Standard 6 syllabus is repeated in Standard 7, although greater emphasis is placed on the definition and aims of the enemy. Students learn about the 'importance of enemy propaganda, and how it places our security in danger', and that they must 'report or hand in anything that comes to their attention'. They are warned that the 'collecting of information can be dangerous, but so is the with-holding of information' (1986: 57–8).

Standard Sevens hear that the propaganda of the enemy is aimed at 'destroying faith in the cadet, his land, his people and his leaders; creating the impression that there is no need for war and that a complete victory over them is impossible; . . . in this way the enemy has succeeded in having economic pressures placed on us' (1986: 60).

In Standard 8, when most cadets register for military service, the focus shifts towards the SADF itself. The topics covered by the syllabus include the 'necessity of compulsory military service', 'the meaning of National Service', and 'protection of hearth and home'. By this stage of training the cadet is seen as being part of the SADF, and 'the enemy' now becomes 'our enemy'. The cadet also learns that the government is responsible for '(a) maintaining law and order, which is the task of every citizen; and (b) seeing to it that the individual is not exploited'. To achieve this 'each citizen must be trained properly . . . physically and spiritually', and cadets are told that the government has the right and power to use force against aggressors. Since this right is 'granted by the population' the state has the right to claim obedience and co-operation from the populace.

Standard Eights hear that 'some governments look with envious eyes at the resources of other countries', and therefore aim at creating 'a revolutionary climate through getting people to create violence' and 'inciting people not to do military training . . . because a person who is not able-bodied cannot resist any aggression'. They are told moreover that 'the strongest will survive'.

The syllabus goes on to state that 'history provides quite a few examples. In the case of Nazi Germany, the physical preparedness of the whole nation was very good, because they used every opportunity by way of physical exercise, sport, etc., to improve the nation physically. Statistics show that 80 per cent of the American youth do not comply with the minimum standards for physical fitness.'

The manual also places emphasis on building manhood: 'National Service may virtually be regarded as a modern initiation school. It is generally considered that the Defence Force makes a man of boys. In between tears and reproaches of loved ones, every national serviceman is nevertheless admired and those who have already completed national service enjoy a particular status in their family circle and in society. As they are denied this opportunity, women especially admire a national serviceman.' (1986: 6)

While participation in the cadet programmes is not compulsory for private schools, it is strongly encouraged by the SADF and the education departments, and several private schools do participate. At some of these schools, the cadet programme is regarded with a sense of traditional military pride by their conservative school boards.

Diocesan College (Bishops) in Cape Town has perhaps the most advance cadet programme in the country, boasting an air section, a naval and a signals section, as well as the traditional cadet menu. However, with the arrival of a new principal in the early 1980s, the school's conservatism was challenged. A non-cadet service option was introduced, and boys were encouraged to attend meetings of the End Conscription Campaign. In June 1988 the principal lost his job; his approach to cadets was cited as one of the main reasons by school board members for his departure.

Similarly at St Andrews, an Anglican private school in Grahamstown, a vigorous cadet programme is run with the close cooperation of the SADF. In 1985 the teacher in charge of cadets took it upon himself to distribute to pupils an edition of the right-wing *Aida Parker Newsletter* which attacked the End Conscription Campaign and was found by the South African Media Council to have been inaccurate and defamatory.

The 'open schools' movement which has seen a shift towards non-racialism at private schools, and pressure from the English churches, have provided a powerful challenge to the cadet system. This is particularly the case at Catholic schools, most of which have abandoned their cadet programmes.

Male teachers are often keen to participate in cadet programmes because this usually exempts them from SADF camps. Most male teachers who begin their national service after completing their teacher's diploma are immediately posted to the Infantry School at Oudtshoorn where they undergo 'Union Leader' courses and are trained in, among other things, cadet leadership. They then go on to become cadet officers at schools. Since 1980 the training of teachers as cadet officers has been revamped: the programme is more intensive and involves a growing number of teachers participating on a more active level. In the Eastern Province, for example, the number of teachers involved increased by 110 per cent between 1981 and 1983. The teachers who are cadet officers are required to wear full military uniform during drilling practice. They are usually incorporated in the local commando unless they choose to remain in the citizen force.

In 1980 Colonel M. J. Viljoen, the Director of Cadets, announced that in 1983 cadets would be made compulsory for girls, but as yet (1988) this has not been implemented (*Paratus* Supplement, February 1980). However, a rapidly growing number of girls' schools and co-ed schools have introduced a form of cadet programme for girls. Some of these 'pigtail platoons' or 'bobby platoons' are involved in uniformed drill, band practice and cadet camps. At many schools the drum majorette programmes are closely integrated into the cadet and Youth Preparedness programmes, and these girls participate in military parades and cadet competitions.

Youth Preparedness, guidance and civil defence

Youth Preparedness is a compulsory subject for two periods a week in all white state schools in the Transvaal, Orange Free State and the Cape, for both boys and girls. YP programmes place considerable stress on civic duties, patriotism, and 'moral preparedness' (Christie, 1985). To an increasing extent they also involve SADF visits to schools, excursions to military bases, and discussions and films on military-related issues.

The Youth Preparedness programmes arose out of the National Education Policy Act of 1967, which set out to ensure that white education would be Christian, have a broad national character and use the mother tongue as the medium of instruction (Crewe, 1987: 3). YP was first launched in the Transvaal in 1972. One rationale for the programme was to make white students accept the new SADF call-up provisions, which extended military service to two years. In motivating the programme the Director of the Transvaal Education Department spoke of the need for a 'moral strength that fortifies the army, the youth and the nation' (TED, 1972: 4).

One notable feature of the YP programme is that no debate or discussion is encouraged. There is a particular world view that both students and teachers are expected to accept. It has been argued that the thrust of the YP programmes can be traced to the 1950s, when through the guidance of the Broederbond and the Federasie van Afrikaanse Kultuurvereniginge, this world view was already central to Christian National Education and was fostered through the Voortrekker youth movement, youth camps and the attitudes of teachers (Crewe, 1987: 6–7).

Direct input by the SADF into YP programmes appears to be widespread. In June 1982, Defence Minister Magnus Malan said in parliament that SADF officers had visited 33 Cape Peninsula schools in the previous five months in connection with Youth Preparedness programmes and other school activities (HAD, 2 June 1982, cols. 971–3).

Over the last decade the area of civil defence has grown in emphasis at white schools throughout the country, both generally and as an aspect of the YP programmes. The construction of bomb shelters, bomb-scare drills, and mock 'terrorist' attacks have become a feature of the school day generally. This process appears to have gone furthest in the Transvaal where an 'emergency plan' to combat 'terrorist attacks' on white schools was launched by the Transvaal Education Department in 1986 in direct cooperation with the Joint Management Centres (*Weekly Mail,* 10.4.1987; *Weekly Mail,* 16.4.1987; *Star,* 25.4.1987; *City Press,* 19.4.1987; *Neusa News,* June 1987).

The plan, outlined in three confidential documents distributed to all TED school principals and selected heads of department, provides for the increased use of young teachers who have completed their national service in implementing the proposed civil–military alert system. One of the documents, entitled 'Emergency Plan for Colleges, Schools and Hostels', notes: 'Training in the use of rifles is essential and will be given to teachers by commandos.' It adds that 'principals should especially use their young teachers who have completed their national service. These teachers have already been trained in particular aspects of dealing with crises and can be used to great benefit for training other teachers for their tasks.' The 40-page document warns that 'the present situation facing our country has made it essential that an EMERGENCY PLAN make provision for the protection and safeguarding of children, staff and black workers'.

Some of the key provisions of the plan are the following: the appointment of a teacher as school security officer who should address staff and pupils monthly on security matters; the selection of block leaders who are to be equipped with two-way radios; a system of checking and controlling all persons and vehicles entering the school site; routine bomb searches in likely bomb sites and in school buses; a warning that people opening school post should be aware of 'possible undesirable reading matter' and bombs; an instruction for staff to 'carefully note telephoned bomb threats'; and the provision of an emergency alarm system, coupled with the instruction that 'when the signal is given all concerned must drop to the ground, crawl or roll to shelter as practised'.

A second document, entitled 'Memorandum to Heads of Education Institutions', states that the SADF and SA Police will provide necessary protection, 'but for day-to-day safety of children entrusted to their care, teachers and parents will have to assume greater responsibility'. For 'selected parents and education officials' this includes carrying firearms – with the proviso that 'as far as possible pupils should not be aware of the firearms'. The document lays down that the decision to carry firearms must be made by the principal 'after consultation with the mini-JMC or the SAP'.

A third document, entitled 'Life or Death', begins with the following disclaimer: 'The heading could equally well have been, "When may I shoot?", as this is a very topical question.' It states that 'one cannot casually shoot someone else' but goes on to explain that 'certain circumstances justify and legalise squeezing the trigger'.

As part of the 'emergency plan', white school principals in the Transvaal were instructed to ensure that teachers patrol their school in pairs on 'sensitive' days in the calendar (*Weekly Mail*, 16.4.1987). Among the days listed were 21 March (Sharpeville Day), 1 May, 16 June (Soweto Day) and 4 September (Sebokeng Day). One of the plan's provisions was that where children were transported to or through 'unrest' areas they should be accompanied by teachers armed with guns.

Commenting on the implementation of the plan, a teacher at a Johannesburg girls' school said there had been a marked increase in manifestations of militarism in the previous year:

On June 16 last year [1986] all of us had to patrol the grounds for the whole day, starting at 7 a.m. We have regular bomb and fire drills at least once a term, but at most other schools it happens more often. All teachers must have stickers on their windscreens so that no strange cars can be parked on the grounds, and the gates are locked at 8 a.m. The girls also have to carry their bags with them at all times and are not allowed to leave them anywhere. (Interview, May 1987)

At Randburg High School, trees were cut down on the property because, according to security force members who visited the school, 'these trees could become hiding places for terrorists'. Hyde Park High School was used as a polling station during the October 1986 municipal elections. For over three weeks before the election, the school was patrolled for 24 hours by six members of the security forces. Over the last year posters depicting 'terrorist weapons' have gone up in most Johannesburg schools.

Asked about the effect of this process on the pupils, a teacher at a Johannesburg girls' school said that militarism penetrated the minds of the girls to a greater extent than in the past. 'The girls are definitely affected by the bomb practices and take it very seriously – they have also become very scared of terrorists. They use the word "terrorist" all the time now and are also becoming more racist. One girl told me, "there's a terrorist lurking inside every black" – that's becoming a fairly typical attitude.' (Interview, May 1988)

There is considerable variation in the ways in which schools deal with YP and civic defence programmes. Most Afrikaans schools encourage the programme vigorously while many English schools merely pay lip service to it. The latter tend to be more relaxed about security while many Afrikaans schools, particularly those in rural areas, have gone as far as erecting high security fences and floodlights, and organising vigilante groups (Crewe, 1987: 6). Over the past four years there has been a growing sense among teachers at many English and some Afrikaans schools that the YP-type programmes are futile, ineffective and inherently deceptive. This has led to a resistance to College of Education for Further Training in-service courses, which are run for teachers on Youth Preparedness. However the extent of this resistance has been muted by the fact that promotion opportunities and merit awards are linked to teachers attending the courses (Crewe, 1987: 7).

The extent of militarisation can also be seen in the contents of several school subjects, but it is in the guidance programme that it has been most marked, both through the content of the curricula and through its role in channelling pupils into military careers. In white high schools there is at least one guidance period a week, as well as careers and psychological counselling. Guidance syllabi appear to be closely co-ordinated with YP and cadet programmes. A special Human Sciences Research Council report on General School Guidance suggested an approach aimed at helping pupils deal with a variety of individual and social needs, including 'problems relating to National Service' (HSRC, 1981). Departmental guidelines for the primary standards suggest a syllabus which closely complements that of YP – teaching about citizenship, the flag, national monuments and the 'communist threat'.

Careers councillors are responsible for liaison with the SADF to ensure that all pupils register for military service when they are 16 years old. At most schools this compulsory process involves more than the completion of forms. It is accompanied by talks by SADF personnel on what to expect during military training, on how pupils should prepare themselves and on whether students should go to university or college before doing military service. The role of guidance teachers in this process is stressed by the HSRC: 'Since large numbers of young men go to the SADF directly after school, . . . it has become essential to provide them with guidance. Consequently liaison between the SADF and the Guidance Centres is essential.' (HSRC, 1981: 13)

In addition, the SADF regularly sends circulars to guidance teachers stressing the need for pupils to be channelled into the permanent force. At many schools, particularly Afrikaans schools, the guidance programme tends to be directive in this regard. The SADF also plays a prominent role in careers evenings for pupils and in holding careers exhibitions.

Veldschools

The origin of veldschools (which exist only in the Transvaal) goes back to 1972 when a speech by the Transvaal Director of Education suggesting methods of countering the 'total onslaught' was sent to principals. The programme was officially launched in 1976 under the Transvaal Education Department Auxiliary Service of Youth Affairs (whose terms of reference included liaison with the SADF).

According to the TED, veldschools are an extension of the Youth Preparedness programmes and are designed to instil in pupils a greater awareness of their social and natural surroundings, as well as to 'counter-act those things which prevent our youth from adopting a meaningful style of life based on accepted norms' (HSRC Institute for Educational Research, 1979: 21).

Veldschools last a week and are run all year round, with pupils being expected to attend twice during their schooling – in Standard 5 and in Standard 8. By the late 1970s most white pupils in the Transvaal were attending veldschool. In 1981 there were 11 veldschools which catered for 62 548 pupils and teachers (TOD *Onderwysnuusflitse,* February 1982: 5). It is compulsory for all state schools to participate, and each school has a resident staff member (*Neusa News,* June 1987). While attendance is not compulsory for pupils, at many schools teachers and principals make it extremely difficult for them to avoid participating. The veld-schools are run by permanent staff, assisted by teachers from schools involved. The camps are divided by sex and language, but the curricula at all schools are identical.

Although veldschools are publicised as being environmental in orientation, this aspect appears to have become largely incidental to their major function. Discussion topics are preceded by set lectures, with discussion not being permitted until all lectures are completed. According to a 1981 Johannesburg College of Education report on veldschools, both content and method are 'tantamount to indoctrination which is educationally reprehensible' (JCE, August–September 1981: 27).

The stated aims of the veldschools include the following: 'to lead the pupil to maturity and reinforce the norms, values and morals of our society'; to encourage pupils to be 'better South Africans and better Christians'; to provide adventure, to 'show that a threat to South Africa's existence and stability does exist, and what we can do about it'; to provide pupils 'with an opportunity to get to know and appreciate nature'; to assess leadership qualities and to impart knowledge (Human Awareness Programme, 1986).

One way of achieving these aims is to isolate children geographically and distance them from family, school and community. The isolation is compounded by exhaustion caused by long hours of physical activity, and by the frequent use of corporal punishment on boys, and other forms of punishment for girls (interview with teacher at Johannesburg school, June 1988). The camps have a paramilitary nature. During the journey to the camp, leaders are instructed to maintain firm discipline. Pupils are woken at 5.40 a.m., inspection following fifty minutes later. The mornings and early afternoons consist mainly of physical activities, including 'survival, tracking and camouflage', compass marches, obstacle courses and 'practical field training'. The later afternoons are filled with lectures, discussions and films. Rigid regimentation is maintained at all times (interview with Johannesburg school teacher, May 1988).

Some of the extremes in lecture content and militaristic ethos appear to have been eased as a result of widespread criticism of the veldschools from parents, teachers, educational authorities and the media in the early 1980s.

In general, today's veldschool lectures focus on the dangers of communism and the ANC, the need for improved race relations and the importance of working with 'moderate' blacks who have 'turned their backs on violence' (interview with Johannesburg teacher, May 1988).

The SADF has a direct relation to the veldschools and is involved with their initial planning. Close contact is maintained between the camp instructors and SADF personnel from nearby military units. Army lecturers wearing combat uniform are sometimes used, and many of the teachers who participate are cadet instructors at their schools. The SADF also assists with tasks like the building of obstacle courses (Evans, 1983; *Neusa News,* June 1987). However, because of the negative publicity concerning the SADF presence at the veldschools, and opposition from both the Progressive Federal and Conservative parties, the direct presence of SADF personnel at the camps has been reduced over the past five years (*Neusa News*, June 1987).

For many teachers there is considerable pressure to participate. Veldschools are sometimes linked to a system of merit promotion. If teachers are unwilling to participate, they receive negative points which affect their salaries and promotional possibilities, while if they do attend they receive positive points. Principals are informed in advance that a camp will be taking place, and that they will be required to provide a certain number of teachers.

Interviews with teachers and pupils have shown that the response of the latter to these camps varies considerably. For some children at the more liberal, English-medium schools the effect of the propaganda appears to be undermined by the regimentation and the overtly pro-government perspective. Other pupils, perhaps the majority, seem to have an apathetic or ambiguous response. But many come back more conservative and more convinced of the effectiveness and justness of the government's strategy for dealing with its problems (*Neusa News*, June 1987; interviews with five TED school teachers, January–June 1988). As one Johannesburg school teacher put it: 'It's true that some of the girls think the whole thing is a bit of a joke or a bit of a pain, and they complain like hell, but I'd say the majority are definitely influenced. They come back more closed-minded, less liberal and often more racist.' (Interview, May 1988)

Other forms of militarisation in white schools

Outside of the forms of militarisation mentioned above, there are several other direct and indirect ways in which the SADF asserts its influence in the schools. One of these is an annual essay competition organised by the SADF with cash prizes as an incentive. Another is the special schools the SADF runs for immigrant children. Organisations like the Southern Cross organise fundraising drives at schools for the 'boys on the border', and many schools organise fundraising drives of their own for this end. At most schools there is an ample supply of teachers who, outside of the formal curricula, are eager to recount their own 'heroic' experiences in the SADF and to emphasise the importance of the military to the country's future (interviews with Johannesburg teachers, May–June 1988).

More generally, in most white schools there prevails a militaristic ethos which facilitates the acceptance, whether passive or active, of militarisation and the role of the SADF. This applies both to the content of subjects – for example, the glorification of wars of conquest against blacks in history textbooks – and to educational methods – school uniforms, corporal punishment, tight regimentary discipline, a prefect system and a strong emphasis on hierarchy, conformity, obedience and physical prowess.

Opposition to the militarisation of white schooling

In each of the areas mentioned above there have been numerous expressions of opposition and resistance to the militarisation of white schooling. However, this is invariably confined to a small minority of pupils, teachers and parents, mainly at the more liberal English-medium schools. Public expressions of opposition have come from several quarters. The Progressive Federal Party has raised questions in parliament and other forums about the nature of veldschools, cadets and the prevalence of SADF visits to schools. Extra-parliamentary groups such as the End Conscription Campaign and the National Education Union of South Africa or Neusa (both now restricted under the emergency regulations) have initiated campaigns dealing with these issues, and the English press has responded in turn.

Where this pressure has been combined with opposition from parents and educationists, it has sometimes borne fruit. The clearest example of this was the outcry following the exposures about the nature of the veldschools in the early 1980s, which eventually contributed to reforms of the system.

Opposition from white teachers and educationists has taken both individual and collective forms. Many liberal and left-wing teachers, and some principals, play a role in breaking down militaristic influences through their teaching as well as through their participation in extra-curricula activities. One example of this is the reluctance of some school principals and teachers to do more than the minimum in promoting the cadet programme. At many private schools, particularly over the past five years, a more overt form of opposition has been generated. One example of this was the call for alternatives to military service made in 1985 by the Conference of Private School Headmasters and Headmistresses.

There are also several examples of a more collective expression of opposition to militarism among teachers. Some have joined groups like Neusa and others in the extra-parliamentary sphere, which have taken strong public stands on the role of the military in white schooling. At times even the establishment English teachers' associations have come out in opposition to aspects of militarisation.

In 1987 the newly appointed Director of Education in Natal, Arthur Olmesdahl, suspended the cadet programme at all Natal high schools for 'safety' reasons. 'I felt it wise, in the present political atmosphere and with the [general] election coming up, to suspend cadet activities until further notice', he said (*Eastern Province Herald*, 17.4.1988). According to *Southscan*, the decision was motivated by both the fear of ANC attacks on cadets as well as 'the increasing involvement of the SADF in school cadet programmes' (*Southscan*, 29.4.1987). The decision was welcomed by the PFP, several prominent educationists and the Natal Teachers' Society. PFP member and former Natal Teachers'

Society president Mike Ellis said cadets did not fit in with Natal's liberal policy towards education. 'I believe in view of the two-year call-up for young men, cadets is a waste of time and is a highly provocative issue in many white homes, not to mention the way it is seen in the black, coloured and Indian communities. My personal view is that the suspension of cadets should become permanent,' he said (*Daily Dispatch*, 27.4.1987). The decision, which affected over 25 000 cadets, was overruled a week later by Education Minister Piet Clase.

While there is widespread avoidance of cadets by pupils at many schools, there are very few known cases of open resistance. The law allows parents to refuse to permit their children to take part in cadets, but there are few schools where cadets is not, *de facto*, compulsory. Aside from the ignorance of parents and pupils of their rights, the stigma felt by pupils whose parents refuse permission is enough to make this an extremely difficult option.

The father of a Standard 9 pupil at a Cape school explained the reaction as follows: 'My son is one of three pupils at the school who are not doing cadets – the other two kids are Jehovah's Witnesses, so we're the only ones refusing to allow our son to do cadets for political reasons. Because the school is very militaristic it's not looked on too kindly by the teachers, although they're now getting used to it. Some of the other kids are quite envious, but others are resentful. He does things like gardening during cadet periods.' (Interview, September 1988)

Over the last three years, several groups involving white school pupils in anti-apartheid activities have emerged. These groups, such as the Pupils Awareness Action Group and the Pupils United for Peace and Awareness in Cape Town, and Linx in Johannesburg, are based mainly at English-medium schools. The groups have run campaigns and education programmes around issues such as cadets and militarisation.

The End Conscription Campaign also focused on the militarisation of white schooling and on cadets, and attracted the direct support of white pupils in some centres. In 1985, for example, the Cape Town ECC branch ran an anti-cadets programme which led to the formation of an ECC schools group involving several teachers and concentrating on work among school pupils. A pupils' debate forum was held at the July 1985 ECC National Festival, and shortly after the start of the 1986 state of emergency, the Johannesburg ECC distributed a pamphlet entitled 'Wondering What It's All About?' to 15 schools (*Star*, 4.10.1986). Similar activities were organised by the other ECC branches.

Given the ability of the state to determine the direction and content of white schooling, the effect of these activities should not be over-emphasised. However, despite their limited scope, they do feed into other forms of counter-cultural expression which provide a challenge to militarism. But it seems to be only in Cape Town, with its less rigid separation between coloureds and whites and its more liberal tradition, that the anti-war culture has had a significant impact on school pupils.

Conclusion

It is clear that over the past decade the SADF has stepped up its influence over white schooling. It is now a major actor in the white secondary educational sphere and plays an important policy-making role in this area. Through the cadet and Youth Preparedness programmes and guidance classes, it has been able to insert its ideological perspective into the white classroom. It has used the white school as a site of preparatory military training, mainly through cadets, to an extent that would have been inconceivable 15 years ago.

This, however, does not mean that white schools have simply become a conduit for military concerns. For a number of reasons, a fuller insertion of SADF interests into white schooling has not occurred. The one that has already been touched on is the liberal ethos within some English-speaking homes and schools. Perhaps more significant has been the rapid growth of the right-wing over the past five years. One of the key bases of the political right is the educational sphere: in the Transvaal and Orange Free State, Conservative Party supporters play a powerful role as teachers, school-board members, inspectors and officials. This presence has prevented the SADF from using schools unchallenged as a means of selling a National Party reformist perspective.

The most notable feature of the SADF's presence in white schools has been the pace and scale of its expansion since 1976. There are two reasons for this expansion: firstly, the need for white support for the role of the military, and secondly, the desire to increase the level of school boys' military preparedness before undergoing national service. Given the intensifying civil war in the country, it seems likely that the pace of militarisation of white schooling will not slow down.

22 Shopping for war: an analysis of consumerist militarism

KAREN JOCHELSON & FRAN BUNTMAN

The new South Africa? Gone are the space ships, carousels and animal character merry-go-rounds for children and in their places new fun toys are available. D. S. spotted the latest amusement for the little ones at the Cresta Shopping Centre. Put your money in the slot and the kiddies can enjoy a ride in a tank. It's almost as good as the real thing. (Sunday Star, 28.2.1988)

Young Rambos dressed in army fatigues are waging a disturbing 'war' against each other – and it's become the latest party game. . . . Says bruised birthday boy G. S., . . . 'It's much better than having a braai, disco, or even playing snooker. . . . My friends can't stop talking about what a great party we had.' (Sunday Times, 20.3.1988)

In recent years there has been a growing consumer market among whites in South Africa for militarist goods. As Michael Mann has noted (1987: 35–6), militarism is 'a set of attitudes and social practices which regards war and the preparation for war as a normal and desirable social activity. . . . contemporary militarism is not up-front. It is subtle and diverse.' Militarist ideology penetrates social life and the civilian sphere in insidious and often inconsistent ways. It embraces consumer products and advertising, which directly or indirectly present and market war as a natural and unavoidable part of human existence. In this way, military consumerism comes to mirror and reinforce a militarised society.[1]

The consumer militarist market has international and local sources. Most of South Africa's militarist goods sold to the public are imported and reflect international consumer trends. However there is a small but burgeoning local production of militarist goods.

We focus in this chapter on military themes in war toys, war-games and war comics as examples of consumer militarism. These commodities are far from banal and trivial, for in fact they may encourage a militarist ethos. War toys channel children's imagination and play activities towards an enjoyment of war and violence. War-games are battle simulations which trivialise war as a recreational activity. War comics romanticise war and soldiers, and propagandise bigoted perceptions of 'us' and the 'enemy'.

Playing with war: war toys and video-games

Design trends in children's toys are not merely the product of patterns of style or fashion. Toys embody social and cultural definitions of what constitutes appropriate interests, activities and behaviour of children. 'Toys are . . . revealing for they almost always contain statements made by adults (often, though not invariably, parents) either about the culture in which they live and/or the values which they think desirable. Toys mirror a culture – or at least aspects of it.' (Brewer, 1980: 32–3) Roland Barthes suggests that toys are a microcosm of the adult world and help prepare children for that world. 'The fact that French toys *literally* prefigure the world of adult functions obviously cannot but prepare the child to accept them all, by constituting for him, even before he can think about it, the alibi of a Nature which has at all times created soldiers, postmen and Vespas. Toys here reveal the list of all the things the adult does not find unusual: war, bureaucracy, ugliness, Martians, etc.' (Barthes, 1973: 53)

War toys enable children to participate through fantasy in an adult world where the most *natural* solution to a problem is a violent one and where a military option serves and saves both the individual and the nation. The acceptance of violence implies that an enemy exists beyond the boundaries of humanity, making killing acceptable (Collins, 1974).

War toys reflect the nature of current military technology. Nuclear and long-range warfare distances the aggressor from the effects of his actions: a soldier presses a button and thousands of miles away, on another continent, a bomb explodes killing faceless civilians. Similarly when a child presses a trigger of a gun and his or her playmate staggers but then recovers to continue the game, the full import of killing is removed.

War toys also reflect the current state of the art in military hardware. For example, a newly established toy company in the Transvaal recently began manufacturing replicas of Casspirs, Buffels, police helicopters and other vehicles used by the security forces (*Sunday Times*, 26.9.1987). The toys are manufactured in terms of an agency agreement with the South African Police, and are distributed by the police and through toyshops. By September 1987, the company had sold 25 000 toy Casspir models. However, such overt links between toy manufacturers and the security forces are not the norm.

Some games have taken realism to an extreme limit. Toy guns spray paint, or set off electronic bleepers so children know when they have hit a target. Skill and strategy are important components of video-games, and the realistic graphics add to the thrill of immediacy. A commentator on video-games praises *Platoon* for its realism: 'it's one of the few games where you actually feel that you're fighting for your life, rather than the glory of it. A brilliant release . . . you can almost smell the fear.' (*ZZap!*, 1988: 89) The magazine adds: 'The deliberately sombre graphics in the tunnels are broken by the sudden appearance of a knife-wielding soldier, or a blood-hungry maniac pointing a rifle straight at you – fail to kill him, and a sickly blood-splurge oozes onto your viewing screen: brilliant!' (*ZZap!*, 1988: 89)

The message is unmistakable: war is a game, killing is fun, combat drives a man to the limit of his endurance, and he emerges stronger and more powerful from the experience. The real horrors of war – devastation, bombed homes, gruesome and undignified deaths, pain, torture and massive social disruption – are reduced to insignificance.

Games set in space are popular. The *Masters of the Universe* television series and figurines are a science-fiction fantasy about clashes between good and evil. Militarism and violence overtly inform the stories constructed around the figurines. Video-games such as *Space Invaders* are similarly constructed around themes of invasion, counterattack and death-counts.

In world politics the realm of space has been colonised on military terms. For example, Reagan's Star Wars programme was intended to put into space military hardware capable of intervening in earth-bound conflicts. Fantasy space games imitate these militarist intentions. The fantasy quality of such games is sometimes quite minimal: science fiction is supplanted by true-to-life scenarios. An advertisement for *Gryzor* urges the player to 'infiltrate the Alien Rebels' headquarters in . . . [a counter-insurgency operation] and negotiate electric force fields and overcome wave upon wave of fanatical guerillas' (*ZZap!*, 1988: 2). Though staged in a mythical world, the characters, story and language are reminiscent of American counter-insurgency campaigns.

New sophisticated advertising techniques for toys determine the parameters of creative imagination in child's play.[2] For example, *Masters of the Universe* was one of the first television series created to market fantasy figurines (*Wall Street Journal*, 3.5.1988). Buying the figurines implies purchasing the whole ready-made fantasy which defines the framework and content of the game. Thus by playing with the figurines, the child may come to accept unconsciously the militarist assumptions of the game. Spontaneous creative play and unrelated fantasy are rendered less important.

The war toys market appears to ignore girls. In real war situations women play vital auxiliary roles, but military consumerism ignores this. The male toy soldier does not have a female war nurse, radio operator or munitions worker as his counterpart, although he would in real life. Such marginalisation is in keeping with militarist ideology which casts all women as 'campfollowers'. Women have to be excluded from the sphere of combat, which is so central to the social construction of masculinity:

The myth of combat dies hard. In today's highly technological societies, there is still the widespread presumption that a man is unproven in his manhood until he has engaged in collective, violent, physical struggle against someone categorised as 'the enemy' – i.e. combat. For men to experience combat is supposed to be the chance to assert their control, their capacity of domination, conquest, even to gain immortality. (Enloe, 1983: 13)

Even on the rugged turf of war toys and video-games, women are excluded as positive actors. When women play partially combatant roles in science-fiction stories, they are inevitably rescued by men when the going gets tough. They are presented for the most part as 'damsels in distress' and as sex objects.

A private Sunday bush war

If video-game combat seems too tame, the consumer can leave his spectator seat and opt for active engagement in war-games. These are paramilitary hunt-and-destroy games in which opposing teams dressed in camouflage uniform stalk, shoot and 'kill' one another with modified weapons in simulated combat situations. A war-games player describes the experience:

Eyes strain to seek out the slightest movements. Your neck aches from constantly watching behind, in front and to the side. . . . Animal instinct takes over. You break cover in a frantic flight for safety . . . and get mown down in a barrage of fire. 'This is what makes it so exciting. In a real bush war all of these things can happen and when they do, you've got trouble,' says George. 'Only bad shooting and a guardian angel will save your hide. And it's exactly the same with us.' (*Sunday Times Magazine*, 13.9.1987)

Participants emphasise that the pleasure of the game lies in its realism. At one site, players use 'guns loaded with pellets that burst on impact and ooze a blood-like red dye. . . . "The bullets do sting a hell of a lot and leave horrible bruises and welts, but it's such fun." ' (*Sunday Times*, 20.3.1988)

Some players seek out the roughest and harshest game conditions. At another site players use 'catapult-action rifles capable of firing a marble every one-and-a-half seconds with an effective range of about 70 m'. The marbles, explain the players, add a touch of realism to the game that paint dye cannot capture.' Carelessness gets you a good bruising. So we are more cautious. And far more serious.' (*Sunday Times Magazine*, 13.9.1987)

The games seem to attract people from all walks of white life: business-men, children and 'even women'. A war-game owner reports the games are popular recreation for businessmen: 'It's a great way to get your own back at your boss. You can shoot him.' (*Sunday Times*, 20.3.1988) They are also seen as an alternative to family therapy:

George blasted the living daylights out of his son with a twin-barrelled machine-gun and loved every second of it. Young Greg, a former Parabat, in his early twenties, was cut to the ground as the rounds kicked up dust and slammed into his writhing body. George smiled to himself. 'That would teach the little beggar to mess with his old man.' (*Sunday Times Magazine*, 13.9.1987)

War-games graphically reinforce the belief that violence is the only solution to endemic social and individual conflict. Killing is represented as such a natural and healthy response that when the game is over the fighters are encouraged to join their families around their picnic baskets. One player commented: 'We've found that we are far more relaxed after a day's fighting in the bush. It gets rid of a lot of pent-up tension and aggression.' (*Sunday Times Magazine*, 13.9.1987)

Contemporary war comics

War magazines sold in South Africa can be divided into three categories according to their content: American mercenary magazines; Vietnam and Second World War comics; and local South African border-conflict stories. The magazines mythologise war and soldiers, demonise the enemy, and reflect rigid gender stereotypes.

Those aimed at adult readers consist of overseas imports such as *Soldier of Fortune* and *New Breed*. They carry stories on current conflicts in the Persian Gulf, Caribbean and Central America, and offer nostalgic trips down Vietnam's memory lane. The magazines trumpet the cause of America's New Right and its brand of Cold War-mongering and moral conservatism. For example, an advertisement in *Soldier of Fortune* (February 1988: i) proclaims, 'while the US Congress delays and whimpers, the freedom fighters need help', and urges readers to make 'an automatic donation to the Cause of Freedom'. *New Breed* carries advertisements for the Conservative Book Club (March 1988: 2), whose latest bestseller examines 'why Congress caves into the Communists', and 'dissects liberalism deep down to its rotten core'. It examines 'the common ancestors of liberalism and Communism' and discusses 'how liberalism lies at the root of race riots, murderous taxes, national surrender and the crime explosion – and why liberals are helpless to do anything about their own follies'.

Since the magazines are imported from North America they are relatively expensive and probably cater to a small, exclusive market. The possible attraction for a South African reader lies in the comparative perspective the magazines give on counter-insurgency warfare.

The second category, primarily aimed at English-speaking male youth, includes American war comics such as *Fightin' Marines* and the British *War Picture Library* which promises 'tension, excitement, drama, thrills' in 'no-nonsense war stories that take you straight to the thick of the action'. *Fightin' Marines* publishes reprints of stories first issued in the early 1970s, which revolve around American heroics in the Vietnam war and distorted depictions of Chinese history. The stories almost always follow a similar line: powerfully built Americans trick the effete, sly, dumb and barbarous 'Orientals'. The *War Picture Library* carries accounts of the Second World War and concentrates on stories of Allied soldiers' personal development in battle, individual sacrifice and valour. Both comic series depend on 'us–them' oppositions constructed through racist stereotypes. Thus the Forces of the Free World pit themselves against Fascism, Oriental despotism or Vietcong depravity.

Grensvegter leads the series of titles comprising the third category, that of local stories written for a white audience. A marketing manager for Republican Press, a Perskor subsidiary, which publishes *Grensvegter,* maintained in an interview that the readership was primarily Afrikaans and concentrated in rural districts, but included English-speakers. The biggest readership was in the 14–19-year-old age group but included readers in their late thirties. About 30 000 copies of each issue are distributed nationally, though before the introduction of television the figure hovered around the 40 000 mark.[3]

Grensvegter, a photo-magazine, was first published in the early 1970s, at a time when the war in Namibia and conflict in southern Africa began to escalate following independence in Angola and Mozambique. The publishers now have a library of titles which they reprint with changes made to the names of characters and titles. The stories are sold on their appeal to certain universal 'truths' about white South African experience, rather than their relation to current events.

The official magazine of the SADF, *Paratus,* defines a *grensvegter* (border fighter) in the 'fighting man's Fanagalo' as a man 'shrouded in myth and legend, a Rambo-type figure. Essentially one who has been to the Operational Area.' (February 1986: 22) The hero of the *Grensvegter* series, Rocco de Wet, is an epic figure who battles against the forces of evil on the terrain of total strategy. He is no mere soldier but a 'Groot Vegter' (Great Fighter), a courageous warrior who enters the lists for noble ends and demonstrates by his actions that war is an honourable practice.

As the guardian of Africa, Rocco fights a lonely 'one-man battle' against communist (mainly Cuban but occasionally Russian and East German) invaders 'who have not come to Africa to serve or promote freedom, but to plan atrocities. They are the real murderers . . . scavenging hyenas, vermin which seek their prey in the evenings' (quoted in *Jodac News,* 1988: 24).[4] The 'enemy' attacks the innocent and helpless, and violent death is therefore their just reward.

In contrast, Rocco's violent deeds are motivated by principled righteousness and are presented as morally acceptable. In combat with the commander of Cuban infiltrators who have killed a defenceless old man, he declares:

You undoubtedly know that I protect certain people . . . those who are good and honourable . . . it makes no difference what skin colour they are. But you also know that there are others . . . people like you . . . who can expect no mercy from me. Above all because people like you come from a foreign land . . . to contaminate the land of Africa! Why did you not stay in Cuba? Africa does not need Cubans or Russians on her native soil. (*GV* 203: 88–90)

The terrorists are always white foreigners who threaten a country by undermining its foundations, or attacking it from without – Mozambique and Angola are their favourite entry routes. A Russian colonel explained his task as furthering the aims of international communism. He was in Africa out of 'a desire to serve the interests of my fatherland and communism. Africa will one day, like the rest of the world, become communist.' (*GV* 202: 20) So Rocco's battle is more than good versus evil. It is symbolic of the defence of the (white) South African way of life against 'communism'.

Black actors in the stories play subsidiary roles. They are faithful servants who address whites as 'great master', though most desert their masters in times of stress (*GV* 203: 23). Or blacks are loyal followers who accept Rocco and all he stands for. A black Zairean soldier who knows the salvation of his country lies in Rocco's hands, describes him as 'a good white man . . . a child of Africa, like myself. He loves Africa like I do.' (*GV* 200: 22)

Heroines are generally blonde, and embody Aryan stereotypes. They are also portrayed in a contradictory fashion. Women are independent pioneers: one runs a rural hospital, another spies in Mozambique, and a third is an investigative journalist. But ultimately a woman needs a man's protection. And only a man's guidance can help Mitzi von Moltke, an East Germany spy, see the light, and join Rocco's side in the war.

Once Rocco has saved the girl from herself and the enemy, it seems that the only possible denouement is love. The last frame in each story is often 'the kiss'. As the pair sinks to the ground they hear 'the singing of the wind, the murmuring of water, the chirping of birds and the call of the bosloerie' (*GV* 205: 98). For the heroine, it is love. For Rocco, it is a little different: 'Love makes a man like me soft' (*GV* 204: 98).

Topping up the shopping trolley

Toys, video-games, comics, and war-games are only a few of the products that catch the consumer's eye. The list is far longer. Guns and military backdrops are sometimes used for mannequin window displays (*Weekly Mail*, 28.2.1986). Clothing styles are often influenced by military themes; for example, double-breasted, brass-buttoned jackets modelled on naval uniform, khaki-coloured clothing, shoulder pads and leather bomber jackets.

War and anti-war messages are prevalent in movies, music, books and theatre. However, a message may miss its mark. A discerning audience may recognise an anti-war sentiment in a graphic war film.

But other viewers may enjoy the movie as a glorification of war.

Other commodities reinforce militarism and are directly related to current events in South Africa. Music request programmes dedicated to 'our boys on the border' remind troopies that the nation loves and misses them. Pre-packaged basic kits for new conscripts ('troopie packs') provide an assured twice-yearly sale for retailers. Popular magazines increasingly include stories relating to war, conscription and violence.

Each year over 200 000 new firearm licences are issued in the country. South Africa's more than a million legal gun-holders own approximately 2,5 million firearms (*Sunday Tribune*, 24.4.1988). Gun sales have risen as social conflict has intensified. The owner of a Durban shooting-range noted that his clientèle increased significantly after serious bomb blasts in the city (*Sunday Tribune*, 24.4.1988).

The home and commercial security industry in South Africa advertises itself as providing protection against crime and violence. But the emergence of security firms as a new growth industry must be considered in the context of current political conflict and turmoil. Firstly, there is a 'commonsense' assumption that a direct relationship exists between political unrest and a rising crime rate. Secondly, there is an unstated social recognition that while the SADF and SAP are fighting on the borders and in the townships, private forces are necessary to provide protection from the 'onslaught' at home. Thus the security industry is perhaps better understood in terms of militarism, rather than crime prevention.

In military ceremonies and festivals, such as the Durban Tattoo, state militarism infiltrates civilian life. Military displays celebrate nationhood and manhood, and glorify physical force. They familiarise civilians with military weaponry and organisation. The overt show of power assures civilians that everything is under control and the defence of the nation is secure. At the 1988 Rand Show, the SADF and SAP displays of bomb blasts and army vehicles drew eager crowds. Audience participation was encouraged by allowing people to find 'landmines' with electronic detectors (*Sunday Star*, 10.4.1988).

Conclusion

Video-games, war-games and war toys transform war into a game, desensitising players to the real effects of war and familiarising them with the idea of war as an unavoidable, if not desirable, reality. The players indulge in war at a distance, on a terrain where rules are clearly defined, and from which the players may emerge bruised but unhurt. unhurt.

Consumer militarist commodities which reflect the current South African experience also allow civilians to participate in real conflict from afar. Every purchase of a yoyo with an SADF insignia (part of a promotional campaign) is a statement of moral support and embodies a hope that an individual's small financial sacrifice will help win greater battles.

Consumer militarism also seeks people's active connivance in creating and reinforcing myths about war. Players learn that aggression is an acceptable solution to conflict. They learn to define an opposing force as 'the enemy' which exists beyond the bounds of humanity: the enemy are outerspace aliens, communists, or people of a different culture or skin colour. They learn that soldiering makes a man, and that war is a male terrain.

Consumer militarism is one aspect of socialisation encouraging acceptance of the inevitability and naturalness of war. In South Africa the consumerist message is reinforced at political and ideological levels. Its full impact may be measured in terms of its interaction with a range of other pro-militarist socialising agents in homes, education and the media. In this light the trivia of war-games, toys and comics assume more serious dimensions.

PART FIVE
Militarisation and resistance

23 'Marching to a different beat': the history of the End Conscription Campaign
LAURIE NATHAN

On 22 August 1988, the End Concription Campaign (ECC) became the first white organisation to be banned by the South African government in over twenty years. The Minister of Law and Order declared that 'the dangers it poses to the safety of the public and the maintenance of public order leave no other choice but to prohibit it from continuing any activities and acts' (*Eastern Province Herald*, 23.8.1988).

The banning was an unintended testimony to the degree of the ECC's success. When the organisation was formed at the end of 1983, its support was limited to radical sectors of the English-language universities and churches; the broader white community regarded it as irrelevant or subversive. Over the next four years it became a significant force in national politics. It mobilised large numbers of whites in anti-apartheid activities, and was regarded by the black community as making a major contribution to building non-racialism. The state, on the other hand, regarded it as a sufficient threat to expend considerable energy attempting to undermine it and counter its arguments.

The ECC's growth and support were the result of a large measure of dissatisfaction in the white community over the system of conscription. Compulsory military service is one of the few aspects of apartheid that lays a real burden on whites. Young men are obliged to serve an initial continuous period of two years in the SADF, and a further 720 days spread out over twelve years. While the majority of conscripts fulfil this obligation willingly, many thousands regard it as a negative experience.

The high level of opposition to conscription is based on several factors: the authoritarianism, physical hardship and boredom of army life, the disruptive effects of military service on careers and families, and the risk of death or injury. Opposition is also increasingly based on conscripts' moral and political objections to the SADF's role inside and outside the country. War resistance has grown steadily since the mid-1970s in direct relation to the intensifying struggles for liberation in South Africa, Namibia and southern Africa, and to the state's response of military force.

The history of the ECC can be divided into four phases. During the first year and a half, it gradually broadened the base of public opposition to conscription and built a national profile. After the widespread deployment of troops in black townships in 1985, it experienced a tremendous groundswell of support; the war resistance movement expanded rapidly beyond its traditional constituencies, and an anti-war culture emerged. The 1986 state of emergency brought this period of growth to an abrupt halt. The ECC was subjected to intense state repression, and for eighteen months struggled to re-establish an effective public presence. In 1988 the war resistance movement entered a dynamic new phase centred around the war in Angola, the ECC's call for alternative national service, and the stands of individual conscientious objectors.

This chapter reviews the different phases of the ECC's development. It describes the organisation's characteristics and campaigns, and analyses the reasons for its success and for the high level of state repression directed against it. It concludes by assessing the future of war resistance in South Africa.

Formation of the ECC

The political phenomenon of war resistance emerged in the mid-1970s as a result of the intensifying struggles of national liberation and the SADF's increasingly prominent role in South Africa and southern Africa. The army was mobilised during the 1976–7 Soweto uprising, and extended its occupation of northern Namibia after the independence of Angola in 1975. Many young people within the English-speaking universities and churches were politicised by these events. From 1975 to 1978, an average of 1 750 conscripts failed to report for their national service call-ups (CIIR, 1982: 38). Between 1978 and 1982, twelve conscientious objectors were imprisoned for refusing to do military service because of their political and religious beliefs.

The objectors' courage and convictions stimulated the development of a war resistance movement. The Conscientious Objector Support Group (COSG) was formed, and the English-speaking churches declared their support for the right of individuals to refuse to do military service on grounds of conscience. COSG and the National Union of South African Students (NUSAS) began campaigning around the objectors' stands and around issues of militarisation.[1]

The broader white community, including the liberal press and parliamentary parties, was extremely hostile to these developments. In 1983 the government indicated its concern by introducing the Defence Amendment Act. The Act aimed to divide the embryonic war resistance movement, coopt the churches, and prevent further cases of political objection. It made provision for 'religious objectors' who would not serve 'in any armed force' to perform community service in government departments. At the same time, it increased the term of imprisonment for objectors who were not religious, or who objected specifically to service in the SADF, from two years to a maximum of six.

The war resistance movement was united in its opposition to the new legislation. It was forced to reassess its direction, however, as it could no longer depend on raising awareness about militarisation through the stands of individual objectors. It required a new focus and an independent programme of action.

The inspiration for the new focus came from the 1983 Black Sash conference, which made the first public call for an end to compulsory military service. The call seemed daring and idealistic, but it provided the war resistance movement with the direction it was looking for. A few months later the COSG national conference resolved to launch a campaign against conscription.

At the end of 1983 ECC branches were established in Cape Town, Johannesburg and Durban. Over the next three years branches were formed in Port Elizabeth, East London, Grahamstown, Stellenbosch, Pietermaritzburg and Pretoria. ECC groups were also set up on most of the English-speaking university campuses.

Objectives

The ECC defined its objectives as follows: to build pressure on the government to end conscription; to raise awareness of and opposition to militarisation and the SADF's role in South Africa, Namibia and southern Africa; to win support for non-military and non-governmental forms of alternative service for all conscientious objectors; and to 'work for peace and justice in South Africa'.

The campaign did not aim to encourage conscripts to refuse to do military service. This would have amounted to telling them to go to jail or into exile. It would also have been a contravention of Section 121(c) of the Defence Act, which carries a penalty of five years' imprisonment.[2] The aim was rather to provide conscripts with accurate information about SADF activities, and allow them to make independent decisions about their call-ups.

The ECC decided to campaign primarily in the white community. One reason for this was that conscription applied only to white men, and was not an issue of great concern to blacks. The second reason lay in a recognition of the divisions that apartheid has created between racial groups. Blacks and whites live in segregated residential areas and have different life-experiences and political traditions. While the ECC and other progressive organisations sought to break down these divisions, they accepted that it was necessary to target separately and work differently in the black and white communities.

A campaign in the white community against conscription and militarisation was seen as having the potential to make an important contribution to the broader struggle against apartheid. This was because the state depends so heavily on the support of whites to maintain its control over the black population. In particular, it depends on them to provide the manpower, financial resources and ideological backing for its army.

By involving whites in the anti-apartheid struggle, the ECC would pursue a further objective of 'building non-racialism'.

Through our political involvement we are saying to black people that not all whites are racist and that not all white men are prepared to take up arms against them. If we as whites want to be accepted in a future non-racial society, we have to work now, and be seen to be working, for the creation of that society. (Interview with ECC member)

The ECC's commitment to non-racialism led to its developing a close relationship with the United Democratic Front (UDF), the largest anti-apartheid organisation in the country. UDF leaders regularly spoke at ECC public meetings, and the ECC participated in various political activities in black communities. For example, it joined UDF Anti-Conscription Committees in opposing the government's plan to extend conscription to coloured and Indian youth in 1983–4.

Structure and composition

The ECC was formed as a coalition of human rights, religious, women's and student groups. These included national bodies like the Black Sash, NUSAS and the Young Progressives, and over fifty regionally based organisations. The involvement of these groups proved to be one of the ECC's greatest strengths. They brought their energy and ideas into the campaign, enhanced its credibility, and took its message back to their own constituencies.

The member organisations spanned a diverse range of perspectives: liberal and radical, religious and secular, pacifist and 'just war'. Despite their differences, the organisations agreed to unite around their common opposition to conscription and militarisation. The ECC consequently regarded itself as a 'single issue campaign', and avoided taking a position on other issues where this would threaten the coalition's unity.

The ECC also recruited individual members into its sub-committees, which were responsible for running campaigns and maintaining the organisation. The members were initially middle-class English-speaking young people who had been politicised in church or student organisations. As the campaign developed, the committees drew in parents and professionals, school pupils and teachers, and Afrikaners.

Early activities

Immediately after its formation, the ECC embarked on the 'No War in Namibia' campaign, which focused on the SADF's occupation of Namibia and on the Namibian people's struggle for independence. This was followed by a series of activities to launch the ECC Declaration and win support for the call to end conscription. The 'Stop the Call-up' Peace Festival in mid-1985 involved the public and several hundred activists in three days of seminars, workshops, cultural events and public meetings.

Through these activities the ECC motivated its opposition to compulsory military service. It argued that conscription was used to defend and implement the policies of apartheid, maintain South Africa's illegal occupation of Namibia, and wage war on the frontline states. Conscription contributed to an acceptance of militarisation and to the government's use of force to solve political problems. It was also a violation of the fundamental right of freedom of conscience.

The ECC Declaration summarised these arguments and called for 'a just peace in our land'. This could only be achieved by 'dismantling apartheid, unbanning resistance organisations, releasing political prisoners and detainees, and recognising all South Africans as equal citizens'. The ECC believed that the solution to the Namibian conflict lay in the implementation of Security Council Resolution 435, which called for South Africa's immediate withdrawal from the territory, and for free and fair elections to be held under UN supervision.

The peace festival and early campaigns were characterised by a level of creativity unknown in white politics. Conventional political activities were complemented by 'creative actions' like fun runs, kite-flying, pavement art and street theatre. There were rock concerts, fairs and anti-war poster exhibitions. Thousands of stickers, buttons, pamphlets and tee-shirts were produced.

The ECC's dynamic style of politics was a large part of the reason for its success.

Our activities were accessible to whole families and not only 'committed activists'. They allowed the broadest range of people to express their unhappiness with conscription in whatever ways they wanted, and gave rise to a popular culture of war-resistance. A useful spin-off was that they generated a high level of press publicity. (Interview with ECC activist)

The peace festival marked the end of the first phase of the ECC's development. It had built regional and national structures, involved a wide range of groups and individuals in organised opposition to conscription, and established a national profile. Its strong stand against one of the cornerstones of apartheid, however, put it well outside the mainstream of white politics. This would soon change as the implications of the government's deployment of troops in black townships sank home in the white community.

Opposition to troops in the townships

In mid-1984, black communities mounted what was to become the most sustained and serious challenge to the apartheid state in its history.

The government responded by mobilising tens of thousands of troops to assist the police in crushing the rebellion. The liberal English-speaking community and radical sectors of the Afrikaans community were outraged by this development. They interpreted it as a declaration of civil war, and repeatedly condemned the 'politicising' of the SADF and the use of soldiers as policemen (*Sunday Star*, 14.10.1984; *Star*, 2.9.1985).

The massive deployment of troops also provoked an upsurge in opposition to conscription. Military service had previously been the preoccupation of a small group of war resisters. It was now an issue of deep and widespread concern among conscripts and their families. For many young people, the prospect of taking up arms against fellow South Africans engaged in a 'legitimate struggle' raised 'a moral dilemma of excruciating complexity' (*Business Day* editorial, 29.10.1986).

Many people seem to think that blacks are the enemy, do not belong in this country and that they must be controlled at all cost. However, I believe that many blacks, like the nanny who brought me up, do not deserve this terrible treatment. I am confused about whether or not to serve in the army. . . . I hope someone can provide me with a solution. (Letter from 16-year-old school pupil, *Rand Daily Mail*, 3.1.1985)

I'd never even thought about how justified the SADF was in being in the townships until one night on patrol, I suddenly looked around from the back of a Buffel [military vehicle] in Tembisa [township] and thought, 'What the hell am I doing here?' I just freaked out after that, because from my point of view we were maybe doing more harm than good. (National serviceman, 'Conscription makes war on love', *Cosmopolitan*, March 1988)

The growing disaffection with conscription manifested itself in a significant increase in draft evasion. In 1985, some 7 589 conscripts failed to report for the first major call-up after the deployment of troops in the townships (*Cape Times*, 13.3.1985). This constituted 50 per cent of the intake and an increase of 500 per cent over previous years. The SADF later announced that the figure was incorrect and that most of the men had been 'accounted for' (*Citizen*, 4.9.1985).

The Minister of Defence refused to disclose the figures for subsequent call-ups. His reason was that they were 'misused by a certain organisation which campaigns for the discontinuation of national service'.[3] The Minister also refused to reveal how many soldiers had been prosecuted for refusing to carry out township duties, as this would be a 'time-consuming process' which would 'not justify the cost in man hours' (HAD, 11 February 1986, cols. 2–3).

Despite this clampdown on information, there were other indications of growing resistance to military service. In 1986 the commanding officers of several military units in the Witwatersrand revealed in court that one in four conscripts were failing to report for army camps (*Out of*

Step, May 1987). In 1986 South Africa experienced a net emigration rate for the first time. From 1984 to 1987 more than 45 000 people left the country (*Weekly Mail*, 27.4.1987). Academics and business leaders regarded the pressure of conscription and the internal deployment of troops as major reasons for the exodus (*Business Day*, 9.7.1987; *Argus*, 8.12.1987).[4] In January 1987 the SA Army Non-Effective Members Unit was formed to track down draft dodgers. Six months later the Unit claimed to have found 72 000 'serving members', about 80 per cent of whom were 'computer adjustments' (*Natal Witness*, 26.6.1987). The status of the remaining 14 000 was not specified.

ECC campaigns

White unease and anger over the SADF's role within the country led to a dramatic growth of support for the ECC. This was evident in the ECC 'Troops Out of the Townships' campaign in September 1985. The campaign centred on three-week fasts observed by several conscientious objectors around the country. Thousands of people visited the objectors, attended daily educational programmes in the venues where they were fasting, and participated in a 24-hour solidarity fast. For the first time in the history of war resistance, Jewish, Hindu and Muslim groups became involved, and Christian involvement went beyond church hierarchies and activists to include clergy and their congregations.

The campaign marked the ECC's development from a marginal pressure group on the fringes of white politics to a credible organisation with legitimate concerns. It also succeeded in uniting people of all races at a time when security force actions in the townships were generating a high level of racial tension.

On Monday night some 4 000 people of all races, colours and creeds packed the Cape Town city hall to demand the removal of troops from the townships. [The ECC rally] was not a gathering of radicals and revolutionaries but a meeting of South Africans concerned about the future. Divided communities came together – black and coloured people who are subject to police and military action, white potential conscripts, their parents and families. It was a meeting such as the National Party, with all its talk of contact and negotiation, could never organize, but one for which Nationalist policies were responsible. (*Cape Times* editorial, 9.10.1985)

The next major ECC campaign, in May 1986, addressed the need for alternative national service. The 'Working for a Just Peace' campaign called specifically for three changes to be made to the law on conscientious objection. Firstly, community service should not be limited to 'religious pacifists', but should be available to all conscripts who in conscience cannot serve in the SADF. Secondly, objectors should be able to do community service in recognised religious and welfare organisations, and not only in government departments. Lastly, community service should be the same length as military service, and not one-and-a-half times as long.[5]

The campaign sought to highlight these demands in symbolic but practical ways. ECC activists and supporters worked for a month on 21 community projects in black residential areas across the country. They planted trees, built a bridge and renovated child-care centres. They also organised non-racial picnics, anti-litter drives and children's holiday programmes.

We want to demonstrate the numerous ways in which a community and country can be served without resorting to military means. This is what a genuinely national service could be like : meeting the real needs of the people, crossing racial barriers, and building bridges to a better future. (ECC pamphlet)

The campaign captured the imagination of a surprisingly large number of people in the white community. More than 600 volunteered to become involved in the projects, and over 6 000 attended the public rallies at the end of the campaign. This support was a significant public endorsement of the demand for non-military national service.

In a period of intense fighting between the security forces and township residents, the volunteers made an important statement by going into black areas.

We were warned that it would be dangerous to go into the townships, but the residents welcomed us with open arms. In contrast to the SADF, we went in without guns and uniforms, and obtained the community's support for our work. In a small way, we helped counter the anti-white feelings developing as a result of police and army actions. (Interview with ECC member)

Broadening the war resistance movement

With the widespread use of troops inside the country, the ECC not only mobilised greater numbers of people but also expanded in several new directions. The most important of these concerned the Afrikaans community. Since the mid-1970s the war resistance movement had been exclusively based in the English-speaking community. Afrikaans churches, schools and families instilled in young people a strong sense of pride in the army and a belief in the absolute necessity of conscription.

The political crisis of 1985 caused a number of Afrikaners to question these attitudes and beliefs. Even if they agreed with the SADF's presence in Namibia and Angola, they regarded its role inside the country as indefensible. The ECC won sufficient support among Afrikaners to establish branches in Pretoria and at Stellenbosch University.[6] Its Johannesburg branch formed a new wing with the name Eindig Nasionale Diensplig (End National Service).

Although relatively few Afrikaners joined the ECC, their involvement was regarded as highly significant. This was particularly the case in relation to the branch in Pretoria, one of the most conservative and militarised cities in the country.

The very fact that a branch of ECC has been formed here is already a victory. Pretoria is the embodiment of Nationalist ideology and adorned with its symbols: Voortrekker Monument, Union Buildings, Paul Kruger statue, Pretoria Central Prison and State Theatre. In addition, Pretoria is the NERVE CENTRE OF THE SECURITY NETWORK in the country. (Pretoria ECC document)

The second new direction in which the ECC expanded involved the development of an anti-war culture. This culture embraced a variety of different forms – art, writing, cabaret and music – and drew in mainstream and alternative artists and performers. The ECC presented their work through rock concerts, film festivals, art exhibitions and multi-cultural events. These reached new audiences who were not attracted to formal political activities.

The dominant message of the anti-war culture was 'look what this war has done to us', rather than 'this is an unjust war'. It reflected the struggle of young whites to come to terms with living in a racially divided society caught between repression and revolution. The dominant moods were anger, guilt and alienation.

The ECC's third area of expansion concerned white schools. Until the mid-1980s, the vast majority of white schoolboys accepted or were at least resigned to participating in the school cadet system and later the SADF. After troops were deployed in black townships, however, pupils at English-medium schools began for the first time publicly expressing their unease about conscription.

I have a huge problem that I cannot talk to anyone about. I tried talking to my father and he got so angry with me, I thought he might actually hit me. I do not want to go into the army. There is no way I can square it with the way I feel and my religious beliefs. . . . I feel terribly isolated, like I don't belong anywhere. It's not because I am a coward. (Letter to *Weekend Star,* 12.9.1987)

The ECC attempted to address these concerns by forming school sub-committees which included pupils and teachers. The committees organised cultural evenings and concerts, and ran skills-training workshops and educational forums. They also distributed pamphlets on cadets and conscription outside schools.

The ECC's fourth area of expansion brought it into the international arena. In mid-1985 it established contact with a wide range of organisations overseas. One aim was to keep them informed about militarisation and conscription in South Africa, and about the extent of white opposition to apartheid. A second aim was to promote the ECC so that it could draw on international support when running campaigns, and rely on international protest when under government attack. The third aim was to learn about conditions and anti-conscription struggles in other countries.

Over the next few years the ECC developed a significant international profile. Pacifist, religious and anti-apartheid organisations participated in its campaigns, and major newspapers and TV networks reported its activities. The New York City Council and the European Economic Community passed special resolutions supporting its work. ECC members went on speaking tours of Europe and the United States, and attended several international conferences.

In mid-1986 Archbishop Tutu declared: 'the ECC's rapid growth and popularity are signs of hope in this crazy, crazy but beautiful country' (ECC rally, Cape Town, May 1986). His statement reflected the feelings of the black community and a growing number of whites. The campaign was in fact expanding faster than its activists could have imagined or could cope with organisationally. A few weeks later the government declared a national state of emergency, and the ECC was suddenly fighting for its survival.

Harassment

The ECC's growth from mid-1985 was matched by the development of an extensive and sophisticated smear campaign targeted against it. Right-wing organisations produced thousands of glossy pamphlets that 'exposed' the ECC's 'hidden links to Moscow and support for violence'. They sent the pamphlets to school heads and teachers, and the army distributed them amongst pupils and soldiers (*Eastern Province Herald*, 3.3.1987). Afrikaans newspapers and churches and the state-controlled radio and television contributed their part to the offensive.

Government and military spokespersons lambasted the ECC's 'propaganda, suspicion-sowing and misinformation' (Minister of Defence, *Citizen*, 14.4.1987). They described its members as 'lacking the moral fibre to defend the country against Russia and its surrogates' (Deputy Minister of Defence, *Citizen*, 15.8.1987). They accused the organisation of being part of the 'revolutionary onslaught', and linked it to banned groups.[7]

The aim of the smears was to criminalise the ECC, to portray it as unpatriotic and 'dangerous for South Africa' (Deputy Minister of Defence, *Citizen*, 15.8.1987). If the labels stuck, many people (it was hoped) would be frightened to support the organisation even if they agreed with its position. They would see opposition to conscription as inherently subversive, and would also accept direct repression against the ECC as justified.

The repression reached a peak in mid-1986 with the imposition of the national state of emergency. Altogether 75 ECC activists were detained, many went into hiding, and 25 were served with restriction orders. Security police raided over 90 ECC offices and homes, and confiscated hundreds of documents. The official harassment was accompanied by a spate of terror tactics. Motor-car tyres of ECC members were slashed, wheel nuts were loosened, and brake fluid was drained. On at least eight occasions, ECC members were assaulted by soldiers or right-wing thugs.

The central thrust of the crackdown lay in special emergency regulations which prohibited the making or publication of 'subversive statements'. These included statements that 'undermined or discredited the system of compulsory military service'. The offence was punishable by ten years' imprisonment or a R20 000 fine. These measures were widely understood as intended to ban the ECC.

The repression experienced by the ECC in this period was part of a broader state clampdown on all extra-parliamentary opposition to apartheid. There were, in addition, specific reasons for the intensity of state action against the ECC. These lay in the central role that the SADF plays in maintaining minority rule, at both a physical and an ideological level. Since the mid-1970s the SADF has increasingly been used in Namibia and southern Africa as apartheid's front-line of attack, and inside the country as its last line of defence. More than 100 000 troops have been stationed in Namibia, and up to 45 000 have been used annually in South Africa in 'ordinary police work' or against black resistance (*Cape Times*, 19.5.1984; House of Assembly, Parliamentary Questions no. 878, 1986). The 1986 Defence White Paper stated that conscription, which provides 70 per cent of the SADF's manpower, is essential for enabling the army to play these roles. The state consequently viewed draft evasion and opposition to conscription as real threats to its defence capability. It perceived the ECC as 'aiming to leave South Africa defenceless' (Major-General Van Loggerenberg, *Natal Witness*, 21.10.1985), and therefore as a 'direct enemy of the SADF' (Minister of Defence, *Citizen*, 14.4.1987).

War resistance also threatens state ideology in a fundamental way. The government places as much emphasis on maintaining the morale of the white population as it does on repressing the black community. It regards the physical and psychological preparation of whites for protracted war as a priority. This preparation takes place through the militarisation of key areas of civil society, and through the military doctrine of 'national security'. This doctrine presents the conflict in South Africa as a struggle between 'communism' and 'Western Christian civilisation'. It seeks to win acceptance for the use of state force as an appropriate response. It inculcates military values of obedience and discipline amongst the populace, and projects the SADF as a unifying institution and symbol.

The very existence of the war resistance movement challenges these notions. It casts doubt on the government's interpretation of the nature of society, conflict and the required solutions. But the movement goes even further than this – it implicitly questions the legitimacy of the state and its armed forces. The ECC was thus seen by the government as attempting to undermine not only the country's physical ability to defend itself but, more important, its will to do so. In the terminology of the 'total onslaught–total strategy' discourse, the ECC was engaged in 'warfare in the indirect mode', that is, at the psychological and ideological levels. By doing this from within the white community, it was perceived not just as 'the enemy', but as a traitor.

The ECC under the state of emergency

The first six months of the state of emergency proved traumatic for the ECC. It put a hold on all public activities until the legality of further campaigning could be established. The ECC's immediate priorities became those of supporting activists in hiding and detention, maintaining the cohesion and morale of the organisation, and developing security procedures that would make it less vulnerable to further harassment.

Once the initial shock of the emergency had worn off, however, the ECC decided to begin campaigning again. It acknowledged that there was a high risk of further detentions and even criminal prosecution, yet it was determined 'that we do not ban ourselves'.

The government is attempting to outlaw all opposition to apartheid outside of parliament. Together with other democratic organisations we have to contest its ability to do this. The people of South Africa are not about to give up their struggle. Now more than ever they are looking to the white community to join them. This means that we must 'get back onto the streets'. (ECC document)

The ECC was nevertheless careful to avoid contravening the emergency regulations. Its national campaigns – 'Let ECC Speak', 'War is No Solution' and 'War is Not Compulsory, Let's Choose a Just Peace' – called for the right to oppose conscription, and focused on various aspects of militarisation. The central themes revolved around the 'economic, physical and psychological costs of the intensifying civil war'.

At the end of 1987 the ECC assessed its work under the state of emergency. Eighteen months after a crackdown that many thought would break it, the organisation was intact and active. '[The government has] taken some of the excitement and exhilaration out of our work, but in its place is a dedication and a life-long commitment. The State of Emergency is its own school, and we have sharpened our skills and learned to maximise our human resources.' (*Out of Step*, September 1987)

The repression had undoubtedly taken its toll, however, and had forced the ECC onto the defensive. In shifting its focus from conscription to militarisation, the ECC no longer generated the same level of public interest as before the emergency. The press were often scared to report its activities, and the smear campaign had done it considerable damage in the Afrikaans-speaking white community and among conservative English-speakers.

The ECC in 1988

From the beginning of 1988 until its banning in August, the ECC enjoyed the highest profile and broadest support it had ever won. Its successful recovery was due both to its formulating new strategies, and to independent political developments. The new strategies involved abandoning the broad focus on militarisation, and responding more directly to the immediate needs and concerns of conscripts and their families.

One such need was for information about the legal and illegal alternatives to military service, and about conscripts' rights and obligations under the Defence Act. To meet this need, the ECC introduced a series of 'Know Your Rights' meetings and pamphlets. This public service boosted its credibility, and underlined the fact that it was not 'anti-conscript', as the government claimed.

A second area of major concern in the conscripted community centred on the SADF's deepening involvement in Angola. In mid-1987 the army had begun what was to be its most extensive military operation in that country. By early 1988 it had failed to meet its objectives, and faced the possibility of a serious defeat. The shift in the balance of forces resulted in a significantly higher number of South African troop casualties than before. Although the official figure of 52 white deaths was relatively small for a conventional war, it provoked unprecedented opposition from people who had previously been uncritical of SADF activities outside the country.

Pro-government newspapers and conservative parents of soldiers killed in action questioned the army's presence in Angola for the first time.

> You know I often do think of how it happened. There were ten of them in a Ratel [military vehicle] and it was one of those new bombs, a missile, something like that. He was in a convoy of Ratels and it was the only one bombed. Can you believe it? Isn't it terrible that it should be *my* son? Personally I feel that our children should not be fighting in that war. It is our duty to give our sons to the army – nobody really wants them to go, but it is our duty to send them. But . . . we are not told that our children are being sent into Angola. We think they are in South West Africa. Since Pieter died I have had a lot of phone calls. People are unhappy that their children are being sent into Angola. (Mother of a 19-year-old soldier killed in Angola, 'Killed in Action', *Fair Lady*, 17.4.1988)

The most dramatic indication of the mainstream Afrikaans community's opposition came in the form of a critical editorial in *Die Kerkbode,* the official publication of the Nederduitse Gereformeerde Kerk (Dutch Reformed Church).

Without attempting to discuss the issue out of its political or military context, we nevertheless want to raise the question of whether it would not be morally and ethically correct for South Africa to withdraw its troops completely from Angola. The fact of the matter is that Angola is not its territory. It seems to us that the more or less permanent presence of troops in this foreign country can be questioned on Christian-ethical grounds. (*Die Kerkbode*, 8.6.1988)

Although these protests were not linked to the ECC in any way, they created the space for it to campaign systematically against SADF external aggression. The ECC organised a series of protest meetings around the country, and produced pamphlets explaining developments in Angola. It also delivered a protest statement to army headquarters in Cape Town, and sent a more detailed memorandum to the Minister of Defence.

The ECC's major activity in 1988 was the Alternative Service Campaign. The campaign called on the government to give conscripts the right to do 'non-government and non-military national service that is in the interests of the nation and its people as a whole'. The call was endorsed by a wide range of academics, business leaders, parliamentary parties, welfare organisations, and English-language churches and newspapers, many of whom did not support the more radical demand to end conscription.

The need for alternative national service was highlighted in the most powerful way by the stands of individual conscientious objectors. Dr Ivan Toms and David Bruce were imprisoned for eighteen months and six years respectively for disobeying their call-ups, and in early August 143 conscripts collectively announced their refusal to serve in the SADF. These events provoked a public clamour for the introduction of alternative service.

What is needed is a nation-building exercise in which the budding doctors, engineers and other objectors can offer their skills. As one civil engineer protested: 'I want to build bridges, not destroy them.' And as numbers of objectors have spelt out: 'I am a patriot who will not leave my country. But I will not serve apartheid. Please let me contribute in another way.' (*Star* editorial, 10.8.1988)

As the war resistance movement expanded, the government realised that its attempts to restrict and discredit the ECC had failed. More drastic measures were required. The immediate catalyst of its move against the ECC was the stand of the 143 conscripts, one of the most extraordinary acts of white opposition to apartheid. The Minister of Defence was infuriated by it: 'The ECC is the vanguard of those forces that are intent on wrecking the present dispensation and its renewal. . . . Those who support and propagate campaigns against national service have overplayed their hands.' (*Citizen*, 4.8.1988)

Two weeks later the government banned the ECC. Anti-apartheid groups and the liberal parliamentary parties condemned the action as 'outrageous', 'crude' and 'counter-productive'. They dismissed the allegation that the ECC was subversive as 'absurd'. According to the Black Sash, 'ECC has done more to create goodwill and understanding than any action of the government' (*New Nation*, 25.8.1988).

Shortly after the ban, the SADF suffered an embarrassing setback when the Supreme Court in Cape Town ordered it to refrain from 'unlawfully harassing or interfering with the ECC'. In the course of the hearing, the SADF acknowledged responsibility for a series of 'legitimate secret counter-measures' against the ECC. The SADF argued that its actions were justified and that the Supreme Court had no jurisdiction to hear the matter because the army was 'on a war footing' (*Sunday Star*, 4.9.1988). The military's arguments and revealed actions provoked a storm of protest. As the ECC's lawyer, Sydney Kentridge SC, argued, 'the generals have declared martial law by means of an affidavit. These are the pretensions of a junta of South American generals.' (*Weekly Mail*, 2.9.1988)

Conclusion

A review of the history of opposition to conscription suggests that the ECC's banning will be a severe but not fatal blow to the war resistance movement. Over the past decade the state has repeatedly attempted to silence the movement. It introduced Section 121(c) of the Defence Act in 1974, the Defence Amendment Act in 1983, and the state of emergency regulations in 1986. On each occasion the war resistance movement was temporarily thrown into disarray, but was able to define a new direction and emerge stronger than before.

State action against organised opposition to conscription has had limited success because it does nothing to resolve the dilemma of conscripts unwilling to serve in the SADF. Their dilemma is not the creation of anti-apartheid organisations, but the result of a widespread belief that the army plays an aggressive role in defence of an unjust system. This assertion is borne out by the fact that the war resistance movement experienced its most rapid growth in periods when the SADF was playing a new or more prominent coercive role: in the mid-1970s when the army invaded Angola, intensified its occupation of Namibia, and was mobilised against the Soweto uprising; in 1985–6 when it was used extensively against black resistance inside the country; and in 1987–8 when it escalated its involvement in Angola.

When *Die Kerkbode* published its critical editorial on the SADF's presence in Angola, the Minister of Defence replied with a scathing attack. The response of the DRC Moderator, Professor Johan Heyns, captured the essence of war resistance in South Africa: 'the questions raised [in the editorial] are perfectly legitimate. Those are the questions in the hearts of our people.' (*Star*, 8.7.1988) The banning of the ECC will not change this.

The hope seems to be that bans will make unpleasant ideas go away. Of course they won't. Young men with strong moral or political views against serving in the army will still feel the need to go to jail for their principles, or to sever their ties with the country or disappear 'underground'. (*Star* editorial, 23.8.1988)

24 Waging peace: church resistance to militarisation

HARALD E. WINKLER &
LAURIE NATHAN

In the South African situation, conscientious objection should be adopted as a principle by the churches. I believe that the churches should adopt this view, even at the risk of open confrontation with the government. Confrontation has to occur some time. (Archbishop Hurley speaking in 1974; quoted in Methodist Church of Southern Africa (MCSA), 1986: 15)

Since 1974, the English-speaking churches' stand on conscientious objection and the role of the SADF has been a source of conflict both with the state and within the churches themselves. The churches' position on these issues evolved on the basis of their theological teachings and their understanding of the nature of South African society. Their fundamental belief in the right of freedom of conscience in relation to military service is strongly reinforced by the view that the SADF is an aggressive force in the defence of apartheid inside and outside the country.

The English-speaking churches initiated public debate around issues of militarisation in the mid-1970s. They have since been an important part of the war resistance movement, with their stand being strengthened over time as a result of intensifying black resistance. This chapter examines their role, the reasons for its development, and church debates around issues of militarisation like chaplaincy in the SADF. It also considers briefly the position of the Afrikaans-speaking churches.[1]

Early war resistance

The struggle of the Jehovah's Witnesses

In response to the militant campaigns of the African National Congress in the 1950s, the government introduced a system of conscription for white men in 1957. In 1961 the Defence Act made limited provision for conscientious objectors. Non-combatant service in the SADF was available to conscripts who belonged to recognised peace churches. These churches – Jehovah's Witnesses, Seventh Day Adventists, Quakers and other small pacifist groups – do not allow their members to participate in any armed force.

Many Jehovah's Witnesses rejected the concession. They refused to serve in the SADF in any capacity and were sentenced to repeated three-month periods in military detention barracks. Some Witnesses spent up to four years in DB. Conditions there were harsh, and the objectors were treated more severely than other offenders. They frequently endured periods of solitary confinement for not obeying commands. Some spent the entire winter in their underclothes for refusing to wear military uniform (CIIR, 1982: 26–7).

The Jehovah's Witnesses have in the past gone through a lot of suffering. A lot of them had been put in solitary confinement for periods much longer than I. A lot of them had been put into dark cells. They had been beaten up. They had been dragged out at midnight and told to douse themselves under a cold shower. They had been treated in a most disgusting and abominable way. I really do not know how the Defence Force could bear to treat people like animals as they did. (Conscientious objector Peter Moll; in Louw, 1984)

In 1972, the government finally made concessions to the Jehovah's Witnesses. Their sentence for refusing to serve was increased to 15 months, but was no longer repeatable. In practice they would only spend a year in DB. They were issued with neutral blue overalls, segregated from other prisoners, and excused from military drill.

The SACC resolution

The mainstream English-speaking churches were slow to respond to the issue of military service and the broader militarisation of South African society. This was the result of the traditional Protestant reluctance to become involved in matters 'political', and the failure among white South Africans to see the connection between military structures and apartheid.

Against the background of growing internal resistance and liberation wars in neighbouring countries, the South African Council of Churches passed a landmark resolution at its 1974 conference at Hammanskraal. The resolution marked the first concrete statement by churches on the issue of conscientious objection. In debate at the conference Douglas Bax, a Presbyterian minister, stood up and remarked that 'neither the churches nor the SACC have been in the lead of doing something practical to change the status quo in South Africa. Isn't it time for us to consider seriously whether the SACC should challenge young men on the score of conscientious objection?' (CIIR, 1982: 28) After heated discussion and several amendments, a motion proposed by Bax and seconded by Dr Beyers Naudé was passed unanimously by the conference. The resolution noted:

(1) 'that Christians are called to strive for justice and the true peace which can be founded only in justice';
(2) that the conference did not see that it is automatically the

Christian's duty to obey his or her nation's call to commit violence;

(3) that both Catholic and Reformation theology justify taking up arms, but only in order to fight a 'just war';

(4) that 'the theological definition of a "just war" excludes war in the defence of an unjust and discriminatory society';

(5) that the Republic of South Africa is a fundamentally unjust and discriminatory society; and

(6) that the South African military forces are defending this society.

In the light of these arguments, the conference therefore resolved to:

(1) deplore 'violence as a means to solve problems';

(2) call on its member churches 'to challenge all their members to consider in view of the above whether Christ's call to take up the cross and follow him in identifying with the oppressed does not, in our situation, involve becoming conscientious objectors'; and

(3) commend 'the courage and witness of those who have been willing to go to jail in protest against unjust laws and policies in our land'. (CIIR, 1982: 78–9)

The SACC resolution was a dramatic departure from previous church statements. It located the issue of participating in the SADF in the context of the justice of the cause being fought for. The system of apartheid, and not war in itself, was being questioned. As a result of the resolution the member churches of the SACC, which had previously not discussed the issue, were challenged to formulate their own positions.

Reaction to the resolution

Within the English-speaking churches a split occurred between those who supported the resolution and those who did not. Negative responses came from those churches dominated by white minorities. Black sections of segregated churches came out in support of the resolution, as did all the multiracial denominations (see CIIR, 1982: 31–4).

Within the broader white community the reaction to the SACC resolution was overwhelmingly negative. The liberal opposition in parliament was scathing in its criticism of it, and the entire English and Afrikaans press, with the sole exception of the *Rand Daily Mail,* condemned it. Clearly the notion of conscientious objection had raised the question of patriotism sharply for whites.

The government indicated how seriously it viewed war resistance from any quarter, even from the churches, by immediately amending the Defence Act. Section 121(c) made it an offence, punishable by R6 000 or six years' imprisonment, to encourage or assist any person to refuse or fail to render military service. The draconian legislation had the effect of uniting 'pacifist' and 'just war' theological positions, and of further alienating the church from the state. Numerous individuals and organisations condemned it. The administrative board of the

Southern African Catholic Bishops' Conference (SACBC) declared that if the bill became law, it would be bound by conscience to disobey it, and would encourage its clergy and members to do the same (CIIR, 1982: 34).

Despite these protests against Section 121(c), however, the legislation had the effect of inhibiting church debate. The individual churches went no further than resolving to educate their members about the issues surrounding conscription. At the 1975 SACC conference a motion proposing new action and thought on conscientious objection was shelved. At the 1976 conference the issue was only referred to in passing. In required, as before, broader social and political developments to provoke the churches into strengthening their stand.

The call for the recognition of conscientious objectors

The independence of Angola in 1975 marked the start of the full-scale border war in Namibia, and led to the introduction of three-month border camps for national servicemen. In 1976 student protests in Soweto grew into a national uprising. The government declared a state of emergency, mobilised the army and eventually crushed the rebellion. Many young blacks left the country to join the armed struggle of the African National Congress. The government responded to these developments by doubling the total length of military service to nearly three years.

These events had a politicising effect on many white conscripts and led to an increase in draft evasion. From 1975 to 1978, about 3 500 men failed to report for duty each year. A small number, mostly Jehovah's Witnesses, were charged and imprisoned. The remainder presumably went into exile or evaded the authorities inside the country (CIIR, 1982: 38).

The events of this period also radicalised the churches further. Under pressure from small groups of committed whites and predominantly black memberships, all the English-speaking churches by the late 1970s had declared their support for the right to refuse military service on grounds of conscience. Significantly, this position was based on a critique of the SADF's role inside and outside the country, and applied to both Christian and non-Christian conscientious objectors.

The churches also pressed the government to make practical arrangements whereby objectors would be recognised. For example, in October 1979 at its annual conference, the Methodist Church made a concrete proposal to the Minister of Defence that 'a commission of enquiry, comprising a fair cross-section representative both of the church and the Department of Defence, be established to test the convictions of any person claiming to be a conscientious objector' (CIIR, 1982: 53).

The churches' stand was grounded in the theological traditions of the various denominations. The Catholic bishops appealed to authoritative church teaching on the issue. Vatican II in *Gaudium et Spes* held that those who perform military service for their country fulfil a role of upholding the long-term peace and security of that country. But it also held that 'it seems right that laws make humane provisions for the case of those, who for reasons of conscience, refuse to bear arms, provided, however, that they accept some other form of service to the human community' (MCSA, 1986: 5). Both Pope Paul VI in 1967 and the Roman Synod of Bishops (1971) endorsed this position, recognising the right to object conscientiously to military service and the need for alternative forms of national service.

In its public statements the Church of the Province of South Africa seemed to be acting in the spirit of the 1978 Lambeth conference. The conference had made a clear statement on war and violence (though not dealing specifically with conscientious objection). It condemned violence and its many forms – exploitation, open war, and misdirection of resources: 'In the face of the mounting incidence of violence today, and its acceptance as a normal element in human affairs, we condemn the subjection, intimidation, and manipulation of people by the use of violence and the threat of violence' (MCSA, 1986: 8).

The conscientious objectors

The intensifying conflict in the mid-1970s also prompted the first objectors from the English-speaking churches to take a stand. They differed from the peace-church objectors in two respects. They sought to publicise their stands, and they spoke out strongly against the SADF's role in defending apartheid against the majority of the South African and Namibian people.

In 1979 and 1980 two Baptists, Peter Moll and Richard Steele, disobeyed their call-ups and were sentenced to a year in detention barracks. There they were punished with repeated periods in solitary confinement for refusing to wear military uniform and perform drill. The public outcry that ensued eventually led to their being treated in the same way as the Jehovah's Witnesses.

Over the next three years a further eight objectors from the English-speaking churches were charged and imprisoned. Their reasons for objecting indicated the diversity and unity of the emerging war resistance movement. Some refused specifically to undergo service in the SADF while others said they would not serve in any army. Some grounded their objection in religious beliefs, others in political convictions. All stated their abhorrence of apartheid and their commitment to 'working for peace and justice'. All were willing to perform non-military alternative service.

The Christian objectors drew on two major church traditions – pacifism and the just war theory. The pacifist tradition goes back to the early church – there is no record of Christians serving in the Roman army prior to A.D. 170 (Resource Group on Military Service, 1984: 2). Pacifists take the Fifth Commandment, 'Thou shalt not kill', to apply in all situations. The Sermon on the Mount (Mt. 5–7) is possibly the most powerful argument for their position. In it, Jesus calls on Christians to love even their enemies, and blesses 'the peacemakers, for they shall be called the children of God' (Mt. 5: 9).

The just war tradition, which guides selective objection to participation in particular wars, evolved in the thinking of the church over centuries. According to this tradition, only if the following criteria are met can participation in war be considered justified: the war must be declared by a legitimate authority; the war must be waged for a just cause; the war must be motivated by a right intention, the goal of justice; there must be a reasonable chance of success; the suffering caused by the war must be proportionate to the ends achieved by it; just means must be used; a just peace must be envisaged.

Objectors from the English-speaking churches drew on both traditions, as is evidenced by these extracts from their statements.

Selective conscientious objection is the refusal to engage in a particular war, while making no necessary statement about war in general. I have decided to be a selective conscientious objector because in terms of Christian moral standards, South African society is fundamentally unjust [and because] the insurgents are generally not foreigners but South African citizens – i.e. the situation is one of civil war. This makes one question very seriously just what one is required to fight for, and what one is required to die for. (Extract from Peter Moll's letter to the SADF stating his refusal to obey his call-up; cited in CIIR, 1982: 80)

I object to *all* military training. The only way a soldier can be effective is to deny the humanity of his opponent: he is a terrorist, a communist, a racist – whatever word in a given context that makes him better dead than alive. . . . In dehumanising the other, you lessen your own humanity as well. Military training relies on this process of repression, seeks to obliterate individual identity and to introduce unquestioning obedience without consideration of generally accepted moral values of not killing or desecrating another person. (Extract from interview with Richard Steele; cited in CIIR, 1982: 83)

The objectors went to jail at a time when the white community was overwhelmingly hostile to their beliefs and actions. Yet their stands were so remarkable that they opened up public debate about military service and the SADF's role, and forced other conscripts to think critically about their own participation in the army. They also compelled the churches to move beyond merely passing resolutions on conscientious objection to engaging in concrete support action.

The most important consequence of the objectors' stands was that they gave rise to the first local organised form of war resistance. Conscientious Objector Support Groups (COSGs) were established as friends came together to support the objectors in prison. COSG began to raise public awareness about militarisation and conscientious objection through meetings and a national publication, *Objector*.

The Afrikaans churches on war resistance

At the same time that the English-speaking churches were moving closer to supporting the right of conscientious objection, the Afrikaans churches were moving further away. The 1982 General Synod of the Nederduitse Gereformeerde Kerk (NGK) expressed the official position of the church on conscientious objection, war and revolution. This position, formulated at a time when Afrikaner nationalism held undisputed power, differs dramatically from that of the period when Afrikaner nationalism was seeking to assert itself against British imperialism. Durand and Smit have illustrated the irony of this shift with examples from the 1914–15 rebellion, the Second World War and the present conflict (Durand and Smit, 1987: 31–49).

In 1914 Afrikaner nationalists objected to the Botha–Smuts government's decision to participate in the First World War in support of Britain. They were deeply opposed to fighting alongside an army that had defeated them only twelve years previously. When Smuts decided to occupy German South West Africa, thousands of men in the Union Defence Force followed their generals – Maritz, Beyers and De Wet – in rebellion, and some joined with the German forces.

The response of the Afrikaner churches was ambivalent. They did not explicitly support the rebels, but they refused to condemn them or their use of force against the state. The most important consideration for the churches seemed to be the maintenance of Afrikaner unity (Durand and Smit, 1987: 34).

In the Second World War, Afrikaner nationalists were again asked to participate in what they saw as an imperialist war. Many refused. One prominent soldier who refused to fight outside South Africa, General Hiemstra, became Chief of the Army under the Nationalist government after 1948. Another future Defence Force chief and Minister of Defence, Magnus Malan, refused to enlist on the grounds that the war 'was not his war but Britain's war' (McIntosh, 1980: 7).

In this situation the Afrikaner churches argued for the right of the individual to refuse to fight. The 1937 Cape Synod of the NGK stressed 'the limitations of obedience to the state in so far as the Christian conscience and the demands of the Word of God forbid an absolute and unlimited obedience to anyone but God' (Durand and Smit, 1982: 40).

This position has been turned on its head since the National Party came to power in 1948. Conscientious objection now entails refusing to fight for the SADF on 'the border' or in the townships. It entails refusing to defend Afrikaner nationalist (and, more broadly, white) interests. The document accepted at the 1982 Synod rejected total pacifism as 'unChristian', and refused to consider seriously the case of

selective objection to participation in the SADF.
According to Durand and Smit:

At the time of the rebellion in 1914 and during the Second World War the idea of overriding obedience to God vis-à-vis the state, and accompanying this the acceptance of the possibility of a right to resist, formed an intrinsic part of [the Dutch Reformed Church's] line of argument. In its 1982 document on conscientious objection the argument is virtually reversed, to such a degree that neither the church nor individual Christians are allowed to challenge the state in the name of God on the issue of an unjust war. (1982: 45)

The Defence Amendment Act (1983) and the Board for Religious Objection
By 1983 the war resistance movement in South Africa had developed considerable momentum and was becoming increasingly active around the individual stands of conscientious objectors. The state's response to this and to the churches' call for non-military national service was the 1983 Defence Amendment Act. The Act established the possibility of objectors performing community service in government departments. This option was limited, however, to objectors who could satisfy a Board for Religious Objection that they would not serve 'in any armed force' because of their religious convictions.[2]

At the same time, the amendment increased the term of imprisonment for other objectors to one-and-a-half times the length of their outstanding military service. Non-religious objectors, or those who refused specifically to serve in the SADF, now faced a maximum of six years in jail. The amendment represented an attempt to defuse and minimise conscientious objection as a political issue by offering a significant concession to religious pacifists, while making objection by non-religious or non-pacifist objectors prohibitively costly. The legislation was also intended to divide the war resistance movement by seeking to coopt the churches and pacifist groups, and separating 'religious' objectors from 'political' ones. It aimed moreover to create division within the churches between pacifists and just war theorists.

The churches, however, were united in their opposition to the new legislation. As a Congregational Church statement declared,

the churches cannot accept a law that provides solely for religious objectors while it imposes severe penalties on others. To do so would amount to condoning privileges for the religious and persecution of the non-religious – a complete anomaly in a state which is opposed to religious discrimination. (Cited in Law *et al.*, 1987: 292)

The SACC summed up the churches' objections in a resolution passed at its 1984 national conference. The resolution noted that the legislation contained some positive aspects: it accepted the principle of non-military national service, broadened the recognition of conscientious objection beyond members of the peace churches, and established a civilian rather than a military board to hear applications from objectors.

However, the resolution stated that these positive aspects were outweighed by the negative consequences of the Act, whose 'ultimate effect is to make conscientious objection more difficult than before'. The resolution condemned 'the failure of the legislation to recognise as conscientious objectors all those who are non-religious or who only object to some wars'. It also rejected the punitive prison sentence for objectors not recognised by the Board, and the 'unreasonably' long period of alternative service for those that were recognised. The conference strongly affirmed 'that the state has a duty to recognise the right of any individual to object in conscience to military service and be given a fair non-military alternative' (SACC Resolution no. 21 of 1984).

Bishop Tutu, then general secretary of the SACC, said in support of the resolution:

The Gospel demands that each person should obey his own conscience, and that imperative implies an inalienable right to do so. It is pernicious in the extreme therefore for the state to force people to violate their consciences, especially for a state that claims to be Christian. (*Rand Daily Mail*, 27.12.84)

The Board for Religious Objection

The Board for Religious Objection was set up to test the sincerity of objectors on the basis of two criteria – whether their objection is 'religious', and whether it is based on universal pacifism. From August 1984 to August 1986 there were 1 059 applications. The vast majority were from Jehovah's Witnesses.[3] Some 123 applications were withdrawn and 16 were refused because they did not meet the criteria of being religious and universally pacifist. Altogether 70 per cent of those accepted were granted the option of community service, and the rest were given non-combatant status in the SADF (*Weekly Mail*, 27.4.1987).

Over the following two years, church commentators expressed criticisms of the functioning of the Board. The first major criticism was related to the Board's composition and task. It is made up of theologians from various churches (including that of the applicant), SADF officers, military chaplains and a Supreme Court judge as chairperson. The majority appear to believe that the SADF is engaged in a 'just war'. They are not themselves conscientious objectors and are unlikely to be sympathetic to such a position. 'It is inconceivable that a man with thirty years' military service behind him could even comprehend the convictions of a conscientious objector, much less come to a reasoned judgement as to how sincere the objector is' (Moll, 1986).

A second criticism is that the Board tends to view religion and politics as mutually exclusive. An applicant who shows liberal or radical political beliefs may be rejected by the Board even if he is genuinely religious and pacifist. Some applicants are therefore inhibited from expressing their true feelings. 'To convince narrow-minded people that you adhere to a set of beliefs that they have defined narrowly, one has to become (or convey the impression of being) as narrow-minded as one's interlocutors' (Moll, 1986).

The third criticism is that community service is limited to working in government departments at military pay rates. The objector may or may not be placed in a position which allows him to use his professional skills. For many objectors this is not real national service. Work within the churches or welfare or community organisations is seen by many as far more constructive.

In view of these criticisms, some churches – Catholic, Presbyterian, Congregational and Anglican – have refused to allow their clergy to serve on the Board.

The churches after 1983

Troops in the townships

In late 1984 black opposition to apartheid entered its most intense phase. Over the next two years thousands of white conscripts were deployed in the townships to assist the police in suppressing the uprising. The English-speaking churches expressed outrage at this development, which they saw as amounting to a declaration of civil war. The churches compiled documents on security force actions and petitioned the government to withdraw its troops. The Church of the Province of South Africa sought an urgent meeting with the State President to present the 'emerging mass of documents' alleging brutality and harassment of township residents (*Argus*, 23.10.1986). It called on the government to establish an independent judicial inquiry into police and army activities in black areas.

The Methodist synod resolved to educate its membership that young people who entered the townships under SADF orders were acting contrary to church principles (*Citizen*, 23.10.1986). It outlined its position in a telex to the State President.

We call on you to withdraw all National Servicemen immediately from the townships where a situation has now arisen in which white and black Methodists are facing each other in armed confrontation. We know that this situation is leading to a crisis of faith among our young Methodists whose loyalty to their country is unquestioned but [who] also cannot accept that that requires of them to take up arms against their fellow South Africans. (Extract from telex, October 1986)

The on-going deployment of troops inside the country led the churches to strengthen their stand on compulsory military service. They shifted their position from demanding the recognition of the right of freedom of conscience, to calling for an end to the system of conscription itself.

This call was based on several arguments: conscription compels young men to fight in an unjust war in Namibia and against fellow South Africans, requires them to assist in the implementation and defence of apartheid policies, intensifies rather than resolves the escalating conflict in the region, and does not allow for the right of conscientious objection.[4]

The churches also reiterated their call for constructive alternative service while the system of conscription remained in force. They demanded that three fundamental changes be made to the law regarding conscientious objection: community service should be available to all conscripts who in conscience cannot serve in the SADF; objectors should be able to do community service in recognised religious and welfare organisations; and community service should be the same length as military service.

In August 1985 the SACC, on behalf of its member churches and the SACBC, presented memoranda along these lines to the Geldenhuys Committee, an SADF committee investigating various aspects of military policy. The committee rejected the proposed changes as 'unacceptable' as they would 'result in the Defence Force being reduced to inefficiency [and] encourage an attempt against national service' (White Paper on Defence, 1986: 6).

The churches and the End Conscription Campaign

The widespread deployment of troops also encouraged liberal and radical members of the English-speaking churches to become active in the End Conscription Campaign (ECC), formed at the end of 1983. This involvement consolidated the alliance of secular organisations and religious groups of different denominations and faiths in the area of war resistance.

Church youth groups and social action committees became affiliated to the ECC, religious leaders frequently spoke on its platforms, and the churches as institutions participated in its activities. Church members were particularly involved in the 'Troops out of the Townships' and 'Working for a Just Peace' campaigns of 1985 and 1986. The churches also provided an important source of solidarity when the organisation came under state attack, and when its activists were detained and conscientious objectors imprisoned in the mid-1980s.

Christian activists, however, were dissatisfied with the extent of church action around conscription and militarisation. They felt that insufficient work was being done to educate and involve white clergy and congregations at the grassroots level. In 1985 they formed ECC churches groups around the country to address this need.

Some of these groups offered a counselling service to conscripts. Others provided educational resources to clergy, and held programmes for youth groups, social action committees, and school and university societies. They also successfully encouraged the participation of clergy and lay people in ECC activities.

Christ has called all Christians to be peacemakers. This call becomes particularly significant in times of conflict and violence. We need to promote peace by working for an end to injustice in whatever ways lie open to us. Involvement in the ECC is a concrete way for Christians to express their commitment to peace and justice for all people. (Extract from ECC press statement, 1985)

The Churches' Alternative National Service Project

The Churches' Alternative National Service Project (CANSP) was initiated by the SACBC in 1986 and is currently being discussed by other denominations. The programme will offer conscripts the kind of alternative service which the churches have long demanded of the government. Conscripts who are unwilling to serve in the SADF, and who are either not eligible for or do not want to go before the Board for Religious Objection, will be able to work in a church or welfare organisation for the same length of time as military service.

Churches that agree to participate in the programme will be responsible for placing the conscript in a suitable body and for paying him. Since the conscript's work will not free him from his military obligations, the churches will also undertake to support him if he is prosecuted for disobeying a call-up.

The chaplaincy debate

One of the most controversial church debates throughout the 1970s and 1980s has centred on the participation of religious ministers, from all denominations, as military chaplains in the SADF. Chaplains wear military uniform, are paid by the SADF according to their rank, and are subject to army discipline. They are required to undergo military training, including combat training with weapons (CIIR, 1982: 67).

The position of the SADF Chaplains' Corps is that 'the church cannot detach itself from the struggle of the SADF' (*ibid.*). Chaplains are expected to identity fully with the SADF and to boost the morale of the fighting men. 'When the men in uniform defy the Marxist danger with arms, they are assisted by the Chaplain with the weapon of the Gospel. A man in uniform is made aware of his calling, to live and if need be to die for his country, South Africa.' (SADF publication quoted in *Objector*, 2, 4)

The partisan nature of military chaplaincy gave rise to a concern within the churches that it provides the army with theological and moral legitimacy. The 1974 Hammanskraal resolution of the SACC called 'on those of its member churches who have Chaplains in the military forces to reconsider the basis on which they are appointed and to investigate the state of pastoral care available to the communicants at present in exile or under arms beyond our borders and to seek ways and means of ensuring that such pastoral care may be properly exercised' (quoted in CIIR, 1982: 68).

Black Christians began to challenge their white fellow Christians to consider the contradiction of criticising the actions of the SADF, yet continuing to provide it with moral support. They issued a statement in preparation for the SACC national conference in 1976:

Black Christians call on all churches in South Africa to withdraw recognition of chaplains appointed and paid by the SADF, and to make their own independent arrangements for pastoral care of all persons involved in armed struggle on both sides of the border *(ibid.)*.

The debate was particularly sharp in those churches whose membership was predominantly black but whose leadership was largely white. Two central issues emerged – the 'demilitarisation' of the chaplaincy and ministry to the guerilla forces operating against the apartheid state. The 1984 SACC national conference adopted a statement urging its member churches 'to demilitarize their chaplains by relieving them of the symbols of military status like rank and uniform; . . . to undertake all training and financing of their chaplains; . . . [and] to bring their chaplains under church authority, thereby releasing them from military influence' (quoted in Moll, 1984: 304). The Methodist Church in 1976 and the SACBC in 1978 had set themselves similar guidelines (CIIR, 1982: 70–2). The Namibian churches have taken an even stronger stand. They do not allow SADF personnel to attend their services in uniform, and have refused to allow their clergy to participate in the chaplaincy programme of the 'foreign army' (*Cape Times,* 10.7.1985).

The churches' response to the challenge to minister to 'the other side' in the conflict has been slower. Only a few churches have responded in practice. The Anglican church in Namibia has established a presence in SWAPO camps (CIIR, 1982: 72). The Methodist Conference of 1980 decided to extend its chaplaincy to the guerilla forces, accept financial responsibility for that ministry, and call for volunteers to serve in it *(ibid.)*.

Conclusion

The English-speaking churches have traditionally been engaged in protest against apartheid, but have been reluctant to become involved in active opposition (Kairos Document, 1986: 9–16). The tension between the churches' white-dominated leadership and their pre-dominantly black membership has prodded them into 'protest' but kept them from 'challenge'.

In matters of war resistance, however, the churches have moved further. Their latest initiative, CANSP, for example offers a concrete alternative for conscientious objectors and comes close to civil disobedience. The churches' militancy in this area has been the result of the external context of growing militarisation, and internal pressure from black Christians and small groups of white activists. In particular, the churches have felt obliged to express solidarity with, and pastoral support to, Christian conscripts unwilling to serve in the SADF.

The CANSP initiative is a direct challenge to the government and will undoubtedly heighten church–state conflict around the issue of military service. This conflict will not be resolved until the government recognises the fundamental right to freedom of conscience.

References

Introduction

1. I would like to express my thanks to a number of friends who read and commented on the first draft of this chapter, particularly Laurie Nathan, David Shandler, Mark Swilling, Kathy Satchwell, Graeme Simpson, Rob Davies, Jean Leger, William Cobbett and Jon Hyslop.

2. While it seems accurate to describe the pattern of violence as 'episodic', it is important to note how this violence is escalating. According to official statistics a total of 238 guerilla attacks took place in the first 10 months of 1988, compared with 234 during 1987, 230 in 1986, 136 in 1985 and 44 in 1984. This means that there has been a 640 per cent increase in the number of guerilla attacks; from 3,6 a month in 1984 to 23,4 a month in 1988 (*Weekly Mail*, 23.12.1988).

3. However, there is legislation on the statute books to enable such requisitioning.

4. While they are often associated, there is no one-to-one relationship between militarism and repression. 'One cannot look at the extent of militarism in a given country – whether judged in terms of military expenditure as a percentage of GNP, the number of soldiers per head of population, or the size and sophistication of the weapons system – and draw any automatic conclusions about the intensity of repression there . . . The US is more heavily armed and has a higher number of soldiers per head of the population than Guatemala or Haiti or Indonesia; yet repression and social exploitation is far more intense in these countries than it is in the US.' (Randle, 1981: 86)

5. Grundy defines the 'security establishment' as 'all those individuals and institutions, whether a formal part of the government and administrative apparatus of the state, or attached to private and parastatal organisations, that are concerned with the maintenance of the South African state primarily by developing and employing the coercive instrument of the state or by weakening by various means the coercive arms of hostile states' (Grundy, 1983: 2). A further difficulty about lumping the SADF and the SAP together is that it ignores the tensions between competing factions within the state's coercive apparatus. The SADF and the SAP represent organisational bases for different leadership groupings, which are often in conflict over the control and direction of state-security strategy.

6. The structure of the SADF shows an extensive reliance on conscripted manpower. The periods of compulsory military service have been progressively extended over the last 20 years in a chronology that parallels increasing black resistance to the apartheid state.

7. Lasch sees this siege mentality infiltrating all aspects of cultural, social and political life in advanced capitalist societies. It is a mentality he attempts to capture in his concept of 'the minimal self'. He writes, 'people have lost confidence in the future. Faced with an escalating arms race, an increase in crime and terrorism, environmental deterioration, and the prospect of a long-term economic decline, they have begun to prepare for the worst, sometimes by building fallout shelters and laying in provisions, more commonly by executing a kind of emotional retreat from the long-term

commitments that presuppose a stable, secure and orderly world.' (Lasch, 1985: 16) This response is dramatically evident among many South African whites.

1. The nuts and bolts of military power: the structure of the SADF

1. The most widely reported of the South African hit squads is the 'Z Squad', allegedly formed under the Bureau for State Security, then transferred to the National Intelligence Service (see Davies *et al.*, 1986: 194; *Sunday Star*, 10.4.88).

2. Tens of thousands of activists have experienced harassment, attacks and threats to their persons, property and families (see *Sunday Star*, 30.10.88; *Sunday Tribune*, 25.9.88).

3. The best-known incident involved Recce Major Wynand du Toit, captured in Angola by FAPLA on 21 May 1985. He and his fellow commandos were to have sabotaged the Gulf Oil complex in Cabinda and attributed the action to UNITA. Du Toit's capture exposed a number of realities about the SADF's destabilisation campaign and UNITA's dependency on it.

4. See the chapter by Swilling and Phillips in the present volume.

2. 'Platskiet-politiek': the role of the Union Defence Force, 1910–1924

1. I am extremely grateful to David Everatt, who typed and undertook to edit this text. His encouragement and support were invaluable.

2. For a full account of the strike see Katz, 1976, and U.G.55 and 56–1913.

3. The Defence Act of 1912 was based on the military system which pertained in Britain, but it incorporated the commando system used in the former Boer Republics and a diluted commando system extant in the former Cape and Natal colonies.

4. See works by Davenport, Garson and Spies listed in the bibliography.

3. The power to defend: an analysis of various aspects of the Defence Act

1. See also judgment in *State* v *Ivan Peter Toms* who was sentenced to serve a period of 630 days' imprisonment in the Regional Court at Wynberg on 1 March 1988. Charles Bester, an 18-year-old matriculant, was sentenced to 6 years' imprisonment in September 1988.

2. A plethora of legislation pertaining to secrecy exists but is not dealt with in this chapter: National Key Points Act No. 102 of 1980; Internal Security Act No. 74 of 1982; Protection of Information Act No. 84 of 1982; Police Act No. 7 of 1958; Prisons Act No. 8 of 1959; Nuclear Energy Act No. 92 of 1982; and so on.

4. Manpower and militarisation: women and the SADF

1. Women's employment in armaments production is only a fraction of the work that maintains militarisation. 'Militarised work refers to any labour organised and exploited in the allegedly civilian sector of the economy to produce goods and services that military officials claim they need' (Enloe, 1983: 175).

2. From this premise flows James's main argument, that military conflict will persist until anti-militarists find an adequate substitute (the 'moral equivalent') for this function. See James, 1966: 179-90.

3. The Council decided that only women employees whose husbands are doing or have done military service would be eligible to receive up to 96 working days' leave on full pay, on condition they pledged to work for the Council for a further year. All other women employees would have to apply for the normal government maternity allowance based on a percentage of their salaries (*Weekly Mail*, 24.1.1986). Controversy resulted but the Council's Staff Board Chairman defended the proposal saying it was 'merely a gesture' similar to that made in wartime to women whose men had gone off to fight (*Star*, 28.1.1986). After numerous objections were lodged the decision was dropped.

4. This theme of sacrifice was poignantly expressed after the 1973 Yom Kippur War in Israel by Naomi Zorea whose second son died in that war (her first having died in the

Six Day War of 1967). In an open 'Letter to the Daughters of Israel' she spoke of women's role in Israel at war. 'No, ours is not an impotent participation in the process of human history . . . we bestow things that are as basic as sun and soil. We bestow life itself, and the first pleasures, food, feel, smell, the beginnings of the capacity to love.' In her view 'the mothers are the strong, the determiners of fate, not the determined.' This was referred to by Yitzhak Rabin, then premier, as 'the supreme sacrifice – not her own death, but that of her husband or son' (Hazelton in Herschel, 1983: 83).

5. As 'God's police' women are a source of moral authority; as 'damned whores' a source of dangerous sexuality (Summers, 1975).

6. Other white women who became ANC activists have met a worse fate than prison. Jeanette Curtis and Ruth First were both killed by parcel bombs allegedly sent by South African agents.

5. Troops in the townships, 1984–1987

1. This was not the first time the SADF was deployed inside the country. Troops were mobilised in 1961 after the Sharpeville massacre and in 1976–7 during the Soweto uprising. The Defence Act (1957) provides that the SADF's secondary function is 'service in the prevention or suppression of internal disorder in the Republic' (Section 3(2)a). Soldiers have also increasingly been employed to assist the SAP in 'crime-prevention operations' – between 1983 and 1984 some 43 000 soldiers were used in 'ordinary police work' (*Cape Times*, 19.5.1984).

2. The paramilitary character of the SAP has its roots in the role of the colonial police force, and in the cultural tradition of the Afrikaans community which fused civil and military activities. Police training currently includes instruction in the use of military weaponry, and SAP members are routinely sent on 'operational duty' to northern Namibia (Brewer, 1988: 177).

3. The incidents referred to were revealed in the Kannemeyer Commission of Enquiry into the police shootings at Langa, Uitenhage, on 21 March 1985, and in a court case involving police officers who had 'panel beaten' an elderly black man to death (Shärf, 1988).

4. The survey was conducted by Dr Mike Sutcliffe of the University of Natal, and reported in *At Ease*, May 1986.

5. See for example Southern African Catholic Bishops Conference, 1984; Cooke, 1986; Black Sash, 1986; Detainees' Parents Support Committee, 1986.

6. The psychological experiences of white conscripts in the black townships

1. The chapter is based on my BA Hons dissertation, 'Plucking the wings off butterflies: a phenomenological investigation of the experiences of white SADF conscripts in the black townships', Department of Psychology, University of the Witwatersrand, January 1986.

2. Some of the most useful are: Lifton, 1971; Gault, 1971; Haley, 1974; Borus, 1973; Brett and Ostroff, 1985; Hendin and Haas, 1984; Hendin *et al.*, 1981; Laufer *et al.*, 1985; Van der Kolk *et al.*, 1984; and Yager *et al.*, 1984.

9. The South African Defence Force in Angola

1. The nature of the various movements, and their social composition, base and leadership, have all been the subject of an extensive literature. Some characterisations, such as Marcum's (1969), give ethnic and linguistic factors greatest weight. Other writers like Davidson (1972) tend to view ideology as the defining characteristic of the various movements. My approach derives from my reading of Heimer (1979).

2. Documents published in *Afrique-Asie*, 61, July 1974, reproduced correspondence between Savimbi and the Portuguese military on collaboration in mutual avoidance in the east in 1972, and exchanges regarding joint plans to identify and attack the MPLA and FNLA.

3. The Angolan civil war of 1974–6 is well documented. Because of its significance

much effort has been devoted by various writers in showing that one side or other in the conflict began the process of armed escalation. Among the more useful sources are Hallett (1977), a very thorough and careful piece of research, Marquez (1977) which presents the Cuban version, and Stockwell (1978) which provides an insider's view of the CIA role in the conflict.

4. The details of the invasion are well covered elsewhere, e.g. by Wolfers and Bergerol, 1983, and Hallett, 1977. The discussion here deals with the broad outlines only.

5. This became possible in the absence of large-scale support for UNITA from South Africa.

6. For discussion of these issues, see Hanlon, 1986: 46-7. The issues were never officially disclosed, but were leaked through press reports, and included MPLA talks with UNITA, clamps on the ANC and SWAPO by the MPLA, and Cuban troop withdrawals.

7. Du Toit's subsequent account of his mission, published on his release, avoids all important details and holds to the reconnaissance version put out by the SADF.

10. State power in the 1980s: from 'total strategy' to 'counter-revolutionary warfare'

1. This framework is adapted from a work on the Latin American military by A. Stepan (1988).

2. According to Webster (1988), trade unions have 'two faces', one located in the formal industrial relations system in political society and the other a component of the social movements in civil society.

3. For more detailed analyses of the relationship between overall structural contradictions and reform policy, see W. Cobbett *et al.*, 1986.

4. To argue these policy shifts were *ad hoc* responses to popular pressure emanating from black communities and liberal white sectors (e.g. big business) is to question a previous assumption held by Cobbett *et al.* (1986) that they flowed from a coherent policy package worked out by a cabal of top-level reformers in the state and business. The pressures, contradictions and incoherencies produced a series of policy reversals that were reactive rather than proactive in character. They may have been part of an overarching 'regional federal' programme in the minds of some, but there is no evidence of a hegemonic consensus.

12. The militarisation of urban controls: the establishment of a security management system in Mamelodi, 1986–1988

1. For a full account of this period, and an analysis of the political and strategic implications of 'people's power', see Boraine, 1987.

2. Nationally, the SADF has erected 14 military bases in black residential areas, at a total cost of R5,7 million (*Cape Times*, 8.6.1988).

3. A detailed summary of the regulations is provided by SAIRR, 1986: 830-45. Also see D. Webster, 1987.

4. An alternative name given to the municipal police by some residents is 'Sunlights', after a soap commercial on TV2 'promising a fast response to your washing problems'. Note that municipal police, set up in the wake of political unrest in September 1984, are different from the 'special' police (or 'kitskonstabels'), first recruited in September 1986 and sent into action after three weeks' police training.

5. My understanding of the NSMS has been drawn from five sources in particular. They are Selfe, 1986; Philip, 1987; Merrifield, 1987; Seegers, 1988; and Grundy, 1986.

6. For various examples of the Bureau for Information's disinformation campaigns, see Black Sash, 1987.

7. See joint statement issued by the Mamelodi Youth Organisation and the Mamelodi Civic Association on the alleged escape of Stanza Bopape and the detention of other Mamelodi leaders, 11 July 1988.

13. The militarisation of the bantustans

1. The author would like to acknowledge the help of Karen Schreiber with some of the research which went into this chapter and for reading and commenting on the draft.

2. The Lebowa Act passed in 1986 was declared null and void after court action in 1987.

3. For further debates on the army and modernisation in Africa, see, for instance: K. Fidel (ed), *Militarism in developing countries* (Brunswick, N.J., 1975); H. Bienen (ed), *The role of the military in underdeveloped countries* (Princeton University Press, 1967).

15. The private sector and the security establishment

1. The Old Mutual defines inward industrialisation as 'domestically generated growth based upon supplying basic consumer products (e.g. clothing, shoes, furniture, basic foodstuffs) and facilities (e.g. low-cost housing) to the rapidly urbanising black population, with the increasing labour force coming from the rural areas simultaneously finding employment in these expanding industries'.

16. The politics and economics of the armaments industry in South Africa

1. 'My kinderlewe was een van kleilat gooi saam met die bruin seuns en groot word met my ouers se belangstellings.'

2. Frankel talks of a 'lower-order military-industrial complex', while much of Ratcliffe's discussion is focussed on the existence in South Africa of a 'Department III' within the South African economy.

3. See here R. Vayrynen, 'The role of transnational corporations in the military sector of South Africa', *JSAA*, 5, 2 (1980); Submission by the Anti-Apartheid Movement of Great Britain to the Public Hearings on the Activities of Transnational Corporations in South Africa and Namibia, 'How Britain arms apartheid' (United Nations, New York, September 1985); and Western Massachusetts Association of Concerned African Scholars (eds), *US military involvement in southern Africa* (South End Press, Boston, 1978), pp. 131-249.

18. Defence expenditure and arms procurement in South Africa

1. I am indebted for comment and the loan of material to Anton Eberhard, Peter Moll, Laurie Nathan, Mary Reynolds, Annette Seegers and James Selfe.

2. Throughout the paper 'defence expenditure', 'military expenditure' and 'military outlays' are used interchangeably.

3. Blackaby and Ohlson comment: 'in the six years up to 1981 the British Government spent some £1 billion on developing a new warhead for its Polaris missiles. The student of British military statistics would not have been able to discover this fact . . . [except] that the new Conservative government found the revelation of the figure was a useful way of discomforting the Labour Party.' (1987: 13)

4. As Seegers notes: 'the NSMS has driven government spending on security issues deeper into the recesses of the state . . . [in addition to] the national tier . . . it has created several other secret levels of expenditure on the regional, sub- and mini-regional, and local levels . . . [and] thus has driven state expenditure on security further away from the white electorate's inspection . . .' (1988: 17, 19).

5. Total defence expenditure for 1987/8 has been deflated (by the production price index) up to the end of 1987; because the budget year is longer than the calendar year this may slightly exaggerate the calculated real increase.

6. 'Between 1971 and 1985, major conventional weapons valued at $286 billion in constant (1985) US dollars were imported by countries in the Third World. That is almost four times the value recorded for the previous two decades . . . .' (Brzoska and Ohlson, 1987: 1) One hypothesis is that increased numbers of 'military-controlled governments' may influence this trend (Sivard, 1985: 23).

7. Recent contributions are by Brzoska and Ohlson, 1986; Deger, 1986; Deger and Sen, 1987; Katz, 1984; Neuman, 1984; and Wulf, 1987a, 1987b.

8. The average cost per barrel of crude oil imported into South Africa in 1986 was R33–41 (HAD, June 1987: 57).

9. 'Economic sanctions, 17 per cent inflation, high unemployment and the lack of investments describe the economic situation in South Africa, which is financing a big military machine' (SIPRI, 1987: 148).

19. A 'battlefield of perceptions': state discourses on political violence, 1985–8

1. This is not to deny the relevance of the material context and configuration of class and other interests, which have underpinned the development of these discourses. Indeed, to see these state discourses as a carefully fashioned (albeit not fully controllable) instrument in the current political struggle, is to set the content analysis within this wider context from the start.

2. However, the television channels aimed at a black audience were not monitored.

3. See also TV1 news of 23 March 1985 (8 p.m.), 24 April 1985 (6 p.m.), 9 May 1985 (8 p.m.), 9 July 1985 (8 p.m.), 7 August 1985 (6 p.m.), 11 August 1985 (8 p.m.), 19 May 1986 (5.45 p.m.), 22 May 1986 (8 p.m.), 3 February 1987 (Network), 11 June 1987 (Network), 5 May 1988 (8 p.m.).

4. See also TV1 news of 17 October 1985 (late), 16 October 1985 (7 p.m.), 25 October 1985 (7 p.m.), 11 August 1985 (8 p.m.), 20 May 1986 (5.45 p.m.), 11 June 1986 (5.45 p.m.), 3 February 1987 (Network).

5. See also TV1 news, 12 April 1985 and 9 May 1985.

6. See also TV1 news of 24 March 1985 (8 p.m.), 27 March 1985 (6 p.m.), 23 March 1985 (6 p.m.), 5 April 1985 (8 p.m.), 12 April 1985 (8 p.m.), 24 April 1985 (8 p.m.), 9 July 1985 (8 p.m.), 2 October 1985 (7 p.m.), 11 August 1985 (8 p.m.), 23 April 1986 (5.45 p.m.), 20 May 1986 (5.45 p.m.), 9 June 1986 (8 p.m.), 3 February 1987 (Network).

7. Media representation of Inkatha's role in township conflict must, however, be contrasted with coverage of Inkatha's stance against sanctions. In the latter case, Inkatha is vaunted as a champion of reason and restraint.

8. For example, see television coverage of the launch of the Inkatha-controlled union, UWUSA, 1 May 1986. This discussion of the portrayal of Inkatha is still tentative, requiring further research. But it suggests a contradiction between the visual images of Inkatha, and the state's verbal affirmation of Chief Buthelezi as the champion of 'law and order and peaceful change' (*Citizen*, 30.9.1985).

20. Works of friction: current South African war literature

1. 'New' only in the sense that the theme of border war has resurfaced in South African literature in the last ten years after a lull of several decades. There is a significant number of writings on the earlier frontier wars, as well as on the Anglo–Boer wars, where the notion of frontiers and group divisions and loyalties are predominant.

2. The original term *grensliteratuur* was used specifically to refer to Afrikaans literature on war, but currently the term is used more broadly to include English writings.

3. In, for example, S. Muller, *Alleenduif en ander vertellinge* (1981), a situation is described where the mother of a prospective soldier visits a camp, and is made to lose her reservations, when she encounters the warmth, compassion and helpfulness of young soldiers and army personnel.

4. See, for example, P. Wilhelm, *At the end of a war* (1981), in the short story 'Zimbabwe', where the narrator is a war journalist recounting his experiences in Africa, and juxtaposing those experiences with his disintegrating personal life.

5. As in the poem 'A child who survived the soldiers' by Shadrack Pooe in *Staffrider* (7, 1, 1988), where the poem ends as follows:

They asked where I came from,
I told them my mother, father, grandmother,
    brother and I
All fled from the country.
To find this life, this death, this horror in
    Azania.
These, they told me, were the doings of oppressors,
These, they told me, were the doings of racialists,
These, they told me, were the massacres of
    Azania.

6. P.C. Jones, *War and the novelist* (1976), sets out the following characteristics as being definitive of war literature: war is used as the context within which to explore moralistic-didactic notions of 'human nature'; war provides the framework for the examination of violence, authoritarianism and compliance; war is seen as the ideal arena for the investigation of psychological dynamics such as the relationship between sexuality and violence, deprivation and violence, repression and violence, etc.; the technology of war, especially in relation to nuclear war, becomes a major theme; often accounts of war are attempts to counteract distorted media perspectives.

7. This novel is based on true events, according to the author.

8. South African whites, other than the police and the army, are not exposed to these situations, either physically, or through the media, but because they are aware that 'something is going on', and do not know the extent of it, they psychologically feel intensely threatened.

22. Shopping for war: an analysis of consumerist militarism

1. A crude Marxist analysis assumes that capital has an economic interest in war production and that the state, as a representative of capital, wages war on capital's behalf (Shaw, 1984: 7-13). Thus the creation of militarised consumer markets is a consequence of the drive to create new profitable markets and to socialise the populace into accepting war. This instrumentalist relationship is too simple. For example, consumer products may originate from research for the military, but lose their military function when marketed for mass consumption. The video-camera was developed for the United States army, but Japanese manufacturers developed its commercial possibilities. Video-game war simulations, in contrast, have retained their military connotations even though they are sold as games of skill and strategy.

2. Studies on the effect of television violence suggest that a direct unmediated promotion of aggressive and violent behaviour is unlikely. Violent behavioural scripts depicted on visual media must be reinforced by similar norms in other areas of social interaction. See for example a special issue on media violence and anti-social behaviour in *Journal of Social Issues*, 42, 3 (1986). However, concern about the effects of war toys and television violence has led to a declaration of an international War Toy Boycott which now covers 28 countries. The International Coalition Against Violent Entertainment is supported in 17 countries. Such public lobbying against war toys has affected sales. War toys continue to be favourite purchases but their rating amongst the top twenty best-selling toys has dropped. In 1985 war toys made up 9–13 of the best sellers. In 1987 they constituted 6–8 of the top twenty placements (*Star*, 13.1.1988).

3. This is still relatively small compared to *Your Family*'s or *Femina*'s print-run of 150 000 each.

4. The photo-mag is written in Afrikaans. These are the authors' translations.

23. Marching to a different beat: the history of the End Conscription Campaign

1. For a history of war resistance until 1982, see CIIR, 1982.

2. Section 121(c) makes it an offence to do anything to support or encourage any person to fail or refuse to render military service.

3. See for example *Cape Times*, 13.2.1986; *Cape Times*, 24.2.1987; and *Weekly Mail*, 4.3.1988.

4. A University of Cape Town faculty dean worked out that 80 per cent of the chartered accountants who had qualified in his department over the past twenty years had emigrated. They left 'primarily because of the waste of their time and skills when in the army and because of the army's role in the townships' (Jasper Walsh MP, ECC public meeting, 10.12.1987).

5. In August 1985 the ECC and the South African Council of Churches presented memoranda along these lines to the Geldenhuys Committee, an SADF committee investigating various aspects of Defence Force policy. The Committee rejected the proposed changes as 'unacceptable', as they would 'result in the Defence Force being reduced to inefficiency [and] encourage an attempt against national service' (Defence White Paper, 1986: 6).

6. The Stellenbosch University administration banned the ECC from operating on the campus within two months of the formation of its branch there. The branch was forced to work through other student organisations and off-campus.

7. According to one National Party MP, Mr Fick, 'the ECC is linked to the United Democratic Front, the African National Congress, the SA Communist Party and the Communist parties in Britain, the US and the Soviet Union. Where does the ECC get its funds? I will say no more than that it gets them from the same international sources as the African National Congress'. (*Citizen*, 11.2.1987)

24. Waging peace: church resistance to militarisation
1. This article draws substantially on an earlier paper by Law, Lund and Winkler, 'Conscientious objection: the church against apartheid's violence', 1987.

2. Religious objectors may apply to a Board for Religious Objection for one of three alternatives to military service: (a) non-combatant service in the SADF for the same period as military service; (b) non-combatant service in a non-military uniform in the SADF for one-and-a-half times the length of military service; and (c) community service in a government, provincial or municipal department for one-and-a-half times the length of military service.

3. However, in terms of their faith, the Witnesses do not recognise the authority of the state to decide over their conscience, and thus reject the findings of the Board. In practice, they apply to the Board but refuse to render their community service. They appear before a military court which sentences them to a six-year jail sentence. They are then granted parole from this sentence and are allowed to do community service instead.

4. Resolutions of the Methodist Church (1985), Catholic Bishops Conference (1984) and Presbyterian Church (1984).

Bibliography

Adams, G. 1986. Pentagon maneuvers for high funding. *Bulletin of the Atomic Scientists*, 42

Adorno, T. 1969. *The authoritarian personality.* New York: Harper

Aitcheson, J. 1988. *Numbering the dead: political violence in the Pietermaritzburg region.* Pietermaritzburg: Centre for Adult Education, University of Natal

Andreski, S. 1968. *Military organisation and society.* Berkeley: University of California Press

Archer, S. 1987. South African industrial experience in perspective. *Social Dynamics*, 13

Archibald, H.C. and Tuddenham, R.D. 1965. Persistent stress reactions after combat – a twenty year follow-up. *Archives of General Psychiatry*, 12

Armstrong, A. 1987. 'Hear no evil, see no evil, speak no evil': media restrictions and the state of emergency. In *South African Review 4*, ed. SARS. Johannesburg: Ravan

The art of counter-revolutionary warfare. 1987? Unsourced document circulated by DMI

Bahro, R. 1982. *Socialism and survival.* London: Heretic Books

Barthes, R. 1973. *Mythologies.* London: Paladin

Bell, P. 1988. General manoeuvres. *Leadership SA*, 7, 1

Berghahn, V.R. 1981. *Militarism: the history of an international debate.* Cambridge: Cambridge University Press

Birmingham, D. 1978. The twenty-seventh of May: an historical note on the abortive 1977 coup in Angola. *African Affairs*, 77

Blackaby, F. 1983. Introduction: the military sector and the economy. In *The structure of the defence industry*, ed. N. Ball and M. Leibenberg, London: Croom Helm

Blackaby, F. 1987. Preface. In *Peace, defence and economic analysis*, ed. C. Schmidt and F. Blackaby. London: Macmillan

Blackaby, F. and Ohlson, T. 1987. Military expenditure and the arms trade. In *The economics of military expenditure*, ed. C. Schmidt. London: Macmillan

Black Sash. 1986. *Memorandum on the suffering of children.* Johannesburg: Black Sash

Black Sash. 1987. Introduction to the National Security Management System. Paper presented to Black Sash National Conference, 1987

Black Sash. 1988. *'Greenflies': municipal police in the Eastern Cape.* Cape Town: Black Sash

Blatchford, M. 1988. The last drop of blood. *Work in Progress*, 55

Boraine, A.M. 1987. Mamelodi: from parks to people's power; a survey of community organisation in South Africa, 1979-1986. Unpublished B.A. (Honours) thesis, University of Cape Town

Boraine, A. 1988. Security management and urban upgrading under the state of emergency: a case study of state strategy in Mamelodi township, 1986-1988. Paper presented to ASSA conference, Durban

Borus, J.F. 1973. Reentry: 1. Adjustment issues facing the Vietnam returnee. *Archives of General Psychiatry*, 28

Davies, R. 1987. South African strategy towards Mozambique since Nkomati. *Transformation*, 3

Davies, R. 1987a. South African regional policy post-Nkomati: May 1985-December 1986. In *South African Review 4*, ed. SARS. Johannesburg: Ravan

Davies, R. and O'Meara, D. 1985. Total strategy in southern Africa: an analysis of South African regional policy since 1978. *Journal of Southern African Studies*, 11, 2

Davies, R., O'Meara, D. and Dlamini, S. 1984. *The struggle for South Africa*. London: Zed Books

Deger, S. 1986. *Military expenditure in Third World countries*. London: Routledge

Deger, S. and Sen, S. 1987. Defence industrialisation, technology transfer and choice of techniques in LDCs. In *Structural change, economic interdependence and world development*, vol. 2, ed. S. Borner and A. Taylor. London: Macmillan

Detainees' Parents Support Committee. 1986. *Abantwana bazabalaza: memorandum on children under repression in South Africa*. Johannesburg: DPSC

De Villiers, M. and Roux, M. 1988. Restructuring apartheid: terror and disorganisation in the Eastern Cape, 1986-1988. Paper presented to the Nineteenth ASSA Conference, University of Durban-Westville, July 1988

Diokno, M.S. 1988. Self-styled guardians of democracy: vigilantes in the Philippines. Paper presented to CIIR conference on Death Squads and Vigilantes, London, May 1988

Drechsler, H. 1980. *Let us die fighting*. London: Zed Books

Dubow, S. 1987. Race, civilisation and culture: the elaboration of segregationist discourse in the inter-war years. In *The politics of race, class and nationalism in twentieth century South Africa*, ed. S. Marks and S. Trapido. London and New York: Longman

Durand, J. and Smit, D. 1987. The Afrikaner churches on war and violence. In *Theology and violence: the South African debate*, ed. C. Villa-Vicencio. Johannesburg: Skotaville

ECC. 1985. The 'internal enemy' – civil war in South Africa. *South African Outlook*, April 1985

ECC. 1988. *Angola: the war and the prospects for peace. Documents and articles*

Economist Intelligence Report. 1987. *Angola to the 1990s: the potential for recovery*. Special report no. 1079 by T. Hodges. London

Eide, A. and Thee, M. (eds). 1980. *Problems of contemporary militarism*. London: St Martin's Press

Eisenhart, R.W. 1975. You can't hack it, little girl: a discussion of the covert psychological agenda of modern combat training. *Journal of Social Issues*, 31, 4

Enloe, C. 1983. *Does khaki become you? The militarization of women's lives*. London: Pluto Press

Evans, G. 1983. The role of the military in education in South Africa. Unpublished B.A. (Honours) thesis, University of Cape Town

Evans, G. 1983a. SADF and the Civic Action Program. *Work in Progress*, 29

Evans, M. and Phillips, M. 1988. Intensifying civil war: the role of the South African Defence Force. In *State, resistance and change in South Africa*, ed. P. Frankel, N. Pines and M. Swilling. London: Croom Helm

Feinstein, A. *et al.* 1986. Some attitudes towards conscription in South Africa. *Psychology in Society*, 5

Ferreira, J. 1985. *Sitatie vir 'n rewolusie*. Cape Town: Human and Rousseau

Fine, P. and Getz, A. 1986. An examination of the role of women in the militarisation of South African society. Unpublished paper, Department of Sociology, University of the Witwatersrand

Flower, K. 1987. *Serving secretly: Rhodesia's CIO chief on record*. Alberton: Galago Books

Frankel, P.H. 1984. *Pretoria's praetorians: civil–military relations in South Africa*. Cambridge: Cambridge University Press

Brett, E.A. and Ostroff, R. 1985. Imagery and post-traumatic stress disorder: an overview. *American Journal of Psychiatry*, 142, 4

Brewer, J. 1980. Childhood revisited: the genesis of the modern toy. *History Today*, 30

Brewer, J.D. (eds.) 1988. *The police, public order and the state.* London: Macmillan

Breytenbach, W. 1987. Federation of a special kind: the South African case. Paper presented to conference on South Africa in Transition, City University of New York, September–October 1987

Bridgland, F. 1986. *Jonas Savimbi: a key to Africa.* Johannesburg: Macmillan

Brooks, H. 1986. The strategic defence initiative as science policy. *International Security*, 11

Brownmiller, S. 1976. *Against our will: men, women and rape.* Harmondsworth: Penguin

Brzoska, M. and Ohlson, T. (eds). 1986. *Arms production in the Third World.* London: Taylor and Francis

Brzoska, M. and Ohlson, T. (eds). 1987. *Arms transfers to the Third World, 1971-1985.* New York: Oxford

Bureau for Information. 1987. *The national state of emergency.* Pretoria: Bureau for Information

Campbell, J. 1956. *The hero with a thousand faces.* New York: Meridian

Cape Education Department. 1986. *Cadet Training Manual.* Cape Town: CED

Cars, H.C. 1987. Negotiations to reduce military expenditures – problems and possibilities. In *The economics of military expenditure,* ed. C. Schmidt. London: Macmillan

Cawthra, G. 1986. *Brutal force: the apartheid war machine.* London: IDAF

Cawthra, G. 1988. South Africa at war. In *South Africa in question,* ed. J. Lonsdale. London: James Currey

CENE-DPCCN. 1988. *Rising to the challenge: dealing with the emergency in Mozambique.* Maputo: CENE-DPCCN

Central Statistical Services. 1988. Production and sales – manufacturing. *Statistical News Release,* P.3041.2, February 1988

Chan, S. 1985. The impact of defense spending on economic performance: a survey of evidence and problems. *Orbis*, 29

Christie, P. 1985. *The right to learn.* Johannesburg: Ravan

CIIR. 1982. *War and conscience in South Africa: the churches and conscientious objection.* London: CIIR–Pax Christi

CIIR. 1988a. *Now everyone is afraid: the changing face of policing in South Africa.* London: CIIR

CIIR. 1988b. Vigilantes and the new policing in South Africa. Anonymous paper presented to CIIR conference on Death Squads and Vigilantes, London, May 1988

Cobbett, W., Glaser, D., Hindson, D. and Swilling, M. 1986. South Africa's regional political economy: a critical analysis of reform strategy in the 1980s. In *South Africa Review 3,* ed. SARS. Johannesburg: Ravan

Collins, R. 1974. Three faces of cruelty: towards a comparative sociology of violence. *Theory and Society,* 1

Cooke. 1986. *The war against children: South Africa's youngest victims.* New York: Lawyer's Committee for Human Rights

Crewe, M. 1987. Black and white in khaki: education and militarization in South Africa. Unpublished paper

Davenport, T.R.H. 1963. The South African Rebellion of 1914. *Economic History Review,* 77, 306

Davey, D. 1988. A phenomenological explication of problems in intimacy experienced by the returned conscript, as a result of military experiences in the South African Defence Force. Unpublished Honours thesis, Rhodes University

Davidson, B. 1972. *In the eye of the storm: Angola's people.* Harmondsworth: Penguin

Fraser, C. *Lessons learnt from past revolutionary wars.* Unpublished document
Garson, N.G. 1962. The Boer Rebellion of 1914. *History Today,* 12
Gault, W.B. 1971. Some remarks on slaughter. *American Journal of Psychiatry,* 128, 4
Gavshon, A. 1981. *Crisis in Africa.* Harmondsworth: Penguin
Geldenhuys, D. 1981. Some strategic implications of regional economic relations for the
 Republic of South Africa. *ISSUP Strategic Review,* January 1981
Geldenhuys, D. 1984. *The diplomacy of isolation: South African foreign policy-making.*
 Johannesburg: Macmillan
Geldenhuys, D. and Kotze, H. 1983. Aspects of political decision-making in South
 Africa. *Politikon,* 10, 1
Geldenhuys, D. and Venter, D. 1979. Regional cooperation: a constellation of states?
 South African Institute of International Affairs Bulletin, December 1979
Gersony, R. 1988. *Summary of Mozambican refugee accounts of principally conflict-
 related experience in Mozambique.* Washington: Department of State
Gordon, R. 1984. The San in transition: what future for the Ju/Wasi of Nyae Nyae? In
 Cultural Survival
Grundy, K. 1983. *Soldiers without politics: blacks in the South African armed forces.*
 Berkeley: University of California Press
Grundy, K. 1986. *The militarization of South African politics.* London: I.B. Tauris
Haasbroek, P.J. 1974. *Heupvuur.* Cape Town: Human and Rousseau
Haasbroek, P.J. 1976. *Skrikbewind.* Cape Town: Human and Rousseau
Haley, S.A. 1974. When the patient reports atrocities. *Archives of General Psychiatry,* 30
Hallett, R. 1978. The South African intervention in Angola 1975-76. *African Affairs,* 77
Hancock, W.K. 1962. *Smuts: the sanguine years, 1870-1919.* Cambridge: CUP
Hancock, W.K. and Van der Poel, J. 1966. *Selections from the Smuts papers,* vols. 4-6.
 Cambridge: CUP
Hanlon, J. 1986. *Beggar your neighbours: apartheid power in southern Africa.* London:
 CIIR
Hanlon, J. and Omond, R. 1987. *The sanctions handbook.* Harmondsworth: Penguin
Hartley, K. 1987. The evaluation of efficiency in the arms industry. In *Structural change,
 economic interdependence and world development,* vol. 2, ed. S. Borner and A.
 Taylor. London: Macmillan
Hartung, W. 1987. Nations vie for arms markets. *Bulletin of the Atomic Scientists,* 43
Haysom, N. 1983. *Ruling with the whip.* Johannesburg: Centre for Applied Legal
 Studies, University of the Witwatersrand
Haysom, N. 1986. *Mabangalala.* Johannesburg: Centre for Applied Legal Studies,
 University of the Witwatersrand
Hazelton, L. 1983. Old myths and images. In *On being a Jewish feminist,* ed. S. Hershel.
 New York: Schocken Books
Heitman, H.R. 1988. *South African arms and armour.* Cape Town: Struik
Heimer, F.W. 1979. *The decolonization conflict in Angola: an essay in political
 sociology.* Geneva: Institut Universitaire de Hautes Etudes Internationales
Hendin, H. *et al.* 1981. Meaning of combat and the development of post-traumatic
 stress disorder. *American Journal of Psychiatry,* 138, 11
Hendin, H. and Haas, A.P. 1984. Combat adaptations of Vietnam veterans without post-
 traumatic disorders. *American Journal of Psychiatry,* 141, 8
Hindson, D. 1987. *Pass controls and the urban African proletariat.* Johannesburg:
 Ravan
Hirson, B. 1987. Whatever did happen at Jaggersfontein? Unpublished paper presented
 at History Workshop, University of the Witwatersrand
HSRC, 1981. Work Committee Report on Guidance. Pretoria: HSRC
Human Awareness Programme. 1986. *Militarisation dossier.* Johannesburg: Human
 Awareness Programme
Huntington, S.P. 1968. *Political order in changing societies.* Princeton: Yale University
 Press

IISS. 1987. *The military balance 1987-1988*. London: IISS

International Maritime Organisation. 1986a. 'All states shall cease forthwith.' The Security Council and its arms embargo. Paper presented to the International Seminar on the UN Arms Embargo Against South Africa, London, May 1986

International Maritime Organisation. 1986b. Techniques for the procurement of military supplies. Paper presented to the International Seminar on the UN Arms Embargo Against South Africa, London, May 1986

International Maritime Organisation. 1986c. 'Self-sufficiency' and internal arms production. Paper presented to the International Seminar on the UN Arms Embargo Against South Africa, London, May 1986

Jackson, R. L. (ed.). 1987. *Security: a national strategy*. Johannesburg: Lex Patria

James, W. 1966. The moral equivalent of war. In *The pacifist conscience*, ed. P. Mayer. Harmondsworth: Penguin Books

Johnson, P. and Martin, D. 1986. *Destructive engagement*. Harare: Zimbabwe Publishing House

Jones, P.C. 1976., *War and the novelist*. Missouri: Columbia University Press

Kairos Document. 1986. *The Kairos document: challenge to the church*, 2nd ed. Johannesburg: Skotaville

Kaldor, M. 1982. Warfare and capitalism. In *Exterminism and cold war*, ed. New Left Review. London: Verso

Katjavivi, P. 1988. *A history of resistance in Namibia*. London: James Currey

Katz, E. 1976. *A trade union aristocracy*. Johannesburg: African Studies Institute, University of the Witwatersrand

Katz, J.E. (ed.) 1984. *Arms production in developing countries*. Lexington: Lexington Books

Keegan, J. 1985. *The strategic dimensions of military manpower*. Washington DC: Center for Strategic and International Studies, Georgetown University

Kennedy, G. 1983. *Defense economics*. New York: St Martin's

Kidron, M. and Smith, D. 1983. *The war atlas*. London: Pan Books

Kiljunen, K. 1981. National resistance and the liberation struggle. In *Namibia: the last colony*, ed. R. Green, M.L. Kiljunen and K. Kiljunen. London: Longman

King, W. 1986. In Symposium on Stress, Medical Association of South Africa

Klare, M.T. 1988. Secret operatives, clandestine trades: the thriving black market for weapons. *Bulletin of the Atomic Scientists*, 44

Koeberg Alert Research Group. 1987. The power of the state and the state of power: recent developments in South Africa's nuclear industry. In *South African Review 4*, ed. SARS. Johannesburg: Ravan

Konig, B. 1983. *Namibia: the ravages of war*. London: IDAF

Kruger, L. 1984. *'n Basis oorkant die grens*. Cape Town: Tafelberg

Lakob, M. 1984. *Human rights in South Africa's homelands: the delegation of repression*. New York: Fund for Free Expression

Lacey, M. 1981. *Working for boroko*. Johannesburg: Ravan

Larteguy, J. 1988. South Africa (transl. P. Cockayne). *Paris Match*, 1.7.1988

Lasch, C. 1985. *The minimal self: psychic survival in troubled times*. London: Pan Books

Laufer, R. and Gallops, M.S. 1985. Life-course effects of Vietnam combat and abusive violence – marital problems. *Journal of Marriage and the Family*, 2

Laufer, R.S., Brett, E. and Gallops, M.S. 1985. Symptom patterns associated with post-traumatic stress disorder among Vietnam veterans exposed to trauma. *American Journal of Psychiatry*, 142, 11

Law, L., Lund, C. and Winkler, H. 1987. Conscientious objection: the church against apartheid's violence. In *Theology and violence: the South African debate*, ed. C. Villa-Vicencio. Johannesburg: Skotaville

Lawyers' Committee for Human Rights. 1987. *Crisis in Crossroads*. New York: Lawyers' Committee for Human Rights

Leonard, R. 1983. *South Africa at war*. Westport: Laurence Hill

Lifton, R.J. 1971. *Home from the war: Vietnam veterans: neither victims nor executioners*. New York: Simon and Schuster

Lipton, M. 1988. *Sanctions and South Africa*. Economist Intelligence Unit Special Report No. 1119. London

Lombard, J. 1988. Housing finance and the national economic scenario. Paper presented to the conference on Finance: The Pathway to Housing, CSIR, June 1988

Louw, R. (ed). 1984. *Detention barracks*. Cape Town: Mission of the Churches for Community Development

Lowy, M. and Sader, E. 1985. The militarization of the state in Latin America. *Latin American Perspective*, 12, 4

Luckham, R. 1971. A comparative typology of civil–military relations. *Government and Opposition*, 6

McCuen, J.J. 1966. *The art of counter-revolutionary war*. London: Faber and Faber

McIntosh, G. 1980. Paper presented to COSG conference

McKenzie, D. 1983. Militarism and socialist theory. *Capital and Class*, 19

Maddison, A. 1984. Origins and impact of the welfare state, 1883-1983. *Banca Nazionale del Lavoro Quarterly Review*, 148

Malan, M. 1980. Die aanslag teen Suid-Afrika. *ISSUP Strategic Review*

Mann, M. 1987. The roots and contradictions of modern militarism. *New Left Review*, 162

Manning, P. and Green, R.H. 1986. Namibia: preparations for destabilization. In *Destructive engagement*, ed. P. Johnson and D. Martin. Harare: Zimbabwe Publishing House

Marcum, J. 1969. *The Angolan revolution. Vol. 1: The anatomy of an explosion, 1950-1962*. Cambridge, Mass.: M.I.T. Press

Marcum, J. 1978. *The Angolan revolution. Vol. 2: Exile politics and guerilla warfare 1962-1976*. Cambridge, Mass.: M.I.T. Press

Marcum, J. 1986. Angola: twenty-five years of war. *Current History*, 85

Maré, G. 1982. Repression in/through the Bantustans. In *'Homeland' tragedy, function and farce*. Braamfontein: DSG–SARS

Maré, G. and Hamilton, G. 1987. *An appetite for power: Buthelezi's Inkatha and the politics of 'loyal resistance'*. Johannesburg: Ravan

Marquez, G.G. 1977. Operation Carlotta. *New Left Review*, 101-2

Marshall, J. and Ritchie, C. 1984. *Where are the Ju/Wasi of Nyae Nyae?* Cape Town: Centre for African Studies, University of Cape Town

Martins, J.H. 1986. *Income and expenditure patterns of urban black multiple households in Pretoria, 1985*. Pretoria: Bureau for Market Research, University of South Africa

Mason, T. 1976. Women in Germany, 1925-1940. *History Workshop*, 1

Maughan Brown, D. 1984. Racial domination as crowd control: race ideology in some post-1948 liberal fiction. Paper presented to the Conference on Economic Development and Racial Domination, University of the Western Cape, October 1984

Melman, S. 1986. Limits of military power: economic and other. *International Security*, 11

Merrifield, A. 1987. Recent changes in state strategy: JMCs, national security and low intensity warfare. Unpublished paper

Merrit, N. 1988. *Detentions and the crisis in the Pietermaritzburg area, 1987-1988*. Pietermaritzburg: Centre for Adult Education, University of Natal

Merryfinch, L. 1981. Militarization/civilianization. In *Loaded questions: women in the military*, ed. W. Chapkis. Amsterdam: Transnational Institute

Methodist Church of South Africa (MCSA). 1986. Church and conscience: a collection of church and other statements on conscientious objection in South Africa. Unpublished: Christian Citizenship Department of the Methodist Church

Miliband, R. 1973. The coup in Chile. *Socialist Register*

Ministry of Law and Order. 1988. White Paper on the Organization and Functions of the South African Police. Pretoria

Moll, P.G. 1984. A theological critique of the military chaplaincy of the English-speaking churches. Unpublished M.A. thesis, University of Cape Town

Moll, P.G. 1986. Conscientious objectors under renewed attack. *South African Outlook*, October 1986

Moorsom, R. 1982. *Transforming a wasted land.* Nottingham: CIIR

Mozambique National Planning Commission. 1984. *Economic report.* Maputo

Muller, J. 1987. People's education and the National Education Crisis Committee. In *South African Review 4,* ed. SARS. Johannesburg: Ravan

Muller, J. 1982. *Alleenduif en ander vertellinge.* Pretoria: Van Schaik

Neuman, S.G. 1984. International stratification and Third World military industries. *International Organization,* 38

Niddrie, D. 1988. Namibia: a nation in waiting. *Work in Progress,* 55

NUM. 1988. Collective bargaining at Anglo American mines: a model for reform or repression. Unpublished research report

Orr, R. 1983. *Women, militarism and non-violence.* London: Peace Pledge Union

Philip, K. 1987. Total strategy and the rise of the National Security Management System in South Africa. Unpublished paper presented in Department of Sociology, University of the Witwatersrand

Phillips, M. 1988. Exploiting divisions: vigilantes and state objectives in Crossroads. Paper presented to CIIR conference on Death Squads and Vigilantes, London, May 1988

Posel, D. 1987. The language of domination. In *The politics of race, class and nationalism in twentieth century South Africa,* ed. S. Marks and S. Trapido. London and New York: Longman

Prendes, J.P. 1988. Violence, national security and democratisation in Central America. Paper presented to CIIR conference on Death Squads and Vigilantes, London, May 1988

Randle, M. 1981. Militarism and repression. *Alternatives,* 7

Ratcliffe, S. 1983. Forced relations: the state, crisis and the rise of militarism in South Africa. Unpublished Honours thesis, University of the Witwatersrand

Reppy, J. 1985. Military R & D and the civilian economy. *Bulletin of the Atomic Scientists,* 41

Republic of South Africa. 1985. *The monetary system and monetary policy in South Africa: final report of the commission of enquiry,* RP70/1984. Pretoria: Government Printer

Republic of South Africa. 1985-1988. *Estimates of the expenditure to be defrayed from state revenue account,* RP2 & 4 1985, 1986, 1987, 1988. Pretoria: Government Printer

Republic of South Africa. 1987. *Third report of the standing committee on public accounts,* G5-87. Pretoria: Government Printer

Resource Group on Military Service. 1984. *Resource booklet on military service.* Cape Town: Ezempilo Press

Rivlin, P. 1983. The burden of defence: the case of Israel. In *SIPRI Yearbook 1983 World Armaments and Disarmament.* London: Taylor and Francis

Rivlin, P. 1987. The burden of defence in developing countries. In *The economics of military expenditures,* ed. C. Schmidt. London: Macmillan

Roberts, B. 1984. The death of machothink: feminist research and the transformation of peace studies. *Women's Studies International Forum,* 7, 4

SA Barometer. 1987. The structure of the South African Defence Force. *SA Barometer,* 1, 20

SACBC. 1984. *Report on police conduct during township protests.* London: SACBC-CIIR

SACBC. 1987. *The last affidavits.* Pretoria: SACBC

Sahak, I. 1988. Israeli apartheid and the *intifada. Race and Class,* 30, 1

Schärf, W. 1988. Police abuse of power and victim assistance during apartheid's emergency. Paper presented to the Sixth International Symposium on Victimology, Jerusalem, August 1988

Schweik, S. 1987. Writing war poetry like a woman. *Critical Inquiry*, 13

Seegers, A. 1986. The military in South Africa: a comparison and a critique. *South African Internatinal*, 16, 4

Seegers, A. 1987. Apartheid's military: its origins and development. In *The state of apartheid*, ed. W. James. Boulder, Colorado: Lynne Rienner

Seegers, A. 1988. The National Security Management System: a description and theoretical inquiry. Paper presented to the Africa Seminar, Centre for African Studies, University of Cape Town, October 1988

Seegers, A. 1988a. Extending the security network to the local level. In *Government by the People?*, ed. C. Heymans and G. Tötemeyer. Johannesburg: Juta

Seekings, J. 1985. Probing the links. *Work in Progress*

Selfe, J. 1986. Democracy and militarisation: the National Security Management System. Unpublished paper

Shaw, M. (ed). 1984. *War, state and society*. London: Macmillan

Shaw, M. 1988. *Dialectics of war*. London: Pluto Press

Simpson, M.A. 1986. Post-traumatic stress disorder – a scarring of the soul. In Symposium on Stress, Medical Association of South Africa

SIPRI. 1983. *SIPRI Yearbook 1983 World Armaments and Disarmament*. London: Taylor and Francis

SIPRI. 1987. *SIPRI Yearbook 1987 World Armaments and Disarmament*. Oxford: Oxford University Press

Sivard, R.L. 1985. *World military and social expenditures 1985*. Washington: World Priorities

Sköns, E. 1983. Military prices. In *SIPRI Yearbook 1983 World Armaments and Disarmament*. London: Taylor and Francis

Smith, R.P. 1977. Military expenditure and capitalism. *Cambridge Journal of Economics*, 1

Smith, R.P. 1987. Military expenditure. In *New Palgrave Dictionary of Economics*. London: Macmillan

Smith, D. and Smith, R. 1983. *The economics of militarism*. London: Pluto Press

Soggot, D. 1986. *Namibia: the violent heritage*. London: Rex Collings

Somerville, K. 1986. *Angola: politics, economics and society*. London: Francis Pinter

South African Institute of Race Relations (SAIRR). *Annual Survey*. Johannesburg: SAIRR

South West Africa Administration. 1988. *Official Gazette Extraordinary* No. 5582. Windhoek: John Meinert (printer)

South West Africa Administration. 1988. *Official Gazette Extra-ordinary* No. 5582. Windhoek: John Meinert (printer)

Spies, S.B. 1963. The rebellion in South Africa, 1914-1915. Unpublished M.A. thesis, University of the Witwatersrand

Steenkamp, W. 1983. The South African Defence Force. *Leadership SA*, 2, 4

Stepan, A. 1988. *Rethinking military politics*. Princeton: Princeton University Press

Steyn, J.C. 1976. *Op pad na die grens*. Cape Town: Tafelberg

Steyn, J.C. 1978. *Dagboek van 'n verraaier*. Cape Town: Tafelberg

Stiehm, J. (ed). 1983. *Women and women's wars*. Oxford: Pergamon Press

Stockwell, J. 1978. *In search of enemies*. New York: W.W. Norton

Strachan, A. 1984. *'n Wêreld sonder grense*. Cape Town: Tafelberg

Strockenström, W. 1988. Agter die ysterhekke van 'Turf'. *Die Suid-Afrikaan*, 14

Summers, A. 1975. *Damned whores and God's police: the colonisation of women in Australia*. Sydney: Penguin Books

Swilling, M. 1988. Whamming the radicals. *Weekly Mail*, 20.5.1988

Swilling, M. and Phillips, M. 1988. Reform, security and white power: rethinking state strategy in the 1980s. Paper presented to ASSA Conference, Durban, 1988

Thompson, E.P. 1982. Notes on exterminism, the last stage of civilization. In *Exterminism and cold war*, ed. New Left Review. London: Verso

Thorsson, I. 1982. Study on disarmament and development. *Bulletin of the Atomic Scientists*, 38

Tomaselli, R. 1988. Social construction of the enemy: SABC and the demonisation of the ANC-terrorist. In *Hawks and doves: the pro- and anti-conscription press in South Africa*, ed. M. Graaf. Durban: Contemporary Cultural Studies Unit, University of Natal

Van der Byl, P. 1971. *From playgrounds to battlefields*. Cape Town: Timmins

Van der Kolk, B. *et al*. 1984. Nightmares and trauma: a comparison of nightmares after combat with lifelong nightmares in veterans. *American Journal of Psychiatry*, 141, 2

Van der Spuy, E. 1988. Policing the eighties: servamus et servimus? Paper presented to the Annual Congress of the Association of Sociologists in Southern Africa, University of Durban-Westville, July 1988

Vanrynen, R. 1980. The role of transnational corporations in the military sector of South Africa. *JSAA*, 5, 2

Van Zyl, J.C. 1979. Some economic aspects of national defence. The re-allocation of resources. *ISSUP Strategic Review*, April 1979

Viljoen, Lettie. 1984. *Klaaglied vir Koos*. Emmarentia: Taurus

Walker, E. 1959. *A history of southern Africa*. London: Longmans

Wandrag, A.J. 1985. Political unrest: a police view. *ISSUP Strategic Review*, October 1985

Weaver, T. 1987a. The war in Namibia: social consequences, and documentary on torture in Namibia. In *Namibia in perspective*, ed. G. Tötemeyer, V. Kandetu and W. Werner. Windhoek: Council of Churches in Namibia

Weaver, T. 1987b. Witbooi's Gibeon. *Leadership SA*, 6, 6

Weaver, T. 1988. An ordinary tale of life and death in the bush. *Weekly Mail*, 9.9.1988

Webster, D. 1987. Repression and the state of emergency. In *South African Review 4*, ed. SARS. Johannesburg: Ravan

Webster, E. 1988. The rise of social-movement unionism: the two faces of the black trade union movement in South Africa. In *State, resistance and change*, ed. P. Frankel, N. Pines, and M. Swilling, London: Croom Helm

Western Province Council of Churches. 1988. *Crisis news*.

Wilhelm, P. 1986. *At the end of a war*. Johannesburg: Ravan

Williams, R. 1985. *Towards 2000*. Harmondsworth: Penguin

Wiseman, J. 1988. Militarism, militarisation and praetorianism in South Africa. *Africa*, 58, 2

Wolfers, M. and Bergerol, J. 1983. *Angola in the front line*. London: Zed Books

Women for Peace. 1985. *'Voices from the townships': a survey on black opinion in the townships*. Johannesburg: Women for Peace

Woolf, V. 1957. *A room of one's own*. London: Hogarth Press (first edition, 1928)

World Bank. 1988. *World Development Report 1988*. Washington: World Bank

Wulf, H. 1987a. Arms industry unlimited: the economic impact of the arms sector in developing countries. In *Structural change, economic interdependence and world development*, vol. 2, ed. S. Borner and A. Taylor. London: Macmillan

Wulf, H. 1987b. Arms production in Third World countries: effects on industrialisation. In *The economics of military expenditures*, ed. C. Schmidt. London: Macmillan

Yager, J. 1975. Personal violence in infantry combat. *Archives of General Psychiatry*, 32

Yager, J. *et al*. 1984. Some problems associated with war experience in men of the Vietnam generation. *Archives of General Psychiatry*, 41

Index

Acts of Parliament: Abolition of Influx Control (1986), 141–2; Armaments (1964), 222; Armaments Development and Production (1968), 222; Armaments Development and Production (1977), 222; Atomic Energy, 206, 225; Civil Defence (1977), 52; Defence (1912), 38; Defence (1957), 40, 41; Defence (1974), 322; Defence Amendment (1982), 211; Defence Amendment (1983), 309, 322, 331; Group Areas, 139; Industrial Disputes Prevention, 29; Internal Security, 48–9; National Education Policy (1967), 289; National Key Points (1980), 206, 213; National Supplies Procurement (1970), 206, 225; Natives Land (1913), 36, 205; Official Secrets, 48; Petroleum Products Amendment (1970), 206, 225; Protection of Information, 8, 48; Publications, 48; South African Citizenship (1944), 41

African National Congress, see ANC
Afrikaner Weerstandsbeweging, 271
Alexandra, 1, 9, 167, 173, 199, 211–2
Algeria, 9
alternative service campaign (ECC), 321
Alvor Accord, 121
Ama-Afrika, 189; see also vigilantes
Amabutho, 189; see also vigilantes
ANC, 1, 21, 49, 63, 67, 69, 72, 109, 111, 142–3, 178, 204, 207, 221, 327
Anglo American Corporation, 204, 206, 211, 215
Angola, 20, 23, 40, 92, 107, 109, 149, 242, 309; attempted coup (1977), 123; economic crisis, 123, 126, 129; setbacks to SADF in, 115, 126, 229; strategic importance of, 116; war in, 5, 6, 90–1, 112, 115, 118–31, 320
'area war', concept of, 178–9
Arendt, Hannah, 1
armaments industry, 5, 16; acquisition of skills, 221; constraints on arriving at facts of, 256–8; integration of political and economic features of, 217; involvement of leading industrial corporations in, 219; procurement through production and trade, 253–6; spin-offs from, 230, 250–3; trading with Israel, 239–40
Armscor, 5, 16, 24, 52, 54, 137, 217, 229, 235, 246, 248; composition of Board, 222–3; as exporter, 223, 229, 258; history of, 220–4; links with private sector, 206–7, 224–6; objects of, 222; self-sufficiency of Armscor questioned. 224. 228
arms embargo, 23, 219, 222, 229, 232, 241–3; circumvention of, 234–5; co-production and licensing agreements as loopholes in, 234; covert action in, 235–6, 238–9; failure of, 236–8; history of, 233–5; international conference on, 234; suppliers of arms, 234
Assocom, 208, 211
Atomic Energy Corporation, 248
bantustans: corruption in, 182–3; on SA, 178, 186; intervention in by SA, 177; to maintain white power, 174, 187; as sources of instability, 182, 185, 187; vigilantes in, 190; working together with SADF and SAP, 179, 185; see also militarisation

Kabwe Conference, 1
Kentridge, Sydney, 95
kitskonstabels, 8, 16, 76–7, 199
Koeberg Alert Research Group, 6
Koevoet, 22, 26, 98
'Koornhof Bills', 192
labour unions, 141
Lawyers' Committee for Human
Rights, 7
Lesotho, 6, 17, 40, 109, 179
Lesotho Liberation Army, 17, 27, 109,
179
liability for service in SADF, 41–6
Lloyd, Major-General C., 143, 145,
180
local black authorities, 139–40, 193–4,
199
low-intensity conflict, 2, 8, 103
Lusaka Accord (1984), 126–7
Malan, D.F., 17
Malan, General Magnus, 5, 6, 9, 55,
112, 126, 127, 136, 203, 289
Malawi, 109
Malebane-Metsing, Rocky, 183–6
Mamelodi: assessment of NSMS strat-
egy in, 169–73; financing develop-
ment in, 168–9; Joint Operations
Centre in, 164–6, 169; mini-Joint
Management Centre in, 166–7,
169; National Security Management
System applied in, 159–173; Opera-
tion Upgrade, 167–8, 169; as part of
Pretoria JMS, 163–4; security forces
in, 160–2; Mamelodi Youth Or-
ganisation, 165, 170
Mamelodi Civic Association, 165, 170
Mangope, Lucas, 183, 185
manpower: and SADF, 51
MARNET, 22
martial law, 31–2, 37, 69; in Transkei,
183
Matanzima, George, 183–4
Matanzima, Kaiser, 185
Mavinga, 129
Mbokotho, 189, 199
McCuen, J.J., 9, 144
Merriman, J.X., 37, 38
militarisation, 2–4, 12; of bantustans,
174; consumer militarism reinforc-

ing myths about war, 306; at economic level, 5–6, 218, 230; as ideology, 2; at ideological level, 10; and
links with masculinity, 55; and
links with private sector, 205–7,
220; and manpower, 51; at political
level, 6–10, 137; reinforcing militarism, 305; resistance of white women
to, 63–5; and schooling, 11, 25, 283,
290, 294, 295; as social process, 2;
South Africa as militarised society,
3, 83; of SAP, 70; and state decision-
making, 8; of youth in bantustans,
181–2
military area radio network, see
MARNET
military consumerism, 298
military-industrial complex, 217–20
Military Intelligence and Counter-
Intelligence, 16
MK, 2, 63
MNR, see Renamo
Mozambique, 6, 20, 23, 40, 103, 109,
115, 149; damage to economic and
social fabric, 112; economic action
against, 107, 110; Pretoria's covert
war in, 107–15; resistance movement, see Renamo
MPLA, 107, 117–25
municipal police, 8, 76–7; in Mamelodi, 162; vigilantes as community guards, 197–8
mythology of war, 83
Namibia, 6, 26, 40, 90, 318, 327; destruction of peasant agriculture, 97;
disease in, 99; forced removals in,
97–9; intensification of conflict,
92–4, 115; military occupation of,
96–100
National Education Crisis Committee,
74
National Education Union of South
Africa, 295
National Intelligence Service, 16
National Key Points Committee, 16
National Security Management System, 8, 17, 25, 77, 143, 145, 202,
207–10, 245; and the future, 156–8;
growth of, 149–50; non-account-